AF695284

The Value and Limits of Academic Speech

Free speech has been a historically volatile issue in higher education. In recent years, however, there has been a surge of progressive censorship on campus. This wave of censorship has been characterized by the explosive growth of such policies as "trigger warnings" for course materials; "safe spaces" where students are protected from speech they consider harmful or distressing; "micro-aggression" policies that often strongly discourage the use of words that might offend sensitive individuals; new "bias-reporting" programs that consist of different degrees of campus surveillance; the "dis-invitation" of a growing list of speakers, including many in the mainstream of American politics and values; and the prominent "shouting down" or disruption of speakers deemed inconsistent with progressive ideology. Not to be outdone, external forces on the right are now engaging in social media bullying of speakers and teachers whose views upset them.

The essays in this collection, written by prominent philosophers, political scientists, sociologists, and legal scholars, examine the issues at the forefront of the crisis of free speech in higher education. The contributors address the broader historical, cultural, legal, and normative contexts of the current crisis, and take care to analyze the role of "due process" in protecting academic freedom and individuals accused of misconduct. Additionally, the volume is unique in that it advances practical remedies to campus censorship, as the editors and many of the contributors have participated in movements to remedy limitations on free speech and open inquiry. *The Value and Limits of Academic Speech* will educate academic professionals and informed citizens about the phenomenon of progressive censorship and its implications for higher education and the republic.

Donald Alexander Downs is the Alexander Meiklejohn Professor of Political Science, Law, and Journalism at the University of Wisconsin-Madison, and the Glenn B. and Cleone Orr Hawkins Professor of Political Science at the University. He is also the director and co-founder of the University's Wisconsin Center for the Study of Liberal Democracy.

Chris W. Surprenant is an associate professor of philosophy at the University of New Orleans, where he is the founding director of the Alexis de Tocqueville Project, an interdisciplinary center for research and programming focusing on issues at the intersection of ethics, individual freedom, and the law.

Routledge Studies in Contemporary Philosophy

101 **Formal Epistemology and Cartesian Skepticism**
In Defense of Belief in the Natural World
Tomoji Shogenji

102 **Epistemic Rationality and Epistemic Normativity**
Patrick Bondy

103 **From Rules to Meanings**
New Essays on Inferentialism
Edited by Ondřej Beran, Vojtěch Kolman, and Ladislav Koreň

104 **Toleration and Freedom from Harm**
Liberalism Reconceived
Andrew Jason Cohen

105 **Voicing Dissent**
The Ethics and Epistemology of Making Disagreement Public
Edited by Casey Rebecca Johnson

106 **New Directions in the Philosophy of Memory**
Edited by Kourken Michaelian, Dorothea Debus, and Denis Perrin

107 **A Pragmatic Approach to Libertarian Free Will**
John Lemos

108 **Consciousness and Physicalism**
A Defense of a Research Program
Andreas Elpidorou and Guy Dove

109 **The Value and Limits of Academic Speech**
Philosophical, Political, and Legal Perspectives
Edited by Donald Alexander Downs and Chris W. Surprenant

The Value and Limits of Academic Speech

Philosophical, Political, and Legal Perspectives

Edited by Donald Alexander Downs and Chris W. Surprenant

Routledge
Taylor & Francis Group
LONDON AND NEW YORK

First published 2018 by Routledge

2 Park Square, Milton Park, Abingdon, Oxfordshire OX14 4RN
52 Vanderbilt Avenue, New York, NY 10017

Routledge is an imprint of the Taylor & Francis Group, an informa business

First issued in paperback 2020

Library of Congress Cataloging-in-Publication Data
A catalog record for this book has been requested

ISBN: 978-1-138-47989-0 (hbk)
ISBN: 978-0-367-59102-1 (pbk)

Typeset in Sabon
by Apex CoVantage, LLC

Contents

Acknowledgement

This publication volume would not have been possible without a generous grant from the Institute for Humane Studies at George Mason University. We are incredibly thankful for their support of this project and the scholars who have contributed to this volume, as well as their support for other scholars working on a wide range of projects in the area of free speech and open inquiry.

Introduction

Donald Alexander Downs and Chris W. Surprenant

This book addresses a matter that has provoked much attention and debate in recent years: the status and fate of free speech, open inquiry, and academic freedom in higher education. While the recent string of inviting, and then either disinviting, protesting, or otherwise interfering with a controversial speaker being brought to campus has drawn public attention to this issue, at its heart is a more fundamental concern about the appropriate function (or functions) of colleges and universities as institutions and what types of rules or safeguards must be in place to allow them to fulfill this aim. In this discussion, we (the editors of this volume) are not impartial observers, having taken speech-libertarian positions in writing and action. But our motivation for gathering together this collection of essays is to draw more attention to a discussion that seems to be going in the wrong direction. And as advocates of free speech and intellectual diversity, we feel obligated to include a variety of points of view from respected scholars and practitioners whose diverse ideas can help citizens in liberal democracies come to more informed conclusions regarding the present controversy. Rather than staking out our own positions, in this Introduction we strive to place the debate in a broader historical context while addressing the major points raised by our contributors.

Most universities and colleges remain publicly committed to long-established liberal principles of academic freedom and freedom of speech. Princeton's Keith E. Whittington captures the essence of what we will call the "liberal model" in his contribution to this volume:

> Freedom of thought is the lifeblood of a university. Universities are dedicated to the advancement and dissemination of knowledge. In order to fulfill that mission, universities must nurture an environment in which scholars can ask difficult questions and follow their evidence and analysis wherever they lead and teachers can expose their students to the unvarnished truth and press them to reexamine their most fundamental commitments.

Human truth and truth in the physical world are elusive things, requiring a capacity to face difficult matters, ambiguity and contradiction, as Edward Johnson discusses in his essay on humor. As Hamlet related to his friend, “There are more things in heaven and earth, Horatio/Than are dreamt of in your philosophy.” Furthermore, education is not simply about what transpires in the classroom, but also what happens in the countless open-ended encounters—intellectual and interpersonal—that students and other campus citizens experience every day. At its best, a university is a kind of intellectual *polis*.

Though the intellectual freedom of the liberal model has been the predominant principle of higher education for over century, it has often co-existed or dealt with other values. Most ominously, historians of academic freedom have chronicled several periods of political and moral “zealotry” during which moralistic and political pressures emanating from outside or inside higher education have engendered extensive censorship, including during World I, the McCarthy period of the 1950s, and the recent decades of so-called “political correctness.” (Hamilton)

In a legitimate vein, as John Hasnas discusses, certain non-liberal values—what we will call “proprietary”—have often characterized non-liberal colleges and universities while vying for respect in many liberal institutions as well. In addition, as noted by James R. Stoner, Jr., even the most liberal of institutions and political regimes properly abide principled limits to freedom of speech and academic freedom that are consistent with their missions.

> The different purposes of free speech and the different inherent limits on speech that they allow or require sum up to make questions of free speech enormously complex—and the complexity itself can be a problem, for if one needs to consult a lawyer on a regular basis to determine what one can or cannot say, it would be hard to claim one has free speech.

Accordingly, we may construe the recent heated debate over free speech in higher education as the most recent chapter in a longer book. The pertinent question is what is new under the higher education sun, and what is not. Hopefully this volume will help to illuminate, if not to answer this question.

Today’s conflict regarding free speech in higher education comes to us largely on the tail of numerous policies and programs that can inhibit or even censor speech in the name of promoting a diverse, respectful, and inclusive campus. The goals of promoting inclusion and due respect are not only consistent with the missions of liberal education and liberal democracy but are also obligatory to it. Problems arise, however, when such policies chill or proscribe speech that is properly part of the discourse that a challenging college education should encourage. Are such programs and policies valid partners of liberal freedom? Or are they weapons in the hands of ideologically driven pedagogues? The fate of liberal education hangs in the balance.

The list of policies at stake are now well known to those who follow the folkways of higher education, including such things as speech codes; often overly expansive anti-harassment codes pushed by internal campus constituencies and the federal government; sensitivity and diversity training that can either enlighten or open the door to ideological bullying and intolerance of intellectual diversity; trigger warnings that can signal trauma and emotional danger in great literature; anti-microaggression policies that can inhibit intellectual honesty and the interpersonal exchanges that are essential parts of college education; safe-space policies that can either protect the sanctity of unpopular campus groups or be applied to prevent legitimate speakers from coming to campus; and often extensive bias-reporting systems that can have Orwellian implications.[1] Meanwhile, a growing list of speakers who would be welcome in the polity at large have been shouted down (some even physically threatened) at several prominent schools, while even more have continued to be "dis-invited"—or not invited in the first place—because their views are deemed contrary to regnant campus orthodoxies.[2]

As some of our contributors point out, surveys of student attitudes and feelings toward speech indicate a growing willingness to deem disrespectful and unwanted speech as "harmful" or even "dangerous," thereby creating fertile ground for the restriction of discourse. Others maintain that such speech is inconsistent with the normative obligations of higher education. A major issue lying in the background of the debates in this volume is over the meaning of "harm" itself. Free speech may be restricted if it causes a significant harm. Several of our writers refer to the "harm principle" in John Stuart Mill's classic work, *On Liberty*, which requires a direct harm to the significant interests of another person before liberty—especially liberty of *speech*—may be limited. But like so much else in our modern or post-modern age, the concept of harm has been expanded and "problematized."[3] Before recent decades, for example, society did not countenance such things as widespread environmental harm, discriminatory—as opposed to traditional moral—harms associated with pornography, harm due to "micro-aggressions," and the like. Four major speech-related questions loom regarding claims of harm: Are they reasonable? Are they genuine? Are they political weapons in disguise? What impact does their recognition have on the higher education mission?

Building on the famous harm principles of Mill and philosopher Joel Feinberg, Andrew J. Cohen strives to distinguish what types of speech and conduct constitute sufficient harm to justify restriction.

> On the account defended here, *to undergo a harm is to be the subject of an event wherein one's interests are wrongfully set back and*

> *wherein the status of the undergoing of the harm derives from its being the sort of event that it is (namely, a setting back of interests), independently of the badness of any resulting state.*
>
> (emphasis in original)

Michael Joel Kessler wrestles with similar questions, paying particular attention to the claim that one of higher education's mission is to "challenge a student's intellectual comfort zone." Drawing upon the premise that universities constitute distinctive intellectual spaces as distinct from the broader marketplace of ideas—a view shared in varying degrees by many of our contributors, as we will see later—Kessler argues that "in many cases it will be possible to accommodate the fact of offense without compromising on a commitment to freedom of thought." Other authors evince greater concerns about the new claims of "offense." As editors, we leave this question for our readers to decide.

In addition to the problems posed by the new policies and the mentalities associated with them, broader psychological, sociological, structural, and economic forces are affecting the status of academic freedom. In his essay for us, French social theorist Frank Furedi cites the rise of psychological and therapeutic trends that amount to the "infantilization" of students, contributing to a fear of challenging or disagreeable discourse. (Hence, Furedi discerns deep problems with the expansion of the "harm principle" to such emotional states.) Meanwhile, attorney Rima Najjar Kapitan delineates the numerous legal difficulties of defending the rights of faculty members today in the new environment.

> In fact, academic freedom is emerging as one of the casualties of the ever-expanding power and corporatization of university administrations. Academic freedom is losing ground due to the decreasing number of tenure line positions, the scarcity of jobs relative to the number of applicants, and the willingness of some administrators to terminate the positions of even tenured faculty members when their power is challenged.

Broader Questions Posed

What should we make of this situation, and how should we deal with it in a manner suitable to the purposes of higher education institutions? What are those purposes? The status and fate of campus free speech and open inquiry are important not only to higher education and its standing—which is now questioned by many—but, more broadly, to democratic regimes themselves. By virtue of teaching and training a large portion of a nation's citizens and future leaders, what happens in higher education can significantly affect the polity, and vice versa. As social psychologist Jonathan Haidt has observed, the principles and practices that have supported the unique and challenging historic experiment of liberal democracy are similar to those that have built and sustained the modern university as an institution (Haidt 2017). The fates of "liberal democracy" and "liberal education" go hand in hand.

The scholars and practitioners who have contributed to this volume come from different fields and backgrounds, and they present different perspectives on the various issues at hand. They also focus on different contexts and dimensions of the campus free speech/academic freedom debate, obligating us to try to find common themes and threads. Most are Americans, but some hail from other liberal democracies. Our contributors disagree over several matters, including the normative dimensions of academic freedom and free speech, the extents to which colleges and universities should accommodate new student demands and political aspirations, how to apply these principles in the different institutional contexts, what limits to discourse are justified or required in different institutional contexts, what they perceive as problems and the extent to which problems exist, and over what to do about the conflicts and problems that confront higher education today. While our authors share a common commitment to higher education as an essential institution, are the differences reflected in these pages indicative of a debate within a community of shared values? (The "uni" part of the term "university"?) Or do they signify a more fundamental dispute over the very meaning of higher education today and the proper course for the body politic? Are we engaging in a vibrant debate over potentially valid reform? Or, in Yeats's terms, are we confronted with a situation in which "Things fall apart; the centre cannot hold"?

Three possible models for higher education present themselves for our consideration: the liberal model, the proprietary model, and the mixed model. Clear lines do not distinguish the models we discuss here. Rather, they constitute "ideal types" that roughly yet heuristically reflect reality.

The Liberal Model

The first outcome is the preservation of the liberal model, perhaps fitted to accommodate the needs and claims of an increasingly diverse polity, which includes the fomenting of equal respect and inclusion. The liberal model received one its most famous American voices in the 1915 *General Report of the Committee on Academic Freedom and Academic Tenure* of the American Association of University Professors (AAUP 1915). Inspired by the thought of such nineteenth-century intellectual activists as Mill and the German William von Humboldt (see the essay by Brian Leiter), the *Report* declared that the central purpose of the modern research university is "to advance knowledge by the unrestricted research and unfettered discussion of impartial investigators."[4]

Writing from England, Arianne Shahvisi argues that such new policies as trigger warnings and safe-space provisions are not inconsistent with the liberal model of education. Accordingly, she disagrees with those who claim we are dealing with a crisis.

> Free speech is widely declared to be endangered, and we are told that students are responsible. Yet on the ground, things feel much the same as ever. Lively debates *do* continue to happen, and students are in fact generally polite, deferential, and heterogeneous in their views. Eruptions of protest concerning permissible speech are rare. Where they do happen, they seem consonant with the ideals of the university.

In a similar vein, Ryan Muldoon maintains that policies designed to promote diversity and inclusion can be properly balanced with a strong commitment to freedom of speech and inquiry. Muldoon seeks an approach that appropriately balances what he calls the "distribution of burdens" that results from exposure to strong viewpoints. "As such, we need to look for a compromise between inclusion of ideas and inclusion of people as a deliberative principle."

Other of our contributors are less sanguine. Frank Furedi contends that higher education's excessive catering to the emotional demands and vulnerabilities of students undermines the character needed to sustain the demands of serious intellectual engagement.

> The call to immunize students from distress and pain underlines the call for trigger warnings and safe spaces. From this perspective, security and safety constitute first-order values, which clearly trump the value of free speech and academic freedom. This transformation of freedom into a second order value in campuses is the inexorable consequence of the psychological turn of socialization.

Furedi's concerns parallel those of Northwestern University's Laura Kipnis, who was the target of a Title IX investigation for writing an op-ed in the *Chronicle of Higher Education* in which she criticized what she and other observers consider "sexual paranoia" in higher education today. In her book on this matter and the broader issue, Kipnis critiques what she perceives as higher education's emphasis upon "feelings" at the expense of intellectual "distancing." "The result is that higher education has been so radically transformed that the place is almost unrecognizable." (Kipnis, 2–3)

Furedi's view contrasts with Shahvisi's as well with that of our contributor Michael Joel Kessler.

> My argument is that universities should approach trigger warnings the same way we approach accessibility accommodations. If there are accommodations that we can make to enable as many students as

> possible to learn then we should do so. Like any accessibility accommodation trigger warnings pertain to the way material is presented rather than the content of what is taught. This does not mean ceding control over syllabi. That would be an unreasonable expectation by students. . . . Unfortunately control over content is how many have chosen to frame the issue.

Furedi's position brings to mind a section of the AAUP's 1915 *Report* in which it portrayed the type of character faculty members should possess in order to meet their intellectual obligations. The section on "The Nature of the Academic Calling" extolled certain character traits in addition to the "impartial" and trained pursuit of truth.

> If education is the cornerstone of the structure of society and if progress in scientific knowledge is essential to civilization, few things can be more important than to enhance the dignity of the scholar's profession, with a view to attracting into its ranks men of the highest ability, of sound learning, and of strong and independent character.

Three goods are linked here: intellectual advance, the good of the polity, and individual self-reliance and character. Such character attributes are also part of the theoretical foundation of liberal First Amendment jurisprudence in the United States, as reflected in key Supreme Court decisions.[5] Consistent with this portrayal of academic character in its 1915 *Report*, in 2015 the AAUP published a statement criticizing trigger warnings. "The presumption that students need to be protected rather than challenged in a classroom is at once infantilizing and anti-intellectual" (AAUP 2015). In a similar vein, J.K. Miles holds that the sensitivity-oriented regulatory agendas that have come to populate higher education are inherently at odds with the intellectual "conscience" and give and take that are essential to the "First Amendment culture" of the liberal model.

The Proprietary Model

Some of the essays of our contributors point in varying degrees to a second possibility: a return of the "proprietary model" of higher education to the prominence that it enjoyed before the rise of the liberal model, this time with a progressive twist. The AAUP discussed this model of the university in its 1915 *Report*. Rather than the unending pursuit of truth through impartial critical thinking and research, the mission of the "proprietary" institutions that preceded the modern research university was "to subsidize the promotion of opinions held by the persons, usually not of the scholar's calling, who provide the funds for their maintenance" (AAUP 1915). Proprietary institutions at the time existed for *a priori* ends, usually religious or moral. They were typically more conservative in nature, which led during the Progressive Era to prominent battles over academic freedom that eventually gave birth to the AAUP and the type of university it championed. In terminology we borrow from libertarian philosopher Robert Nozick (Nozick 1974), the liberal research university is not dedicated to any particular "end state," but rather, in the words of the official motto of the University of Wisconsin—itself fashioned after a nationally prominent academic freedom dispute in 1894—"that continuous and fearless sifting and winnowing by which alone the truth can be found" (Hansen 1998).

The type of proprietary institutions the AAUP discussed in its 1915 Report continue to exist, as contributor John Hasnas points out in his essay. As Hasnas suggests, such institutions are consistent with the American constitutional polity for several reasons, including the right of free association and the concomitant promotion of cultural pluralism befitting a civil society free from state control. (Our author Andrew J. Cohen also acknowledges that private schools are entitled to define speech-related "harms" as they see fit, but stresses that as educational institutions, it would not behoove them to do so.) And some responsible critics lament the secularization of the modern research university for lacking "soul" or "spirit"—for being "disenchanted" in Max Weber's terms (Madsen 1994). A truly pluralistic constitutional regime characterized by exit, voice, and loyalty legitimately features both liberal and proprietary educational institutions (Hirschman 1970).

As several contributors note, as state actors, public colleges and universities are obligated to adhere to libertarian First Amendment doctrines appropriately tailored to educational institutions. Independent of law, such obligation is normatively required in a highly pluralistic polity dedicated to individual rights, self-government, consent of the governed, and the liberty of association. Given the ubiquity and power of the state and its proper relation to its citizens, it would be wrong for the state to tip the scales of self-determination by inhibiting or censoring some ideas unless it is clearly necessary to do so. (See our discussion of American First Amendment law following.) Allowing public institutions to engage in propriety forms of censorship would violate the proper relationship between the state and We the People. As Alexander Meiklejohn, the great American philosopher of education, free speech and self-government, wrote, "To be afraid of ideas, any idea, is to be unfit for self-government" (Meiklejohn, 28). This principle applies regardless of which political or ideological direction the justification for "propriety" as the AAUP defines it comes from. "Progressive" censorship is no more justified than "conservative" censorship. The principle of self-government also allows private schools to choose to act differently, so long as they are honest about it.

That said, another kind of proprietary institution has emerged in the wake of the 1960s student revolts that has influenced some of the policies that lie at the heart of the contemporary conflict over campus free speech: what Haidt and others have labeled the "social justice" vision of the university (Haidt 2016). This type of university is dedicated to the promotion of progressive and egalitarian ends, sometimes—or often, depending upon the eyes of the beholder—as a priority over intellectual freedom and the pursuit of truths when they allegedly run counter to social justice visions.

Peter Singer pivots upon the different type of censorship pertinent to the social justice university. In a personal memoir in which he presents examples of his own struggles with censors of various stripes, Singer begins by citing threats to his own freedom that have come from the right, the traditional direction of censorship. He then cites three recent famous incidents of censorship at the behest of progressive causes—now famous incidents at Middlebury, Berkeley, and Google.

> Recently, however, we have seen something different: a section of the left actively opposing freedom of speech. . . . What are we to make of all this? Should we echo the famous remark commonly, though apparently, erroneously attributed to Voltaire: "I disapprove of what you say, but I will defend to the death your right to say it"? Or should we say that some speakers cross a line, and should not be tolerated?

In the classic liberal tradition, Singer then offers a strong defense of freedom of speech as the best means to counter false or malicious ideas without censoring them. Calum Miller refers explicitly to the Singer case in his essay.

A major critique of the social justice university is its overt politicization at the price of intellectual values and diversity. The question of "how should we live?" is perhaps the fundamental question in the history of political theory, and this history is replete with different and competing answers to this ongoing question. It is one thing to be devoted to the *question* of social justice, yet another to enforce a particular *answer*. In intellectual institutions, social justice should be a question, not an *a priori* conclusion.

Furedi perceives the return of *in loco parentis* in higher education in new progressive forms as one suspect aspect of this model. The return of *in loco parentis* in this guise entails the institutionalization of regulatory regimes within higher education that are part and parcel of the burgeoning of campus administrative offices that enforce internal and external mandates. Furedi concentrates on the proliferation of mental health administrative regimes. Three other of our other authors present critical pictures of the regulatory machinery and mandates that have posed challenges for academic and other freedoms on campus. In addition to the aforementioned essays by Miles and Kapitan, legal scholar Evan Gerstmann delineates the ways in which new "affirmative consent laws" and other policies and rules regarding sex affect sexual relations in detrimental ways, including harming "the right of sexual autonomy" and intellectual freedom on campus. While correctly condemning unwanted sexual advances, Gerstmann critiques laws that, in words that echo Laura Kipnis, "turn many, if not most students, into expellable perpetrators of sexual assault." A Harvard undergraduate presented a noteworthy—if extreme—version of the "social justice" position in a 2014 op-ed in the *Harvard Crimson*: "If our university opposes racism, sexism, and hetero-sexism, why should we put up with research that counters our goals?" (Korn 2014).

Many critics of higher education today point to Herbert Marcuse's famous 1965 essay "Repressive Tolerance" as a founding document of the social justice model of higher education. Marcuse made a case for restricting speech he considered detrimental to progressive rationality. As Miles points out in his essay, the list of ideas Marcuse deemed out of bounds could be quite extensive, suffering from what Miles calls "concept creep."

Leiter provides a different and provocative take on Marcuse that is not based upon a progressive notion of the proprietary institution as we have defined it here, but rather on the pursuit of truth itself—the hallmark of the liberal research institution. Leiter employs Marcuse's logic to highlight the type of discourse and inquiry befitting an institution dedicated to the difficult task of finding truth. Like Mill, Marcuse emphasized the pursuit of truth, as well as the necessity of limiting the liberty principle to those who possess emotional maturity and the requisite attributes of rationality. This logic provides a rationale for treating higher education institutions with professionally trained staff as special places for the dissemination of ideas, *so long as they are true to their fiduciary intellectual obligations*:

> Universities will be in no position to defend academic freedom in capitalist societies—given the powerful interests aligned against such freedom for reasons unrelated to the value of truth—unless they are prepared to insure that the fields of inquiry they nurture and protect aim for truth, and do so utilizing methods of inquiry that have truth not simply as their aim, but as their reasonably frequent result.

Sarah Conly presents a similar perspective. In her estimation, speech appropriate *to the academy* requires suitable delimitation.

> That, however, doesn't mean that the expression of any and all ideas should be permitted, much less encouraged. Since education is schools' mission, speech can and should be avoided when it is not educational. It should especially be avoided if it doesn't merely fail to educate but actually promotes the acceptance of false views. This

> is the standard we use in the classroom, and it is the standard we should use outside the classroom as well.

As several of our contributors observe, Mills's support of wide-open freedom of speech is predicated in major part upon the fallibility principle: ineradicable human error and bias call for appropriate intellectual tolerance because no person or group can possibly possess all of the truth. Marcuse, however, notoriously did not apply this principle to those—invariably progressive—who would bear the responsibility to engage in censorship in his ideal polity. But Leiter's use of Marcuse is fundamental in a different sense: It conditions universities' special status upon their actually living up to the standards required for the rigorous and impartial pursuit of truth. This move does two things. First, it beckons us to determine the *raison de entre* of higher education, which is essential to any institutional analysis.[6] Leiter stresses the rational pursuit of truth. Second, it poses the question of which forces undermine this mission. Like Marcuse, Leiter claims the key culprit is the exertion of self-interested forces in capitalist society. But the progressive policies that have precipitated today's free speech conflict can also have this effect, as our more liberal-libertarian commentators observe. Leiter himself targets fields that rely upon insufficiently rigorous intellectual standards and methods, or which deny the possibility of truth (e.g., post-modernists). In addition to Furedi's critique of campus therapeutics, we have Whittington's analysis regarding threats to impartiality stemming from a lack of intellectual diversity on campus; Jason Brennan's defense of outside funding as a partial antidote to an institution that is already "corrupt" due to what he sees as widespread ideological bias and uniformity (interestingly, Brennan's point in this regard dovetails from a different ideological direction with Shahvisi's notion of "epistemic privilege" and bias); and the analyses of Gerstmann and Miles on overly zealous applications of Title IX's rules against sexual misconduct.

Drawing from the Declaration of Independence at Gettysburg, Lincoln declared that the United States was "conceived in liberty and dedicated to the proposition that all men are created equal." Liberty and equality are core principles of what Tocqueville called "Democracy in America," and the proper balance between the two is necessary to the legitimacy of liberal democratic polities. But Tocqueville also famously warned us of what can happen when the drive for equality becomes unmoored from intellectual liberty and respect for the restraints and manners attendant to rule of law and its living reality. A "tyranny of opinion" can result which is oppressive in its own right. The proprietary social justice university runs this risk.

As Hasnas observes, public universities in the United States are constitutionally obligated to abide by the First Amendment; however, many of the proprietary programs and policies public institutions adopt in the name of social justice can conflict with this obligation. Whereas the First Amendment does not bind private schools, most officially extend similar protections to their faculty and students on their own volitions. As Hasnas points out, however, private schools are known to compromise this protection when internal proprietary pressures intercede. (The same can be said for public schools as well.) He calls on private schools to be clear about where they stand regarding academic freedom and free speech, and to abide by what they proclaim.

The Mixed Model

The complexity of the situation in higher education today points to a third possible model that balances liberal and proprietary missions: How should we react in a macro sense to the apparent resurgence of the different proprietary missions within higher education today? As Hasnas suggests, let proprietary missions—of whatever ideological bent—prevail as institutional missions, so long as they are honest about what they are up to so the students and parents who bear the escalating costs of higher education today can know what they are getting into. If the norms of Mill, Humboldt, and their protégé maintain the most legitimacy or highest prestige in society when it comes to education—as we editors hope they do—they will be in the majority while the different types of proprietary institutions remain available for others. The modern research university was itself ultimately the product of an historical struggle that began at least with the Enlightenment, and today the struggle is apparently being renewed in a new way with the outcome still unclear. As the best theorists of liberal democracy have told us, liberty of thought is not manna from heaven: It has to be fought for and renewed on an ongoing basis. Is higher education up to this task?

Limits Commensurate with the Liberal Educational Mission

As our author James R. Stoner, Jr. and several other contributors write, principled limits on free speech and academic freedom have always coexisted with liberal education and liberal democracy. Stoner and Leiter also point out that some of the most profound works have been produced under conditions of oppression, not freedom. (Stoner begins his essay with a discussion of Leo Strauss's great essay, "Persecution and the Art of Writing.") Freedom is sometimes most appreciated when it encounters resistance.

Though American First Amendment law is probably the most libertarian in the world, it features several long-standing "exceptions" to free speech. In a nutshell, the state may *not* censor ideas because it disapproves of the message or because it has an "undifferentiated" or non-demonstrable fear that radical or dangerous ideas will be acted upon.

And it must not allow hostile audiences or "hecklers" to "veto" the rights of unpopular speakers. These standards are readily applicable to higher education and its free speech question: In censoring or inhibiting speech, higher education institutions must not use sensitivity as a pretext for expunging unpopular ideas, and it must not be influenced by unreasonable claims of emotional harm attached to speech.

But First Amendment law allows speech to be proscribed if doing so is demonstrably "necessary to protect a compelling social interest" (strict scrutiny), such as when it constitutes a clear criminal threat, when it is part and parcel of criminal conduct, when it directly incites unlawful action, when it constitutes libel and defamation, if it constitutes obscenity (e.g., extreme or "hard core" pornography), if it invades substantial privacy concerns, if it interferes with the rights of other speakers or other rights, or if it constitutes clear disturbance of the peace. In addition, speech may be restricted to certain subjects and topics in special contexts, as in special types of forums created for specific purposes, or be appropriately limited by time, place, and manner regulations so long as such regulations are no more extensive than necessary and avoid limiting speech because of its viewpoint.

In a similar vein, as many of our authors stress, principled limits are applicable in certain domains of higher education, notably those that are most central to the core scholarly mission: those settings involving pedagogy, research, and scholarly gatherings. These are the domains in which the principle of "academic freedom" applies as distinct from other realms of the campus, where more general free speech principles can apply, at least in the case of public schools and private schools that voluntarily adopt these principles as part of their official rights and privileges.

The proper balance between academic freedom and scholarly standards can be difficult to navigate; as academic scholars know, many conscientious debates over hiring and tenure entail adhering to standards while also striving to ensure that this effort does not serve as a smokescreen for infringing academic freedom simply because one does not like the conclusions the person at stake has reached for ideological or other biased reasons. But such necessary freedom does not mean that "anything goes" in *academic* settings.

In thinking about the campus realms we are about to discuss, a point should be born in mind: The university is a kind of intellectual *polis*. What happens in one domain can have effects on the other. If a speaker is deemed inappropriate for the public forum, in the real world, this decision can have an impact on what is deemed acceptable in class.

Domain # 1: Speech in Formal Academic Settings

As Erwin Chemerinsky and Howard Gillman teach in their 2017 book *Free Speech on Campus*, the academic freedom core of the university entails "a professional zone, which protects the expression of ideas but imposes an obligation of responsible discourse and responsible conduct in formal educational and scholarly settings." (75) The distinction between the "professional zones" of higher education and the more libertarian zones is one reason that "academic freedom" is distinct from "freedom of speech." Chemerinsky and Gillman emphasize that all "ideas" must be protected in this realm, no matter how offensive. As Jonathan Rauch famously taught in *Kindly Inquisitors*, many of the most important truths in the history of knowledge, such as evolution, have been deeply offensive to many people.

The general societal "marketplace of ideas" can be considerably less demanding than the "professional zone." Like Dostoyevsky's Underground Man, you may preach to your heart's content in the marketplace that "two plus two equals five." But don't expect to be hired to teach college math. And universities and colleges would be laughing stocks if they hired or retained incompetent instructors or researchers, or did not fail or grade down students whose work fell short of valid academic standards. In a similar vein, an institution can become a laughing stock if it allows itself to be overwhelmed by politicization, which apparently transpired at Evergreen State in 2017, and which happened when Middlebury activists physically attacked Charles Murray and the faculty member who deigned to moderate his talk there in 2017.

A major domain subject to academic standards is the classroom. Longstanding principles espoused by the AAUP and other sources have conditioned freedom in the classroom in common sense ways: What is taught and discussed must be generally "germane" to the subject matter and competently taught. Where to draw the line in class is a controversial matter, but liberal standards require that we err on the side of freedom, allowing what the Supreme Court has called "breathing space" for error.[7]

Earlier we discussed Conly's position regarding speech that is clearly "untruthful," such as Holocaust denial. It is one thing to teach Holocaust denial as an issue, another to teach it as truth. In her essay, Christina Easton does not deal with disciplining classroom speech but rather with how teachers should handle comments that threaten disruption or the "silencing" of other students through "wounding speech." Her effort is an attempt to preserve the liberal foundation of education while duly accommodating student sensitivities.

Readers should compare Easton's analysis with the essays by Shane D. Courtland and Calum Miller. Courtland discusses the "inevitability of offense" that adheres to the open and honest pursuit of truth, especially when value judgments are at stake. Assuming the "truthfulness" of certain offensive ideas, he concludes, "If we are to allow the banning of offensive discussions and/or speakers, then such policies are not, epistemologically, without their costs." Costs are especially likely given contemporary students' hypersensitivity to speech, which Courtland and several of our authors cite. Meanwhile, Miller makes an argument in favor of "the plausibility of bad views." Though he acknowledges the standard arguments for allowing bad or evil speech—e.g., exposing it to critical scrutiny, minimizing the extent of limiting it wrongly, on the deontological grounds of individual liberty—Miller chooses a different tack.

> I do not pursue any of these lines of argument here (though they link closely to my main argument). Rather, I suggest that the character of moral epistemology itself suggests no clear connection between the (apparent) heinousness of a view and its obvious falsehood—at the very least, there is no reason to think that wicked views will always be obviously false.

Edward Johnson provides a different interesting take on this question, looking at the state and role of "humor" in education. He begins by discussing the harm principle and the self-banishment of such comedians as Jerry Seinfeld and Chris Rock from campuses because of the censorship pressures that reign there. Johnson claims that the moral climate of higher education today is inhospitable to such things as ambiguity and irony, and that such intolerance shackles the pursuit of knowledge, which is often ambiguous and elusive. He quotes Furedi in agreement: "Hostility to ambiguity speaks to a pedagogic ethos that has become estranged from the open-ended pursuit of ideas. . . . In demanding that the outcome of learning should be stated in advance, this technique undermines the freedom that is required for intellectual exploration."

Domain #2: The Public Forum and Campus Encounters

Campuses are not limited to the professional realm. Chemerinsky and Gillman properly stress that there is a second realm that has come about in reaction to the Berkeley Free Speech Movement of 1964.

> [T]he [Berkeley] students demanded that [the university] also be recognized as a public forum for free speech. . . . We should think of campuses as having two different zones of free expression: a professional zone, which protects the expression of ideas but imposes an obligation of responsible discourse and responsible conduct in formal educational and scholarly settings; and a larger free speech zone which exists outside scholarly and administrative settings where the only restrictions are those of society at large.
>
> (Chemerinsky and Gillman, 75, 77)

This realm welcomes or tolerates speech that would lie outside the responsible bounds of "academic freedom" per se.

We editors would extend this sphere further to the campus at large. While upholding the right of an Iowa high school student to wear a black armband in class to protest the Vietnam War in *Tinker v. Des Moines School District*, the US Supreme Court wrote that a student's speech rights also exist in "the cafeteria, or on the playing field, or on the campus during the authorized hours."[8] In a recent op-ed in *Vox*, former Yale Law School dean Robert Post (and also lead counsel of the AAUP's Committee on Academic Freedom) asks if universities are obligated to provide forums for such highly offensive speakers as Milo Yiannopolous and Richard Spencer of the alt-right. Similar to our authors Leiter, Conly, and Shahvisi, Post writes, "No university, public or private, could perform its mission were it not permitted to evaluate the merit of ideas," including those in the campus public forum (Post). Among our contributors, Kessler presents perhaps the strongest case in support of this logic. His argument

> supports rejecting controversial speakers who are controversial because they adopt morally offensive positions. In addition to being a waste of resources, hosting such speakers contributes harm by presenting certain ideas as up for debate. Hosting the Holocaust denier implies that there is value in hearing these ideas. However, no credible faculty would teach these same ideas as true, so there is no reason to change our standards simply because this takes place elsewhere on campus.

Other contributors (Miles, Furedi, and Brennan) pose challenges to this position, citing the undue expansion of what is considered acceptable academic discourse and the need to distrust "who decides." Such mainstream speakers as Charles Murray, Heather MacDonald, Janet Napolitano, George Will, and Michael Bloomberg have either been shouted down or dis-invited in recent years. Though an ostensibly simplistic maxim, those experienced in free speech conflicts know that "who decides" is often the single most important question in the real world.

Post is certainly right that no one has a right to be invited as a speaker to any college or university. (Dis-invitations are a different matter, as they unavoidably raise the specter of censorship of disfavored ideas.)[9] But his limitation is more questionable if applied to those domains of public universities that qualify as "public forums" under First Amendment case law. And it is also open to question if applied to speakers invited by student or other academic groups as part of a program that gives them the right to invite speakers at their own discretion. (What lesson, except in extraordinary circumstances, is taught if administrators may broadly "veto" speakers whom students invite?) In 2000, the Supreme Court ruled that programs designed to promote student speech at public colleges must abide by the constitutional requirement of viewpoint neutrality.[10] And, as several of our authors maintain, it is often quite hard to distinguish between an "academic" motive for disallowing a speaker in the forum and an ideological motive, especially in today's environment.

Third Realm: The Forum of Private Association

Like some other authors in our volume, Burkay T. Ozturk and Bob Fischer question the applicability of the "marketplace of ideas" concept to higher education. In a kind of thought experiment, they suggest that another concept might be more helpful in judging the legitimacy of limitations on speech: just war theory. Just war theory is

> designed to provide an account of when actions that would normally be impermissible are, in fact, permissible. After all, its sole purpose is to answer the question: What makes it morally acceptable to engage in conduct—such as killing and maiming—that is normally wrong? In the present context, that helps us answer a parallel question: What makes it permissible to restrict speech, which would normally be a serious violation of a basic interest?

The "basic interest" of universities is the pursuit of truth.

Building on the work of political theorist Jacob Levy and the constitutional doctrine of private association rights, Ozturk and Fischer also refer to what we may discern as a third realm of campus speech activity. Unlike the second campus domain that is premised upon the right to present views and speakers to the public or campus community as a whole—the classic foundation of the "public forum" concept—this domain honors

> the right of individuals and communities to pursue their lives quite independently of one another, at least in certain crucial respects. So perhaps, the Framers established a system of rights in which speech isn't just a tool for the dissemination of ideas: It's also a way of telling the world who you are, and for aligning yourself with like-minded people.

In an influential 1982 essay, the late constitutional scholar Robert Cover analyzed this important aspect of freedom of thought and conscience, which harkens back to the original landing of the Pilgrims at Plymouth Rock: the right to establish your own community of meaning and truth contrary to state and community truths, so long as you abide by legitimate general laws that do not unnecessarily infringe upon this right. Similar to political scientist Samuel Huntington, Cover argues that constitutional meaning is forged by the "constant struggle" of groups to define their own meanings and to "maintain the independence and authority of their own *nomos*" (Cover, 4; Huntington). Hasnas's defense of proprietary institutions is indebted to this constitutional right; and the rights inherent in this domain also support certain versions of the erstwhile controversial policy of "safe spaces" that Shahvisi and Muldoon support. A private campus group is indeed a kind of safe space, and the right to only entertain certain voices is an aspect of this space. Problems arise when the doctrine of safe spaces is extended to the campus as a whole, thereby violating the rights congruent with the second "public forum" domain (e.g., the shouting down and bullying of Charles Murray and his host at Middlebury). We should also note that progressive forces of censorship are now impinging upon the private rights of student groups whose views that they consider politically incorrect, as in the efforts of administrations to crack down on Greek organizations and campus clubs that disavow or contradict reigning notions of "diversity"—a way of restricting diversity of groups in the name of diversity itself.[11]

Notes

1. See, e.g., Jeffrey Aaron Snyder and Amna Khalid, "The Rise of 'Bias Response Teams,'" *The New Republic*, March 30, 2016. The authors deal with bias report teams, but place them in the context of these other programs in an interlocking campus system.
2. The Foundation for Individual Rights in Education keeps a long list of dis-invited speakers on its webpage: www.thefire.org/resources/disinvitation-database/
3. See, e.g., Bernard E. Harcourt, "The Collapse of the Harm Principle," *Journal of Criminal Law and Criminology*, Vol. 90 (1999).
4. AAUP, *1915 Declaration of Principles on Academic Freedom and Tenure*, www.aaup.org/NR/rdonlyres/A6520A9D-0A9A-47B3-B550-C006B5B224E7/0/1915Declaration.pdf
5. Most notably, see *Whitney v. California*, 274 U.S. 357 (1927), Brandeis, concurring.
6. In his book, *Visions of Academic Freedom*, Stanley Fish says institutions and practices should be defined by their central purposes and missions, in legal scholar's Ernest Weinrib's term, their "immanent intelligibility." "It is a 'this,' not a 'that.'" (61)
7. *New York Times Co. v. Sullivan, 376 U.S. 254 (1964).*
8. *Tinker v. Des Moines Sch. Dist.*, 393 U.S. 503 (1969).
9. See, e.g., *Board of Education v. Pico*, 457 U.S. 853 (1982): removal of library books from public school library, as opposed to initial acquisition, creates a presumption of idea-based censorship.
10. *Board of Regents of University of Wisconsin System v. Southworth*, 529 U.S. 217 (2000).
11. See, e.g., Harvard's recent ruling against fraternities, sororities, and clubs: www.harvardmagazine.com/2017/11/harvard-final-clubs-and-faculty-governance-challenges In *Christian Legal Society v. Martinez*, 561 U.S. 661 (2011), the Supreme Court narrowly ruled in favor of a law school's rule that required

officially recognized student groups to allow admission to individuals even if those individuals did not share the beliefs of the group. Many free speech advocates disagree with this decision.

Works Cited

"1915 Declaration of Principles on Academic Freedom and Tenure." *American Association of University Professors*. www.aaup.org/NR/rdonlyres/A6520A9D-0A9A-47B3-B550-C006B5B224E7/0/1915Declaration.pdf

Chemerinsky, Erwin and Gillman, Howard. *Free Speech on Campus*. New Haven, CT: Yale University Press, 2017.

Cover, Robert. "Forward: Nomos and Narrative." *Harvard Law Review*, Vol. 97 (1983): 4–68.

Fish, Stanley. *Visions of Academic Freedom*. Chicago: University of Chicago Press, 2014.

Haidt, Jonathan. "A Conversation With Jonathan Haidt." *Minding the Campus*. February 3, 2016. www.mindingthecampus.org/2016/02/a-conversation-with-jonathan-haidt/

———. "Wriston Lecture." *Manhattan Institute*. November 15, 2017. www.wsj.com/articles/notable-quotable-jonathan-haidt-on-identity-politics-1511464920

Hamilton, Neil. *Zealotry and Academic Freedom*. Piscataway, NJ: Transaction Publishers, 1995.

Hansen, W. Lee. *Academic Freedom on Trial: 100 Years of Sifting and Winnowing at the University of Wisconsin-Madison*. Madison, WI: University of Wisconsin Press, 1998.

Harcourt, Bernard E. "The Collapse of the Harm Principle." *Journal of Criminal Law and Criminology*, Vol. 90 (1999): 109–194.

Hirschman, Albert. *Exit, Voice, and Loyalty*. Cambridge, MA: Harvard University Press, 1970.

Huntington, Samuel. *American Politics: The Promise of Disharmony*. Cambridge, MA: Belknap Press, Harvard University, 1981.

Kipnis, Laura. *Unwanted Advances: Sexual Paranoia Comes to Campus*. New York: Harper Collins, 2017.

Korn, Sandra Y. "The Doctrine of Academic Freedom: Let's Give Up on Academic Freedom in Favor of Justice." *Harvard Crimson*. February 18, 2014. www.thecrimson.com/column/the-red-line/article/2014/2/18/academic-freedom-justice/?page=single

Madsen, George. *The Soul of the American University: From Protestant Establishment to Established Nonbelief*. Oxford: Oxford University Press, 1994.

Meiklejohn, Alexander. "Free Speech and Its Relation to Self-Government." In Meiklejohn, *Political Freedom: The Constitutional Powers of the People*. Oxford: Oxford University Press, 1965.

Nozick, Robert. *Anarchy, State, and Utopia*. New York: Basic Books, 1974.

"On Trigger Warnings." *American Association of University Professors*. www.aaup.org/report/trigger-warnings

Post, Robert. "There Is No First Amendment Right to Speak on a College Campus." *Vox*, October 25, 2017. www.vox.com/the-big-idea/2017/10/25/16526442/first-amendment-college-campuses-milo-spencer-protests

Rauch, Jonathan. *Kindly Inquisitors: The New Attacks on Free Thought*. Chicago: University of Chicago Press, 1993.

Snyder, Jeffrey Aaron and Khalid, Anna. "The Rise of 'Bias Response Teams.'" *The New Republic*. March 30, 2016.

Strauss, Leo. "Persecution and the Art of Writing." *Social Research*, Vol. 8 (1941): 488–504.

1 Philosophy, Controversy, and Freedom of Speech[1]

Peter Singer

Freedom of speech has traditionally been a cause championed by the left and liberal side of the political spectrum, against conservatives who have sought to limit the expression of radical ideas. In fact, the last time I spoke on this subject, about ten years ago, was to receive the Scott Nearing Prize from the Department of Political Science at the University of Pennsylvania. Scott Nearing was a radical economist who advocated reducing the gap between rich and poor. In 1915, he lost his teaching position at the University of Pennsylvania because powerful people at the university and its Wharton School of Business did not share his values and did not want him teaching there. Edgar Smith, the university's provost at the time, said that academics should not spend their time "meddling in political questions." Nearing went on to become an advocate of simple living and self-sufficiency on the land. With his wife Helen he wrote *Living the Good Life: How to Live Sanely and Simply in a Troubled World*.[2] Thanks, perhaps, to their vegetarian diet and healthy lifestyle, the couple lived long enough to see their book become a kind of bible among the "back to the land" hippies of the 1970s.

Today we still see some cases in which conservatives seek to keep people from the left off the campus. When I was appointed to Princeton University in 1999, Steve Forbes, whose father had endowed Forbes College, a residential college at the university, called for my appointment to be rescinded and pledged that he would not donate to the university as long as I was on the faculty. It is perhaps relevant that Forbes was, at the time, running for the Republican nomination for president. More recently, in 2014 the University of Illinois withdrew an offer of appointment to Professor Steven Salaita because he posted tweets that were highly critical of Israel and Prime Minister Netanyahu. In September 2017 Harvard's Kennedy School withdrew Chelsea Manning's appointment as a visiting fellow after CIA Director Mike Pompeo called her a "traitor" and cancelled a lecture he had been scheduled to give at the school.

Recently, however, we have seen something different: a section of the left actively opposing freedom of speech. Here are three recent examples.

At Middlebury College in Vermont, Charles Murray, the co-author of the controversial book *The Bell Curve*, about race and IQ, was shouted down. As he left the building, masked protesters pushed and shoved him and his faculty interviewer, Alison Stanger, who suffered concussion after her hair was pulled and her neck twisted.[3]

At Berkeley, a planned event featuring the alt-right journalist Milo Yiannopoulis was cancelled after violent protests.[4]

Outside the universities, at Google, James Damore, a software engineer, was fired after he circulated a memo suggesting that there are differences between men and women that may explain, in part, why there are fewer women than men in his field of work.[5]

What are we to make of all this? Should we echo the famous remark commonly, though apparently, erroneously attributed to Voltaire: "I disapprove of what you say, but I will defend to the death your right to say it"? Or should we say that some speakers cross a line and should not be tolerated?

***

There is nothing like being silenced to make one feel vividly the importance of freedom of expression. In 1989, and for several years thereafter, announcements of lectures that I was scheduled to give in Germany, Austria, and the German-speaking part of Switzerland led to protests and threats of violence that caused the complete cancellation of two conferences and the withdrawal, at late notice, of several invitations to speak at universities and conferences. In Zurich, I had to stop lecturing after I was physically attacked on the stage, and my glasses were ripped off my face and smashed under the boot of a protester.[6]

The protesters were opposed to my view that parents should be permitted to make life and death choices for their severely disabled infants, including, if they wish, the option of active euthanasia. Many of my German opponents were not interested in the reasons why a professor of philosophy might take this view. Rather they held that, irrespective of the merits of the arguments, it is impermissible to question the inviolability of human life in general or the right to life of disabled human beings in particular.[7] Some values, in other words, are so sacrosanct that they must not be challenged.

This type of objection to freedom of speech is discussed by John Stuart Mill in his famous defense of freedom of expression in *On Liberty*. Mill begins his defense by arguing that to prohibit disagreement with a widely shared view is to assume infallibility in the belief that the view is true. He cites many examples to show that what has been believed to be the most certain truth has often turned out to be false. It is only by allowing views to be contested that we can really be justified in claiming to know that they are true. Moreover, he adds, even if a view is true, to prevent it being challenged is to risk it becoming dead dogma, rather than a living truth.

Mill also considers a different ground for suppressing dissent. There are some, he tells us, who would deny the right to challenge a belief, not because they are certain the belief is true but because the belief is "indispensable to well-being" and "none but bad men would desire to weaken these salutary beliefs." Mill responds that this objection seeks to separate the usefulness, or otherwise, of a view from the question of its truth. But surely, Mill says, we are no more infallible in assuming that a view is harmful than we are in assuming it to be false. We have to be able to discuss whether a view really is useful or harmful.[8]

That was the approach that I took on the one occasion during those years when a fruitful discussion did take place in Germany between me and those who had sought to silence me (at the University of Saarbrücken, under the auspices of Professor Georg Meggle). Since the protestors blew whistles and made too much noise for me to be able to speak, Meggle invited one of them up on the stage to state why I should not be allowed to speak. That revealed some basic misconceptions about my views—including the belief that I was politically on the right—but also included the claim that Germany's past shows the danger of regarding some human lives as more valuable or "worthy of life" than others. After the spokesperson for the protestors had been heard, Meggle said that, in fairness, I should be allowed to respond, not to discuss the sanctity of human life, but rather to discuss the claim that there must be no discussion of the sanctity of human life. That led, inevitably, to a discussion of my claim that no reflective society can avoid raising the issues that my opponents thought should not be raised. My views about the sanctity of human life have arisen in the context of a society with sophisticated and expensive medical technology. That we *can* save a life does not imply that we *ought* to save that life. We need to ask whether our medical technology should always be used to preserve human life to the maximum extent possible. If the answer is "maybe not," and it is acknowledged that sometimes the patient is incapable of expressing a preference for continuing to live or for dying, then some important questions must be asked:

- On what grounds are decisions to discontinue treatment to be based?
- Should these grounds include judgments about the quality of the life that the patient can be expected to live if he or she survives?
- Who should make such a decision when the patient cannot?
- If the decision is to bring about the patient's death, does it make a morally significant difference whether that is done by the withdrawal of life-support, such as a ventilator, or by a lethal injection?

There is room for different views on these questions, but I find it hard to understand those who do not even think the questions should be asked.

On one point, my experience does not entirely support what Mill writes. He asserts: "And it will not do to say that the heretic may be allowed to maintain the utility or harmlessness of his opinion, though forbidden to maintain its truth. The truth of an opinion is part of its utility." That is no doubt correct, if we are concerned with opinions about something that can be true or false. But, arguably, that is not the case with moral opinions. My German opponents seemed divided on this question. Some of them were conservative Christians who thought that the sanctity of human life is God's law and hence a moral truth that I was denying. To this group, Mill's point would apply. Others, however, were from the left and regarded morality and politics as simply a power struggle. They saw themselves as on the side of the oppressed, whereas my views were part of a capitalist-fascist attempt to eliminate all who are not productive workers. It was precisely because they saw ethics as relative to economic interests that they rejected the idea of debate and discussion as a way of reaching truth. They represent a different kind of challenge to free speech, one that sees ethics as mere camouflage for the real issues of power and dominance that, they say, inevitably lie beneath its surface.

This approach was not entirely unknown when Mill wrote *On Liberty*—it is outlined in *The Communist Manifesto* and can be traced back to Thrasymachus, who in Plato's *Republic* defines "justice" as "whatever is in the interests of the stronger"—but it has become more popular since, especially among postmodernists, deconstructionists, and critical theorists of various kinds.[9] It is alien to Mill's philosophical outlook, however, and so requires a separate refutation. That refutation should start from the fact that those who oppose freedom of expression while denying that reason plays a role in ethical argument are undermining their own ethical stance, for they thereby admit it to be no more true, and no better justified, in terms of reason and argument, than the view they would suppress. Once we grant that, we rapidly arrive at an argumentative stalemate and open the door for those willing to use force to impose what we might call the Thrasymachus solution: to impose their own "justice," which in fact becomes "whatever is in the interests of the stronger."

***

In arguing against those who tried to prevent me speaking, I have been focusing on views that I believe to be sound or true. What about views that are palpably false? Even here it is important to defend the right to free speech. As an example, I will take David Irving, whose failed lawsuit against the historian Deborah Lipstadt is the subject of the 2016 film *Denial*. Irving has served time in an Austrian prison for saying that the Holocaust never happened.[10]

The best way to persuade people of the reality of the Holocaust is to confront them with some of the evidence, which is in fact completely overwhelming. In contrast, how is imprisoning someone who denies the existence of the Holocaust going to persuade anyone that the Holocaust happened? Would it be unreasonable to think that if a government locks people up for saying something, they may be in possession of facts that the government wants to keep secret?

But, it may be said, to deny the existence of the Holocaust is deeply offensive to those who survived it or to the descendants of those who were victims of it. It is. I know because I am among those descendants: Three of my four grandparents died in the Holocaust, and the fourth endured terrible years before managing to live through to her liberation. Nevertheless, I agree with Mill that causing offense is not sufficient reason for restricting free speech because there are so many different views to which someone can take offense that this restriction would utterly destroy freedom of expression. Without the freedom to criticize in ways that risk causing offense, progress will always be running up against a roadblock. The benefits of freedom of speech outweigh the harms of offense.

This is especially true in philosophy. The Western philosophical tradition goes back to Socrates, who spent a lot of time demonstrating to his fellow Athenians how little they knew and pushing them to examine the way they were living. He undoubtedly offended many of them. For this he was condemned to death by drinking hemlock. Today, philosophers are still challenging conventional beliefs and values, encouraging us to ask ourselves how we ought to to live, and in the process changing the lives of many people. To do this properly, philosophy needs a license to cause offense.

Nevertheless, aren't there defensible limits on freedom of speech? Mill thought that there are: "even opinions lose their immunity, when the circumstances in which they are expressed are such as to constitute their expression a positive instigation to some mischievous act." That sentence immediately precedes his oft-quoted distinction between publishing in a newspaper one's opinion that corn dealers are starvers of the poor and saying the same to an excited mob in front of a corn-dealer's house.[11]

Today we are less worried about violence to corn dealers and more concerned about incitement to racial or religious hatred. Consistently with the distinction Mill was trying to draw, I believe that the right of free speech does not extend to a right to incite racial hatred, which often leads to violence against members of racial or ethnic minorities. Racial vilification, sometimes referred to as hate speech, can be distinguished from other forms of speech because it is an appeal to our emotions rather than to our intellect or our finer feelings. Granted, the line is not always easy to draw, and where it is not, drawing it will be a task for the courts. But the principle is tolerably clear.

It is also clear that some speakers and authors who have recently been shouted down are not engaging in racial vilification. Charles Murray's work is not racial vilification, for it is aimed at our intellect, presenting complex evidence and making arguments based on that evidence. You may think the evidence is selective and the arguments unsound. You may point out that some will find his conclusions offensive. The proper response to that is to refute the evidence, or present contrary evidence, and to point to holes in the argument. Preventing Murray speaking will only give him more publicity and boost sales of his books.[12] Moreover, it seems likely to encourage those predisposed to his view to conclude that his opponents have no answer to his position. For if there is an answer, these people will ask, why would Murray's opponents need to prevent him speaking, especially in a university that has many people who would, one can reasonably assume, have the resources and ability to scrutinize his arguments and the data on which he relies?

At Middlebury College last March, after the events involving Murray, a number of faculty members wrote and signed onto a statement of principles under the heading "Free Inquiry on Campus."[13] The principles included such points as:

- Genuine higher learning is possible only where free, reasoned, and civil speech and discussion are respected.
- Only through the contest of clashing viewpoints do we have any hope of replacing mere opinion with knowledge.
- The incivility and coarseness that characterize so much of American politics and culture cannot justify a response of incivility and coarseness on the college campus.
- A protest that prevents campus speakers from communicating with their audience is a coercive act.

The statement prompted a counter-statement by a group of Middlebury students entitled "Broken Inquiry on Campus."[14] The counter-statement offers us an opportunity to examine the thinking of some of those who prevented Murray from communicating with those who had turned up to hear him. Here is one revealing passage, written in response to the faculty assertion that "Only through the contest of clashing viewpoints do we have any hope of replacing mere opinion with knowledge." To this the students reply:

> By elevating bigotry and engaging with it in open debate under the misguided view that all ideas must be respected, we risk elevating biased opinions with no solid, factual foundation into the realm of "knowledge" and affirming the unconscious biases many hold. . . . If we hold that the contest of clashing viewpoints is the only way to solidify knowledge, it naturally follows that we have a responsibility to articulate some parameters for which viewpoints are worthy of such a process.

The students assume that Murray's work consists of biased opinions with no solid, factual foundations; but that is precisely what needs to be demonstrated. By silencing Murray and preventing any debate, the protesters passed up an opportunity to show that his conclusions lack a solid factual foundation. Perhaps, instead of pressing the university administration to cancel Murray's visit, they should have pressed for a debate in which an expert opponent of his views—and there are many such people—could have exposed the flaws in his argument.

The students also appear to believe that it is possible to articulate parameters for deciding which viewpoints are worthy of entry into the contest of clashing opinions. Presumably, since Murray's work attempts to appeal to our reason rather than to our emotions, the students believe that these parameters can be set on the basis of an assessment of the content of the work, rather than, as I have suggested, its tone and the nature of its appeal. But how is that to be done without debating and discussing the content of Murray's work? And why do the students think that they are in a position to decide this for others—for those who had come to the event to hear what Murray had to say, and, presumably, to hear other members of the university community respond critically to it? If they simply assert that they know that Murray is wrong, Mill's assumption of infallibility is squarely applicable.

The students do have more to say on this matter, but it cuts directly against what I have been arguing are key values for a university and for any community that values an open search for knowledge:

> We contend that experiences and emotions are valid ways to see the world, and that the hegemony of rational thought-based perspective often found in a university setting limits our collective creativity, health, and potential. If we are to move from opinion to knowledge, it is truly imperative to listen, understand, and reflect upon the various lenses members of our community use to view the world.

It is, of course, important to listen to a range of different opinions, and to know how other members of our community view the world. That includes knowing what they are experiencing and what emotions they are feeling. The assertion that emotions are "valid ways to see the world," however, should be firmly rejected, and we should uphold what is here referred to, critically, as "the hegemony of rational thought." Otherwise, we open the door to all the nationalist, racist, sexist, homophobic, and transphobic emotions that, as we saw only too clearly in the 2016 presidential election, are very widely held in this country. I doubt that the Middlebury protesters would regard these emotions as "valid ways to see the world." How then are we to decide which emotions are valid ways of seeing the world, and which are not? Not, I presume, by counting which emotions are most widely held by members of our community. I can see no other way than holding them up to rational examination.

I need to respond to one other ground that the students give for disrupting Murray's speech, rather than presenting arguments against his views. They ask, "is it reasonable for students or community members to be asked to debate someone who has presented their intellectual inferiority as an irrefutable fact?" The reference, of course, is to Murray's claim that there is a genetic basis for the lower average IQ scores of African Americans, when compared to whites. I am not aware of any place in which Murray has presented this "as an irrefutable fact." I presume that he would acknowledge the possibility of new evidence emerging that would refute his views. More importantly, he is talking about averages, not about the intellectual inferiority of any particular African Americans—it is of course obvious, and Murray states it clearly, that some African Americans are intellectually superior to most whites. Nevertheless, it is doubtless troubling for African Americans, and indeed for anyone hoping for a more egalitarian and less racially divided society, to hear claims that there are genetic differences in intelligence that align in any way with racial differences. Is this a reason for not allowing such claims to be discussed in a university?

In October 2017, Yale University dedicated a new residential college named for Pauli Murray. Born in 1910, Pauli Murray was the granddaughter of a slave. She became a civil rights activist. She spent time in jail for refusing to sit in the "Negro" section of the bus. She led sit-ins to desegregate white-only eating places in Washington DC. When she studied law at Howard University in the 1940s, she was the only woman in the class and her professors were also all male. One of them announced to the class that he didn't know why a woman would want to study law. She graduated first in her class and applied to Harvard Law School to do graduate work, only to be turned down because at that time Harvard Law School did not admit women. She did her own legal research on segregation, which was later drawn upon by the legal team that won the landmark desegregation case, *Brown v. Board of Education*. Later Pauli Murray was a co-founder, with Betty Friedan, of the National Organization for Women.

In 1963 Pauli Murray was studying for a doctorate at Yale Law School when the Yale Political Union invited George Wallace, the governor of Alabama, to speak on campus. In his inaugural speech as governor, Wallace had called for "Segregation now, segregation tomorrow, segregation forever!" In the wake of that speech, members of the Ku Klux Klan bombed a church in Birmingham, Alabama, killing four African American schoolgirls and injuring twenty-two others. Many blamed Wallace for inciting violence.

By that time, opposing segregation had been Pauli Murray's life's work for more than twenty years. She had described segregation as "a monster, dividing peoples, thwarting personalities, breeding civil wars." She said that she would picket any event at which Wallace spoke. Nevertheless, she wrote to the president of Yale urging him not to "compromise the tradition of freedom of speech and academic inquiry" by preventing Wallace speaking on campus. Her experience in the civil rights movement had given her a strong sense of the importance of maintaining these rights for everyone. In her letter to the president of Yale, she wrote: "This has been the principle behind the enforcement of the rights of the Little Rock Nine, James Meredith and others to attend desegregated schools in the face of a hostile community and threats of violence. It must operate equally in the case of Governor Wallace."[15]

Pauli Murray was an African American woman living in a climate of racism and sexism more hostile than anything that exists today, and she was fully aware of how mistaken and harmful racist and sexist views are. Yet this did not lead her to seek to suppress them, nor did it blind her to the fundamental importance of freedom of thought and expression. We should follow her example.

Notes

1. This essay is based on an invited lecture given at Wellesley College on November 30, 2017, and sponsored by The Freedom Project and the Philosophy Department. I am grateful to Tom Cushman, Director of The Freedom Project, for the invitation, and also to Chris Surprenant for suggesting that it would be suitable for publication in this volume.
2. (New York: Schocken Books, 1970; first published 1954).
3. Stephanie Saul, "Dozens of Milddlebury Students Are Disciplined for Charles Murray Protest," *New York Times*, May 24, 2017.
4. Thomas Fuller, "A Free Speech Battle at the Birthplace of a Movement at Berkeley," *New York Times*, February 2, 2017.
5. Daisuke Wakabayashi, "Contentious Memo Strikes Nerve Inside Google and Out," *New York Times*, August 8, 2017.
6. For details, see "On Being Silenced in Germany," *The New York Review of Books*, August 15, 1991, reprinted in *Practical Ethics* (Cambridge: Cambridge University Press, 1993): appendix, and in *Writings on an Ethical Life* (New York: Ecco, 2015): 303–318.
7. See, for example, Franz Christoph, "(K)ein Diskurs über 'lebensunwertes Leben,'" *Der Spiegel*, No. 23/1989 (June 5, 1989); O. Tolmein, *Geschätztes Leben* (Hamburg: Konkret Literatur Verlag, 1990); T. Bastian, editor, *Denken, Schreiben, Töten* (Stuttgart: Hirzel, 1990); Franz Christoph, *Tödlicher Zeitgeist* (Cologne: Kiepenheuer und Witsch, 1990).
8. John Stuart Mill, *On Liberty* (London: John W. Parker & Son, first published 1859), Chapter 2.
9. See, for example, Richard Rorty, "Does Academic Freedom Have Philosophical Presuppositions," *Academe*, Vol. 80, No. 6 (1994): 52–63.
10. Mark Landler, "Austrian Court Frees Jailed Holocaust Denier," *New York Times*, December 20, 2006.
11. Mill, *On Liberty*, Chapter 3.
12. Eric Siegel has written: "Recent college protests have propelled Charles Murray into the news cycle again, and his resurging book sales show the public-ity's not all bad." See Eric Siegel, "The Real Problem With Charles Murray and 'The Bell Curve,'" *Scientific American* blogs, August 12, 2017, https://

blogs.scientificamerican.com/voices/the-real-problem-with-charles-murray-and-the-bell-curve/

13. https://freeinquiryblog.wordpress.com/
14. https://brokeninquiryblog.wordpress.com/
15. See Kathryn Schulz, "Saint Pauli," *The New Yorker*, April 17, 2017, published online as "The Many Lives of Pauli Murray," www.newyorker.com/magazine/2017/04/17/the-many-lives-of-pauli-murray; and Peter Salovey, "Free Speech Personified," *New York Times*, November 26, 2017.

Works Cited

Bastian, T. *Denken, Schreiben, Töten*. Stuttgart: Hirzel, 1990.

"Broken Inquiry on Campus." https://brokeninquiryblog.wordpress.com/

Christoph, Franz. "(K)ein Diskurs über 'lebensunwertes Leben.'" *Der Spiegel*. June 5, 1989.

———. *Tödlicher Zeitgeist*. Cologne: Kiepenheuer und Witsch, 1990.

"Free Inquiry on Campus." https://freeinquiryblog.wordpress.com/

Fuller, Thomas. "A Free Speech Battle at the Birthplace of a Movement at Berkeley." *New York Times*. February 2, 2017.

Landler, Mark. "Austrian Court Frees Jailed Holocaust Denier." *New York Times*. December 20, 2006.

Nearing, H. and Nearing, S. *Living the Good Life: How to Live Sanely and Simply in a Troubled World*. New York: Schocken Books, 1970.

Rorty, Richard. "Does Academic Freedom Have Philosophical Presuppositions." *Academe*, Vol. 80 (1994): 52–63.

Salovey, Peter. "Free Speech Personified." *New York Times*. November 26, 2017.

Saul, Stephanie. "Dozens of Milddlebury Students are Disciplined for Charles Murray Protest." *New York Times*. May 24, 2017.

Schulz, Kathryn. "Saint Pauli." *The New Yorker*. April 17, 2017. Published online as "The Many Lives of Pauli Murray." www.newyorker.com/magazine/2017/04/17/the-many-lives-of-pauli-murray

Siegel, Eric. "The Real Problem With Charles Murray and 'The Bell Curve.'" *Scientific American* blogs. August 12, 2017. https://blogs.scientificamerican.com/voices/the-real-problem-with-charles-murray-and-the-bell-curve/

Singer, Peter. "On Being Silenced in Germany." *The New York Review of Books*. August 15, 1991. Reprinted in *Practical Ethics*. Cambridge: Cambridge University Press, 1993 and *Writings on an Ethical Life*. New York: Ecco, 2015: 303–318.

Tolmein, O. *Geschätztes Leben*. Hamburg: Konkret Literatur Verlag, 1990.

Wakabayashi, Daisuke. "Contentious Memo Strikes Nerve Inside Google and Out." *New York Times*. August 8, 2017.

2 Why Academic Freedom?

Brian Leiter

Why protect *academic* freedom? We cannot answer that question until we specify what *kind* of freedom that involves. The American legal scholar William Van Alstyne noted more than a generation ago, in his seminal 1972 essay, that "academic freedom" has migrated "from a close association with protection of the academic in his professional endeavors and assumed a new synonymy with the general civil liberties of academics (and especially their general *political* liberties)" (1972, 62). Citizens in a decent society should enjoy political liberties, of course, including liberties of expression and thought, and they should enjoy them without threat to their livelihood, but the justification of those liberties is independent of, even if (as we will see) related to, the justification of distinctively *academic* freedom.

The confusion between specifically *academic* freedom and general political freedom is incorporated, as it happens, into the influential 1940 statement by the Association of American University Professors (hereafter "AAUP"), which defines the contractual entitlements enjoyed by most American university professors as follows:

1. Teachers are entitled to full freedom in research and in the publication of the results, subject to the adequate performance of their other academic duties.
2. Teachers are entitled to freedom in the classroom in discussing their subject, but they should be careful not to introduce into their teaching controversial matter which has no relation to their subject.
3. College and university teachers are citizens, members of a learned profession, and officers of an educational institution. When they speak or write as citizens, they should be free from institutional censorship or discipline (AAUP 1940).[1]

Freedom in research and teaching are the central components of distinctively academic freedom, and not only in the United States (a point to which I return, following). It is the third provision in the AAUP definition, protecting "extramural speech" by academics from institutional censure, that has muddied the waters in the ways that Van Alstyne noticed. Why should a professor, after all, when speaking as a citizen, enjoy a freedom from employment repercussions that most other citizens, including highly educated professionals, do not enjoy? This is the aspect of the AAUP definition of academic freedom most vulnerable to attack in a capitalist society where at-will employment is the norm.[2] As Van Alstyne quipped, ordinary citizens might be forgiven for thinking it "odd" that,

> professors . . . insist that professors have an *extra* right to be protected in these aprofessional pursuits [i.e., extramural speech] . . . a claim sublimely stronger than [ordinary citizens], insisting as professors do that such activities are part of their "academic freedom" and a special contribution to the social good, whereas such activities by others are merely an ordinary matter of common liberty to be tolerated in a liberal society but not, of course, of the same rank of special good as the protection of academic freedom.
>
> (Van Alstyne 1972, 64)

In a free and democratic society, one may hope that no citizens would suffer employment repercussions for their political speech, regardless of their employers, unless (perhaps) that political speech runs afoul of *general* legal regulations (e.g., prohibitions on sexual harassment or, as in many countries, hate speech). But the defense of that broad right of political expression by citizens is not the same as the defense of *specifically* academic freedom, which is my topic here.

Van Alstyne is, again, a useful guide to what distinctively *academic* freedom involves. He writes:

> Insofar as it pertains to faculty members in institutions of higher learning, "academic freedom" is characterized by a personal liberty to pursue the investigation, research, teaching, and publication of any subject as a matter of professional interest without vocational jeopardy or threat of other sanction, save only upon adequate demonstration of an inexcusable breach of professional ethics in the exercise of that freedom. Specifically, that which sets academic freedom apart as a distinct freedom is its vocational claim of special and limited accountability in respect to all academically related pursuits of the teacher-scholar: an accountability not to any institutional or societal standard of economic benefit, but solely to a fiduciary standard of professional integrity. . . . The maintenance of academic freedom contemplates an accountability in respect to academic investigations and utterances solely in respect of their professional integrity, a matter usually determined by reference to professional ethical standards of truthful disclosure and reasonable care.
>
> (Alstyne 1972, 71)

This captures the kind of academic freedom defended in other countries with major university systems as well. For example, Germany's post-war constitution—"the Basic Law"—enshrines core academic (and artistic) freedom in the text: "Arts and sciences, research and teaching shall be free" (German Basic Law 1949, Art. 5(3)). Protection for *Wissenschaftsfreiheit*—"scientific freedom"—dates back to the early nineteenth century, when Germany was the birthplace of the modern idea and reality of a university (Barendt 2010, 120–121). In German, *Wissenschaft* or "science" has a much broader connotation than the Anglophone "natural science": It includes any systematic form of inquiry into nature, history, literature, or society marked by rigorous methods that secure the reliability or truth of its findings.[3] In Germany—as in Van Alstyne's account of academic freedom—it falls to academic professionals in each *Wissenschaft* to determine what constitutes failure to live up to scientific standards (Barendt 2010, 125).[4]

Similarly, in the United Kingdom, after the elimination of university tenure in 1988, academic freedom was secured by statutory provision (Barendt 2010, 93), according to which,

> academic staff have freedom within the law to question and test received wisdom, and to put forward new ideas and controversial or unpopular opinions, without placing themselves in jeopardy of losing their jobs or privileges they may have at their institutions.
>
> (Education Reform Act 1988, §202(2)(a))

As one English commentator notes, "the freedom is not explicitly limited to the communication of ideas in lectures and seminars," so would presumably cover *some* extramural speech insofar as it was related to the area of academic expertise of the faculty member (Barendt 2010, 94).

Note that academic freedom so-conceived has definite limits, but those limits are to be set by those with expert competence in the relevant *Wissenschaft*, not by offended members of the polity at large or by politicians or business leaders whose interests might be adversely affected by *wissenschaftlich* research or teaching. The limits inherent in the idea of academic freedom derive from academic expertise as manifest in the *Wissenschaft* in question.[5] That, of course, makes the very idea of a *Wissenschaft* centrally important to understanding academic freedom, a topic to which we will return at the conclusion of this essay.

If the preceding constitutes the core of distinctively *academic* freedom, why protect it? The central rationale for academic freedom in the Western universities has always been that such freedom makes discovery of the truth more likely, and that knowledge of the truth contributes to the well-being of individuals and society at large. In the Anglophone world, these ideas were famously articulated in the mid-nineteenth century by John Stuart Mill in *On Liberty* (1859), though Mill's account was, by his own admission, heavily influenced by Wilhelm von Humboldt's writings on this topic (Mill [1873] 1975, 179–180). Humboldt, of course, was also the primary architect of the idea of a modern research university in Germany (which became the model everywhere else) and for the attendant *Wissenschaftsfreiheit* that was deemed essential to its success (Forster 2010, 244, 246–247). So this tradition of defense of academic freedom has been central in the two Western countries, Germany and Britain, responsible for the shape of the modern research university.

We can summarize the Millian argument briefly as follows: Mill believed that knowing the truth would maximize human well-being or happiness; and he believed we are more likely to find out what is true—in both theoretical and practical matters—if we permit people wide latitude to express their views and opinions, even when those turn out to be mistaken.[6] Mill's core rationale for these beliefs was twofold (I simplify a bit, for ease of exposition): first, we are fallible, so we may be wrong (wholly or partially) about what we take to be true, but we are less likely to discover our errors unless others with opposing views enjoy the freedom to challenge us; and second, even if we believe what is true already, being challenged by false beliefs insures that we hold our beliefs for sound reasons, not just dogmatically.

Mill's view has been hugely influential in both the thinking and the jurisprudence of the Western democracies, but it has had some trenchant critics, one of whom will help us bring out the special force of the Millian argument in the case of academic freedom. In a famous 1965 essay—or "infamous," depending on whom one asks—the German Marxist philosopher Herbert Marcuse argued against liberty of expression for those defending imperialist aggression and oppression (he was thinking, in particular, of the recent US invasion of South Vietnam in 1962, the subsequent assassination of its president, and the ensuing military violence): no tolerance, according to Marcuse, should be accorded that kind of harmful expression (Marcuse 1965). Marcuse, it bears emphasizing, did not think of "harm" in the expansive sense now favored by some college students in the capitalist countries: hurting feelings and saying mean things were of no interest to Marcuse. He was concerned with public defenses of state policies and practices that killed and maimed people. Many who have not read the essay but know Marcuse only by "reputation" are surprised to learn that his argument was, in fact, explicitly Millian. Marcuse's claim was that toleration of expression of certain views harms human well-being (because it contributes causally to state actions that physically harm people), and so could not be justified on utilitarian grounds. As Marcuse put it:

> [S]ociety cannot be indiscriminate [in what it tolerates] where the pacification of existence, where freedom and happiness themselves are at stake: here certain things cannot be said, certain ideas cannot

> be expressed, certain policies cannot be proposed, certain behavior cannot be permitted without making tolerance an instrument of the continuation of servitude.
>
> (Marcuse 1965, 88)

Marcuse's suggestion is that restrictions on speech in support of, e.g., chattel slavery or *de jure* segregation, would in fact have hastened the end of both horrific institutions. *If* that were true, the burden on a utilitarian justification of such expression would be very high indeed.

The key to understanding both Mill and Marcuse is to realize that neither of these thinkers believed that liberty of expression was *intrinsically* valuable. Rather, they thought that liberty of expression was only valuable *in virtue of its actual consequences*—the consequences being hostage to facts about the world in which such expression occurred. This is clear enough in Mill himself, in a passage in *On Liberty* that many commentators pass over in silence. For Mill wrote that his doctrine of the harm principle—"that the sole end for which mankind are warranted, individually or collectively, in interfering with the liberty of action of any of their number is self-protection" or "to prevent harm to others"—

> is meant to apply only to human beings in the maturity of their faculties. We are not speaking of children or of young persons below the age which the law may fix as that of manhood or womanhood. Those who are still in a state to require being taken care of by others must be protected against their own actions as well as against external injury. For the same reason we may leave out of consideration those backward states of society in which the race itself may be considered as in its nonage. . . . Despotism is a legitimate mode of government in dealing with barbarians, provided the end be their improvement and the means justified by actually effecting that end. Liberty, as a principle, has no application to any state of things anterior to the time when mankind have become capable of being improved by free and equal discussion.
>
> (Mill 1859, 13–14)

This passage is easy to dismiss as Mill's rationalization for British dominance of its colony in India. But such a dismissal would merely be an objection *to the empirical facts* as Mill understood them, not to his understanding of the principle. Mill also claims that "mankind" has "in all nations with whom we need here concern ourselves" now "attained the capacity of being guided to their own improvement by conviction or persuasion," but that empirical assertion deserves as little credence as his assertion about the "barbarians" on the Indian subcontinent (Mill 1859, 14).

Marcuse's case against broad tolerance of even harmful speech is, in short, a version of Mill's case against free speech in colonized India: The facts about expression in many modern societies, including capitalist America on Marcuse's view, make clear that its consequences are also harmful—American citizens are more like the "barbarians" of Mill's colonial imagination than one might have supposed, at least according to Marcuse.

We need not adjudicate here the merits of Marcuse's objection,[7] because for our purposes—namely, understanding the justification of academic freedom—there is a far more striking fact about his theoretical position. Marcuse accepted the Millian rationale but doubted that the preconditions for truth-maximizing speech existed in society as presently constituted. Yet at the same he recognized that the university was (or, in principle, should be) different. While he rejected "indiscriminate" toleration that "protect[s] false words and wrong deeds which demonstrate that they contradict and counteract the possibilities of liberation," he went on to write: "Such indiscriminate tolerance is justified in harmless debates, in conversation, in academic discussion; it is indispensable in the scientific [*wissenschaftlich*] enterprise, in private religion" (Marcuse 1965, 88). Marcuse, as a German, undoubtedly understood the *wissenschaftlich* enterprise quite broadly, going well beyond natural science, which is how the notion should be understood.[8] And that means that Marcuse thought that in the scholarly enterprise (unlike in the polity at large), *everything goes*, at least subject to the constraint imposed by disciplinary competence. In short, the dispute between Mill and Marcuse about the background conditions in which utility-maximizing speech can take place actually suggests an important conclusion with respect to academic freedom. For *even Marcuse*—the Hegelian-Marxist skeptic about free expression in the political sphere—recognized the sphere of academic debate as one in which "indiscriminate" toleration, as he would put it, should prevail.

Why would Marcuse have thought that? I suspect two basic ideas were at work. On the one hand, Marcuse thought the immediate consequences of academic debate were harmless, only affecting opinion in the journals and the seminar room (to the extent they are harmful elsewhere, the regulation of such speech would fall within the purview of general norms of speech regulation in a society); but, at the same time, as an heir of the Humboldt tradition, he no doubt believed that academic debate held to *wissenschaftlich* standards would maximize the discovery of truth over the long term. After all, Marcuse was as much a Hegelian as a Marxist: He thought there were truths, including moral truths, to be discovered.[9] Indiscriminate toleration of *wissenschaftlich* expression in the universities was the way to reveal them.

Thus, we may say that on what I will call henceforth the Mill/Marcuse view, the special role of the universities is to provide a forum in which the vigorous pursuit of knowledge and truth is free from sanction or censure (unless, of course, there is a violation of *wissenschaftlich* standards), since (1) the results of such inquiry harm no one immediately, and (2) universities satisfy (or aspire to satisfy) the Millian (and Marcusian) conditions in which truth is more likely to be discovered over the long-term, at least insofar as *wissenschaftlich* standards of disciplinary expertise are honored, the crucial point to which we must now turn. The reason to think (2) is true is easy to specify: In universities, at least when functioning properly, all views can be aired and defended with appropriate evidence and reasons, and all such views can be subject to scrutiny from skeptics based on evidence and reasons—that is, when academic freedom prevails, truth is more likely to win out.[10]

What I am calling the Mill/Marcuse rationale for academic freedom depends crucially, as I emphasized earlier, on the idea of a *Wissenschaft*. Like Mill, I am an empiricist and fallibilist—that is, someone who thinks knowledge comes from experience and we could always be wrong—so I do agree with him that we can never be confident in the truth of what we believe, and thus our beliefs demand constant challenge. Marcuse was neither an empiricist nor fallibilist, at least as far as we can tell, but he arrived at a similar place, perhaps because of the influence of Humboldt and the historicist tradition in German thought, which emphasized the historical relativity and evolution of conceptual schemes and moral ideas. Hegel perverted the historicist tradition in German thought in a Whiggish direction, which no doubt influenced Marcuse, but in its origins, in Herder, there was no assumption of progress towards the truth. One who is a genuine historicist must be open to the possibility that one's current understanding will evolve dramatically with the passage of time and in a way that does not build on the current *Geist* but repudiates it.

Empiricists and historicists can agree that challenge can only be useful for discovering the truth if we are in a cognitive position to assess the challenge. Universities are—at least in the capitalist world, a fact presumably vivid to Marcuse—the primary sites of such challenges, the only ones outside of courts of law in which knowledge of the truth stands some chance of prevailing subject to rigorous disciplinary interrogation. The unmediated Internet, with its blogs and tweets, as well as television and the mass media, are largely worthless on this score. In all these fora, no one really listens to what anyone else says, arguments and evidence are never evaluated seriously, and the absence of mediators guarantee that any ignoramus or maniac with a computer—or a sympathetic billionaire backer—can be "heard."

In universities, at least while academic freedom prevails, the situation is different: Certainly, professors propagate bogus ideas, and whole dubious *Wissenschaften*—think of behaviorism in psychology, or neoclassical economics, or deconstructionism in literary studies—can flourish for decades. Partisan agendas can claim the mantle of scientific knowledge across the spectrum of political opinion; but in the end, all these views have to answer to inquiry and critique, and as long as academic freedom prevails, we have reason to be optimistic that truth will win out in universities committed to the *Wissenschaften*.

But what then are *Wissenschaften*? If Humboldt's ideal was to create a place where rigorous methods for the discovery *of truth* could flourish, then there is a serious problem for fields that deny there is such a thing to discover. Postmodern skeptics about truth probably have no claim to the protections of academic freedom, unless they wish to claim that their inquiries reveal the truth that there is no truth, which would thrust them back into the relativist paradoxes diagnosed by Plato in antiquity. More generally, when methods of inquiry are *explicitly* subsumed to moral or political ends, rather than epistemic ones, the defense of academic freedom will be in trouble—assuming, as I do, that epistemic ends (knowing what is true) can be independent of moral and political ones—and that is true even if, as the American empiricist Quine held, and as I accept, that our epistemic norms are at bottom adopted for pragmatic reasons (Leiter 2015, 67–68).

But postmodern skeptics about knowing the truth are not the real problem for the defense of academic freedom, since their influence is limited already to the more feeble parts of the humanities and social sciences. The problem with behaviorism in psychology, let alone with neoclassical economics—the only putatively scientific field in which scholars whose views contradict each other—Eugene Fama and Robert Schiller—were deemed worthy of a Nobel Prize in the same year[11]—is obviously not that both fields were not interested in discovering what was true. To the contrary, both fields thought they were deploying rigorous methods aimed at discovery of the truth. The problem was that their methodologies were not, in fact, epistemically reliable, even if (in the case of behaviorism) that took decades to discover and even if (in the case of economics) that fact continues to meet with massive ideological resistance. Psychology, for example, underwent a major scholarly self-correction beginning with Chomsky's critique of behaviorism in the late 1950s, and economics too has been marked precisely by ideological rifts that insure lively competing research programs persist. Academic freedom makes this possible, even if falsehood triumphs for decades.

The more serious worries arise about those academic subjects that are not organized around *wissenschaftlich* techniques, but around the moral and political concerns of (often justly) aggrieved social groups seeking "recognition,"[12] as well as (once again) the more feeble academic disciplines, like literary studies,[13] not to mention some parts of academic law, one of my fields, which sometimes emulates the worst features of the pseudo-disciplines.[14] Universities will be in no position to defend academic freedom in capitalist societies—given the powerful interests aligned against such freedom for reasons unrelated to the value of truth—unless they are prepared to insure that the fields of inquiry they nurture and protect aim for truth, and do so utilizing methods of inquiry that have truth not simply as their aim, but as their reasonably frequent result.

Unfortunately, as the great American philosopher of science Larry Laudan (1983) demonstrated, we have no criteria for demarcating even genuinely successful natural science from pseudo-science, so it should hardly be surprising that we have no simple way of demarcating *Wissenschaften* from pretenders. University administrators would no doubt welcome simple criteria—at least those administrators not already committed to turning universities into simulacra for the kind of justice unrealized in society at large[15]—since they are charged with ensuring their institutions are sites of only such inquiry.

Since there are no necessary and sufficient conditions for what makes a mode of inquiry epistemically reliable, the only evidence we have to go on is the *actual track record*, i.e., the extent to which its claims generate good predictions and survive scrutiny and apparently contrary evidence. Although these are far from clean demarcation criteria, they still give us indicators that a field is a *Wissenschaft*, one deserving of a place in a university as Humboldt understood it. There are others useful indicators: For example, the possession of and ability to teach *methods* of inquiry for epistemic ends is another good sign of a *Wissenschaft*; and receptiveness to critique from other *Wissenschaften* in the university is probative. (Academic fields that want to insulate themselves from assessment by "outsiders" should be treated as inherently suspect, though not necessarily pretenders to being a *Wissenschaft*.) But, again, we must remember that the evidential standards for truth regarding, for example, the authenticity of ancient texts, the correct translation of Augustine, the causes of suicide bombing, and the relative contribution of natural selection and genetic hitchhiking to evolution will be multivarious, and admit only of evaluation by reference to preexisting expert opinion. This is the potentially dangerous circularity of academic freedom based on disciplinary expertise, but I see no way around it, except to require that all university disciplines be open to critique from other university disciplines.

Most fields in most major Western research universities these days probably qualify as *Wissenschaften* in the relevant sense: biology, psychology, the cognitive sciences, mathematics, chemistry, linguistics, much of philosophy,[16] physics, the applied sciences (including engineering), even most of what goes on in political science, sociology, history, and economics. And the crux of academic freedom in this context is that faculty are not censured for their views arising from their disciplinary competence; arguments and evidence are the central currency of the exchange of ideas, consistent with the *wissenschaftlich* ideal; and tolerance of minority viewpoints is actively encouraged by those who administer university life. Not all minority viewpoints need be encouraged, only those that can claim that they arise from methods of inquiry and analysis that are relevant to ascertaining what is true. Academic freedom, in short, is the hallmark of a serious university, and disciplinary competence in the *Wissenschaft* is the benchmark for the freedom in question.[17]

Let me conclude with some skeptical doubts and challenges about the kind of academic freedom articulated and defended here.

Marcuse suggested, and I agree, that in the context of the academic or "scientific" enterprise, freedom of expression and inquiry should be "indiscriminate" (in Marcuse's terms). But does that mean academic freedom should protect academic defenses of Nazism or slavery, or the inferiority of certain races or religions? The answer is, "yes, it should," subject to the demand that these defenses meet the standards of a *Wissenschaft*.[18] I am not much worried about "scientific" Nazism gaining traction in universities, but it is clearly the case that other "morally suspect" views might gain traction within existing university disciplines—but that is precisely why academic freedom is important. The empirical bases for claims about racial or gender-based differences should be seriously scrutinized, and I expect they will be rejected as they have been before, but they are fit subjects for research and debate—for "indiscriminate" toleration, again, as Marcuse would put it. (After all, if there were cognitive differences that tracked racial, ethnic, or gender differences, that leaves wholly open what ought to be done about them.)

The much harder cases will involve the kind of non-cognitive normative advocacy that characterizes parts of many humanistic and social science fields. While all criteria of "scientific" inquiry are socially constructed—there is, per Laudan (1983), no line drawn by nature between science and pseudo-science—one may still hope that in *wissenschaftlich* fields, the criteria of success (knowledge, truth) answer primarily to the facts about the world, not facts about the community of inquirers, as seems to be true in most of the moral and political philosophy of the last generation in the capitalist democracies. That way of framing the problem plainly presupposes substantive views about the cognitive status of forms of inquiry that are themselves subjects of contestation in various disciplines—and Millian fallibilism and academic freedom suggests we should try to be agnostic about them!

A more serious challenge, by my lights, is skepticism about the supposition that academic freedom in the universities actually increases the discovery and dissemination of knowledge, the central purpose of the universities on everyone's account. Many of the great discoveries of modernity occurred under conditions where academic freedom did not prevail. In the natural sciences, think of Copernicus, Galileo, Lavoisier, Priestly, Darwin, Einstein, and Heisenberg; in the human sciences, think of Hobbes, Machiavelli, Hume, Herder, Marx, Hayek, and Benjamin. (Of course, many of these thinkers were not even professional academics!) The results of the modern, largely post-World War II era of "academic freedom" seem paltry by comparison. To be sure, any judgment about the value of particular "results" already implicates scholarly judgments that are highly contested and about which the ultimate verdict would itself be distorted by limitations on academic freedom.

There are also crucial differences between the human and natural sciences to which any discussion of academic freedom must attend. The main threats to academic freedom in the natural sciences in the capitalist democracies come from powerful business interests that disfavor, for profit-seeking reasons, certain discoveries: for example, concerning the human contribution to climate change, to take the most important example in the present, but also findings about the inefficacy of particular pharmaceuticals and medical treatments. Businesses have a strong interest in the correct natural scientific understanding of the causal order of nature, to be sure, since the extraction of profit from nature requires it. At the same time, businesses also have strong interests in concealing certain scientific results that might impede popular acceptance of their business practices and consumption of their products. Academic freedom is a crucial bulwark in favor of discovering truths about the natural world even in the relatively free capitalist societies.

In the human sciences, the issues are usually different: It is, shall we say, rare for international corporations to get exercised about the latest developments in the history of early modern Europe or philosophy of the social sciences. The threats to academic freedom in the human sciences come less from the business sector and more often from political and religious interest groups whose normative commitments are threatened by the findings of the human sciences. In the United States, for example, external pressure is frequently brought upon universities who try to employ critics of Israeli policy towards the Palestinians.[19] But the pressure to violate academic freedom comes from within the universities too. Indeed, some humanists have concocted a whole new metaphysics of "silencing" and "marginalizing" and "violence" to describe the expression of ideas that are offensive and insulting to certain minority groups. For these academic insiders, Marcusian "indiscriminate" toleration in academic discourse is not acceptable, since the expression of ideas that might be hurtful to individuals based on group membership—in particular, membership in groups that have been victims of historical practices of subordination (e.g., African-Americans in the United States, though more recently, transgender individuals)—is alleged to "silence" members of that group and do "violence" to them.

Marcuse himself wanted to suppress speech advocating for actual violence against and silencing of human beings: murdering their political leaders, dropping chemical bombs on their country, destroying their society and livelihood through military violence. But neoliberalism—the idea that the preferences of the consumers of products, including education, determine the value of what is offered—now rules in the capitalist universities too, with the result that some self-styled "progressive" faculty and students—even in institutions of higher education that protect expressive rights quite resolutely—believe that denigrating and offensive ideas "silence," "marginalize," and "do violence" to them. (Ironically, one need only watch videos, easily available on-line, of minority students challenging and ridiculing the pathetic neo-Nazi Richard Spencer on various campuses to realize that no one was "silenced" and no one suffered actual "violence.") In both research and teaching in the human sciences, such metaphysical flights of fancy deserve no consideration at any university committed to academic freedom. The dismissal of this melodrama is, of course, compatible with full commitment to laws, common in most Western democracies these days, prohibiting racial, gender, or sexual orientation discrimination.

In sum, we protect academic freedom to protect the discovery and dissemination of truths about the world. And there is a final consideration in favor of such protection that deserves notice, pertaining to the epistemological crisis of the twenty-first century, namely, the Internet. Remember that most of what any of us know about the world is due to "epistemic authorities," that is, individuals or institutions that tell us what we ought to believe about Newtonian mechanics, evolution by natural selection, climate change, resurrection from the dead, or the Holocaust. The most practically fruitful epistemic norm of modernity, empiricism, demands that knowledge be grounded in sensory experience, but almost no one who believes in evolution by natural selection or the reality of the Holocaust has any sensory evidence in support of those beliefs. Instead, we rely on epistemic authorities—biologists and historians, for example—who, in turn consult testimony, texts, physical evidence, and the like.

Epistemic authority cannot be sustained by empiricist criteria, for obvious reasons: salient anecdotal evidence, the favorite tool of propagandists, appeals to ordinary faith in the senses, but is easily exploited given that most people understand neither the perils of induction nor the finer points of sampling and Bayesian inference. Sustaining epistemic authority depends, crucially, on social institutions that inculcate reliable second-order norms about whom to believe about what: Here academic institutions, insofar as academic freedom prevails, have been hugely important. From their regime of "indiscriminate" toleration should emerge the ideas about the world most likely to be true, or at least in the vicinity of the truth. The media of mass communication have also been crucial, in the age of mass democracy, with promulgating and sustaining such norms, at least insofar as they defer to the epistemic authorities in institutions where academic freedom prevails.

The Internet is, alas, the great eliminator of intermediaries. This has been its great appeal for all those excluded in the past, justly or unjustly, from public discourse. But as cyberspace, with its lack of mediators and filters, has become the primary source of information for most people in the economically advanced nations, its ability to undermine epistemic authority has become alarmingly evident. The barriers to entry on the

Internet in the relatively free capitalist societies are "low," as the economists like to say, and they do not include knowledge, intelligence, competence, or even good mental health. The Internet is the epistemological crisis of the twenty-first century: It magnifies ignorance and stupidity and is now leading hundreds of millions of people to act on the basis of the fantasy world it constructs. That fact makes academic freedom even more important than ever before for two reasons. First, groups outside the universities, influenced by the Internet fantasy world, are ever more likely to demand that actual scholars conform to their fantasies, thus increasing the traditional non-epistemic pressures on academic inquiry. Second, the intermediaries for public discourse that remain—those that check facts, consult experts, exclude cranks—will be increasingly dependent on an academy in which robust Marcusian academic freedom prevails if it is to offer a reliable counterweight to the "nonsense and misinformation superhighway" that is the modern Internet. Academic freedom is now a crucial safeguard for knowledge and for truth in the Internet era.[20]

Notes

1. I omit here the "good manners" provisions about faculty speech that even the AAUP itself has effectively disowned, since they would impose upon the political speech of academics standards of decorum that do not apply to anyone else in the polity.
2. In an at-will employment regime, employees can be fired for any reasons not otherwise prohibited by law (e.g., the employee cannot be terminated for his race or her gender). The contrast is with employment laws that permit firing employees only "for cause," i.e., for failure to perform their occupational duties. "Tenure" is such a system, though it has migrated at far too many universities into a system that insulates even incompetent employees from repercussions.
3. Interestingly, in the German case, scientific freedom has been held by the Constitutional Court to create positive entitlements, not just protection from interference: "the state is under a constitutional duty to safeguard the value by making some provisions for the effective exercise of academic freedom" (Barendt 2010, 118). It is even a right enjoyed by non-academics, insofar as they are engaged in *Wissenschaft* (Barendt 2010, 119).
4. Whether all disciplines in the modern university are *Wissenschaften* is a topic to which I return, following.
5. Academic freedom can and is limited in all jurisdictions by general legal prohibitions. A German academic cannot invoke academic freedom to teach the merits of Nazism to his students, and an American academic cannot appeal to academic freedom to justify creating a hostile environment for women in his classroom. Whether such limits on academic freedom are compatible with its principled rationale may be debated in particular cases, though in general, they are probably sound.
6. I am skeptical of this assumption, as I argued in Leiter 2016.
7. I think it has merit, as I argue in more detail in Leiter 2016.
8. Marcuse no doubt thought that an obscurantist Christian metaphysician like Hegel was also a purveyor of a *Wissenschaft*, but that is doubtful: Hegel should be taught as a matter of intellectual history, of course, but he cannot

be invoked as a guide to truth, let alone as evidence of the harm of certain kinds of speech.

9. I disagree with both Mill and Marcuse on this point, but whether or not they are correct is clearly a crucial topic for scholarly inquiry.
10. This defense of academic freedom does not cover freedom in the creative arts, including the teachers of those arts, since such freedom of artistic expression is not, directly in any case, connected to discovery of the truth. The German "Basic Law" takes the right approach by protecting such freedom *in addition* to *Wissenschaftsfreiheit*. The general justification of artistic freedom is not my topic here.
11. Economics, as critics external to the field have frequently pointed out, has fairly obviously been subject to an ideological capture that insulates it from the failure of its predictive models, in a way no actual science could withstand. See, e.g., Hausman 1992 and Rosenberg 1993. And for a fascinating history of how the quasi-Nobel Prize in Economics was created in 1969 to legitimize the discipline and mobilize it against social democracy, see Offer and Söderberg 2016.
12. The tragedy here is that many disciplines ignored these groups for non-epistemic reasons, e.g., racism, sexism, and other parochial prejudices. Unfortunately, at many, but not all universities, programs devoted to neglected groups have evolved in ways that reflect non-epistemic normative agendas.
13. Literary studies used to be a clear *Wissenschaft* in the Humboldt sense when it presupposed a high level of technical competence with languages, diction, the history of texts, and the formal features of expression.
14. For an early exposé of this problem in academic law, see Leiter 1992, which made me many long-standing enemies.
15. Just to be clear about my own views on this score: American society is horribly "unjust" on any conception of justice, but the idea that infringing the academic freedom of scholars and teachers has any impact in rectifying the actual injustice is delusional. Nothing in the argument in the text turns on whether I am correct about the injustice of American society.
16. Philosophy I know well, and here the situation is complex. Much of Anglophone philosophy has adopted a *wissenschaftlich* self-conception, but there are still outliers where in-group cults, usually inspired by Heidegger or Wittgenstein, dominate and the result is not a truth-oriented community but an academic community whose goals are self-congratulation and solidarity. I wish this were only true at marginal universities!
17. Note that "academic freedom" so conceived does not protect students, except indirectly. Students lack a *Wissenschaft*, they attend university in order to acquire one (or more). To the extent their freedom of expression contributes to successful research or teaching, their expression should be treated as instrumentally important. But all competent teachers limit expression in the classroom, and they are right to do so, insofar as the purpose of such restrictions is to facilitate the dissemination of knowledge. (This is why, as the AAUP statement notes, academic freedom does not protect off-topic pontificating by faculty: The job of faculty is to disseminate the knowledge distinctive of their disciplines, and that is all.) Student groups who invite speakers to campus are also not protected by academic freedom. There may be strong reasons related to general freedom of expression to give wide latitude to such invitations, but universities are well within their academic freedom rights to reject those speakers that fall short of *Wissenschaften* standards—but that is a judgment to be rendered by scholars in the relevant *Wissenschaft*, not by offended students or members of the public

at large. In the United States, there is a significant constitutional limitation on the ability of public universities to restrict speakers this way, but private university can plainly do so consistent with academic freedom.

18. Academic freedom, as noted *supra* n. 5, is also subject to general legal regulations.
19. For an example, see Salaita 2015, Schmidt 2015, Leiter 2014a, and Leiter 2014b on the Steven Salaita case at the University of Illinois.
20. Thanks to my former colleague David Rabban for helpful guidance on the legal issues, and to Taylor Coles, University of Chicago Law School class of 2018, for his characteristically excellent research assistance. I also benefitted from discussion of many of the ideas here at workshops at the law schools at Brooklyn, Columbia, Chicago, and Utah, and the philosophy departments at Iowa and Colorado. I also thank the Alumni Faculty Fund of the University of Chicago Law School for support.

Works Cited

American Association of University Professors. "1940 Statement of Principles on Academic Freedom and Tenure." 1940. www.aaup.org/report/1940-statement-principles-academic-freedom-and-tenure.

Barendt, Eric. *Academic Freedom and the Law: A Comparative Study*. Oxford: Hart, 2010.

Basic Law for the Federal Republic of Germany in the revised version published in the Federal Law Gazette Part III, classification number 100–1, as last amended by the Act of July 21, 2010 (Federal Law Gazette I, p. 944). https://germanlawarchive.iuscomp.org/?p=212.

Education Reform Act 1988. c. 40 §§1–238. United Kingdom.

Forster, Michael N. "The Liberal Temper in Classical German Philosophy: Freedom of Thought and Expression." Chap. 7 in *After Herder: Philosophy of Language in the German Tradition*. Oxford: Oxford University Press, 2010.

Hausman, Daniel. *The Inexact and Separate Science of Economics*. Cambridge: Cambridge University Press, 1992.

Laudan, Larry. "The Demise of the Demarcation Problem." In *Physics, Philosophy and Psychoanalysis: Essays in Honour of A. Grünbaum*, editd by Robert S. Cohen and Larry Laudan. Boston: D. Reidel, 1983: 111–127.

Leiter, Brian. "Intellectual Voyeurism in Legal Scholarship." *Yale Journal of Law & the Humanities*, Vol. 4, No. 1 (1992): 79–104.

———. "University of Illinois Repeals the First Amendment for Its Faculty." *Huffington Post*. August 23, 2014a. www.huffingtonpost.com/brian-leiter/university-of-illinois-re_1_b_5703038.html.

———. "Salaita v. University of Illinois: The Constitutional Issues." *Huffington Post*. August 27, 2014b. www.huffingtonpost.com/brian-leiter/salaita-v-university-of-i_b_5726034.html.

———. "Normativity for Naturalists." *Philosophical Issues*, Vol. 25 (2015): 64–79. http://dx.doi.org/10.1111/phis.12046.

———. "The Case Against Free Speech." *Sydney Law Review*, Vol. 38, No. 4 (2016): 407–439.

Marcuse, Herbert. "Repressive Tolerance." In *A Critique of Pure Tolerance*, edited by Robert Paul Wolff, Barrington Moore, Jr. and Herbert Marcuse. Boston, MA: Beacon Press, 1965: 95–137.

Mill, John Stuart. *On Liberty*. London: John W. Parker & Son, 1859.
———. *Autobiography of John Stuart Mill*. Reprint, Oxford: Oxford University Press, (1873) 1975.
Offer, Avner and Söderberg, Gabriel. *The Nobel Factor: The Prize in Economics, Social Democracy, and the Market Turn*. Princeton, NJ: Princeton University Press, 2016.
Rosenberg, Alexander. *Economics: Mathematical Politics or Science of Diminishing Returns*. Chicago: University of Chicago Press, 1993.
Salaita, Steven. "Why I Was Fired." *Chronicle of Higher Education*. October 5, 2015. www.chronicle.com/article/Why-I-Was-Fired/233640.
Schmidt, Peter. "AAUP Takes Illinois to Task in Report on Salaita Case." *Chronicle of Higher Education*. April 28, 2015. www.chronicle.com/article/AAUP-Takes-Illinois-to-Task-in/229715.
Van Alstyne, William. "The Specific Theory of Academic Freedom and the General Issue of Civil Liberty." In *The Concept of Academic Freedom*, edited by E. L. Pincoffs. University of Texas Press, 1972: 59–85.

3 Free Speech and Ideological Diversity on American College Campuses[1]

Keith E. Whittington

Freedom of thought is the lifeblood of a university. Universities are dedicated to the advancement and dissemination of knowledge. In order to fulfill that mission, universities must nurture an environment in which scholars can ask difficult questions and follow their evidence and analysis wherever they lead and teachers can expose their students to the unvarnished truth and press them to reexamine their most fundamental commitments. Restrictions on the freedom of thought are antithetical to the most basic commitment of the member of the campus community to pursue the truth. Skepticism of received wisdom and free inquiry into what lies at the boundaries of human knowledge are organizing principles of the university (see Whittington 2018).

It is not easy creating and maintaining the conditions in which freedom of thought can thrive. The temptations to limit the scope of that freedom are myriad. Orthodoxies arise and demand fealty. Conformity can be comforting though stifling. Dissent can be disagreeable and offensive. The toleration of free-ranging thought and speech often means tolerating the erroneous, the embarrassing, the odious, and even the dangerous. The benefits of a culture of free inquiry are not always obvious and immediate, but the costs often are.

Freedom of thought is most useful when there is openness to disagreement. The English philosopher John Stuart Mill (2015, 20) noted,

> while every one well knows himself to be fallible, few think it necessary to take any precautions against their own fallibility, or admit the supposition that any opinion, of which they feel very certain, may be one of the example of the error to which they acknowledge themselves to be liable.

"Absolute princes" tended to be particularly confident in their own opinions precisely because they were surrounded by sycophants who were unwilling to voice any disagreement with their ruler. The political leadership is subject to "groupthink," unless active steps are taken to discourage conformity and encourage independent thought (Janis 1982). Individuals gain confidence in the infallibility of their own opinions when those opinions are reinforced by "'the world' in general," but too often "the world, to each individual, means the part of it with which he comes in contact; his party, his sect, his church, his class of society." (Mill 2015, 20).

The process of free inquiry in pursuit of the advancement of knowledge functions best when diverse voices can be heard. Universities should strive to cultivate that intellectual diversity. Scholarship advances and students learn by exposing ideas to the test of skeptical examination. We should want to see ideas advanced by those who actually believe them and are capable of presenting them within their most thoughtful and persuasive form. We should want to see those ideas dissected by those who are genuinely critical of them and can subject them to the most withering criticism and analysis. Our convictions are most justified when out ideas have withstood careful scrutiny. We benefit from surrounding ourselves with those who disagree with us. We should not merely tolerate disagreement; we should welcome it.

Of course, universities do not desire indiscriminate diversity. We should value the productive exchange of ideas, not mere cacophony. We should wish to hear from those who have something useful to say, and not simply from those who are strident. The advancement of knowledge requires discernment, and the modern university is organized to promote those who have mastered a body of knowledge, who can claim expertise, who can claim to operate on the frontiers of knowledge and not simply in the intellectual wastelands. Intellectual diversity, if it is to be useful, need not extend so far as to include the crank and the propagandist. Even so, universities should seek to engage the intellectual world around them, to hear from those who are active in the public sphere as well as those who rove the groves of academia. If it is to be vital and relevant, the campus community should not be sealed off from the world. The university should expose scholars and students to the ideas shaping society as well as the ideas sparking academic debate.

The failures of universities to live up to their own ideals and to be tolerant of dissenting ideas have been increasingly documented. Controversial speakers are disinvited or shouted down. Troublesome faculty are harassed or fired. Outspoken students are ostracized or disciplined. Social media is scrutinized for unorthodox thoughts and careless phrasing (See, e.g., Downs 2005; Lukianoff 2012; Furedi 2016).

Although attacks on freedom of thought and free speech on American college campuses can and do come from both the left and the right, there may be particular reason to worry that the internal pressures for conformity come from the left. American universities face substantial and growing pressures from the political right, and they increasingly operate in an environment in which conservatives distrust universities and are eager to expose the missteps of academics. But on campuses themselves, the conservative perspective is often not well represented.

There has been growing attention paid to what is sometimes called ideological or viewpoint diversity on American college campuses. Critics worry that academia itself has become an intellectual echo chamber in which only the left side of the political spectrum is heard, an intellectual bubble from which conservative voices are excluded. The effort to map intellectual diversity on American college campuses has been somewhat limited, however.

This chapter brings some empirical evidence to bear on this issue. In particular, the chapter examines college commencement speakers and summer common readings for incoming first-year college students in the spring and summer of 2017. Commencement speakers and common readings have been periodic subjects of controversy on college campuses, with some students objecting that the selections have strayed too far from the political and social mainstream, as they understand it. Particular examples of disputes over speakers and readings have drawn attention to campus intolerance, but such isolated episodes and anecdotal evidence tell us little about how such common features of campus life help shape the intellectual environment that students experience. A more systemic look at these materials can provide some further evidence on how narrow or how broad the intellectual horizons are on American college campuses.

Viewpoint Diversity on Campus

It is no secret that American college campuses skew to the political left. This has been a source of near-constant conservative complaint for much of the twentieth century. William F. Buckley (1951), who helped create the modern conservative movement, came to national attention on the eve of the Eisenhower administration with a scathing critique of the liberal tilt of his alma mater, Yale University. The ascent of Ronald Reagan was accompanied by conservative denunciations of the "tenured radicals" occupying the universities (Bloom 1987; Kimball 1990). As time has worn on, conservative denunciations of academia have become a growth industry (D'Souza 1991; Horowitz 2006; Maranto, Redding and Hess 2009).

Although many of these jeremiads against academia are sensationalized and focus their fire on extreme examples, there are also careful studies detailing the political views of the university faculty. As soon as social scientists began to study political attitudes and voting behavior, they turned the microscope on themselves and started to survey academics to assess their political leanings. A survey of academic political scientists at the end of the 1950s revealed that they were overwhelmingly supporters of the Democratic Party and held liberal political views (Turner, McClintock and Spaulding 1963). A decade later, broader surveys of university professors found similar results, though they noted that more conservative faculty members could be found in some disciplines (such as engineering) and in lower-prestige institutions (Lipset and Ladd 1972). More recent surveys have found that the dominance of Democratic-voting, liberal-thinking academics has only become more pronounced over time, and the number of conservatives found anywhere in academia had shrunk (Rothman, Lichter and Nevitte 2005; Klein and Stern 2005). Whether measured by professed policy commitments, self-described ideology, self-reported voting habits, voting registration records, or campaign donation histories, the evidence is overwhelming and consistent that American academics cluster on the left end of the political spectrum.

It is much less clear how these political leanings matter to daily life within the universities. Knowing that members of the university faculty lean to the left does not necessarily tell us that teaching or research is similarly politically skewed. Surveys of college students suggest that they view their professors as predominantly on the left end of the political spectrum, but student assessments seem to significantly underestimate how left-leaning the professoriate is, which might suggest that professors in the classroom are not always politically transparent. There is little evidence that exposure to left-leaning academics has the effect of indoctrinating college students and pushing their own political values to the left (Mariari and Hewitt 2008; Woessner and Kelly-Woessner 2009; Linvill and Havice 2011; Wills 2013; Braidwood and Ausderan 2017).

Even so, there is reason to think that greater viewpoint diversity would be beneficial. Conservative students are more likely than their liberal peers to perceive political bias in the classroom. Conservative members of the faculty often find it easier to conceal their own political views in order to better fit in to their work environment. It seems likely that important research questions and angles of research are underexplored because they escape the notice of an ideologically homogeneous university faculty. Conservative ideas might not be presented as often or as well in classrooms populated overwhelmingly by liberal instructors. Liberal conventional wisdom might not be exposed to the kind of skeptical scrutiny that would foster greater dialogue and deeper knowledge. Although there may be no easy remedies to the situation, the lack of ideological diversity on American college campuses is a troubling flaw in a set of institutions dedicated to freedom of thought and the exploration of the unknown (Rothman, Kelly-Woessner and Woessner 2011; Yancey 2011; Gross 2013; Shields and Dun 2016).

Commencement Speakers

Commencement speakers are a somewhat unusual feature of the intellectual environment of most American college campuses. The ceremony to honor graduating seniors serves as an opportunity for universities to celebrate what their students have achieved and to show off for parents what the university has to offer. The combination of prestige, speaking fee, and honorary degree is enough to allow many colleges to attract an unusually visible figure to campus capable of entertaining a general audience. Commencement speakers bring a dash of celebrity to university proceedings. A successful choice of a commencement speaker should raise the visibility of the campus and impress assembled guests, but generate no real controversy. The commencement ceremony is one of the few occasions on a college campus when a sizable portion of the campus community is gathered together to listen to a common address.

The commencement speaker is expected to add to a celebratory occasion and not necessarily elevate the intellectual discourse on campus. The speaker is not generally expected to push intellectual boundaries, raise difficult questions, or lay out provocative arguments. There is no give-and-take with the audience or other speakers. The speaker is expected to say something suitably soothing and gratifying, to provide a bit of motivation and inspiration, and perhaps hit a note of nostalgia and acclaim. The speaker might challenge the graduating seniors to go out into the world and do well, but will probably not challenge them to reassess their most firmly held convictions. The commencement speaker lifts up, but does not unsettle.

Nonetheless, commencement speakers have become an increasingly visible point of contention on college campuses. Commencement controversies seem to come in waves. Over the course of the 1990s, the *Chronicle of Higher Education*, perhaps the most visible national source of news about American universities, published only a handful of articles taking note of campus protests over the selection of commencement speakers. No doubt there were more dissenters who made themselves known on individual campuses but who did not attract the attention of a larger audience. Harvard University caused a slight stir in 1993 when it selected General Colin Powell as the commencement speaker, leading some gay students to say that they were "insulted" by the choice a general at a time when the military's policy on homosexuals openly serving in the ranks was a matter of controversy. Meanwhile, some students at the University of Texas grumbled that their college had chosen a "boring weenie" (the incoming university president) to give the commencement address, and the students at William and Mary College were put out that they "end[ed] up with Bill Cosby," after expecting to be fêted by President Bill Clinton. The disappointed students thought they should have a greater say over speaker selection in the future (*Chronicle of Higher Education*, May 19, 1993). Some students at Evergreen State College walked out of their graduation ceremony in protest in 1999 at the videotaped appearance of the student-chosen commencement speaker, Mumia Abu-Jamal, who sat on Pennsylvania's death row for the killing of a police officer but who had become something of a celebrity in left-wing circles as a black nationalist (*Chronicle of Higher Education*, June 25, 1999).

The pace of protests seemed to pick up in the new century. Vice President Richard Cheney met with demonstrations denouncing him as a "war monger" at Michigan State University (*Chronicle of Higher Education*, May 24, 2002). Members of the faculty walked off the stage at Georgetown University during the remarks of the conservative Catholic cardinal from Nigeria, Francis Arinze. Saint Louis University disinvited the CEO of American Airlines in response to student protests of executive pay and replaced him with a local newspaper columnist who had helped rally the protestors (*Chronicle of Higher Education*, June 6, 2003). By the time of the Obama administration, spring-time protests over commencement speakers had become an annual ritual and colleges had become the butt of jokes. The president of Worcester Polytechnic Institute negotiated an elaborate plan to accommodate the protestors of Exxon CEO Rex Tillerson as commencement speaker (*Chronicle of Higher Education*, June 13, 2011). Rutgers University disinvited former Secretary of State Condoleezza Rice in the face of extended protests. Conservative neurosurgeon and future presidential candidate Ben Carson withdrew from a planned commencement address at Johns Hopkins University given expected protests. University of California president and former secretary of homeland security Janet Napolitano resolved to ride out the protests over her selection as the commencement speaker for the Hastings College of Law (*Chronicle of Higher Education*, May 7, 2014). The selection of the commencement speaker had become a political "minefield" that university presidents approached with angst and trepidation (*Chronicle of Higher Education*, May 11, 2015). Rather than a feel-good moment of celebration, graduation ceremonies had become a potential source of negative publicity.

After years of campus protests over commencement speakers, how bold are universities willing to be in extending invitations? Some have charged that the "intolerant left" has cowed campus administrators and truncated the acceptable range of campus speakers, assuming that college leaders would have been willing to invite more conservative speakers in the first place. We might worry that university presidents have chosen to play it safe with commencement speakers and have shied away from anyone who might spark controversy. But, perhaps, despite the stress that can be associated with the selection of a commencement speaker, colleges nonetheless offer seniors a diverse range of speakers who can challenge students and enliven the intellectual environment. While the occasional high-profile protest can paint universities in an unpleasant light and suggest that students will only tolerate speakers operating within narrow ideological bounds, a broader look at the line-up of commencement speakers might provide a different perspective.

To that end, this chapter considers a database of 444 commencement speakers whose selection was reported in a national news site covering higher education, *Inside Higher Ed*, in the spring of 2017. Although this selection certainly does not include all the commencement speakers who spoke that year, it represents a large sample of American colleges and universities. Rather than focusing on the small number of commencement speakers who spurred protests or disinvitations, this sample based on the public announcement of speakers encompasses the run-of-the-mill speakers who were able to deliver their remarks without a hitch (as well as, no doubt, a few who encountered criticism). It ranges across a wide array of institutions of higher education from small liberal arts colleges to flagship state universities and across the nation as a whole.

Colleges invite a wide range of figures to campus to serve as commencement speakers. Some are figures of national or even global renown, but many others are most likely to be familiar primarily to a local audience. Some are known for their ideas and ability to spin words in the public sphere, but many are known more for their actions than for their rhetoric. For some speakers, the strength of their ideas recommends them to speak before a university audience. More often, their record of personal accomplishment brings them to the commencement platform as a symbol of inspiration.

Perhaps to a surprising degree, colleges and universities seem to favor business leaders over nearly any other category of speaker. Such choices often allow universities to show off for its graduates an alumnus who has been successful in the world, while perhaps deepening a relationship with a current and future donor to the school. For its commencement address, Oklahoma State University tapped Larry Bryce, the president of Kohler Company, a producer of power generators, and a graduate of the university's undergraduate engineering program. Kennesaw State University in Georgia turned to Michael J. Coles, a long-time benefactor of the school, co-founder of the Great American Cookie Company, and president of Caribou Coffee Company. Franklin & Marshall College welcomed back to campus its first female African American alumna, Wanda Austin, who had recently retired from the presidency of the Aerospace Corporation. The graduates of Broward College in Florida heard from the president of the nearby retail company, City Furniture, while the seniors of Ohio's Otterbein University heard inspiring words from the chairman of a local food service company, Donatos Pizza, Inc.

Some business leaders cross the line into celebrity. They are aspirational figures who can be expected to excite and not merely impress the seniors and their parents. Landing such a luminary might be beyond the reach of a small public university or liberal arts college, but some institutions of higher education can boast a brand powerful enough to provide an attractive platform for business titans to promote their own public image. Apple's Tim Cook graced the stage of the Massachusetts Institute of Technology, Facebook's Mark Zuckerberg returned to Harvard University, and former eBay chief Meg Whitman came to Carnegie Mellon University.

If colleges want a celebrity to spice up the commencement exercises, many simply turn to the entertainment industry. University of Southern California might have an advantage in that regard, and in 2017 they landed comic actor Will Ferrell. But plenty of colleges drew from that well. Tulane University in New Orleans brought in actress Helen Mirren. The University of Houston turned to action star Arnold Schwarzenegger. New York University got singer Pharrell Williams. Plenty of lesser known entertainers found work on college campuses during commencement season as well, including *Black-ish* creator Kenya Barris at Tufts University, actor Bill Pullman at Warren Wilson College in North Carolina, stage actor Stephen Henderson at Julliard, actress Octavia Spencer at Kent State University, actress Eva Longoria at Knox College in Illinois, comedian Kumail Nanjiani at Grinnell College in Iowa, *Tonight Show* band leader Kevin Eubanks at the University of the Redlands, and country music singer Jimmy Wayne at Missouri's William Woods University. Athletes such as tennis player Billie Jean King, gymnast Carly Patterson, basketball player Julius Erving, and football player Emery Moorehead, as well as coaches such as Mike Tomlin and Shaka Smart, fall into a similar category.

Media figures put a more intellectual spin on the celebrity genre of commencement speaker, though whether their remarks are likely to be more elevated might be an open question. Oprah Winfrey kept herself busy with three separate addresses to graduates (in this sample) in the spring of 2017. Colleges heard from myriad radio and television news reporters, including CNN's Wolf Blitzer, Christiane Amanpour, Jake Tapper, and Fareed Zakaria; CBS's Vladimir Duthiers; NBC's Anne Thompson; MSNBC's Stephanie Ruhle; NPR's Arun Rath and Guy Raz; *New York Times*' Frank Bruni; the *Washington Post*'s Eugene Robinson; the *Boston Globe*'s Sacha Pfeiffer and Thomas Farragher; *Teen Vogue*'s Lauren Duca; FiveThirtyEight's Nate Silver; public radio's Virginia Prescott; and syndicated radio host Tom Joyner. Notably colleges seemed to lean toward relatively centrist figures for commencement speakers. CNN anchors predominated over MSNBC or Fox News anchors, though left-leaning opinion columnists like Lauren Duca and Eugene Robinson make an appearance while more right-leaning opinion leaders are absent.

Speakers drawn from higher education itself might be expected to have more of an ideological edge, but here too colleges seemed to prefer to play it safe. Many academic figures chosen to speak to graduates occupied positions in the senior administration of universities and colleges, and presumably could be counted on to keep their remarks suitably neutral. Active academics might be somewhat more pointed in their remarks, but universities in the spring of 2017 tended to favor professors with relatively unobjectionable research agendas. The Harvard political scientist Robert Putnam, speaker at Suffolk University, is best known for his advocacy of greater social bonds. The Wharton School's decorated management professor Adam Grant spoke at Utah State. The historian of race relations in the American South, Edward Ayers, was invited to the University of Mary Washington. Harvard's Kimberlyn Leary, who spoke at Widener University, made her reputation studying how to improve public health for diverse populations.[2]

Activists, politicians, and public officials are the most likely to wear their ideological commitments on their sleeve, and it has often been the announcement of government officials as commencement speakers who have sparked controversy. Despite such controversies in the past, universities have not stopped inviting such speakers, and this sample of speakers in the spring of 2017 included numerous speakers in that category.

After the 2016 elections, Republicans dominated both state and federal offices, and thus colleges looking for high-ranking government officials to speak to graduates might naturally find themselves drawing on more conservative figures. Some colleges did go that direction, generating some controversies on campus, but not many. President Donald Trump received a warm welcome at the religiously conservative Liberty University. Notre Dame broke with its tradition and did not invite the newly inaugurated President Trump to campus, but instead went with the more conventional conservative and former Indiana governor, Vice President Mike Pence. Even so, students staged a silent walk-out of Pence's commencement address (*Inside Higher Ed*, May 22, 2017). Pence might have expected a less contentious environment at the religiously conservative Grove City College, but nearby residents mounted their own protest of his speech there (*Pittsburgh Post-Gazette*, May 20, 2017). Secretary of Education Betsy DeVos spoke at historically black Bethune-Cookman University, requiring the university's president to intercede at one point to try to calm student hecklers (*Inside Higher Ed*, May 11, 2017). A number of smaller state universities invited local Republican politicians to speak to their graduates, as did a couple of private colleges. Republican Massachusetts governor Charlie Baker attributed his invitation to speak at Hamilton College in New York to his high-profile campaign comment that his biggest regret was that he did not attend Hamilton and to his relatively non-partisan governing philosophy. When New York's St. Lawrence College announced the selection of Republican US senator from Maine, Susan Collins, as the commencement speaker, it made sure to mention that she was an alumna of the college and was the "most bipartisan member" of the Senate.

Far more common at college commencements in the spring of 2017 were Democratic political figures. While the local Republican member of the state legislature might get a speaking invitation to the small college in his district, nationally known Democratic and left-wing politicians and activists were fêted on college campuses. Veterans of the Obama administration graced numerous graduation stages, including multiple appearances by former Vice President Joe Biden, his wife Jill Biden, former Secretary of State Hillary Clinton, cabinet member Julian Castro, and White House advisors Valerie Jarrett and Knatokie Ford. Democratic congressional leaders like Nancy Pelosi, John Lewis, and Tim Ryan greeted graduates. Commencement speakers included Hillary Clinton's 2016 running mate, Tim Kaine, as well as veterans of the Clinton administration such as former President Bill Clinton and Clinton confidante Vernon Jordan. Former and future Democratic presidential aspirants from Bill Bradley, Howard Dean, and Bill Richardson, to Bernie Sanders, to Kamala Harris, Elizabeth Warren, Tammy Duckworth, and Cory Booker crisscrossed the country to deliver commencement addresses. Liberal activists and media figures such as Van Jones, Bakari Sellers, Dolores Huerta, and Gloria Steinem were welcomed as commencement speakers.

On the whole, universities do not seem to prefer to use the selection of commencement speakers as an opportunity to advance a particular ideological message. Less than a fifth of the spring 2017 speakers in this sample had a clear political orientation, though among those who did the left side of the political spectrum was far better represented than the right. No doubt this is a somewhat conservative estimate, for surely many nominally non-ideological speakers like the heads of nonprofit organizations or artists and authors have distinct political and social commitments of their own. It would be interesting indeed to see an analysis of the actual content of commencement addresses and the political valence of the messages being delivered to graduates. But campus protests over speaker selection usually have little to do with the content of the commencement address. It is the identity of the speaker that generates the controversy, not the substance of the speech. For many colleges, the safest route appears to be to turn to prominent alumni, wealthy benefactors, and individuals with inspirational life stories. Pizza magnates, musicians, and astronauts are presumably less likely to stir up protests on campus than presidential aspirants and opinion columnists. But if playing it safe with anodyne speakers is what it takes to allow a graduation ceremony to go off smoothly, then the intellectual climate on college campuses may not be as robust as one would like.

Common Readings

Many American universities have taken to adopting a common summer reading for incoming first-year students. The goals of such programs are various, but they are often used as a vehicle for encouraging students to begin to assimilate into an academic environment even before they reach campus and to provide a common experience for the entire cohort of first-year students. Like social book clubs, common readings are often presented as something other than "homework." They encourage students to think about reading as enjoyable and valuable on its own terms, without necessarily being driven by some extrinsic consideration like its appearance on a test. The expectations that such works might play in the university experience no doubt varies substantially depending on the nature of the institution. Some colleges are working with students coming from a wide variety of academic environments, and thus the common reading can be considered as something of an entry point that puts them on a path toward being active participants in the college-level academic experience. They are viewed as potentially valuable components of an effort to successfully transition students from high school to college and to retain students once they matriculate on campus. The summer readings are often selected in order to be somewhat provocative and engaging. Students are being prodded to think a bit and to take ideas seriously. At the same time, the readings must be sufficiently universalistic and accessible to be appropriate for students, regardless of whether they are arriving from American public schools or schools abroad or are entering an engineering academic track or the humanities (Garcia 1991; Stone, Higginson and Liljequist 2004; Ferguson 2006; Laufgraben 2006; Nadelson 2012).

As a consequence, the common readings are often value-laden. Books are often chosen for their "ability to 'stir' discussion," and are often specifically aimed at raising "questions of meaning and value" (Twiton 2007). Universities often incorporate the books into small-group discussions in freshman orientation programs or writing seminars. As a reading designed to complement the orientation process, the books are often selected to convey an appropriate theme. Very often, that theme is diversity. Frequently, the common readings are situated within a larger program of activities that are intended "to inspire action and community engagement" (Randall 2017). As the *New York Times* (July 2, 2017) found, "the books are almost always tied to current events and often make strong statements on issues like immigration, race and the perils of technology."

As a result, the common book selections have given rise to conservative complaints that the programs are used for ideological indoctrination. On occasion, students object to having to read books that expose them to themes or ideas that they find disagreeable or offensive. An incoming Duke University student spurred headlines when he launched a boycott of a summer reading assignment on the grounds that "I would have to compromise my personal Christian moral beliefs to read it" (*USA Today*, August 24, 2015). Courts have been forced to rule on whether common readings are "part of an academic exercise" or an effort at religious indoctrination (*Yacovelli v. Moeser* 2004). State legislators have threatened university funding over common readings that they regard as "purely promotion of a lifestyle" (*Inside Higher Ed*, February 20, 2014). Conservative watchdog groups view the book selections as college administrators "pushing their political agenda" (*Campus Reform*, August 31, 2017). Although college officials emphasize that the summer reading program "isn't explicitly political," their choices of readings routinely engage with themes of "social justice" and more often than not from a perspective that conservatives are likely to find objectionable (*Inside Higher Ed*, June 28, 2017). Some enterprising groups have begun to publicize their own counter-programming of "conservative summer reading books" (Crocker 2017).

The method of selection for summer pre-readings is various. Often college administrators have a strong role in choosing the books, in part because the discussion of the books in the academic year are often housed in administrator-run freshman orientation, freshman writing, "co-curricular" or inclusion and diversity programs. Since it has often proven difficult to get faculty and student "buy in" to the common reading, some colleges have adopted committee structures or nomination procedures that solicit contributions from a broader constituency on campus. Given an often explicit goal of fostering "civic engagement" and a selection process that deemphasizes academic considerations, common readings can wind up insuring that the incoming students' first exposure to campus is ideologically charged and noticeably tilted.

As the number of common reading programs has grown, and become more politically controversial, efforts to survey book selections have become more common. A few years ago, the number of books included in such surveys might number in the dozens. Now, they number in the hundreds. The conservative academic watchdog group National Association of Scholars produces an annual review of college common readings, and it offers an alternative list of recommended readings that emphasizes more classical choices. The National Resource Center for First-Year Experience and Students in Transition has begun to conduct its own survey on common readings. The publisher Random House has posted its own roundup of over 400 college common reading selections, reflective of the interest in book publishers to encourage the trend and market their own books as appropriate for selection. It has become apparent that colleges seeking "accessible" and "engaging" books have tended to gravitate toward a distinctive genre of "flavor of the week," socially conscious, least-common-denominator non-fiction (Thorne 2015). *Nickel and Dimed*, a 2001 first-person journalistic narrative style book on income inequality, was once a popular (and controversial) choice for such programs, but is now rarely chosen as colleges have moved on to more recently published fare, such as Ta-Nehisi Coates's *Between the World and Me*, a 2015 personal narrative of the author's awakening to racial consciousness and America's history of racial conflict.

Conservative groups like the National Association of Scholars have complained that the common readings chosen by universities not only systematically lean to the left, but also lack the kind of depth and rigor that one would expect from a university. Universities have largely shed much of the common core curriculum that once provided undergraduates with a common educational experience in the liberal arts. The residue of a general education distributional requirement pushes students toward sampling classes from a variety of disciplines but imposes little structure on the undergraduate degree and refrains from ushering students through a specific set of materials or classes that have been deemed particularly worthy and fundamental to a modern undergraduate education. The common summer reading for incoming first-year students provides at least one point of commonality for a cohort of students, but does so wholly outside the context of any rigorous disciplinary framework. Critics have found the introduction of a common reading into undergraduate education more akin to a social book club than the beginning of a general collegiate education.

A handful of colleges in the spring of 2017 selected classical works of literature for the common reading. Those selections, however, are not particularly taxing, and few would regard them as appropriate entry points into the canon of American, Western, or global literature. Science fiction and fantasy were popular selections for those who wanted to go the fiction route. Four colleges chose Mary Shelley's *Frankenstein* (and another assigned a graphic novel version of Shelley's tale). Bram Stoker, George Orwell, Virginia Wolfe, and Erich Maria Remarque made fleeting appearances on the list. Many more colleges eschewed fiction that had been written before the students had been born. Popular contemporary options were the recent science fiction novels, Ernest Cline's *Ready Player One*, Emily St. John Mandel's *Station Eleven*, Dave Eggers's *The Circle*, and Margaret Atwood's *The Handmaid's Tale*. Perhaps not coincidentally, three of those four had just been adapted to the screen (though *The Circle* proved to be a box office failure). Some chose social novels of immigration, race, and hardship, such as Cristina Henriquez's *Book of Unknown Americans*, Jennine Capo Crucet's *Make Your Home Among Strangers*, and Colson Whitehead's *The Underground Railroad*. Colleges assigned serious fiction and chose novels that wrestled with real ideas, but such selections would not have been out of place as summer reading for incoming high-school students and were unlikely to signal to students what they might be expected to read in a freshman literature class.

Colleges were far more likely to select works of non-fiction rather than fiction for their summer common reading. Vanishingly few, however, assigned scholarly works published by university presses of the type that one might expect to find on a college syllabus and informing current scholarly research. Nor did colleges take the opportunity to assign foundational or canonical works in any of the academic fields of study in which college student might soon be expected to embark. Colleges instead uniformly sent students to the books that might be found on the entry way table at the local Barnes & Noble. Serious commentaries on contemporary society, but nothing that would require any knowledge of the subject matter or lay the foundations for any further study. The selections position the modern undergraduate experience as more akin to Dwight Macdonald's "middlebrow" culture than Mortimer Adler's "great books" culture.

While colleges seemed to prefer books that address contemporary social issues, they avoided books that were explicitly about public affairs, contemporary politics, or public policy. Journalistic narratives and memoirs predominate over political tomes; grounded reporting was favored over either speculative theorizing or scholastic empiricism. Books by Barack Obama, Cory Booker, John Lewis, and Sonia Sotomayor make an occasional appearance, but not more analytical best-selling works by public figures such as Newt Gingrich, Al Gore, Thomas Friedman, or Charles Murray.

The most popular choices all shine a spotlight on societal inequalities, whether those are driven by race or income. The most widely-used texts for the summer of 2017 included Ta-Nehisi Coates's *Between the World and Me*, Matthew Desmond's *Evicted*, J.D. Vance's *Hillbilly Elegy*, Bryan Stevenson's *Just Mercy*, and Wes Moore's *The Other Wes Moore*. The inequality angle was also reflected in the more historical works favored by some colleges, such as Rebecca Skloot's *The Immortal Life of Henrietta Lacks* and Margot Lee Shetterly's *Hidden Figures*. Given the thematic concerns of the common readings and the authorial perspective in considering those themes, it is not surprising that the conservative National Association of Scholars would conclude that the common reading genre was "ideologically constrained." Although most common readings were readily aligned with the "progressive political culture in higher education," relatively few were explicit pieces of advocacy (Randall 2017, 32, 38). No doubt, for some students these readings were provocative and challenged their assumptions, while other students would have found them agreeable in general perspective though perhaps illuminating in some specifics. For the faculty and administrators who made the book selections, however, the common readings uniformly reinforced rather than questioned regnant ideological assumptions.

Conclusion

Universities are dedicated to the pursuit of truth. That project is most effectively fulfilled if competing arguments can be heard and carefully examined. It is easy to assume that weak arguments and flawed ideas are in fact strong when they are not seriously put to the test. If scholars and students are not confronted with competing ideas, they risk falling into complacency. If students are not exposed to a wide range of ideas, their education will be shallow and their intellectual growth stunted. Freedom of thought makes space for intellectual diversity, and intellectual diversity makes freedom of thought more valuable.

Of course, it is not necessary or useful for universities to encourage diversity just for diversity's sake. Indiscriminate intellectual diversity has little value. Once ideas have been tested and found wanting, they should be discarded. The goal of critical inquiry is to identify and weed out error. Universities need not invest in junk science in the name of collecting one of every type. They suffer, however, if they narrow the bounds of inquiry and debate so tightly that they are only left with affirming orthodoxy. They forsake their own values if they cannot tolerate hearing from dissenting voices.

Commencement speakers and common readings are not at the heart of the academic mission of the university. They are, however, among the very few common intellectual experiences shared by a cohort of students who are otherwise spread across the fragmentary byways of the modern university. The selection of such speakers and books reflect university values, and the breadth of offerings in those areas says something about the robustness of intellectual life on campus. The evidence suggests that universities rarely use these opportunities to challenge students or push against the predominant climate of opinion on campus. Universities have instead preferred to avoid controversy. They would rather cater to self-satisfaction than unsettle expectations. The safe choice often tilts left, and very rarely tilts right, but most often it simply aims low.

Notes

1. My thanks for Nathaniel Hyman and Taylor Whittington for their research assistance.
2. My sample did not include Princeton African American Studies professor Keeanga-Yamahtta Taylor, whose 2017 anti-Trump commencement address at Hampshire College gained national notoriety and led to death threats against her (*Inside Higher Ed*, June 1, 2017).

Works Cited

Bloom, Allan. *The Closing of the American Mind: How Education Has Failed Democracy and Impoverished the Souls of Today's Students.* New York: Simon & Schuster, 1987.

Braidwood, Travis and Ausderan, Jacob. "Professor Favorability and Student Perceptions of Professor Ideology." *PS: Political Science and Politics*, Vol. 50 (2017): 565–570.

Buckley, William F. *God and Man at Yale: The Superstitions of "Academic Freedom."* Chicago: Regnery, 1951.

Crocker, Auberon. "The Top 10 Conservative Summer Reading Books." *Conservative Book Club.* 2017. www.conservativebookclub.com/19781/featured-article/top-ten-conservative-summer-reading-books

Downs, Donald Alexander. *Restoring Free Speech and Liberty on Campus*. New York: Cambridge University Press, 2005.

D'Souza, Dinesh. *Illiberal Education: The Politics of Race and Sex on Campus.* New York: Free Press, 1991.

Ferguson, Michael. "Creating Common Ground: Common Reading and the First Year of College." *Peer Review*, Vol. 8 (2006): 8–10.

Furedi, Frank. *What's Happened to the University? A Sociological Exploration of Its Infantilisation.* New York: Routledge, 2016.

Garcia, Philip. "Summer Bridge: Improving Retention Rates for Underprepared Students." *Journal of the First-Year Experience & Students in Transition*, Vol. 3 (1991): 91–105.

Gross, Neil. *Why Professors Are Liberal and Why Do Conservatives Care?* Cambridge, MA: Harvard University Press, 2013.

Horowitz, David. *The Professors: The 101 Most Dangerous Academics in America.* Washington, DC: Regnery, 2006.

Janis, Irving L. *Groupthink: Psychological Studies of Policy Decisions and Fiascoes.* Boston, MA: Houghton Mifflin, 1982.

Kimball, Roger. *Tenured Radicals: How Politics Has Corrupted Our Higher Education.* New York: Harper & Row, 1990.

Klein, Daniel B. and Stern, Charlotte. "Professors and Their Politics: The Policy Views of Social Scientists." *Critical Review*, Vol. 17 (2005): 257–303.

Laufgraben, Jodi Levine. *Common Reading Programs.* Columbia, SC: University of South Carolina National Resource Center for First-Year Experience and Students in Transition, 2006.

Linvill, Darren L. and Havice, Pamela A. "Political Bias on Campus: Understanding the Student Experience." *Journal of College Student Development*, Vol. 52 (2011): 487–496.

Lipset, Seymour Martin and Ladd Jr., Everett Carl. "The Politics of American Sociologists." *American Journal of Sociology*, Vol. 78 (1972): 67–104.

Lukianoff, Greg. *Unlearning Liberty: Campus Censorship and the End of the American Debate.* New York: Encounter Books, 2012.

Maranto, Robert, Redding, Richard E. and Hess, Frederick M. *The Politically Correct University: Problems, Scope, and Reforms.* Washington, DC: AEI Press, 2009.

Mariari, Mack D. and Hewitt, Gordon J. "Indoctrination U? Faculty Ideology and Changes in Student Political Orientation." *PS: Political Science and Politics*, Vol. 41 (2008): 773–783.

Mill, John Stuart. *On Liberty, Utilitarianism and Other Essays.* New York: Oxford University Press, 2015.

Nadelson, Sandie G. "In Search of the Right Book: Considerations in Common Reading Book Selection." *Journal of College Reading and Learning*, Vol. 43 (2012): 60–66.

Randall, David. *Beach Books, 2016–2017: What Do Colleges and Universities Want Students to Read Outside Class?* New York: National Association of Scholars, 2017.

Rothman, Stanley S., Kelly-Woessner, April and Woessner, Matthew. *The Still Divided Academy: How Competing Visions of Power, Politics, and Diversity Complicate the Mission of Higher Education.* Lanham, MD: Rowman & Littlefield, 2011.

Rothman, Stanley S., Lichter, Robert and Nevitte, Neil. "Politics and Professional Advancement among College Faculty." *The Forum*, Vol. 3 (2005). DOI: https://doi.org/10.2202/1540-8884.1067

Shields, Jon A. and Dun Sr., Joshua M. *Passing on the Right: Conservative Professors in the Progressive University*. New York: Oxford University Press, 2016.

Stone, Staci, Higginson, Bonnie and Liljequist, Laura. "Summer Reading Programs: Perceptions of a University Freshman Reading Experience." *College Reading Association Yearbook: Celebrating the Power of Literacy*, Vol. 26 (2004): 423–437.

Thorne, Ashley. "Common Reading Programs: Trends, Traps, Tips." *Academic Questions*, Vol. 28 (2015): 138–146.

Turner, Henry A., McClintock, Charles G. and Spaulding, Charles B. "The Political Party Affiliation of American Political Scientists." *Western Political Quarterly*, Vol. 16 (1963): 650–665.

Twiton, Andi. "Common Reading Programs in Higher Education." 2007. https://gustavus.edu/library/Pubs/Lindell2007.html.

Whittington, Keith E. *Speak Freely: Why Universities Must Defend Free Speech*. Princeton, NJ: Princeton University Press, 2018.

Wills, Jeremiah B. "Political Ideological Distance Between Sociology Students and Their Instructors: The Effects of Students' Perceptions." *Sociation Today*, Vol. 11 (2013). www.ncsociology.org/sociationtoday/v111/studentpol.html

Woessner, Matthew and Kelly-Woessner, April. "I Think My Professor Is a Democrat: Considering Whether Students Recognize and React to Faculty Politics." *PS: Political Science and Politics*, Vol. 42 (2009): 343–352.

Yacovelli v. Moeser. 324 F.Supp. 2d 760 (2004).

Yancey, George. *Compromising Scholarship: Religious and Political Bias in American Higher Education*. Waco, TX: Baylor University Press, 2011.

4 Are Academic Freedom and Freedom of Speech Congruent or Opposed?

James R. Stoner, Jr.

The question I wish to explore in this essay is the relation of freedom of speech in the university to freedom of speech in the polity at large. I will do so beginning with an examination of the writings of two seminal thinkers from the middle of the twentieth century.

Leo Strauss on Freedom of Thought

On the eve of American entry into the Second World War, in exile from his German homeland, now under control of the Nazis—conquerors of France, combatants against the Soviets, collaborators of the Fascists—the political philosopher Leo Strauss published an essay, "Persecution and the Art of Writing," that first propounded what was to become his sometimes-celebrated, frequently-reviled mode of interpreting great texts in the philosophical tradition (Strauss 1941). Noting that most thinkers studied in the history of philosophy wrote under the threat of persecution for their ideas—the liberal ideas of freedom of speech and academic freedom being little more than a century-and-a-half old when he wrote, at least on the European continent—Strauss argued that most historians of thought mistook the intention of earlier authors, supposing the outward conformity of their writing to the dominant opinion of their day to be indicative of mental constraints in the human spirit, rather than deliberate, exoteric presentation of thoughts by writers who were under no such mental compulsion. Actually, Strauss wrote, besides conversation in private among trusted friends (possible when every word was not recorded), the most agile minds developed and passed down a number of techniques for communicating with discerning readers, even in published writing, timeless truths that can elude careless censors: voicing received opinions in tedious manner while raising objections with striking lucidity before their perfunctory refutation; reserving radical statements for the middle of a text, where they would be less visible than in an introduction or conclusion; misquoting sources; restating opinions in ways that modify or qualify rather than reiterate; and so forth. Strauss knew perfectly well that the use of such techniques could not be proven beyond doubt, nor could every author be presumed to employ them. But the wisest authors sent signals, sometimes in their discussion of how to read or interpret others, and besides ancient rhetoricians and scholars advised their pupils how to write and how to read "between the lines," an art forgotten only in the previous hundred years, and only in the Western world, where liberalism reigned.

Strauss's article—and the book by the same name that followed a decade later and included examples of his interpretive technique at work in the study of difficult medieval Jewish and Islamic texts (Strauss [1952] 1988)—is presented as an argument concerning historiography, or to use his own ironic indicator, as sociology of philosophy, and it has usually been read as such. But, like a two-way mirror, the essay was simultaneously a critique of liberal doctrines of free speech and academic freedom and offered a trenchant analysis of how persecution actually operates. John Stuart Mill's influential essay, *On Liberty* ([1859] 1978), makes the case for "freedom of thought and discussion" by supposing that the latter is required for the former, but Strauss insists that freedom of thought is possible even when freedom of discussion is not, at least not in public. Strauss is less concerned than Mill about protecting the timid—he explains that expression can be suppressed, but not thought itself, at least not directly—but he agrees with Mill that conformity of opinion destroys philosophy. According to Strauss, this is done by depriving the young of the presence of alternative thoughts, at least until or unless they learn the art of seeking out hidden meaning, an art that itself cannot be openly taught, except in a setting where it is barely needed. Since most people assume that liars get caught and thus that honesty is not only right but "the best policy," they take for granted that public doctrines that are not contradicted must be true; this is how persecution generally works, not by winning over the oppressed but by silencing them and thus leading others, particularly the young, even their own young, to ignore them (Strauss 1941, 488–489).

Like Mill, Strauss thinks that persecution takes many forms and thus can be found in various degrees, from the threat of death to mere social disapproval; the latter, however, being strong enough to cause people to censor themselves, so to speak. Unlike Mill, Strauss does not suppose a "very simple principle" can be successfully inculcated to dissolve the phenomenon: The needs of society and the needs of philosophy are not perfectly congruent, and the continued hostility of public opinion to nonconforming thought confirms this fact (Kendall 1960). Liberal democracies can afford to allow more freedom of speech than other regimes; hence, Strauss freely breaks the secret of esotericism, knowing that either he will be ignored or he can survive (maybe even benefit from) the criticism directed against him (Melzer 2014). But as Alexis de Tocqueville had noted a century before, majority opinion can be tyrannical, bloodlessly but no less effectively ([1835] 2000, 243 ff.). Majorities may not suppress dissenting thought, but they readily marginalize it.

Although Strauss does not mention universities in his "Persecution" essay, he alludes to them in the introduction to his subsequent book. There he draws a contrast between Jewish and Muslim medieval authors, such as Maimonides and Farabi, and Christian ones, like Thomas Aquinas. To the Jew or the Muslim, revelation is contained in the Law; scholarly learning within each tradition was centered around the study of the law, and the philosopher was a suspect outsider. In Christianity, by contrast, "sacred doctrine is revealed theology," so that "in Christianity philosophy became an integral part of the officially recognized and even required training of the student of sacred doctrine" (Strauss [1952] 1988, 19). In the medieval university, philosophy was the fourth faculty, in addition to Theology, Medicine, and Law, a preparatory rather than a practical discipline; this is what distinguishes the university from institutions of higher education in other cultures, places, and times. Strauss adds that the incorporation of philosophy into Christian doctrine and by implication its status as a faculty in the university was a mixed blessing:

> The precarious status of philosophy in Judaism as well as in Islam was not in every respect a misfortune for philosophy. The official recognition of philosophy in the Christian world made philosophy subject to ecclesiastical supervision. The precarious position of philosophy in the Islamic-Jewish world guaranteed its private character and therewith its inner freedom from supervision. The status of philosophy in the Islamic-Jewish world resembled in this respect its status in classical Greece. It is often said that the Greek city was a totalitarian society. It embraced and regulated morals, divine worship, tragedy and comedy. There was however one activity which was essentially private and trans-political: philosophy. Even the philosophic schools were founded by men without authority, by private men.
>
> (Strauss 1952, 21)

Unlike some of his students (Bloom 1987), Strauss wrote little about the university per se, whether Christian or modern. It seems fair to say that he thought the relationship of philosophy to universities was ambivalent, if not problematic, and was at any rate precarious, it being impossible to ensure that every doctor of philosophy is a philosopher in the true sense, much less that every genuine philosopher bothers to earn a doctorate. In other words, the existence of universities cannot guarantee genuine freedom of thought, any more than a polity is likely to encourage it. Fortunately, according to Strauss, philosophers can learn how to take care of themselves and to care for their kind.

Michel Foucault on Free Speaking

The second book I will consider is Michel Foucault's *Fearless Speech* (2001). Actually, it is somewhat misleading to call it a book, since it is a transcription from tape recordings of lectures given by Foucault at Berkeley, apparently in English, during the last year of his life, and the editor chose to eliminate repetition, incorporate discussion, and revise sentences "all in the hope of producing a more readable set of notes," which, however, the speaker "did not write, correct, or edit." Nevertheless, Foucault's characteristic insight emerges through this cloud, and his perspective, not surprisingly, is very different from Strauss's. Foucault explains at the outset: "My intention was not to deal with the problem of truth, but with the problem of the truth-teller, or of truth-telling as an activity." (5) He transliterates and comments upon the Greek term for freedom of speech, *parrhesia*, which can also be translated as "frankness," and literally means "saying everything." True to his described intention, Foucault concentrates especially on the *parrhesiastes*, "someone who says everything he has in mind" (12), though he acknowledges that the latter word does not appear in Greek until long after the former. Characteristically, he gives a genealogy of the use of the term *parrhesia*, from the age of Athenian democracy through the emergence of Christianity in late antiquity, which he describes as "a genealogy of the critical attitude in Western philosophy" (171). What begins as courageous truth-telling in the face of power becomes arduous self-examination; Cartesian doubt, introduced at the beginning of the lectures as the opposite of *parrhesia* (14), is only a step away by the end.

Foucault describes truth-telling as a "parrhesiastic game," in which "you risk death to tell the truth instead of reposing in the security of a life where the truth goes unspoken" (17). The discovery or discernment of the truth is not at issue—on the contrary, the *parrhesiastes* has no doubt of the truth he articulates—but only the courage to speak it in the face of an interlocutor of superior power. To speak up in the assembly for something unpopular or to criticize a ruler to his face are parrhesiastic actions; speech by the powerful or the use of rhetorical technique by an orator is not. "In *parrhesia*, the speaker uses his freedom and chooses frankness instead of persuasion, truth instead of falsehood or silence, the risk of death instead of life and security, criticism instead of flattery, and moral duty instead of self-interest and moral apathy" (20–21).

Foucault illustrates his heroic account of free speech through an analysis of six plays by Euripides, introducing in the course of his discussion the notion of a parrhesiastic contract—a move in the "game," one supposes—where the ruler grants the privilege of free speech "to the best and most honest citizens of the city" by promising not to punish their truth-telling. In democracy, where everyone has an equal right to speak, however, parrhesia becomes "problematized," Foucault writes, and Euripides shows this in his *Orestes*, where the term is used to describe a character's "ignorant outspokenness" (58) rather than his courage or frankness. How is one to distinguish the ignorant speaker from the learned one, the bad from the good *parrhesiastes*, when both speak freely? Euripides in the play invokes a nameless worker, whose sensible speech carries the day; Foucault identifies him as a stand-in for Theramenes (70), a conservative landowner who led the party in favor of making peace with Sparta, and who, by the way, was admired by Aristotle in *The Athenian Constitution.*

Foucault summons Socrates to rescue Athens from this political problematic, so to speak, to address the problem of truth. On his terms, Socrates is a *parrhesiastes*, a truth-speaker, but his peculiarity is in challenging others to tell the truth about themselves, putting them to the test. Foucault is less interested in the fact that most Athenians found this offensive or threatening than in the fact that some—he cites Nicias and Laches in Plato's dialogue named after the latter—welcome his pressure, which he (Foucault) explains through Laches's observation that Socrates's life follows his argument, his *bios* follows his *logos*, particularly regarding courage, which the two generals purport to understand (101). This philosophical *parrhesia*, says Foucault, is different from political speech; it aims at self-understanding and even self-transformation, but it is private speech, raising no claim to rule.

The Socratic model for philosophy is eventually adopted by all philosophic sects, in their distinctive ways, Foucault explains: by the Epicureans in relation to community life, as spiritual guides to happiness (108–115); by the Cynics, politically, in their "aggressive individualism" challenging the people in general and rulers in particular by their preaching, (mis-)behavior, and provocation (115–133); and by the Stoics, in personal relationships, avoiding self-delusion and stressing steadiness of mind (133–142). The self-examination they promoted was not yet the Christian examination of conscience, meditating on sin and the afterlife, for they all focused on happiness in the world and successful living, but it paved the way toward Christian inwardness. The frankness of speaking truth to others turns back upon the speaker, now suspicious of himself instead of righteous; truth itself has been "problematized," according to this genealogy, both with regard to what can be known and with regard to the value knowing and telling the truth (170). The framework is Nietzschean: The will to power becomes the will to truth, then turns on itself and becomes nihilistic. To this problem, Foucault offers no savior.

No more than Strauss does Foucault write about the university in *Fearless Speech*, and he, too, offers a sociology of philosophy, if with a psychological twist. Foucault wrote numerous books of intellectual history, focused on the frame of mind of the sciences and their discursive practices; a quick perusal shows no systematic treatment of the university as an institution or of the place of philosophy within it, although the topic comes up in his interviews (Foucault 1979). What does seem clear is that Foucault does not share Strauss's sense of an intrinsic conflict between the philosopher and the city; he agrees with Strauss that the relation of the two is problematic, but he presents the emergence of the conflict and its consequence as historical, not natural. Like Strauss he sees in Socrates a crucial turning point, but for Foucault Socratic self-examination issues, not in the emergence of political philosophy, but, in his characteristic phrase, in "care of the self" (92). Both are trenchant critics of modernity, and both turn back to the Greeks for contrast and for understanding—for alternative thought—even though Foucault forecloses as much as Strauss invites reflection on whether the Greeks offer ideas contemporary man might credibly adopt. Foucault's editors chose for the cover of *Fearless Speech* a photograph of the author speaking through a bullhorn, but although his politics is a source of contemporary comment, there is nothing explicit in the book that links *parrhesia* with modern protest. Neither Strauss nor Foucault takes for granted the adequacy of the modern notion of free speech, as presented for example by Mill, and each in his own way seems to dispute it; given their respective influence in the modern university, that fact alone suggests that the current liberal orthodoxy is unstable.

Free Speech Principles Today

What can be said on behalf of the liberal principle of free speech today, and what can be learned from Strauss and Foucault about how to make the case for free speech? Both recommend attention to Greek philosophy, which suggests to me that the case for free speech ought to begin with a consideration of the ends it achieves or aspires to. In modern accounts, these are three-fold: for the sake of the truth, for republican government, and for self-expression.[1] For clarity of analysis, let me link them with three leading defenders in the English-speaking tradition, respectively, John Milton, James Madison, and John Stuart Mill. The three ends are widely recognized and often mixed in practice; even the classic defenders of each speak to more than one end. Still, the ends are analytically distinct, and this distinction will help us sort out the difference between free speech in the university and free speech in society at large. It is also important to recognize that defining free speech by its ends will help define the limits of free speech, at least with regard to each end. I should be clear that, while I intend to defend free speech, I do not endorse what is called "free speech absolutism" (Abrams 2017); in fact, I think the successful defense of free speech today requires recognition of the proper limits on speech and thus restoration of the distinction between the liberty of speech and licentious speech, just as the defense of the Constitution in *The Federalist* at the time of the American founding required explanation of the proper limits on, as well as endorsement of, popular rule.

The defense of free speech, or more precisely, freedom of the press, in the name of the pursuit of truth received its classic if not its first expression in the pamphlet, *Areopagitica*, by John Milton. Published in 1644, addressed to the parliament of England, then governing London while Charles I was exiled to the countryside, the pamphlet complains of parliament's renewal of the Licensing Act, under which works could be printed in England only upon approval of the authorities. Milton begins with a quotation from Euripides's *Suppliants*—not one of the plays included in Foucault's analysis, as the word *parrhesia* does not appear in it, though the sentiment seems similar—and in fact he offers a genealogy of his own, from the ancient indulgence of writings even in cities like Athens and Rome, through the invention of licensure by the Roman pontiff upon the invention of printing. Since

> books are not absolutely dead things, but do contain a potency of life in them to be as active as that soul was whose progeny they are . . . as good almost kill a man as kill a good book; who kills a man kills a reasonable creature, God's image, but he who destroys a good book kills reason itself, kills the image of God, as it were in the eye.
> (Milton [1644] 1999, 7)

Of course, no censor claims to suppress good books, only evil ones, but Milton argues this is impossible:

> Good and evil we know in the field of this world grow up together almost inseparably; and the knowledge of good is so involved and interwoven with the knowledge of evil, and in so many cunning resemblances hardly to be discerned, that the confused seeds which were imposed upon Psyche as an incessant labor to cull out, and sort asunder, were not more intermixed. It was from out of the rind of an apple tasted, that the knowledge of good and evil, as two twins cleaving together, leaped forth into the world. And perhaps this is the doom which Adam fell into of knowing good and evil, that is to say of knowing good by evil.
> (17)

And, Milton adds, censorship is not likely to fall into hands that could wield it on Platonic principles, but instead into the hands of the dull or the bigoted, while subjecting true writers to these would be not only unjust but dispiriting, undermining their incentive to write and publish. Besides, censorship is futile, for readers are more apt to interpret works for better or worse according to their characters than to have their characters formed by the books they read: "a wise man will make better use of an idle pamphlet than a fool will do of sacred Scripture" (20). Moreover, it is unnecessary: "And though the winds of doctrine were let loose to play upon the earth, so Truth be in the field, we do injuriously by licensing and prohibiting to misdoubt her strength. Let her and falsehood grapple; who ever knew Truth put to the worse, in a free and open encounter?" (45) Still, Milton was no free speech absolutist: He writes to defend Protestant publication and disputation concerning religious truth, but he would readily suppress Catholic publication: "I mean not tolerated Popery, and open superstition, which, as it extirpates all religious and civil supremacies, so itself should be extirpate, provided first that all charitable and compassionate means be used to regain the weak and the misled" (47).

The defense of free speech for the sake of republican government receives a classic formulation in James Madison's *Report on the Virginia Resolutions* ([1800] 1836), written as a review and defense of the Virginia Resolutions of 1798, themselves a protest against Congress' Alien and Sedition Acts. Although the *Report* is perhaps best known for its account of the compact theory of the Constitution and of interposition as an appropriate stance for states faced with what they consider to be unconstitutional federal laws, Madison includes as well the argument for considering the Sedition Act unconstitutional, relying in part on interpreting "freedom of speech, and of the press" in the First Amendment to go beyond the principle of "no prior restraint," established in English common law once the Licensing Act expired in the early 1700s. Because American governments are republican, not monarchical, English doctrine ought not to be used to interpret American constitutional language, or at least the English notion of free speech needs to be expanded in American circumstances:

> The nature of governments elective, limited, and responsible, in all their branches, may well be supposed to require a greater freedom of animadversion, than might be tolerated by the genius of such a government as that of Great Britain. In the latter, it is a maxim, that the king—an hereditary, not a responsible magistrate—can do no wrong; and that the legislature, which, in two thirds of its composition, is also hereditary, not responsible, can do what it pleases. In the United States, the executive magistrates are not held to be infallible, nor the legislatures to be omnipotent; and both, being elective, are both responsible. Is it not natural and necessary, under such different circumstances, that a different degree of freedom in the use of the press should be contemplated?
>
> (570)

Even in England, greater freedom than implied in their law of sedition has been allowed concerning the elective branch, and likewise the American states have offered more freedom of speech in practice than the doctrine of the common law they inherited: "In every state, probably, in the Union, the press has exerted a freedom in canvassing the merits and measures of public men, of every description, which has not been confined to the strict limits of the common law" (570). Already in colonial times Americans embraced truth as a defense in libel cases. Madison goes a step further, noting that in electoral politics, "opinion, and inferences, and conjectural observations" are a necessary part of debate, even though they cannot always be established by the standards of proof in a court of law. "The right of freely examining public characters and measures, and of communication thereon, is the only effectual guardian of every other right," he concludes (576); elections, essential to republican government, are meaningless without it. Monarchies with established churches have their chief authorities in place; republics with religious liberty depend on free speech if they are to represent the sovereignty of the people as they claim.

John Stuart Mill's defense of "freedom of thought and discussion" in *On Liberty* echoes Milton in emphasizing the claim of truth, his defense of dissent against received opinion being organized according to whether that opinion might be false, might be true, or might be partially true and partially false. The context of the argument, however, not to mention specific points, distances it from Milton's concern with public doctrine or Madison's with electoral politics. Mill's chief concern, instead, is with individuality, which he defines as the freedom each person has to live his own life in his own way, without public pressure from law or opinion except for the sake of other individuals' own self-protection. Writes Mill: "If a person possesses any tolerable amount of common sense and experience, his own mode of laying out his existence is the best, not because it is best in itself, but because it is his own" ([1859] 1978, 64). If that is so, then it seems to me that the truth Mill defends in Chapter 2 of *On Liberty* is simply the truth as it seems to every individual and by which he discerns his own good as Mill expounds in Chapter 3; it is not established by objective reason, but by private reason, or for that matter, unreason, if that seems good to the person in question. Mill's defense of free speech, then, is a defense of the freedom of self-expression, in words as well as in actions. If Milton's emphasis is on learning and Madison's is on politics, Mill's is on civil society and culture, or what today we might connote by economy and identity.

If these are the three ends of free speech, what are the limits implied in each? Insofar as freedom of speech is for the sake of discovering truth, the most obvious limit is that one has no right to lie, that is, to deliberately present an untruth, knowing it is untrue, as though it were a truth. Of course, the weakness and unsteadiness of the human mind ensures that people think many things are true that are false; the friend of freedom of speech replies that this is precisely why people need such freedom, for only when false opinions are contradicted can people be led to change their minds. Of course, such is the weakness and stubbornness of people that they often do not change their minds even in the face of better evidence and argument. The search for truth commends appeal to reason and gives men and women the freedom to express their opinions as reasons, and perhaps the duty to do the same. Nevertheless, given the limits of human reason, the search for truth may require openness to ideas that are not simply rational; for example, religious teaching or artistic insight. Whatever advances knowledge ought to be allowed; whatever impedes it is suspect.

The republican rationale for free speech commends constitutional government and the processes that entails. Those include rules of order in any legislative assembly, which limit who speaks when and on what subject, as well as even stricter rules of proceeding in court. Secrecy may be needed in executive councils, at least in some military affairs, and respect for citizens' privacy requires that government protect the confidentiality of information it collects—although, in modern times, these concerns are balanced against sunshine laws and freedom of information acts, requiring access to records of government proceedings for the sake of holding government accountable to the voters. As Madison explained, elections are free only when the people and the press have ample latitude to comment on men and measures, but he did not deny that candidates ought to have the ability to protect themselves against malicious attacks on their reputations, only required that they do so according to the law of libel in state court. Can the regime defend itself against those who would destroy it? Thomas Jefferson said famously, in his first inaugural address: "If there be any among us who would wish to dissolve this Union or to change its republican form, let them stand undisturbed as monuments of the safety with which error of opinion may be tolerated where reason is left free to combat it" ([1801] 1984, 493). But Jefferson meant, let the law leave them free, not that they were to be free, as Mill might have it, from social disapproval of their opinion. Oliver Wendell Holmes wrote in dissent, "If, in the long run, the beliefs expressed in proletarian dictatorship are destined to be accepted by the dominant forces of the community, the only meaning of free speech is that they should be given their chance and have their way" (*Gitlow* 1925), but the majority has never gone beyond allowing advocacy of overthrowing the government in the abstract; commanding imminent illegal violent action against public order has not been held within the protections of free speech. As Justice Robert Jackson quipped, the Court must not "convert the Bill of Rights into a suicide pact" (*Terminiello* 1949).

Limitations implicit in the principle of self-expression are probably the most extensive, at least potentially. If we follow Mill, who justifies free speech on this ground, the limit that follows would be against speech that harms other individuals, and the law clearly protects against certain forms of harmful speech: true threats, fraudulent speech in commercial transactions, libel and slander, and even certain insults (what were called "fighting words"). Obscenity used to be strictly limited by law, on account of the harm that it might cause to the weak-willed and to minors, but most of those limits have now been relaxed in the name of self-expression. Respect for privacy can be required by law, and violations of privacy punished, even if the violation involves only saying or publishing things that are true. Symbols and other visual and musical modes of communication are expressive, of course, even though they do not strictly speaking entail speech; so are actions, as we saw in Mill, although to protect every action because it is also expressive would incapacitate law. Self-expression seems, of all the justifications for free speech, the most demanding—neither truth nor justice constitutes its natural limit, as for the other forms—but it is also the most readily limited, particularly if one adopts an expansive view of what is harmful or offensive. Most European countries have taken such an expansive view, enforcing laws against "hate speech"; American law thus far has taken a narrower view of harm and so a broader view of what can be said with impunity, at least with legal impunity, it being possible to criticize the expression of hatred thanks to the protection of free speech itself (Waldron 2012; Ash 2016).

The Polity and the University

The different purposes of free speech and the different inherent limits on speech that they allow or require sum up to make questions of free speech enormously complex—and the complexity itself can be a problem, for if one needs to consult a lawyer on a regular basis to determine what one can or cannot say, it would be hard to claim one has free speech. Let me conclude by suggesting in a general way how these principles, purposes, and limits ought to be recognized in the polity on the one hand and in the university on the other. Among private associations in civil society—firms or clubs, churches or schools—it makes sense that agreeing to limits on speech on the part of members is necessary for the association to express a coherent message to society at large, not to mention for there to be harmony among the members. But in the polity—society as a whole, insofar as it is self-governing—it makes sense to allow wide latitude to speech, at least as a matter of law concerning all issues that come before the institutions of government and hence before the voters. Because all citizens in a democratic republic have the right to vote, they can rightly demand respect for their equal rights as citizens from one another, and there are degrees and kinds of insult that I think can sometimes rightly be suppressed and certainly ought to be discouraged. On the whole, democracy itself insures respect, for it is often true that no majority is so entrenched and stable that politicians do not see that those they alienate today might be those whose votes they will need tomorrow. The danger comes when majorities disfranchise those they outnumber, or when differences of opinion on questions of policy, perhaps especially differences that have divers consequences for divers interests, are interpreted as insults against someone else's citizenship. Foucault wrote that the exercise of free speech requires a certain fearlessness; perhaps listening to *parrhesia* requires courage, too, equalizing the players in the parrhesiastic game.

The promise of democracy is that differences can be settled peacefully, not that society itself will be peaceable. The attraction of a peaceable kingdom is precisely the balm of monarchy, which republicans have always held can be purchased only with the sacrifice of liberty. A self-governing people might limit the issues that are open to electoral choice—to an extent Americans have done so by entrenching rights, such as the freedom of speech, in the Constitution and allowing recourse to courts for their protection—but the wider the array of rights thus entrenched, the less the people can be called self-governing. Moreover, because the Constitution is subject to amendment by the people through their representatives, no issue can be wholly removed from public debate; in that sense, one might say freedom of speech is constitutive of republican government. But this argument, remember, is based on the republican rationale, not the case for self-expression. Republican government might, I think, place appropriate limits on merely expressive claims, for the sake of preventing harm and perhaps even for the sake of forming good citizens, able and willing to speak freely to one another and to listen to one another, too.

Free speech in the universities, or academic freedom, seems both less and more than free speech in the polity or in society at large (Downs 2005; Chemerinsky and Gillman 2017). In the first place, while the ability to lie is not generally suppressed in society and cannot be without causing more harm than good, the university depends on academic integrity, since its principal end is the search for and transmission of truth. Plagiarism can and must be punished in the university, even though, so long as copyright is not violated, it is generally immune from the law in society at large. (Copyright law, by the way, contains an exception for "fair educational use," acknowledging that the protection of due profit should not impede the progress of learning itself.) Universities can and must make all sorts of judgments about the truth or value of theories and interpretations, finding some so well established that they are beyond debate—oxygen rather than phlogiston as the cause of fire, for example—while acknowledging the perennial character of debates about, for example, the human good. It would do wrong to promote debates about matters that are clearly known, except for the purpose of requiring that proofs remain known, not just conclusions, and it would also do wrong to suppress debates about matters that are not, perhaps cannot, be settled. The university exists somewhere between the circles of philosophic friends about whom Strauss writes and the wider world of politics and business. Its capacity for freedom of thought can neither be taken for granted, nor will freedom of thought be secure if the concerns of the world and the conditions of competition in the wider polity are merely reproduced within its gates.

Universities are devoted to the pursuit of truth, but also to its transmission; their core activity is not only research but also education. Long experience has shown that teaching young people how to think for themselves requires allowing them ample space for self-expression, not exactly as a right, and certainly not as a right to be oblivious to correction for folly, but as an element of pedagogy, so they learn how to choose wisely, and in the process learn to tolerate one another's choices. Likewise, and as a sort of counter-pressure, experience shows that scholarship, even at the level of the undergraduate, requires certain virtues, and universities ignore the need to cultivate good habits at their peril, or rather, at the peril of their pupils. Much of the controversy about student speech on campuses today results, I think, from a failure to take seriously the need for and the complexity of the moral formation of students, for which political indoctrination is no substitute and is in fact a hindrance. Such formation is impossible, or at least incomplete, if it does not include their initiation into participation in the pursuit of truth and the recognition of its value that comes from such an experience. Whatever choices universities make about free speech on campus ought to be made while remembering that inquiry and learning are their highest and distinctive end. The polity has both more and less to be concerned about, and thus needs both more and less freedom of speech.

Note

1. See, for example, Ash (2016, 73–79), who treats the three in a different order and adds a fourth reason, "it helps us to live with diversity," which I think can be reduced to the second and third.

Works Cited

Abrams, Floyd. *The Soul of the First Amendment*. New Haven, CT: Yale University Press, 2017.

Ash, Timothy Garton. *Free Speech: Ten Principles for a Connected World*. New Haven, CT: Yale University Press, 2016.

Bloom, Allan. *The Closing of the American Mind*. New York: Simon & Schuster, 1987.

Chemerinsky, Erwin and Gillman, Howard. *Free Speech on Campus*. New Haven, CT: Yale University Press, 2017.

Downs, Donald Alexander. *Restoring Free Speech and Liberty on Campus*. Cambridge: Cambridge University Press, 2005.

Foucault, Michel. "Truth and Power: An Interview With Michel Foucault." *Critique of Anthropology*, Vol. 4 (1979): 131–137.

———. *Fearless Speech*. Edited by Joseph Pearson. Los Angeles: Semiotext(e), 2001.

Gitlow v. New York. 1925. 268 U.S. 652.

Jefferson, Thomas. *Writings*. Edited by Merrill D. Peterson. New York: Library of America, 1984.

Kendall, Willmoore. "The Open Society and Its Fallacies." *American Political Science Review*, Vol. 54 (1960): 972–979.

Madison, James. "Report on the Resolutions of 1798–99." In *Debates in the Several State Convention*, Vol. 4, edited by Jonathan Elliott. http://oll.libertyfund.org/titles/elliot-the-debates-in-the-several-state-conventions-vol-4.

Melzer, Arthur. *Philosophy Between the Lines: The Lost History of Esoteric Writing*. Chicago: University of Chicago Press, 2014.

Mill, John Stuart. *On Liberty*. Indianapolis: Hackett Publishing Co., 1978.

Milton, John. *Areopagitica and Other Political Writings of John Milton*. Indianapolis: Liberty Fund, 1999.

Strauss, Leo. *Persecution and the Art of Writing*. Chicago: University of Chicago Press, 1988.

———. "Persecution and the Art of Writing." *Social Research*, Vol. 9 (1941): 488–504.

Terminiello v. Chicago. 1949. 337 U.S. 1.

Tocqueville, Alexis de. *Democracy in America*. Translated by Harvey C. Mansfield and Delba Winthrop. Chicago: University of Chicago Press, 2000.

Waldron, Jeremy. *The Harm in Hate Speech*. Cambridge, MA: Harvard University Press, 2012.

5 Freedom of Expression at the Private University[1]

John Hasnas

Introduction

This chapter explores the obligations, if any, that private universities and colleges have to ensure that their students (and faculties) enjoy the right to freedom of expression on campus. This means that it is not about the First Amendment to the United States Constitution.

The First Amendment restrains the United States Federal Government from enacting legislation that abridges "the freedom of speech, or of the press."[2] In 1925, the Supreme Court of the United States interpreted the due process clause of the Fourteenth Amendment to apply the First Amendment to the state legislatures as well as the Federal Congress.[3] Since that time, the First Amendment has restrained both the federal and state governments from abridging citizens' freedom of expression. This is captured by saying that the First Amendment restrains all "state action"—governmental action at any level—that abridges freedom of speech or press. Because state government legislation that establishes publicly funded universities constitutes such state action, the First Amendment applies to public universities. Therefore, public universities are subject to the same restrictions on actions that abridge freedom of speech and press as are the state and federal governments.

None of this has any bearing on private universities and colleges. Private universities and colleges are not governmental entities. Their actions do not constitute state action. Hence, the First Amendment does not apply to them, and they are not bound by its restrictions. If private universities and colleges have any obligation to ensure that their students and faculties have the right to freedom of expression on campus, it must come from some other source.

Is there such a source? Do private universities and colleges have an obligation to allow their students and faculty to freely express their thoughts on campus?

A Conditional Obligation

The short answer to this question is "no." Private universities and colleges are institutions created by private parties. Private parties are free to pursue whatever ends they believe to be most beneficial to themselves or others as long as they are not violating the law. Therefore, private parties can create universities and colleges to serve whatever ends they deem worthwhile, whether it be the unrestrained pursuit of truth, the propagation of a particular religious faith, the development of a specified art or skill, or the advancement of the members of a particular sex, race, religion, or other social group.

Furthermore, the private parties that create such universities and colleges are free to place any (legally permissible) conditions on matriculation that they judge appropriate. They may require students to promise to refrain from drinking alcohol or engaging in premarital sex while enrolled. They may require students to maintain specified standards of appearance and dress. They may also require students to refrain from the verbal or written expression of certain ideas while on campus, whether these be the advocacy of abortion or the articulation of microagressions that might make the campus an uncomfortable learning environment for members of socially subordinated groups.

There is nothing inherent in the creation of a private university or college that carries with it an obligation to ensure that its students and faculty enjoy unrestrained freedom of expression on campus.

It is perfectly reasonable to argue that the pursuit of truth requires the robust exchange of ideas and rigorous testing of all hypotheses that is facilitated by an atmosphere of uninhibited freedom of expression. Therefore, any university or college that makes the pursuit of truth its essential mission would be well-advised to maintain such an atmosphere on its campus. But the recognition of this connection does not create an ethical obligation for a private university or college to maintain freedom of expression on campus any more than my recognition that my financial interest would be best served by investing in index funds means that I am ethically obligated to refrain from speculating on the commodities market. Private individuals, and private corporate entities, are free to use their resources as they see fit (within the law) regardless of how well- or poorly-adapted these uses may be to the achievement of their desired ends.

But although there is no absolute duty for private universities and colleges to maintain freedom of expression on their campuses, there can be a conditional duty to do so. This is because private universities and colleges are clothed with all the ordinary moral obligations of any individual or group of individual human beings. And one of the most important of these is the duty to keep one's word and deal honestly with others.

All of us are duty-bound to avoid fraud—to avoid making misrepresentations of fact or false promises that induce others to act in ways that they otherwise would not. We need not make any representations as to how we intend to behave; but once we do and another relies on our representation, we are bound to act in accordance with that representation. And this is just as true of corporate entities as it is of individuals.

If private universities and colleges make representations to the public about how they will conduct their business, and members of the public rely on these representations in deciding whether to enroll at, support, or otherwise deal with the universities and colleges, then the universities and colleges are ethically obligated to act in accordance with their representations.

Thus, private universities and colleges, as much as private individuals, have a duty to honor all of their voluntarily-undertaken public commitments. This means that if a private university or college represents itself as maintaining freedom of expression on its campus, it is ethically obligated to do so. Although its obligation is a conditional one, once the representation has been made, the obligation is fully binding.

It is important to note that this conditional obligation carries with it an implicit secondary obligation. For, if private universities and colleges have a duty to honor *all* of their public commitments, then they also have a duty to refrain from making inconsistent public commitments—public commitments that cannot be simultaneously fulfilled. This obligates the institutions to be careful not to make any commitments that a previously undertaken commitment makes it impossible for the institution to honor.

Applying these observations to the case at hand produces three possible scenarios. The first is the case in which the university or college does not represent itself as ensuring full freedom of expression on campus. In such a case, the institution is free to adopt any restriction on expression that it deems appropriate, as long as it does so explicitly. Such an institution can adopt a speech code, limit controversial expression to "free speech zones," and/or prohibit "hate speech" or microagressions, as long as it makes all such restrictions clear to the public. It can also ban the advocacy of disfavored viewpoints on campus—it could prohibit the advocacy of abortion, or laissez-faire capitalism, or same sex marriage, or the condemnation of same sex marriage—again, as long as it does so in an open manner.

The second scenario is one in which the university or college makes a public representation committing itself to maintain freedom of expression on campus. For example, Georgetown University has adopted a Policy on Speech and Expression that states

> Georgetown University is committed to free and open inquiry, deliberation and debate in all matters, and the untrammeled verbal and nonverbal expression of ideas. It is Georgetown University's policy to provide all members of the University community, including faculty, students, and staff, the broadest possible latitude to speak, write, listen, challenge, and learn.[4]

Having undertaken such a commitment, Georgetown University cannot ethically ban the expression of disfavored viewpoints. It is now duty bound to allow its students, faculty, and staff to advocate in favor of or in opposition to abortion, laissez-faire capitalism, and same sex marriage. Indeed, in the absence of an explicit limitation elsewhere in the policy statement, it is also duty bound to permit the advocacy of offensive positions—what is now being called hate speech—such as white supremacy, male domination, or Nazism and to refrain from limiting advocacy to free speech zones. To the extent that a private university or college commits itself to providing the same level of protection to expression that the First Amendment requires public universities to provide, it is ethically obligated to do so.

The third scenario is one in which the university or college has made a public commitment to maintain freedom of expression on campus, and then subsequently makes another public commitment to take action that conflicts with doing so. For example, a university that has adopted a commitment of freedom of expression on campus may also make a commitment to supply an inclusive, safe, and welcoming educational environment for people of all backgrounds.[5] However, the expression of certain ideas can be offensive to the members of some groups and make them feel unwelcome or even unsafe. For example, some members of the university or college community may wish to display the Confederate flag, or believe that homosexuality is a sinful violation of God's law, or that Muslims pose too great a risk of being terrorists to be allowed to enter the country, or that illegal Mexican immigrants are stealing American jobs and should be deported. Their public articulation of these beliefs could well make homosexual, African American, Muslim, and Hispanic students feel unwelcome on campus and in some cases, perhaps even unsafe. This creates a situation in which it is difficult for the university to live up to both of its commitments.

When the third scenario holds, universities and colleges can act with integrity only by clarifying their commitments. Such a university or college could reconcile its commitments by giving priority to freedom to expression. If so, it would have an obligation to make it clear that its commitment to maintaining an inclusive, safe, and welcoming educational environment is limited by its commitment to freedom of expression—that its commitment is to do all that it can to create the most inclusive, safe, and welcoming campus environment *short of restricting any student's or faculty member's ability to express his or her sincerely held beliefs on any controversial matter*. On the other hand, a university or college could decide to give priority to the maintenance of a welcoming environment. In that case, it would have an obligation to make it clear that its commitment to freedom of expression is limited by its commitment to maintaining a welcoming environment—that its commitment is to preserve the widest range of freedom of expression on campus than it can *consistent with not making any member of the academic community feel unwelcome or disrespected*. Private universities and colleges are free to give priority to either of its conflicting commitments, but, because remaining committed to incompatible obligations means that neither can be fulfilled, they are ethically obligated to give priority to one of them.

Meeting the Conditional Obligation

The Contemporary Academic Environment

In the contemporary academic environment, few private universities or colleges are functioning under either of the first two scenarios. There are a limited number of (mostly religiously-based) private universities and colleges that explicitly limit the range of expression they permit on their campuses.[6] There may also be a few that have made an explicit commitment to preserve freedom of expression on campus and have taken steps to ensure that they do not have conflicting commitments.[7] But the overwhelming majority of private universities and colleges exemplify the third scenario. They have made a commitment to preserve freedom of expression on campus, but retain conflicting commitments to other values as well.

It is not difficult to understand why this is the case. Most private universities and colleges have long-standing commitments to freedom of expression on campus. These commitments have typically been on the books for several decades.[8] Commitments to maintain inclusive, or safe, or welcoming educational environments are more recent developments. These have typically arisen over the past ten years. To some extent, these commitments arose as a response to federal law and Department of Education policy on harassment, which holds universities and colleges liable if women or members of other protected classes are subject to an intimidating, hostile, or offensive environment on campus. A commitment to maintain an inclusive, safe, welcoming environment is a natural response to the threat of such liability. To some extent, these commitments arose in response to cultural change. There can be little doubt that the current generation of students has been raised in a social environment that is much more protective of young people's sensibilities and much less tolerant of group-based stereotyping and sexual, racial, or ethnic slurs than in the past.

Whatever the explanation, the commitments to maintain a welcoming educational environment typically post-date the commitments to freedom of expression. And because these subsequent commitments were originally understood as merely positive statements of the institution's rejection of invidious discrimination, they were typically made with no awareness of the potential for conflict with the prior commitment to freedom of expression. It was not until some parties on campus began complaining that other parties' expression of their beliefs made them feel unwelcome or unsafe that the conflict became apparent. As a result, most private universities and colleges now find themselves in a situation in which they have made commitments to the vigorous protection of the full range of freedom of expression and also to protecting students from expressive conduct that makes them feel uncomfortable.

Private universities and colleges that are in this situation are duty bound to resolve the conflict. They may not ethically continue to make representations to the public that they know cannot be simultaneously fulfilled. This means that they must either explicitly identify the limitations they place on freedom of expression on their campus or they must make it clear that all university policies carry an implicit limitation preventing their enforcement in a manner that restricts freedom of expression.

Although either option is equally ethically acceptable, the evidence suggests that few schools are willing to explicitly limit freedom of expression on campus.[9] In response to high profile student protests, university administrations typically underscore their commitment to freedom of expression.[10] Because most private universities and colleges select this option, most private universities and colleges are ethically obligated to ensure that the rest of their policies are consistent with this commitment. What is required for this to be the case?

Harassment Policy

All private universities and colleges have harassment policies designed to discourage the harassment of members of the academic community because of their sex, race, religion, sexual orientation, disability, or membership in any other protected category.[11] A university or college that retains a commitment to freedom of expression must ensure that its harassment policy is consistent with this commitment. And the first thing that this requires is an accurate understanding of the law of harassment.

Legally speaking, harassment is a form of discrimination. Title VII of the Civil Rights Act of 1964 prohibits employment discrimination on the basis of an individual's race, color, religion, sex, or national origin.[12] The Age Discrimination in Employment Act of 1967[13] and the Americans with Disabilities Act of 1990[14] prohibit employment discrimination on the basis of age and disability respectively. The federal courts and the federal Equal Employment Opportunity Commission (EEOC) have held that these statutes "afford[] employees the right to work in an environment free from discriminatory intimidation, ridicule, and insult."[15] Thus, conduct that creates an intimidating, hostile, or offensive work environment for individuals because of their race, color, religion, sex, national origin, age, or disability constitutes illegal discrimination.[16] This form of discrimination is called harassment.[17] As defined by the EEOC,

> Harassment is unwelcome conduct that is based on race, color, religion, sex (including pregnancy), national origin, age (40 or older),

> disability or genetic information. Harassment becomes unlawful where 1) enduring the offensive conduct becomes a condition of continued employment, or 2) the conduct is severe or pervasive enough to create a work environment that a reasonable person would consider intimidating, hostile, or abusive.[18]

Title VI of the Civil Rights Act prohibits discrimination on the basis of race, color, or national origin in any program receiving federal financial assistance. Title IX of the Educational Amendments Act of 1972 prohibits discrimination of the basis of sex in any program receiving federal financial assistance. Because almost all private universities and colleges accept federal financial assistance either directly or indirectly by accepting students who receive federal grants or loans, almost all private universities and colleges are subject to Title VI and Title IX.[19] Title VI and Title IX extend Title VII's prohibition on workplace harassment to the educational environment. Therefore, most private universities and colleges are legally required to ensure that their campuses are not intimidating, hostile, or offensive environments for women and racial and ethnic minorities.

Federal courts and the EEOC have held that more than merely insulting behavior is necessary for conduct to create a hostile environment. In the language of the EEOC, "[p]etty slights, annoyances, and isolated incidents (unless extremely serious) will not rise to the level of illegality. To be unlawful, the conduct must create a work [or educational] environment that would be intimidating, hostile, or offensive to reasonable people."[20] Note however, that the conduct that can create an intimidating, hostile, or offensive educational environment can include verbal and written expression. Once again, in the words of the EEOC, the "[o]ffensive conduct may include, but is not limited to, offensive jokes, slurs, epithets or name calling, physical assaults or threats, intimidation, ridicule or mockery, insults or put-downs, offensive objects or pictures, and interference with work performance."[21] This leads directly to the question of what types of speech or written expression can constitute illegal harassment.

To answer this question, I must give the lie to the first paragraph of this chapter in which I claimed that the chapter is not about the First Amendment. For it is the First Amendment that delimits the scope of harassment law.

The First Amendment restrains the power of the federal government—directly—and state governments—indirectly through its incorporation into the Due Process Clause of the Fourteenth Amendment—to interfere with citizens' verbal and written expression. Yet the government regularly bans or punishes certain forms of expression. For example, treason, criminal solicitation, perjury, and fraud are all crimes that are committed by either saying or writing something, yet they are within the scope of the government's power. This is sometimes expressed by saying that in such cases the speech is "conduct" that is not protected by the First Amendment.[22]

The courts distinguish between protected expression and unprotected "conduct" on the basis of whether the government regulation is content-neutral or content-based. A law is content-neutral, and thus not violative of the First Amendment, when it is "justified without reference to the content of the regulated speech."[23] A law is content-based, and thus potentially violative of the First Amendment, when it is justified with reference to what the speech communicates. Thus,

> [t]he First Amendment generally makes conveying facts and opinions into a constitutionally immunized activity. Normally, the government may punish people for causing various harms, directly or indirectly. But it generally may not punish speakers when the harms are caused by what the speaker said—by the persuasive, informative, or offensive force of the facts or opinions expressed.[24]

A particularly relevant illustration of the range of application of the First Amendment is provided by the Supreme Court's decision in *R.A.V. v. City of St. Paul*.[25] In that case, the Court struck down the St. Paul Bias Motivated Crime Ordinance, which prohibited placing

> on public or private property a symbol, object, appellation, characterization or graffiti, including, but not limited to, a burning cross or Nazi swastika, which one knows or has reasonable grounds to know arouses anger, alarm or resentment in others on the basis of race, color, creed, religion or gender."[26]

Because this ordinance applied only to expression that insulted or provoked violence "on the basis of race, color, creed, religion or gender," the Court held that "the ordinance is facially unconstitutional in that it prohibits otherwise permitted speech solely on the basis of the subjects the speech addresses."[27] The Court explained that "[t]he First Amendment generally prevents government from proscribing speech or even expressive conduct because of disapproval of the ideas expressed. Content-based regulations are presumptively invalid."[28] Thus, because "the only interest distinctively served by the content limitation is that of displaying the city council's special hostility towards the particular biases thus singled out [and because t]hat is precisely what the First Amendment forbids,"[29] the Court struck down the ordinance.

Let us apply this understanding to harassment law. The Civil Rights Act, the Age Discrimination in Employment Act of 1967, the Americans with Disabilities Act of 1990, and the Educational Amendments Act of 1972 that give rise to the legal prohibition on harassment are all federal statutes whose range of application is limited by the First Amendment. This implies that harassment law must be understood as a content-neutral restraint on expression. It can outlaw expression to the extent that it is the equivalent of harm-causing conduct but not to the extent that the harm is caused by the content of what is being expressed. Therefore, harassment law cannot ban or punish expression merely because of its offensive content.

The limited reach of harassment law was illustrated in the case of *Saxe v. State College Area School District*,[30] in which the court reiterated that "[t]here is no categorical 'harassment exception' to the First Amendment's free speech clause."[31] In striking down a school district's harassment policy as unconstitutionally overbroad, the court explained,

> There is of course no question that non-expressive, physically harassing *conduct* is entirely outside the ambit of the free speech clause. But there is also no question that the free speech clause protects a wide variety of speech that listeners may consider deeply offensive, including statements that impugn another's race or national origin or that denigrate religious beliefs. When laws against harassment attempt to regulate oral or written expression on such topics, however detestable the views expressed may be, we cannot turn a blind eye to the First Amendment implications. "Where pure expression is involved," anti-discrimination law "steers into the territory of the First Amendment."[32]

Because "[t]he Supreme Court has made it clear . . . that the government may not prohibit speech under a 'secondary effects' rationale based solely on the emotive impact that its offensive content may have on a listener,"[33] and because the court found that school district's harassment policy did precisely that, it found the policy to be unconstitutional.

Given this understanding of the limits of both federal and state harassment law, let us return to the question of how private universities and colleges can ensure that their harassment policies are consistent with their commitments to freedom of expression. Private universities and colleges must ensure that they are in compliance with the law of harassment. This means that they are legally required to take steps to ensure that women and members of minority groups are not subjected to *conduct* by other members of the academic community that would create an intimidating, hostile, or offensive environment for them. But, as we have just seen, this does not mean that they are required to suppress the expression of any individual's viewpoint or opinion, regardless of how offensive it may be to members of the protected classes. In fact, the Department of Education has issued guidance for complying with the requirements of Title IX[34] that instructs universities and colleges that

> [i]n cases of alleged harassment, the protections of the First Amendment must be considered if issues of speech or expression are involved.

> Free speech rights apply in the classroom . . . and in all other education programs and activities of public schools. . . . In addition, First Amendment rights apply to the speech of students and teachers. . . .
>
> Title IX is intended to protect students from sex discrimination, not to regulate the content of speech. . . .
>
> Moreover, in regulating the conduct of its students and its faculty to prevent or redress discrimination prohibited by Title IX (e.g., in responding to harassment that is sufficiently serious as to create a hostile environment), a school must formulate, interpret, and apply its rules so as to protect academic freedom and free speech rights.[35]

Thus, it is perfectly possible for private universities and colleges to meet their legal obligations while simultaneously preserving freedom of expression on campus. No university or college can correctly argue that it is forced by its duty to obey the law to restrain the freedom of expression of its students or faculty.

Private universities and colleges that voluntarily adopt a commitment to maintain freedom of expression on campus have an ethical obligation to follow the Department of Education's guidance to formulate their harassment policy "so as to protect academic freedom and free speech rights." Fortunately, this is easily done. The university or college can simply insert the following two sentences into its harassment policy:

> An expression of one's religious, philosophical, literary, artistic, political, or scientific views regarding any protected category either in writing or verbally does not constitute harassment and is not prohibited by this policy. The University will dismiss any harassment allegation that it determines to be based solely on such expression.

The first of these sentences provides substantive protection for freedom of expression against restriction by the school's harassment policy. The second provides protection against the self-censorship that results from the desire to avoid the costs and stresses of having to defend oneself against a charge of harassment if one speaks one's mind. That is, the second sentence provides protection against the "chilling effect" of being subject to investigation for speaking.

Chilling Effects

The protection of freedom of expression requires more than the assurance that one will not be punished for expressing one's beliefs and opinions. It also requires the assurance that one will not be subject to the expense and potential public opprobrium associated with having to defend oneself at trial for doing so. The self-censorship that results from the desire to avoid such expense and opprobrium is what the courts refer to as the "chilling effect" of a law or regulation.[36] A university or college that adopts a commitment to freedom of expression adopts a duty to ensure that its polices not only do not punish, but also do not "chill" the expression of its students and faculty. And this means that it has the duty to prevent the academic analog of SLAPP suits.

In the political realm, a SLAPP suit is a strategic lawsuit against public participation. This is a lawsuit brought to intimidate and silence those opposed to the plaintiff's political interests by burdening them with the cost of a legal defense until they abandon their criticism or opposition. Those bringing a SLAPP suit do not expect to win the lawsuit. They simply want to raise the financial and psychological costs of publicly opposing their interests.[37] A typical SLAPP suit might accuse the defendants of defaming the plaintiff in the course of their public opposition to the plaintiff's political position.

The academic analog of a SLAPP suit would be to file complaints against students or faculty for the violation of university policies on the basis of their verbal or written statements. This would force those who hold unpopular positions to devote their time and efforts to answering the complaint and undergoing the hearing that constitutes the academic analog of a trial, all while under a cloud of suspicion of wrongdoing. Even if the complaints had little or no chance of being upheld, they would significantly raise the psychological costs of speaking out. The fear of being subjected to such a process can inhibit individuals from expressing unpopular or controversial opinions.

Perhaps the most famous example of this type of intimidation is the case of Laura Kipnis, a Northwestern University professor who was subject to a Title IX investigation for sexual harassment on the basis of an article that she published in the *Chronicle of Higher Education* criticizing Title IX enforcement policies.[38] Although the investigation ultimately found that the accusation was without merit,[39] Kipnis nevertheless had to endure three months of interrogations, hearings, and vilification before this result was reached.

Further, these academic analogs of SLAPP suits are not limited to university and college harassment policies. Universities and colleges often have civility policies or professional standards that ban certain types of behavior. For example, Northwestern University has a Civility and Mutual Respect policy which prohibits "[d]emeaning, intimidating, threatening, bullying, or violent behaviors that affect the ability to learn, work, or live in the University environment."[40] Similarly, Johns Hopkins has adopted Principles for Ensuring Equity, Civility and Respect for All that state that "[r]ude, disrespectful behavior is unwelcome and will not be tolerated."[41] Students and faculty can be accused of violating such policies for expressing their opinions on controversial subjects and forced to undergo hearings regardless of how outlandish the accusations may be.

An example of this is supplied by a recent event at Georgetown University. Georgetown has a policy denying official recognition and funding to student groups "if their purpose or activities . . . foster hatred or intolerance of others because of their race, nationality, gender, religion or sexual preference, or are inconsistent with acceptable conduct at an American university committed to the Roman Catholic moral tradition."[42] One of Georgetown's officially recognized student groups is Love Saxa, which identifies its mission as follows.

> In a society where dating and courtship are largely forgotten, structures of marriage and family are eroding, traditional understandings of gender complementarity are distant concepts, the use of pornography is prevalent, and sexual assault is rampant, Love Saxa exists to promote healthy relationships on campus through cultivating a proper understanding of sex, gender, marriage, and family among Georgetown students. Many Georgetown students lack a space to discuss their experiences of the harmful effects of a distorted view of human sexuality and the human person. Through programs consisting of discussions, lectures, and campaigns, we hope to increase awareness of the benefits of sexual integrity, healthy dating relationships, and the primacy of marriage (understood as a monogamous and permanent union between a man and a woman) as a central pillar of society.[43]

In October of 2017, a complaint was filed against Love Saxa on the ground that the group's definition of marriage as "a monogamous and permanent union between a man and a woman" fostered "hatred or intolerance of others because of their . . . sexual preference."[44] This forced the group to undergo a hearing before the Student Activities Commission to defend its expression of its belief in monogamous heterosexual marriage. Although the hearing panel voted 8 to 4 that the group did not violate the university policy, the president of the group noted that preparing for and participating in the hearing had required a great deal of time and effort and was a stressful experience.[45]

The notoriety of the hearing on campus—the knowledge that advocating for monogamous heterosexual marriage can result in one being accused of fostering hatred—is enough to make those who oppose same sex marriage think twice before expressing their opinion. This is a classic example of how not merely the threat of sanction but also the threat of trial can chill expression.

Fortunately, as was the case with regard to harassment policy, the problem of chilling effects is easily resolved. The university or college can simply adopt a general policy indicating that no university or college policy can be violated merely by the expression of one's beliefs or opinions. This can be done by adding the following sentence to the school's policy on freedom of expression.

> The University will dismiss any allegation that an individual or group has violated a policy of the university if it determines the allegation

to be based solely on the individual's or group's expression of his, her, or its religious, philosophical, literary, artistic, political, or scientific viewpoints.

Had such a provision been part of Georgetown's Speech and Expression Policy, the Love Saxa group could not have been required to defend its existence at an administrative hearing because the only evidence offered in support of the complaint was the statement of the group's belief in monogamous heterosexual marriage. The existence of such a provision in a university's or college's freedom of expression policy effectively inoculates the campus against the academic analog of SLAPP suits, and thus fulfills the school's obligation to ensure that its policies do not chill the expression of its students and faculty.

Conclusion

Private universities and colleges are under no obligation to maintain freedom of expression on their campuses unless they voluntarily represent themselves as doing so. However, if they make such a representation, they have an ethical obligation to live up to it. And that means that they also have an ethical obligation to ensure that they are not simultaneously undertaking other commitments that make it impossible to do so. The simplest way to assure that this is the case is to adopt a general policy stating that no individual or group will be sanctioned *or subject to investigation and administrative proceedings* based solely on the individual's or group's expression of his, her, or its religious, philosophical, literary, artistic, political, or scientific viewpoints. Finally, given the contemporary academic milieu, any school adopting a commitment to freedom of expression would be well-advised to explicitly reiterate that this general limitation applies to its harassment policy as well by pointing out that under the law of the United States such expression does not and cannot constitute legally prohibited harassment.

Notes

1. The author wishes to thank Ann C. Tunstall of Remedy Pharmaceuticals for her insightful comments on a draft of this essay. The author also wishes to thank Annette Hasnas of the New School of Northern Virginia and Ava Hasnas of the Oakwood School for providing him with first-hand experience of the danger of saying the wrong thing.
2. U.S. Constitution, Amendment I.
3. *Gitlow v. New York*, 268 U.S. 652, 666 (1925) ("For present purposes we may and do assume that freedom of speech and of the press which are protected by the First Amendment from abridgment by Congress are among the fundamental personal rights and 'liberties' protected by the due process clause of the Fourteenth Amendment from impairment by the States.").

4. Georgetown University Faculty Handbook §IV(L), https://facultyhandbook.georgetown.edu/toc/section4/l.
5. To continue using Georgetown University as an example, it makes precisely such a commitment. For example, Georgetown's administration has asserted that "[a]s a Catholic and Jesuit university, we are committed to fostering a community that is welcoming to all people and that values understanding, dignity, inclusion and respect." Broadcast email from the Provost of Georgetown University, on file with the author. See also Georgetown University's website stating that "Georgetown University is committed to creating an inclusive, safe, and welcoming campus for all members of our community across all gender and sexual diversities," https://lgbtq.georgetown.edu/resources.
6. For example, Gonzaga University, Pepperdine University, Brigham Young University, Baylor University, Saint Louis University, Vassar College, and Yeshiva University all have explicit limitation on acceptable expression in their policy statements. See "Spotlight Speech Codes Database," *Foundation for Individual Rights in Education*. www.thefire.org/spotlight/
7. The University of Chicago may be an example of such a private university. There are apparently several public universities that are in this situation, but this is explained by their legal duty under the First Amendment to refrain from interfering with constitutionally protected expression. See "Spotlight Speech Codes Database," *Foundation for Individual Rights in Education*. www.thefire.org/spotlight/
8. For example, Yale University adopted its commitment to freedom of expression in 1974, see Allison Pohle, "A Brief History of Free Speech at Yale," *Boston.com*, December 6, 2015; Harvard in 1990, see Brian R. Hecht, "Faculty Adopts Controversial Proposal Free Speech Policy to Be Consistent With the First Amendment," *The Harvard Crimson*, April 5, 1990; and Georgetown University in 1989, see www.thefire.org/wp-content/ . . . / Georgetown-Speech-and-Expression-13-14.pdf
9. Brown University president Christina Paxson confirms that because private universities and colleges are not bound by the First Amendment, they "could restrict the expression of ideas and beliefs within their campuses, if they chose to do so. But most private colleges and universities wisely do not make this choice. Instead, colleges and universities protect the rights of members of their communities to express a full range of ideas, however controversial." Christina Paxson, "A Safe Space for Freedom of Expression," *Washington Post*, September 5, 2016.
10. For example, following the wave of student protests at Yale in 2015–2016, Yale University president Peter Salovey declared,

    > At Yale, we adhere to exceptionally strong principles of free expression. . . . Yale does not censor invited speakers, nor does the administration discipline faculty members or students for the expression of ideas, no matter how unpopular. The answer to speech one finds offensive is more speech.

    Peter Salovey, "Yale Believes in Free Speech—and So Do I," *Wall Street Journal*, October 17, 2016. Similarly, in response to protests to controversial speakers at Brown, university president Christina Paxson reaffirmed Brown's commitment to freedom of expression stating that "Freedom of expression is an essential component of academic freedom, which protects the ability of universities to fulfill their core mission of advancing knowledge." Christina Paxson, "A Safe Space for Freedom of Expression," *Washington Post,* September 5, 2016. Again, in response to the disruption of a speech by Charles

Murray at Middlebury College, college president Laurie Patton stated when the values of freedom of expression and inclusivity come into conflict "educational institutions have a primary obligation to foster open and civil discourse. . . . Free speech lies at the heart of our purpose as an institution, and we cannot allow force or disruption to undermine it." Laurie l. Patton, "The Right Way to Protect Free Speech on Campus," *Wall Street Journal*, June 9, 2017. See also, "President Lee C. Bollinger's 2016 Convocation Address: Learning From Freedom of Expression," *Columbia News*, August 29, 2016, http://news.columbia.edu/content/1272 stating,

> in the past half century, we have all come to a pretty clear position, rather unique among nations: with extremely few exceptions, speech that is about or relevant to public issues and the search for truth, broadly interpreted, is fully protected against censorship, no matter how offensive or dangerous it might seem to you and me and a majority of the citizens of this country. In this case, what's true for the country is also true for Columbia. We don't ban speech. We don't censor speech.

11. For example, the DC Human Rights Act of 1977 includes age, marital status, personal appearance, gender identity, family responsibilities, genetic information, matriculation, and political affiliation as protected categories.
12. Civil Rights Act of 1964, Pub. L. 88–352, 78 Stat. 241 (1964).
13. Age Discrimination in Employment Act of 1967 (ADEA), 29 U.S.C. §§ 621–634 (2013).
14. Americans with Disabilities Act of 1990 (ADA), 42 U.S.C. §§ 12101–12213 (2013) (amended 2008).
15. *Meritor Savings Bank v. Vinson*, 477 U.S. 57, 65 (1986).
16. For purposes of simplicity, I discuss only federal law at this point. The definition of harassment is the same for state statutes, but often applies to additional protected categories. For example, under the DC Human Rights Act of 1977, there could be harassment on the basis of sexual orientation, gender identity, marital status, personal appearance, family responsibilities, genetic information, matriculation, and political affiliation.
17. There is another form of legally prohibited harassment that constitutes a form of sex discrimination—quid pro quo harassment. This type of harassment occurs when an employer or supervisor makes satisfaction of sexual demand a condition of employment. I do not discuss quid pro quo harassment in this article because its enforcement usually does not generate a conflict with freedom of speech.
18. "Harassment," U.S. Equal Employment Opportunity Commission, https://www1.eeoc.gov//laws/types/harassment.cfm?renderforprint=1
19. There are a few notable exceptions, such as Hillsdale College, Grove City College, and Patrick Henry College, that do not accept any federal assistance and so are not subject to federal anti-discrimination law.
20. "Harassment," U.S. Equal Employment Opportunity Commission, https://www1.eeoc.gov//laws/types/harassment.cfm?renderforprint=1
21. *Ibid.*
22. *See Giboney v. Empire Storage & Ice Co.*, 336 U.S. 490, 498–502 (1949), stating

> [i]t rarely has been suggested that the constitutional freedom for speech and press extends its immunity to speech or writing used as an integral part of conduct in violation of a valid criminal statute . . . [and] it has never been deemed an abridgement of freedom of speech or press to make a course of conduct illegal merely because the conduct was in part

initiated, evidenced, or carried out by means of language, either spoken, written, or printed.

23. *Bartnicki v. Vopper*, 532 U.S. 514, 526 (2001).
24. Eugene Volokh, "Speech as Conduct: Generally Applicable Laws, Illegal Courses of Conduct, 'Situation-Altering Utterances,' and the Uncharted Zones," *Cornell Law Review*, Vol. 90 (2005): 1277, 1301.
25. 505 U.S. 377 (1992).
26. St. Paul, Minn., Legis. Code § 292.02 (1990).
27. 505 U.S. at 381.
28. *Ibid.*, 382.
29. *Ibid.*, 396.
30. 240 F.3d 200 (3d Cir. 2001). The opinion for a unanimous court was written by Justice Samuel Alito, who was then a third circuit judge.
31. *Ibid.*, 204.
32. *Ibid.*, 206 (Citations omitted.).
33. *Ibid.*, 209.
34. And by implication, Title VI of the Civil Rights Act.
35. "Revised Sexual Harassment Guidance: Harassment of Students by School Employees, Other Students, or Third Parties," U.S. Department of Education, Office for Civil Rights, https://www2.ed.gov/about/offices/list/ocr/docs/shguide.html#Guidance
36. See *Walker v. City of Birmingham*, 388 U.S. 307, 344–345 (1967) (Brennan, J., dissenting):

    To give these freedoms the necessary "breathing space to survive" . . . the Court has modified traditional rules of standing and prematurity. We have molded both substantive rights and procedural remedies in the face of varied conflicting interests to conform to our overriding duty to insulate all individuals from the "chilling effect" upon exercise of First Amendment freedoms generated by vagueness, overbreadth and unbridled discretion to limit their exercise.

37. See Carson Hilary Barylak, "Reducing Uncertainty in Anti-SLAPP Protection," *Ohio State Law Journal*, Vol. 71 (2010): 845:

    Corporations, developers, and other private interests use strategic lawsuits against public participation (SLAPPs)—defined as suits that "(1) involve communications made to influence a government action or outcome, (2) which result in civil lawsuits (complaints, counterclaims, or cross-claims) (3) filed against non-governmental individuals or groups (4) on a substantive issue of some public interest or social significance"—to intimidate individuals and organizations that speak out against corporate decisions, development projects, government actions or operations, or other activities that affect their financial interests.

38. See Rachel Cooke, "Sexual Paranoia on Campus—and the Professor at the Eye of the Storm," *The Guardian*, April 2, 2017; Jeannie Suk Gersen, "Laura Kipnis's Endless Trial by Title IX," *The New Yorker*, September 20, 2017.
39. See Brock Read, "Laura Kipnis Is Cleared of Wrongdoing in Title IX Complaints," *The Chronicle of Higher Education*, May 31, 2015.
40. "Human Resources, Civility and Mutual Respect," *Northwestern*. www.northwestern.edu/hr/policies-forms/policies-procedures/civility-and-mutual-respect/
41. "University Policies and Statements," *Johns Hopkins University*. www.jhu.edu/university-policies/

42. "Student Organization Standards," *Georgetown University*, https://studentaffairs.georgetown.edu/policies/student-organizations/standards
43. *Hoya Link, Love Saxa, Love Saxa Constitution 2017–2018*, https://hoyalink.georgetown.edu/organization/lovesaxa
44. *See* Mary Hui, "Georgetown Students Have Filed a Discrimination Complaint Against a Campus Group Promoting Heterosexual Marriage," *Washington Post*, October 25, 2017. www.washingtonpost.com/news/acts-of-faith/wp/2017/10/25/georgetown-students-file-a-discrimination-complaint-against-a-campus-group-that-promotes-heterosexual-marriage/
45. *See* Mary Hui, "Georgetown Students Vote Not to Take Action Against Pro-Heterosexual-Marriage Campus Group," *Washington Post*, November 3, 2017, www.washingtonpost.com/news/acts-of-faith/wp/2017/11/03/georgetown-students-decide-not-to-take-action-against-pro-heterosexual-marriage-campus-group/

Works Cited

Barylak, Carson Hilary. "Reducing Uncertainty in Anti-SLAPP Protection." *Ohio State Law Journal*, Vol. 71 (2010): 845.

"Civility and Mutual Respect." *Northwestern*. www.northwestern.edu/hr/policies-forms/policies-procedures/civility-and-mutual-respect/.

Cooke, Rachel. "Sexual Paranoia on Campus—and the Professor at the Eye of the Storm." *The Guardian*. April 2, 2017.

"Georgetown University Faculty Handbook §IV(L)." *Georgetown University*. https://facultyhandbook.georgetown.edu/toc/section4/l.

Gersen, Jeannie Suk. "Laura Kipnis's Endless Trial by Title IX." *The New Yorker*. September 20, 2017.

"Harassment." *U.S. Equal Employment Opportunity Commission*. https://www1.eeoc.gov//laws/types/harassment.cfm?renderforprint=1

Hecht, Brian R. "Faculty Adopts Controversial Proposal Free Speech Policy to Be Consistent With the First Amendment." *The Harvard Crimson*, April 5, 1990.

Hoya Link, Love Saxa, Love Saxa Constitution 2017–2018. https://hoyalink.georgetown.edu/organization/lovesaxa.

Hui, Mary. "Georgetown Students Have Filed a Discrimination Complaint Against a Campus Group Promoting Heterosexual Marriage." *Washington Post*. October 25, 2017. www.washingtonpost.com/news/acts-of-faith/wp/2017/10/25/georgetown-students-file-a-discrimination-complaint-against-a-campus-group-that-promotes-heterosexual-marriage/

———. "Georgetown Students Vote Not to Take Action Against Pro-Heterosexual-Marriage Campus Group." *Washington Post*. November 3, 2017. www.washingtonpost.com/news/acts-of-faith/wp/2017/11/03/georgetown-students-decide-not-to-take-action-against-pro-heterosexual-marriage-campus-group/

Patton, Laurie L. "The Right Way to Protect Free Speech on Campus." *Wall Street Journal*. June 9, 2017.

Paxson, Christina. "A Safe Space for Freedom of Expression." *Washington Post*. September 5, 2016.

Pohle, Allison. "A Brief History of Free Speech at Yale." *Boston.com*. December 6, 2015.

"President Lee C. Bollinger's 2016 Convocation Address: Learning From Freedom of Expression." *Columbia News*. August 29, 2016. http://news.columbia.edu/content/1272

Read, Brock. "Laura Kipnis Is Cleared of Wrongdoing in Title IX Complaints." *The Chronicle of Higher Education*. May 31, 2015.

"Revised Sexual Harassment Guidance: Harassment of Students by School Employees, Other Students, or Third Parties." *U.S. Department of Education, Office for Civil Rights*. https://www2.ed.gov/about/offices/list/ocr/docs/shguide.html#Guidance.

Salovey, Peter. "Yale Believes in Free Speech—and So Do I." *Wall Street Journal*. October 17, 2016.

"Spotlight Speech Codes Database." *Foundation for Individual Rights in Education*. www.thefire.org/spotlight/

"Student Organization Standards." *Georgetown University*. https://studentaffairs.georgetown.edu/policies/student-organizations/standards.

"University Policies and Statements." *Johns Hopkins University*. www.jhu.edu/university-policies/

Volokh, Eugene. "Speech as Conduct: Generally Applicable Laws, Illegal Courses of Conduct, 'Situation-Altering Utterances,' and the Uncharted Zones." *Cornell Law Review*, Vol. 90 (2005): 1277, 1301.

Cases Cited

Age Discrimination in Employment Act of 1967 (ADEA), 29 U.S.C. §§ 621–634 (2013).

Americans with Disabilities Act of 1990 (ADA), 42 U.S.C. §§ 12101–12213 (2013) (amended 2008).

Bartnicki v. Vopper, 532 U.S. 514, 526 (2001).

Civil Rights Act of 1964, Pub. L. 88–352, 78 Stat. 241 (1964).

Giboney v. Empire Storage & Ice Co., 336 U.S. 490, 498–502 (1949)

Gitlow v. New York, 268 U.S. 652, 666 (1925).

Meritor Savings Bank v. Vinson, 477 U.S. 57, 65 (1986).

R.A.V. v. City of St. Paul 505, U.S. 377 (1992).

Saxe v. State College Area School District, 240 F.3d 200 (3d Cir. 2001).

St. Paul, Minn., Legis. Code §292.02 (1990).

Walker v. City of Birmingham, 388 U.S. 307, 344–345 (1967).

6 Outside Funding to Centers

A Challenge to Institutional Mission?

Jason Brennan

Many colleges and universities have research centers that receive significant funding from outside donors, including private foundations, government agencies, and individuals. Funders give money because there is a congruence of research interests, or of ideology and doctrine, between the funders and the receiving professors and research centers. But inevitably this leads to various faculty, student, and activist groups complaining that the money will have a corrupting effect or will undermine academic freedom. Decades ago, the complaints were against military-funded centers. Then came complaints about conservative centers, religious centers, and centers funded by corporations. Now, the complaints mostly focus on libertarian research centers funded by the Koch Foundation and its allies.

For instance, the Koch Foundation plans to give nearly $4 million over the next five years to the market-friendly Eudaimonia Institute at Wake Forest University. They face derision and deep opposition. Egged on by the George Soros-funded Ralph Wilson of the Soros-funded UnKoch My Campus,[1] the faculty senate voted to demand Wake Forest refuse the money.[2]

In many cases, research centers like this face significant opposition from left-wing faculty. Left-wing students protest. Faculty in other departments demand control and oversight. Left-wing faculty write op-eds and give interviews in which they state how harmful they believe these centers to be. Almost weekly one can find an article in a major press outlet which complains that these centers are undermining, corrupting, or even destroying the academy. Their complaints are manifold, including:

A The centers do not produce honest research, but instead promote an ideological agenda.
B The lure of easy money corrupts professors and graduate students, inducing them to advocate positions they would not otherwise support.
C The money allows libertarians or supporters of free markets to have outsized influence in academia.

D Because the centers are not supervised by other departments, they are a threat to academic freedom at the host institutions.

E The centers in question are governed by different rules from other centers; in particular, they supposedly allow funders to have significant discretion over what these centers do.

In short, critics of free market research centers are quite convinced such centers are a threat to institutional mission. They believe these centers corrupt their host institutions and threaten academic freedom.

In the past, critics of other research centers made similar complaints. Perhaps the Templeton Foundation will corrupt the study of the philosophy of religion by incentivizing philosophers to defend a theistic and Abrahamic worldview. Perhaps Department of Defense money will cause scientists to be pro-military and pro-imperialism. Perhaps corporate money will cause scientists or others to defend their corporate funders and ignore climate change, or whatnot.

My goal in this article is to cast doubt on their complaints. The claim that it corrupts the academy requires empirical evidence which critics have made no attempt to provide, even though they bear the burden of proof. The claim that outside funding threatens academic freedom relies upon a strange conception of academic freedom. Further, I will argue, even if we suppose for the sake of argument that the funders of such centers (such as the Templeton Foundation, the Kochs, or the Kendricks) or the people running such centers (such as philosopher Jim Otteson) are deeply intellectually corrupt, I will argue that academia is already so corrupt and beset by ideological bias that introducing new sources of biases actually *improves* the intellectual atmosphere.

Many of my arguments that follow can be used to defend external research centers in general, regardless of their politics or the politics of their donors. I will tend to use libertarian-oriented research centers as examples not because they are special or a hard case, but simply because—thanks to campus politics—these are the centers that right now face the most opposition.

The Burden of Proof

Suppose I claimed that the government-funding of the humanities and social sciences was corrupting universities and destroying academic freedom. It wouldn't be enough to tell a just-so story about how government funding could harm academia: "Well, obviously, the government's gonna pay people to support increased government power and to promote its agenda. Obviously, the money will lure people to push a statist philosophy."

Since I am the one making the positive claim, I would have to supply strong positive evidence that such corruption is indeed taking place. In the absence of strong evidence on behalf of my claims, people should at most conclude that I merely have a plausible but unproven hypothesis.

Of course, the same point goes for people who claim that private funds (and the funding of market-friendly research centers) corrupts academia. Some of their worries are plausible, but plausible speculations are no substitute for actual evidence.

How might someone prove such claims? If they assert that the funders of such centers have special power over hiring or teaching content, they need to uncover evidence that this is the case. (We could similarly level such accusations against left-wing research centers, but it would be unfair in the absence of substantive evidence.) They might conduct surveys to see if administrators or others have been forced to hire people they regard as unqualified, though such surveys might reflect ideology more than objective measures of quality. (See later in this piece.) They might look for natural experiments, perhaps by examining otherwise largely identical universities that have both approved such centers, but in which some of the centers, for entirely random reasons, failed to be approved. They could then see if afterwards the amount of research produced, the citation indices of the researchers, the number of publications, and so on, increases or decreases once the centers are established. They could measure the effect on graduate student placement or rankings. We could survey attitudes around campus and see if they've gotten worse (though again, this could reflect ideology and bias on the part of the dissatisfied left rather than a real problem with the centers). We could see if the professors at the centers receive unusually low teaching evaluations. (Though, again, this might reflect student bias rather than anything objective.) And so on.

The basic point is that in principle this issue is open to empirical investigation, though researchers must be careful to determine causation, pick apart significant correlations, and control for confounding variables. They would have to check for bias as well: In the same way, if a school composed of white supremacists suddenly had hired a number of black professors, I'd expect to see complaints that the black professors are ruining the school, but I'd wouldn't regard that as serious evidence that there's something wrong with the black professors.

But as of now, we have no such careful studies. We have loud accusations and insinuations, but no actual evidence. For that reason, this essay could just end here: Those who claim outside funding is harming the university bear the burden of proof. They have not begun to meet that burden. Their claims are largely empirical, but they have produced no careful social science to prove these claims. They must come back with real evidence.

But rather than just ignore their complaints on the grounds that they have no evidence, I want to make further trouble. So, here goes.

On the Truth of the "Ism"

Suppose, for the sake of argument, that the easy money associated with, say, libertarian research centers somehow increases the incidence of libertarianism on campus. Suppose it solidifies professors' libertarianism—it prevents current libertarians from changing their minds. Or suppose it induces non-libertarian students and professors to either become libertarian or become at least friendlier toward libertarianism.

Or suppose that the money coming from the Templeton Foundation increases the degree of theism among students and faculty. Or suppose that back in the 1960s, Department of Defense grants tended to make faculty more pro-military and pro-military intervention.

Again, we have no serious evidence that such effects exist, but for the sake of argument, suppose we uncovered firm evidence to that effect.

Would that suffice to prove the money corrupts recipients and that the money is therefore bad? The answer: *It depends*. It depends both on *how* the money caused the change but also on whether the "ism" the money induces people to believe is true. Or, more precisely, it depends on the degree to which the money pushes people closer or farther away from to the truth.

I'll illustrate this point with a thought experiment. Suppose X is the true theory of some intellectual domain. Suppose there is a pill which, if swallowed, will cause one to believe X and also memorize the evidence and arguments for X as well as the arguments and evidence against competitors to X. Suppose I pay you $5,000 to take the pill. You aren't willing to take the pill for free.

Now, we might think the causal story here is troublesome. Your motivation in taking the pill is the wrong kind of motivation. You were motivated by the money rather than the impartial and dispassionate pursuit of truth. You lack virtue as an epistemic agent; if you happen to be a scholar, then your motives are especially troublesome.

Still, it's does not quite follow that bribing you to take the pill was epistemically corrupting. After taking the pill, your epistemic state improves—by hypothesis, you then believe the correct theory and also have the right evidence for it. After taking the pill, your beliefs fit the world better; you are epistemically superior to your state *before* taking the pill.

What if something similar is true for libertarian (or other) research centers and the supposedly easy money attached to them? Suppose for the sake of argument that some form of libertarianism is the correct political theory, or more weakly that libertarianism contains a large number of true claims, such as that we should open borders, end the drug war, reduce prison sentences, pay attention to and correct government failure, and have free trade. Suppose the research funding, fellowships, speaker symposia, or other amenities the centers provide either (A) induce already libertarian-minded professors and students to stay libertarian and/or (B) induce non-libertarian-minded professors and student to move in a libertarian direction. In this case, we may say the same thing we said about the pill thought experiment: Perhaps the causal story is somewhat corrupt—the motive is money rather than a dispassionate pursuit of truth—but by hypothesis, the money improves people's epistemic state (or stops them from having a worse state) because it pushes them or keeps them believing in the correct theory and the evidence in support of that theory.

So, a libertarian might think he has an easy rejoinder to critics: "Even if—and I'm still waiting for you to supply evidence for this claim—the money induces people to believe things they otherwise would not, that's a bonus, not a problem, because libertarianism is correct. It's too bad people didn't believe it on their own, but at least the money sets them on the right track. Libertarian-minded centers are thus at worst helping to improve the epistemic credentials of their host universities. Since libertarianism is the correct theory, these research centers are the *best* places on campus, because they are the only places full of people who support the truth rather than mistakes and falsehoods. As someone who cares about the truth, I should be glad such centers exist." We could imagine others making similar responses. "Since theism is true, taking Templeton money in support of pro-religious research is a good thing."

Or, consider that nearly 18 percent of professors in the social sciences self-identify as Marxist. From a mainstream economist perspective, Marxist economics has been refuted, and so being a Marxist is roughly like being a young Earth creationist in biology. However, suppose the easy money at libertarian research centers lures a few people away from Marxism and toward libertarianism, but does not manage to get them all the way there. In that case, the centers would improve the epistemic state of far left-wing faculty, even if the centers themselves push a view too extreme in a different direction. Extremism of one form might correct extremism of another. After all, even though most economists are not libertarian, it's now standard economics that the robust protection of private property, open markets, and free trade are more or less necessary institutions for sustained economic prosperity.[3] Thus, moving hard-left professors in a market-oriented direction would be a good thing; it would get them to stop believing defunct pseudoeconomics and instead to believe something closer to the truth.

Similar remarks could, in principle, apply to other sources of funding. Suppose, in the 1960s, that the truth of the matter is that a mild and moderate military interventionism is the most just policy. Suppose students and faculty are largely anti-intervention, but the Department of Defense is radically pro-intervention. Suppose the money induces people not to share the DOD's point of view but instead to split the difference—they adopt the moderate position. Here, by hypothesis, the money would tend to improve people's epistemic state rather than corrupt. Perhaps similar remarks apply to other sources of funding.

The upshot is that it is difficult to make an ideological- or doctrine-*neutral* assessment of these centers. At least to some degree, whether these centers are good or bad depends in part on the actual truth of the research they produce, or more modestly, on what effect they have on people's beliefs. If—and this is a big and unsubstantiated if—the money induces people to change their beliefs, that does not yet show the money is corrupting or bad. Rather, it depends in part on whether they change their beliefs toward or away from the truth.

That's not to say it's impossible to make ideologically-neutral arguments for or against such centers; I'll consider some such arguments next. But my point here is that the value of these centers at least in part depends on the truth of the positions they defend and what effect that has on the positions others end up defending. Unfortunately, we don't have some neutral arbiter of truth to refer to. The people in these centers will insist their views are true, so therefore their centers are good. Others might insist their views are false, and so their centers are to that extent bad.

Does External Funding Threaten Academic Freedom?

One ideologically neutral complaint is that external funding threatens and undermines academic freedom. What I mean by saying this complaint is ideological neutral is not that the concept of academic freedom is itself neutral. Rather, I mean that we can hold that an external funding source interferes with faculty freedom without taking on a stance on whether the faculty's beliefs are true. For instance, suppose the state government of Wisconsin threatened to defund any professor who espouses Marxism. I readily admit that this threatens academic freedom, even though I also think Marxism is false.

At Wake Forest University, the faculty senate voted to reject the Eudaimonia Institute's funding on the grounds that it interfered with faculty freedom. To protect academic freedom, the senate demanded discretion over each of the following:

1. Whether the Eudaimonia Institute would be created
2. Whether and from whom the institute would receive funding
3. The right to determine whom the institute may hire
4. The right to decide what the faculty affiliated with the institute may present or publish.[4]

Supposedly, without such rights and powers in place, the Koch funding was a threat to academic freedom.

On its face, this is an odd, almost backward account of academic freedom. In general, individual departments at research universities have tremendous latitude and power to set their own standards and to choose, almost unilaterally, whom to hire. The provost, chancellor, or president may have to sign off on hires, but they nearly always defer to individual departments. While tenure and promotion decisions often require candidates to be screened by an ad hoc committee with professors from around the school, these committees generally just count publications and make sure professors are publishing in the appropriate journals in their field; they do not check the actual quality of the work other professors do. Perhaps this is a mistake, but nevertheless, this is the basic structure of the research university. Further, faculty never have to ask others for permission to present or publish on anything. They write the papers they feel like writing. They present where they are invited to and agree to speak; they publish whatever and wherever they get past double-blind peer review.

Faculty freedom does not mean that the faculty as a collective exercises complete authority and control over each individual professor. Rather, it means that the professors do not have to ask permission from other professors about what to write and say. It means the economics and philosophy departments don't need to ask Marxist studies or English for permission to hire new faculty or publish new books, and vice versa.

Consider an analogy. Suppose billionaire Arnold Cunningham becomes convinced that Mormonism is the correct religion. He pours billions into producing Mormon pamphlets, crafting beautiful and alluring Mormon temples and meetinghouses, funding missionaries, shooting and airing catchy pro-Mormon commercials, and the like. He pumps money into Mormon assistance programs, such that Mormon congregations have significant money to help the poor in their religious communities. Suppose his efforts pay off and Mormonism soon becomes the fastest growing religion around the world.

Now suppose that all the other churches and religious denominations in, say, the United States get angry. They think Cunningham and his money have a pernicious influence. Accordingly, they get a new law passed which states that any new Mormon meetinghouse; any new Mormon bishops; and any new religious material, pamphlets, missionary work, talks, meetings, and commercials must first be approved by a majority vote of *all the other non-Mormon churches, mosques, and temples in the country*. Any new money going to Mormon causes must first get their collective approval.

It would be absurd to cast this new law as a law protecting religious freedom. Rather, it's law clearly curbing religious freedom. If your church has to ask permission from other churches to conduct your activities, you aren't free. Or, if we want to use the language of freedom, we could say this new law which takes away *individual* religious freedom and instead gives a motivated, biased majority the freedom to control what other individuals do. Under this law, the majority of the moment has religious freedom, but no individuals, including the individuals who form that majority, have religious freedom.

Similarly, suppose that in order to expand its business, Bob's Hardware first had to get permission from a hardware guild, with representatives from Home Depot, Lowe's, and Ace. We wouldn't call this system a free market, and we wouldn't say such a law protects economic freedom.

Just as such laws restrict rather than promote religious or economic freedom, so similar rules at universities restrict rather than promote faculty freedom. When faculty complain that Koch money undermines faculty freedom, what they often apparently mean is that they want the freedom to control what their fellow faculty say, think, and do. Concern for "faculty freedom" seems at best to be a conceptual mistake or at worst a thin pretext for demanding power over others.

Nevertheless, one might still have a legitimate complaint about the misuse of the funds. Suppose the Kochs, or George Soros, or anyone else offers to fund a new position but only on the grounds that the faculty hire someone they select, or, more weakly, only if they get veto power over who is hired. Here, the issue is probably not best cast as one of freedom per se. In taking such a deal, the faculty wouldn't exactly lose freedom but rather would agree to use their freedom in a particular way in exchange for funding. Nevertheless, this is potentially problematic: The faculty in question have a fiduciary responsibility to their university to hire the best person they can get, and so would violate their own duties if they were to select a substandard person in exchange for money.

Still, just when faculty should and or should not take such deals is a rather complicated question. It seems plausible to me that I shouldn't agree to hire a substandard professor just to please a donor. On the other hand, it also seems plausible to me that external funders need not make unconditional grants—if a donor offers money to study, say, the problem of free will, she would reasonably be angry if we used her money to hire a person who doesn't study that problem.

There's an interesting question here of how much leeway over a topic external funders should have. Consider: If my department were authorized by the provost to hire a new person, we would not be interested in hiring someone who researches, say, accounting ethics. But if an external funder offered to endow a chair of accounting ethics, we wouldn't see a problem in taking the money and hiring a good person on that topic. In the same way, I'm not planning to buy a Gibson Les Paul any time soon, but if a neighbor offered me one for free, I'd happily take it.

There's also an interesting question here over whether it's permissible to defend a position in print at someone's bequest. Consider that even though I think Marxism is false, it need not violate my integrity to write and publish a paper defending Marxism. After all, I might think that I or the academy could learn from seeing certain ideas and arguments explored. And, in fact, academics often do write papers like that—where they defend a conclusion for the sake of argument, not because they genuinely believe it's correct.[5]

Now, suppose I wrote and published exactly that same paper defending Marxism—where I still believe it's worth considering for the sake of argument—but I also received $10,000 from a Marxist foundation. Would that suddenly make the paper evil, or me corrupt, when it was permissible to write such a paper for free? That's also a rather complicated question; indeed, my frequent co-author Peter Jaworski and I wrote an entire book exploring questions like that.[6]

I don't have space here to adequately explore all these issues. So I admit that in principle it may turn out that certain donor deals could have questionable ethics or involve giving too much power to donors. The complaints are probably not best cast as worries about academic freedom, but instead as worries about professors violating their intellectual integrity or violating their fiduciary responsibility to the university. However, again, I note that the burden of proof is on the critics. They both need (A) to give us a plausible account of what counts as improper donor influence and (B) show us that some actual donors have had this influence. So far, in looking at the myriad articles about the Koch Foundation, the Templeton Foundation, various left-wing foundations, various for-profit corporations, or the Department of Defense, I see only accusations, not evidence.

Could External Funding Improve Debate and Improve Ideological Balance?

In this section, I'll argue that even if such funding is corruptly motivated by false ideology, it might nevertheless improve the university rather than corrupt it. Corrupt money might spoil a pristine academic environment. But the actual academic environment is highly biased and ideological, and so corrupt money might have an ameliorative or balancing effect.

To illustrate what I mean, consider three widely believe sets of ideas about how the university ought to function and how academic discourse ought to go.

> ***The Marketplace of Ideas***
>
> *Academia thrives in an environment of open contestation. People need to be exposed to rigorous defenses of a wide range of ideas, including ideas they find (perhaps rightly find) repugnant, repellant, and abhorrent. Our best ideas, theories, and arguments are improved by having to respond to continual challenges and objections from other camps. We can't really be sure we know what we think we know unless we know others are not only free and indeed do challenge our arguments and conclusions. When the range of ideas becomes narrow, we become less enterprising and innovative. We can have people play devil's advocates, but*

> *frankly, the best challenges come from people who genuinely disagree. Accordingly, academia will thrive best in an arena of massive intellectual diversity.*

To be frank, these are all empirical claims about the value of wide and open discourse. John Stuart Mill defends such ideas in *On Liberty*, largely from anecdotes and armchair analysis. But I haven't seen any vigorous empirical defense of these claims. It's possible they're mistaken. Nevertheless, these ideas are widely shared and believed, and most of our modern pedagogy seems based upon these ideas.

Suppose you agree with the "marketplace of ideas" theory. You might then reason as follows: Even if the external donors are corrupt and simply want to push their own points of view, and even if the faculty recipients of money are just corrupt guns for hire, nevertheless, the academy might benefit from having lots of different people push lots of different ideas so that others can respond to those ideas. For instance, I once debated the issue of immigration with someone from the conservative Heritage Institute; though I think his anti-immigration arguments were bad and his evidence thin, debating him nevertheless helped me write my pro-immigration book.[7] By helping to place and secure faculty with points of view different from the mainstream, certain sources of external funding probably increase the chance that students will be exposed to vigorous debate and good faith defenses of different points of view. It makes it more likely that debate in the academy will be vigorous rather than just fall into a close-minded echo chamber.

And we should indeed worry that the academy is too much of a close-minded echo chamber. I don't want to exaggerate that—there is plenty of vigorous debate in the academy. But at the same time, debate in most social scientific and humanities fields is almost entirely from a left-wing point of view, and if not that, then a libertarian point of view. Conservative voices are largely absent, and though I am not a conservative, I think that's a real problem.

Supposedly, the value in liberal education consists in part in students learning to confront and engage with, and even *learn* from, alien ideas. This means they should encounter vigorous and rigorous defenses of a wide range views, including views they might (rightly) consider wicked and immoral. (For instance, in one of my classes, I have students read vigorous defenses of fascism and Nazism; they regularly report this was one of the best learning experiences.) Scholarship itself presumably improves when academics have to argue against strong defenses of contrary points of view. If academia naturally tends toward narrowing the sphere of disagreement, or to excluding whole certain points of view, then outside money might serve as a corrective.

Academics might claim this is unnecessary—they might say *they* can explain, say, libertarian or conservative thought to students, no need to hire actual libertarians or conservatives—but this claim is shown false by their almost unanimous failure to actually do so in print.[8]

In *Against Democracy*, I introduced three major political archetypes, which I called hobbits, hooligans, and Vulcans. Hobbits won't concern us here. I described the other two as follows:

1. *Hooligans* are the rabid sports fans of politics. They have strong and largely fixed political views. For them, their political affiliation is an essential part of their identity. They tend to befriend those who share their political affiliation, but think those with different ideas are evil or stupid. They tend to be well-informed, but process information in a biased manner. They suffer from confirmation bias, disconfirmation bias, and intergroup bias, among other biases.
2. *Vulcans* are dispassionate truth-seekers. They are well-informed and may have opinions, but they hold their opinions only as strongly as the evidence allows. They actively seek out disconfirmation and regularly change their minds as new evidence comes in.[9]

I argue that the empirical evidence shows us most politically active citizens are hooligans; few are Vulcans.

I invoke the distinction here because it bears on how we evaluate politically-motivated outside grants. Outside funders—whether they come from the left, libertarian quadrant, or right—are not neutral. They have a point of view and they give money in hopes of raising the status of that point of view. They may believe in the importance of free debate, or they may not.

It's tempting, then, to say that because outside funders have political motives, they are thereby corrupting the university. But whether that is so depends in part on what the people at the university are like. If they were mostly Vulcans—rational, disinterested, truth-seeking—then the money would most likely do harm. However, if they are mostly hooligans—biased, activist team-players—then the money might (despite the donors' possibly corrupt motives) improve things.

Now, empirical research overwhelming shows that in day-to-day politics, politically active citizens, or even citizens who have firm opinions at all, tend to be hooligans.[10] In general, the biggest predictor that a person will be well-informed about politics is not education, IQ, or social status, but rather whether that person finds politics *interesting*.[11] But the problem turns out to be that finding politics interesting does not mean one is dispassionately searching for truth. Rather, it usually means one regards one's political as part of one's identity.[12]

In politics (and elsewhere), we suffer from "in-group/out-group bias" or "intergroup bias." In-group/out-group bias means we are tribalistic, in the most negative connotation of that term. We are biased to form groups and to identify ourselves strongly with that group. We tend to develop animosity toward other groups, even when there is no basis for this animosity. We are biased to assume our group is good and just, and that members of other groups are bad, stupid, and unjust. Our commitment to our team can override our commitment to truth or morality.[13]

Political psychologist Geoffrey Cohen did a number of scientific studies in order to determine how partisanship affects people's judgments about policies. As fellow political psychologist Dennis Chong summarizes Cohen's work,

> The experiment presented participants with two contrasting versions—generous or stringent—of a social welfare policy. Judging each policy on its merits, respondents preferred the version that was consistent with their ideological values. But when the policies were attributed to either the Democratic or Republican Party, liberal respondents favored the Democratic-labeled policy regardless of whether it was generous or stringent, and conservatives favored the Republican-labeled policy regardless of details.[14]

Political scientist Diana Mutz finds striking evidence that political "fandom" is what motivates people to get to the polls. The people who are most active in politics tend to have strong hooligan characteristics. Politically active citizens are usually people who have strong opinions but who rarely talk to people who have different opinions and who are unable to explain the rationale behind contrary points of view.[15] Being exposed to contrary points of view tends to lessen one's enthusiasm for one's own political views. Deliberation with others who hold contrary views tends to make one ambivalent and apathetic about politics and less likely to participate.[16] What Mutz calls "cross-cutting political exposure"—exposure to contrary points of view or talking to people who disagree—strongly decreases the likelihood that a person will vote, reduces the number of political activities a person engages in, and makes people take longer to decide how to vote.[17] In contrast, actively participating citizens tend not to engage in much deliberation and tend not to have much cross-cutting political discussion.[18] They people who participate the most are those who spend the most time in echo chambers.

Political scientists Shanto Iyengar and Sean Westwood wanted to determine how much, if at all, political bias affects how people evaluate *job* candidates. They conducted an experiment in which they asked over 1,000 subjects to evaluate what the subjects were told were the résumés of graduating high school students. With this experiment, Iyengar and Westwood could answer questions such as: How much more strongly, if at all, would a Republican evaluator favor a Republican job candidate over an equally qualified Democratic job candidate? Or, if a Democratic evaluator had to choose between a clearly less qualified Democrat and a clearly more qualified Republican, which would he prefer?

The results are depressing: 80.4 percent of Democratic subjects picked the Democratic job candidate, while 69.2 percent of Republican subjects picked the Republican job candidate. Even if the Republican job candidate was clearly stronger, Democrats still chose the Democratic candidate 70 percent of the time. In contrast, they found that "candidate qualification had no significant effect on winner section."[19] In other words, the evaluators didn't care about how qualified the candidates were; they just cared about what the job candidates' politics were

Are faculty any different? Anecdotally, I personally have been on a committee where the chairperson of the committee said, loudly and without restraint, that no libertarian faculty would be considered. He meant it: When the top candidate turned out to be libertarian, the chairperson asked our dean to change the job description from political philosophy/business ethics to moral psychology, in order to exclude the libertarian candidate.[20]

It's well known that academia skews toward the left; conservatives are underrepresented:

> According to data compiled by the Higher Education Research Institute, only 12% of university faculty identify as politically right of center, and these are mainly professors in schools of engineering and other professional schools. Only 5% of professors in the humanities and social-science departments so identify.
>
> A comprehensive study by James Lindgren of Northwestern University Law School shows that in a country fairly evenly divided between Democrats and Republicans, only 13% of law professors identify as Republican. And a recent study by Jonathan Haidt of New York University showed that 96% of social psychologists identify as left of center, 3.7% as centrist/moderate and only 0.03% as right of center.[21]

However, just *why* conservatives in particular are under-represented is a difficult question. Not surprisingly, many on the left claim it has little to do with active discrimination or implicit bias against conservatives; rather, they claim that conservatives simply lack the mindset for academia.[22] They claim that universities encourage open inquiry and rational debate, while conservatives prize the closed passage of received truth.[23] One might wonder if the left's easy willingness to accept this exculpating just-so story is *itself* evidence of bias—conservatives certainly do not regard this as a fair characterization of their mindset.

Empirical work shows that many left-wing professors actively discriminate against conservatives. As Yoel Inbar and Joris Lammers summarize their research:

> conservatives fear negative consequences of revealing their political beliefs to colleagues. They are right to do so: In decisions ranging from paper reviews to hiring, many social and personality psychologists said that they would discriminate against openly conservative colleagues. The more liberal respondents were, the more they said they would discriminate.[24]

In a survey, Inbar and Lammers found about one-third of left-wing professors (and note that left-wing psychologists vastly outnumber everyone else) admitted they would discriminate against conservatives in hiring decision. This doesn't mean the majority would *not* discriminate. Instead, social desirability bias tells us this is a low estimate. If x% admit they would do something bad, the truth is usually that >x% do it. Julie R. Posselt's ethnographic study *Inside Graduate Admissions* similarly describes patterns of mocking dismissal of right-wing and conservative students apply for graduate school admissions.[25]

However, while active and explicit discrimination exists, there's reason to think academia might lean leftward even if all professors were trying to be open-minded and fair. Consider a few more mechanisms:

A *Selection effects*: Most people try to work in professions and live in places where the others around them share the same political beliefs. Once academia acquires—perhaps through pure accident—a reputation for leaning left, we'd expect conservatives to be less interested in working in academia but the left to have more interest.[26]

B *Peer-review and research focus*: In order to succeed in academia, professors must publish in peer-review outlets. But even if reviewers are trying to be fair and open-minded, their politics is likely to affect how they evaluate work. Your political beliefs tell you which topics to regard as most important and worthy of attention. Further, reviewers will naturally find arguments that go along with their preexisting views more reasonable, while they will be more inclined to challenge or doubt the premises of papers going against their preexisting views.[27]

C *The Schelling Segregation Effect*: Suppose most faculty prefer both (A) to be on an ideologically and intellectual diverse faculty, but also prefer (B) not to be in the ideological minority. Suppose they prefer B at least slightly more than they prefer A. Nobel Laureate economists Thomas Schelling famously discovered (using race rather than ideology as his example) that even under such mild conditions, a pattern of radical segregation would emerge.[28]

D *Conformity Effects*: Solomon Asch famously got people in a room to agree that disparate length lines were the same length by surrounding them with peers who claimed the lines were the same. Human beings are naturally conformist; we tend to modulate our beliefs to match those of our peers.

A--D give us reason to think that the academy that starts with a slight leftward slant will tend to lean ever further to the left, and that those on the right will be ghettoized and excluded, even if no one quite intends for this to happen and even if no one intends to discriminate. Similarly, in a parallel universe, where the academy in 1960 had been more right-wing than left-wing, we might expect the academia to become more right-leaning over time. Even if faculty were non-partisan, the gravitational pull of A–D could lead to an ideological effect which is only partially offset by professional diligence.

With all these background dynamics in play, political motivated funding might actually *improve* academia: We have general evidence that people discriminate unfairly against those with different politics. We also have some evidence that academic psychologists will *admit* that they discriminate. Further, there are other sorts of biases and mechanisms which would predict conservatives, libertarians, and others will be treated unfairly in academia or will be underrepresented even if no one intends that. Though we don't know just how big the effect size is of these differing causes, we should presume these causes help explain why genuine social conservatives in particular are unrepresented in academia. However, if such groups receive outside support—which enables such professors to publish more or bolster their résumés—then this might serve partially to level the playfield. Since the academy probably discriminates unfairly against the right, funding right-wing points of view might help to partially correct the improper imbalance and get the academy slightly closer to where it would be if only faculty were not partisan players. This might also hold for other underrepresented non-right-wing points of view.

These points can hold *even if* the funders have corrupt motives. We needn't suppose that outside funders genuinely *care* about correcting discrimination or improving pedagogy or research. Perhaps all they care about is indoctrinating students in their own ideology. Nevertheless, even if funders have bad motives, the actual effect of their money might be positive. Of course, too much money might mean that they *overcorrect* to the point of corrupting the academy. But just where we are on that point is partly open to empirical investigation. So far, no one has any evidence either way.

My point here is that people who complain about outside funding often seem to have in mind an image of the university, whereby pure, disinterested, truth-seeking academics get corrupted by impure, motivated, ideologically-tinged money. In reality, academia is full of ideologically motivated team players, status seekers, activists, and political hooligans. While corrupt funding might corrupt a pure institution, corrupt money might improve a corrupt institution. In principle, the effect of such funding is open to empirical investigation. For now, all we have are some plausible but untested hypotheses.

Conclusion

In this paper, I have not definitely proven that such externally-funded research centers are unproblematic. Really, to take a definitive stance one way or another would not merely require some sophisticated philosophical analysis but would also require significant empirical work.

However, I've made some trouble for the complainants. Their complaints seem unproven and they have not discharged their burden of proof. I've shown that whether money "corrupts" depends in part on the truth of the views the centers support, and, more importantly, on what effect such centers have on the overall level of discourse. The claim that such centers threaten academic freedom also relies on a problematic conception of freedom. It could even be that corrupt money improves the already corrupt political atmosphere of the modern university.

Notes

1. UnKoch My Campus claims its fiscal sponsor is the Center for Media and Democracy. https://centerformediaanddemocracy.salsalabs.org/unkochmycampus/index.html. The center refuses to disclose where it gets its funding, but it has received at least $200,000 from Soros. www.foxnews.com/opinion/2011/12/11/left-obama-escalate-war-on-banks-into-dangerous-territory.html#ixzz1gWfrRwHS. It receives money from a number of other left-leaning foundations: www.sourcewatch.org/index.php/Center_for_Media_and_Democracy#Funding. See also https://fdik.org/soros.dcleaks.com/download/index.html%3Ff=%252Fmemo%2520on%2520climate.pdf&t=us and http://freebeacon.com/issues/soros-tied-networks-foundations-joined-forces-create-trump-resistance-fund/. Note that Lindsey Berger, UnKoch's Executive Director, also works directly for and is paid by Greenpeace.
2. www.jamesgmartin.center/2017/03/wake-forest-faculty-attempt-undermine-koch-funded-campus-institute/
3. Rosenberg and Birdzell, 1986; Acemoglu, Johnson and Robinson 2001; Acemoglu, Johnson and Robinson 2002; Acemoglu, Johnson and Robinson 2005; Acemoglu and Robinson 2005; Acemoglu and Robinson 2013; Glaeser, La Porta, Lopez-de-Silanes and Shleifer 2004; North 1990, 2012; North, Wallis and Weingast 2012; Rodrik, Subramanian and Trebbi 2004; Roland 2014; Weil 2013.
4. www.wsj.com/articles/an-anti-koch-meltdown-at-wake-forest-1491521075
5. Indeed, Brennan 2007 is just such a paper. I wrote that paper because I thought it was worth exploring the ideas, not because I genuinely believe the conclusion.

6. Brennan and Jaworski 2016. We argue that anything it is permissible to do for free can in principle be permissible to do for money.
7. Van der Vossen and Brennan 2018.
8. E.g., consider how the major critiques of Robert Nozick (such as those by Thomas Nagel, David Sobel, or Gerald Cohen) utterly strawman him. See Brennan and van der Vossen 2017.
9. Brennan 2016, 5.
10. See Brennan 2016; Achen and Bartels 2016; Lodge and Taber 2013.
11. Somin 2013.
12. Somin 2013; Simler and Hanson 2018.
13. Haidt 2012; Westen, Blagov, Harenski, Kilts and Hamann 2006; Westen 2008.
14. Chong 2013, 111–112, citing Cohen 2003.
15. See Mutz 2006, 128.
16. Mutz 2006, 120.
17. Mutz 2006, 92, 110, 112–113.
18. Mutz 2006, 30. The more people join voluntary associations, the less they engage in cross-cutting discussions. What demographic factors best predict that one will engage in cross-cutting political discussion? Apparently, being non-white, poor, and uneducated. The reason for this is that white, rich, educated people have more control over the kinds of interactions they have with others. People generally do not enjoy having cross-cutting political discussions. They enjoy agreement. So, those with the most control over their lives choose not to engage in cross-cutting discussions. See Mutz 2006, 27, 31, 46–47.
19. Iyengar and Westwood 2015.
20. My colleague John Hasnas discusses this experience too: www.nationalreview.com/corner/433559/yes-universities-discriminate-against-conservatives
21. www.wsj.com/articles/the-one-kind-of-diversity-colleges-avoid-1459464676
22. E.g., www.slate.com/blogs/quora/2016/07/05/why_are_there_so_few_conservatives_in_academia.html
23. http://dailynous.com/2017/09/18/because-they-are-universities/
24. Inbar and Lammers 2012, 496. However, Gross 2013 argues that discrimination is not so extensive.
25. Posselt 2016, 41–42, 158–159, passim.
26. Gross 2013.
27. Lodge and Taber 2013.
28. Schelling 1971.

Works Cited

Acemoglu, Daron, Johnson, Simon and Robinson, James A. "The Colonial Origins of Comparative Development: An Empirical Investigation." *American Economic Review*, Vol. 91 (2001): 1369–1401.

———. "Reversal of Fortune: Geography and Institutions in the Making of World Income Distribution." *Quarterly Journal of Economics*, Vol. 117 (2002): 1231–1294.

———. "Institutions as a Fundamental Cause of Long-Run Growth." In *Handbook of Economic Growth, Vol. 1A*, edited by Philippe Aghion and Steven N. Darlauf. Amsterdam: Elsevier, 2005.

Acemoglu, Daron and Robinson, James A. "Unbundling Institutions." *Journal of Political Economy*, Vol. 113 (2005): 949–995.

———. *Why Nations Fails*. New York: Crown Business, 2013.

Achen, Christopher and Bartels, Larry. *Democracy for Realists*. Princeton, NJ: Princeton University Press, 2016.

Brennan, Jason. "Dominating Nature." *Environmental Values*, Vol. 16 (2007): 287–299.

———. *Against Democracy*. Princeton, NJ: Princeton University Press, 2016.

Brennan, Jason and Jaworski, Peter. *Markets Without Limits*. New York: Routledge, 2016.

Brennan, Jason and van der Vossen, Bas. "The Myths of the Self-Ownership Thesis." In *The Routledge Handbook of Libertarianism*, edited by Jason Brennan, Bas van der Vossen and David Schmidtz. New York: Routledge, 2017.

Chong, Dennis. "Degrees of Rationality in Politics." In *The Oxford Handbook of Political Psychology*, edited by David O. Sears and Jack S. Levy. New York: Oxford University Press, 2013: 96–129.

Cohen, Geoffrey. "Party Over Policy: The Dominating Impact of Group Influence on Political Beliefs." *Journal of Personality and Social Psychology*, Vol. 85 (2003): 808–822.

Glaeser, Edward L., La Porta, Rafael, Lopez-de-Silanes, Florencio and Shleifer, Andrei. "Do Institutions Cause Growth?" *Journal of Economic Growth*, Vol. 9 (2004): 272–303.

Gross, Neil. *Why Are Professors Liberal and Why Do Conservatives Care?* Cambridge, MA: Harvard University Press, 2013.

Haidt, Jonathan. *The Righteous Mind*. New York: Pantheon, 2012.

Inbar, Yeol and Lammers, Joris. "Political Diversity in Social and Personality Psychology." *Perspectives on Psychological Science*, Vol. 7 (2012): 496–503.

Iyengar, Shanto, and Westwood, Sean. "Fear and Loathing Across Party Lines: New Evidence on Group Polarization." *American Journal of Political Science*, Vol. 59 (2015): 690–707.

Lodge, Milton and Taber, Charles. *The Rationalizing Voter*. New York: Cambridge University Press, 2013.

Mutz, Diana. *Hearing the Other Side*. New York: Cambridge University Press, 2006.

North, Douglass. *Institutions, Institutional Change, and Economic Performance*. Cambridge: Cambridge University Press, 1990.

———. *In the Shadow of Violence: Politics, Economics, and the Problems of Development*. New York: Cambridge University Press, 2012.

North, Douglas, Wallis, John Joseph and Weingast, Barry. *Violence and Social Orders*. Cambridge: Cambridge University Press, 2012.

Posselt, Julie R. *Inside Graduate Admissions*. Cambridge, MA: Harvard University Press, 2016.

Rodrik, Dani, Subramanian, Arvind and Trebbi, Francisco. "Institutions Rule: The Primacy of Institutions Over Geography and Integration in Economic Development." *Journal of Economic Growth*, Vol. 9 (2004): 131–165.

Roland, Gérard. *Development Economics*. New York: Pearson, 2014.

Rosenberg, Nathan and Birdzell, L. E. *How the West Grew Rich*. New York: Basic Books, 1986.

Schelling, Thomas C. "Dynamic Models of Segregation." *Journal of Mathematical Sociology*, Vol. 1 (1971): 143–186.

Simler, Kevin and Hanson, Robin. *The Elephant in the Brain*. New York: Oxford University Press, 2018.

Somin, Ilya. *The Problem of Political Ignorance*. Stanford, CA: Stanford University Press, 2013.
Van der Vossen, Bas and Brennan, Jason. *In Defense of Openness: Global Justice as Global Freedom*. New York: Oxford University Press, 2018.
Weil, David. *Economic Growth*, 3rd edition. New York: Pearson, 2013.
Westen, Drew. *The Political Brain*. New York: Perseus Books, 2008.
Westen, Drew, Pavel S. Blagov, Keith Harenski, Clint Kilts and Stephan Hamann. "The Neural Basis of Motivated Reasoning: An fMRI Study of Emotional Constraints on Political Judgment During the U.S. Presidential Election of 2004." *The Journal of Cognitive Neuroscience*, Vol. 18 (2006): 1947–1958.

7 Harm

An Event-Based Feinbergian Account[1]

Andrew J. Cohen

The essays in this volume are concerned with free speech on college and university campuses. This is an immensely important and timely topic. On my own view, the simplest and clearest way to consider the proper moral limits of free speech on campus is to consider the proper moral limits of any sort of actions. Put differently, we can best address this issue by determining when interference with any given activity—including speech acts—is permissible. As I argue elsewhere,[2] such interference is *pro tanto* permissible when there is significant harm. When one agent harms another, there is *pro tanto* reason to think interference with the first permissible. This holds on college campuses as well as anywhere else. If that is right, though, we need a clear understanding of "harm." The term is used in multiple ways, but when we are speaking of it as providing a normative limit to what must be tolerated, it has—or so I shall argue—a narrow and technical definition.

In this paper, I defend an account of harm as event-based but also in the mold of the account offered by Joel Feinberg in his magnum opus, *The Moral Limits of the Criminal Law*.[3] The analysis I offer is meant, that is, to be serviceable in a project like Feinberg's—that is, it is one of normative political philosophy—and, importantly here, useful for determining when speech might rightly be limited. On the account defended here, *to undergo a harm is to be the subject of an event wherein one's interests are wrongfully set back and wherein the status of the undergoing of the harm derives from its being the sort of event that it is (namely, a setting back of interests), independently of the badness of any resulting state*. When harm in this sense is present, there is *pro tanto* reason to interfere with the actor. In the context of this book, this is when speech might be permissibly limited. Put differently, genuinely harmful speech (where harm is understood as just specified) is the only sort of speech that can possibly be rightly limited—on campus or elsewhere.

It is important to recognize a limit in what has just been said. On one's own property, one can prevent others from speaking even if their speech acts would not, in other ordinary circumstances, be harmful. This is part and parcel of the view that only harm justifies interference, for if you enter my home and start a speech I do not want made therein, you set back my interest in controlling what happens in my home—and absent my permission or some other legitimate justification, you do so wrongly. Put simply, you harm me. This may be a *de minimus* harm that we would not want police to interfere with, but it serves as a limit to what you may morally speak nonetheless. When you act in this way, I can rightly insist we have a different sort of conversation, no conversation at all, or that you leave. On my property, I have the authority to make such rules.

Some colleges, of course, are also private property. The owners (or their agents) of those colleges have the same authority to disallow particular sorts of speech. Using such authority to thus limit speech on campus, however, would be extremely unwise. Private colleges—all colleges—have, as their *raisin d'etre*, to facilitate discussion, enlarge knowledge, and create well-rounded and fully developed human persons. To do that well, colleges must have open and honest inquiry without limits determined by topic or viewpoint. Discussion of even offensive material is part and parcel of college life. Taking part in such discussion is never wrongful and hence never harmful—and so not the sort of speech that is rightly interfered with.[4] Of course, such discussion should be polite and, one hopes, friendly, but open and honest inquiry is the coin of the realm. Some may feel hurt by such discussion, but they are not *harmed* and thus do not warrant protection from said speech. To show this more clearly, I defend the account of harm specified previously.

I proceed as follows: In the first, brief, section, I introduce John Stuart Mill's harm principle in order to situate harm in normative political philosophy. In the next section, I introduce some preliminary distinctions that will be useful later and introduce Joel Feinberg's influential account of harm. In the third section, I flesh out Feinberg's account of harm as an event-based account of harm rather than a state-based account; I continue defending that account in the fourth section. To be clear, while the conception of harm I defend is technical and I readily admit that people use the term in a variety of ways in ordinary usage, I do not shy from using intuitions about ordinary usage to make my case.

The Harm Principle: Harm's Place in Normative Political Thought

A useful place to begin is John Stuart Mill's *On Liberty*.[5] Mill's famous harm principle reads

> the sole end for which mankind are warranted, individually or collectively, in interfering with the liberty of action of any of their number is self-protection . . . the only purpose for which power can be rightfully exercised over any member of a civilized community, against his will, is to prevent harm to others.
>
> (Mill, 9)

This can be read as a principle of non-interference—indeed, a principle of toleration. "Mill's contention is that the only limit to toleration, the only valid reason for not tolerating a kind of behavior, is that this behavior causes harm to people other than those who practice it."[6] So long as an agent does not harm a non-consenting other, she is not to be interfered with. This does not mean that we cannot try to dissuade the agent from her actions. It means only that power—taken as force or coercion—must not be used.

The harm principle indicates when it is permissible to interfere with an individual and does so with reference to harm.[7] It does not say "do no harm"; it indicates that one may rightfully interfere with another only when the other does harm, is about to do harm, or has done harm.[8] In other words, it is not a (mere) prohibition of harm, but a principle that grants *pro tanto* permission to interfere when (and *only* when) harm has been, is, or will be, present. It is a normative jurisprudential principle about what justifies a response (interference, whether by state actors or others) to actions, not a principle about the moral status of those actions. This should not prevent us from seeing that harm itself is what is important.

Harm is not a value. It is, rather, a *disvalue*—a disvalue of such weight that it everywhere makes interference *pro tanto* permissible.

There are two limits built into the harm principle: (1) It forbids only force or coercion, not persuasive rational argument and (2) force or coercion are legitimate in cases where an agent is harming or is going to harm a non-consenting other.[9] These limits are important; we are not prohibited from trying to dissuade others of ill-advised actions, trying to persuade them of beneficial actions, or interfering with their attempts to harm non-consenting others. Thus, one commentator tells us that although we must allow individuals to pursue their own projects, these must "meet a threshold standard of moral justification" such that, for example, those projects do not require the agent to harm others.[10] It is also important, though I will leave discussion of this until later, that the fact that interference is permissible (because there is or will be harm) does not mean interference is necessary. Harm provides a necessary, not a sufficient, condition for interference.

A problem with the harm principle remains: what exactly is "harm"?

The Nature of Harm, Preliminary Distinctions, and Feinberg's Account

What is harm? Harm, as it is used in the harm principle, is conceptually distinct from pain. No one, after all, thinks the pain caused by a strenuous workout provides warrant for interference. (Who would we interfere with?) Nor is it reasonable to seek assistance to prevent such pain. Similarly, harm is conceptually distinct from hurt. I can't, for example, demand interference with anyone because of the hurt of stubbing my toe on my desk when I got up to go to another room. The harm principle is not about all pains or hurts.

I take it pains are often negative—consider the pain of a broken leg or a broken heart. They detract from one's well-being. I also take it, though, that some pains are positive—again, consider the pain one feels with a good workout. They add to one's well-being. I take it all hurts are negative. The pain from a good workout may not be a hurt (the pain from a workout gone wrong may well be). The pain of a broken leg or a broken heart is. The difference between a pain and a hurt is that the latter is *always* a setback to (at least some of) one's interests.[11] While one may want the experience that comes with a hurt or some benefit that is expected if one endures the hurt, one never wants a hurt for its own sake. By contrast, one may want a pain for its own sake. Hence, masochists.

Pains and hurts may be involved in harms, but are neither necessary nor sufficient for harm. The harm principle indicates we can justly interfere with others only when they harm another. I have no claim of justice when I suffer a pain from a tree branch on my property falling on my head. Nor do I have a claim on others to prevent my suffering a hangover if I voluntarily drink too much this evening. I can be free of such suffering by making better choices, but I cannot insist others protect me from my bad choice. These are not harms as that term is used in the harm principle. This is not to deny, of course, that we often have "moral reasons to avoid and alleviate pain,"[12] but it seems clear that those reasons are different (and I think, less morally weighty) than reasons regarding harm—for the latter but not the former necessarily involve an injustice.[13]

According to Joel Feinberg, who has done more to further our understanding of harm than anyone,[14] there are two basic forms of harm. In the first, "harm is conceived as the thwarting, setting back, or defeating of an interest" where to "have an interest" is to "have a kind of stake" (1984, 33). One's "interest," understood as well-being, requires that one's "interests," understood as those things one has an interest in, are not thwarted (1984, 34). In the second sense, harm is understood normatively such that "[t]o say that A has harmed B . . . is to say much the same thing as that A has wronged B, or treated him unjustly" (1984, 34).[15] Feinberg claims that the "sense of 'harm' as that term is used in the harm principle must represent the overlap of [these two] senses . . . only setbacks of interest that are wrongs, and wrongs that are setbacks to interest, are to count as harms in the appropriate sense" (1984, 36). We can thus say that a harm, as we use that term in the harm principle is a *wrongful setback of interests*. (A bit more needs to be clarified, as we will see.)

It should now be clear why the pain of a tree branch on my property falling on me and that of a hangover are not sufficient, according to the harm principle, to warrant even a *pro tanto* reason for interference. In neither case, can I claim to have any interests *wrongly* set back, so in neither case can I claim interference is warranted on my behalf.[16]

Wrongs, of course, are normative; hence, given what has just been said, normativity will necessarily enter into a proper understanding of harm. One of Feinberg's examples makes this clear: "the person who, figuratively speaking, can be blown over by a sneeze cannot demand that other people's vigorous but normally harmless activities be suspended by government power" (1984, 50). We would not declare that the government should interfere with sneezing even if we knew of a particular individual who could be blown over by a sneeze. The individual would certainly suffer a setback of interests: Being knocked down prevents one from accomplishing the (intermediate) goal one pursues. Just as clearly, this is unfortunate. We would not, though, say the "sneezer *wronged* the person blown down." Clearly, defining wrongs involves normative reasoning. With R. H. Dees, we can add that because "we cannot define *harm* in a value-neutral manner . . . the limits of [the harm principle and] toleration will be determined by the needs of a particular context. The demands of toleration must be balanced against other values in the society that help us define what constitutes a *harm*."[17] Some take this to be a criticism. John Horton claims "there is no uncontroversial way in which such a distinction [between harmful and non-harmful actions] can be drawn and, therefore, any attempt to justify toleration which relies on such a supposedly agreed distinction is likely to be seriously defective."[18] Even more forcefully, Ben Bradley argues that the existing definitions of harm are a "mess" so "it should be replaced by other more well-behaved concepts."[19] Needless to say I think Horton and Bradley mistaken.

Horton claims that "the cogency of the liberal's position will depend upon the plausibility of an uncontroversial conception of harm" (1985, 116). His concern, though, is not with the *conception* of harm but with its extension. He cites J. R. Lucas as indicating paradigm cases of harm and argues that even these may sometimes be controversial (Horton 1985, 118). This, though, is not a fatal flaw, for surely there are paradigmatic instances of harm even if there may be other instances of the same sort of thing that would not uncontroversially count as harms; that is, there are uncontroversial tokens, if not uncontroversial types, of harms. There is no reason, then, not to accept that there is a normative component to harm and that this component affects whether tokens are considered harms. This means only that we will inevitably face some indeterminacy of scope regarding harm and thus that "the boundaries of tolerance are indeterminate."[20] We can, nonetheless, use the harm principle as a normative principle of toleration. I do so here, not merely recognizing, but *embracing* the remaining indeterminacy.

Lest it be thought that the indeterminacy here is a drawback, I should make clear why I think it an advantage and embrace it. I believe that indeterminacy is precisely what pushes us to do the right sort of normative work that is required before determining if interference with another is permissible. Given the existence of uncontroversial tokens of harm (and lacks of harm), my Feinbergian account nicely tells us to use those to help in reasoning analogically (as one would expect in juridical situations) about cases that are controversial. It allows us to separate easy and hard cases and pushes us to do the difficult normative work in the latter before concluding that a harm is present and interference permissible. Consider that if you hear that Joe killed Nancy, you might be inclined to think state interference with Joe warranted. If you then hear that the reason Joe killed Nancy was because she was trying to kill him, you might—as I would—conclude that no interference was warranted. What looks to be a case of homicide turns out to be a case of self-defense. Of course, there will be harder cases, but that will be true no matter what one's theory.

The previous discussion concerns primarily the indeterminacy of the wrongfulness element of harm, but much the same can also be said about the second element: the setback to interests. It is often clear when there is a setback to interests. If Nancy stabs Joe, she sets back his interests in bodily integrity, not bleeding, etc. If Miles steals Rachael's computer, he sets back her interests in controlling her property, being able to work, etc. There are times, though, where it will not be clear. In particular, cases where one agent refuses to help another. Imagine Sue is drowning in a lake and I am on a boat going toward her and thus able to forward her interests by saving her. Do I set back her interests if I turn away? Many believe I do, but others point out that her interests are set back *before I came on the scene—so I do nothing at all to her* if I turn away. Failing to promote her interests is not the same as setting them back. This is the baseline problem: If we are asking whether interests are set back, we need to know where they are first. Some insist that the zero line must be (something like) the statistical norm. If that is right, the normal baseline for Sue is presumably one where she is not in danger of drowning, but is on firm ground—in which case, my refusal to help counts as a setback to her interests, keeping them below the zero line. On my view, though, we must take agents *as they are*, not as we wish they would be. If that is right, the appropriate baseline in cases like this is the point at which the other is *when I happen upon them*. Sue's interests are already set back, so I do not set them back by refusing to help. I hence do not harm her.

I must stress here that it will not be a problem for my basic view if my response to the baseline problem is disputed. This too will count as a form of indeterminacy in hard cases that makes it necessary for us to engage in juridical reasoning to determine if a harm is present. I should also note that I agree it would be *wrong* to leave Sue drowning. But wrongs are not sufficient for harms.

As should be clear, I take Feinberg's account of harm to be basically right. There is indeterminacy of both wrongfulness and the concept of setting back of interests, but these simply allow us to know where further moral reasoning is needed. Nonetheless, further elaboration is needed in light of recent debates in the literature.

Feinbergian Harm as an Event-Based Account

Much of the contemporary debate about the nature of harm, in particular whether it is state-based or event-based, comes down to debates about which sort of account best handles possible cases. Theorists give counterexamples to particular forms of each theory and other theorists give responses to those counterexamples. It's not clear what other sort of defense would be possible. Nonetheless, we can take some comfort here in that, as used in the harm principle, what we speak of when we speak of harms are best thought of as events. We can see this by recognizing that what is at issue is the possibility of rightful intervention.

Imagine that Harold surreptitiously stole five dollars from Bill in order to benefit Bill by preventing him from buying a drink that Harold knows would make Bill extremely sick. Despite the good intentions, we would be justified in interfering with Harold's theft if we were to witness it (or in condemning him afterward). We might, all things considered, not suggest punishment for Harold, but only because, though he does harm Bill, it is a *de minimus* harm. If this is right, it cannot be the ending state of affairs that matters. That state of affairs is, by hypothesis, good—Bill is not made sick. He is better off after the theft than he would have been had it not occurred—for then he would have bought the drink that would make him sick. This suggests that the harm is *independent of the final state of affairs*. It is an event.

Consider a slightly different case. If you have less money than you did a year ago, you are less well-off now. You are in a worse condition or state than you were. This is true regardless of how you came to be in this state. While we can reasonably say you are in a hurt state, on the Feinbergian account I am offering, we cannot say you are in a harmed state unless your condition is due to a wrong done you.[21] If you have less money because of a wrong done to you, we can reasonably say you were in a harmed state, by which we mean *you were harmed and as a result are worse off*. It is the fact that you *suffered a harm event* that is relevant for the harm principle or the tasks Mill, Feinberg, or I, use the term.

Consider the financial example again. You have less money now than you did last year. Whether there is any moral or legal concern here depends on *why* it is you have less now. If, for example, you have less money because you chose to use 90 percent of your savings to buy a car (with rapid depreciation of its value), you are not in a harmed state. If, by contrast, you have less now because I stole your money, you are. When we say I harm you by stealing your money, it is *not* explained by the fact that you have less after the stealing. It is explained by that and the fact that *you have less because you were wronged*. How you got to the condition, in another words, matters for the analysis of the condition. The event causing the reduction in your financial well-being is fundamental.

Consider Bill's drink again. If Alan is the purveyor of the drink Bill would buy, Alan may do no wrong to Bill in the process of selling him the drink. He could believe the drink is healthy, that Bill will love it, and that he is merely engaged in an honest and fully ethical trade. Alan does no wrong to Bill, but (absent Harold's interference) Bill is made worse off. If harms were determined by the final state of affairs, we would say that Alan harms Bill. But we would not say that. We would not think any interference with Alan's selling of this drink was warranted. If this is not clear, imagine that there genuinely is nothing wrong with the drink and that it is healthy for 99.99 percent of those who consume it and that they also consider it delicious. Again, harms are independent of the states that someone might be in after they occur.

If this is not clear, consider a parallel: *falling* without hitting the ground. When this occurs, we do not refrain from saying there was a fall just because the end state is not one of hitting the ground. We say there was a fall, but that the agent recovered in time to steady herself without hitting the ground. The *falling* is independent of the end state. In the same way, harming is independent of the states that result from the harms. It's not the end state that matters. What matters, in the language we have been using, is simply whether or not the action that one takes wrongfully sets back the interests of the other. Setting back the interests of the other, wrongfully or not, is an action. When we say, "Joe harms Fred," we use the word "harm" as a verb. The harm is an action or event. It takes time. It is not a state.

Because the harm is an event and not a state, one's interests might be set back while also being forwarded; this would count as a harm regardless of the state one ends in. To see this, imagine I am surreptitiously taking $1 per day from your bank account. This would be an event wherein I wrongfully set back your interest in your property and in controlling your property. Now imagine that unbeknownst to both of us, Warren Buffett is simultaneously depositing $100 per day into your bank account. After a week, I have taken $7 and he has added $700. You end with $693 more then you started. It's still the case that I harmed you. That Buffett benefitted you far more than I harmed you does not mean I did not harm you. I take it all would recognize that my action is morally culpable and, indeed, that interference meant to rectify the harm I have done, is at least *pro tanto* permitted though you are already better off.[22]

Despite what I have just said, most recent writers about harm have considered it to be a state. For these thinkers, *the activity* of harming is defined by the resulting state. They would point out that we say things like "Joe causes a harm to Fred," using the term as a noun, and perhaps less colloquially, "Joe causes Fred to be in a harmed state," turning it into an adjective. Consideration of the different parts of speech will not be of much help here. We are looking to determine the best conceptual analysis of harm.

My view takes a lesson from Matthew Hanser's defense of harms as fundamentally events rather than states.[23] There are two basic components of Hanser's view. First, "It holds that to undergo a harm (or benefit) is to be the subject of an event whose status as the undergoing of a harm (or benefit) derives from its being the sort of event that it is, independently of the badness (or goodness) of any resulting state" (2008, 440). This is the formal component of Hanser's understanding of harm. It leaves open the question "what sort of event?" His answer to that question is in the second, tripartide, component of his view:

(i) Someone suffers a level-1 harm with respect to a certain basic good if and only if he loses some quantity of that good. Someone receives a level-1 benefit with respect to a certain basic good if and only if he acquires some quantity of that good (441).
(ii) Someone suffers a level-(n + 1) harm with respect to a certain basic good if and only if he is prevented from receiving a level-n benefit with respect to that good. Someone receives a level-(n+1) benefit with respect to a certain basic good if and only if he is prevented from suffering a level-n harm with respect to that good. . . .
(iii) Someone suffers a harm if and only if he suffers a harm of some level with respect to some basic good. Someone receives a benefit if and only if he receives a benefit of some level with respect to some basic good (442).

Simplifying, a person suffers a harm if she loses a basic good or is prevented from receiving that good. It is not that the harm is the having less of the good in question, which is the likely state after being harmed. Rather, *the losing of the good* is itself the harm.

Hanser's account has much to recommend it, but it cannot on its own serve the need of the harm principle. Consider that if I am at home in my house, playing with matches on top of a stack of dollar bills and they catch fire, I lose a good. This seems to be a harm on Hanser's account. If it is what is at stake in the harm principle, interference would be called for. Yet interference is not called for.[24] Consider another case: You and I are at my home and I ask if you would like to see a magic trick. You agree and I ask for a one dollar bill. You agree (perhaps, though, you only have a \$20 bill or a \$100 bill). I ask you to mark the bill and then I proceed to light it on fire. You gasp, but when it is completely burned, I go to pull the bill—with the same marking—from behind your ear, expecting you to be impressed with my magic. But instead, I pull out a piece of tissue. Here I have not wronged you, but I have caused you to lose a dollar (a basic good, let us assume). On Hanser's account, I have harmed you and interference is warranted. On my view, that is mistaken as you were a willing participant.

To be clear: Hanser's account is purely descriptive and we need the normative element for the harm principle. Hence, rather than discuss Hanser's account further, I propose a synthesis of the first component of Hanser's definition with Feinberg's definition. On this account, *to undergo a harm is to be the subject of an event wherein one's interests are wrongfully set back and wherein the status of the undergoing of the harm derives from its being the sort of event that it is (namely, a setting back of interests), independently of the badness of any resulting state*. We could add that "someone suffers a level-1 harm with respect to a certain basic good if and only if he loses some quantity of that good" due to a wrong done him and that "someone suffers a level-(n + 1) harm with respect to a certain basic good if and only if he is [wrongfully] prevented from receiving a level-n benefit with respect to that good." The italicized, though, will do the work we need. To be clear, on this account, harms are not symmetrical with benefits;[25] hurts (i.e., setbacks to interests) and benefits are symmetrical.

More on Feinbergian Harm as Event-Based

I take it the account of harm just explicated accommodates all of the cases in which we believe the harm principle applies. Consider the following cases:

MURDER: Nancy kills Bill, unjustifiably setting back his interest in continued living.

THEFT: Nancy takes the cash from Bill's wallet (or digitally empties his bank account), unjustifiably setting back his interest in controlling his money.

In these cases, there is a harm because there is an event wherein the subject's interests are wrongfully (or unjustifiably) set back. Of course, there could be similar cases that had no harms. I consider two in a moment, but first, it is worth considering *Murder* further. Some worry that dying cannot be a harm because it does not result in a bad state. With Michael Rabenberg, I think that worry is misguided. He writes "if we do exist at the moments of our deaths, then I see no barrier to calling death a historical worsening—a crash to axiological absolute zero, as it were."[26] That seems basically right though I would say it is a "historical setting back of my interests to axiological absolute zero." I would also, though, only call it a harm if the dying is caused by wrongful actions. The dying itself is an event, but what sort of event it is will depend on various factors. If I die because I am 102 and have not been able to eat or drink, my interests may be set back but non-wrongfully—hence, my dying would not be harm. But *Murder* is not like that.[27]

Now let us consider two cases that are importantly related to yet different from *Murder* and *Theft*.

EUTHANASIA: Jill kills Frank, because he rationally requested it to avoid further pain and suffering from a condition that could not be cured.
REPAYMENT: Jill takes the cash from Frank's wallet (or digitally from his bank account), per their prior agreement, as a means of collecting what he owes her.

In both pairs of cases, we get the conclusions we would expect: Murder and theft are harms; euthanasia and repayment are not. In *Euthanasia*, arguably, there is no wrong and no setback of interests. In *Repayment*, there may be a setback of interests (Frank would rather keep the money), but there is no wrong.

It's worth considering two more sorts of cases:

RAPE: Bill rapes Nancy, unjustifiably setting back her interests in controlling her body, choosing who can touch her, etc.
TRESPASS: Bill trespasses on Nancy's property (perhaps leaving nothing disturbed), unjustifiably setting back her interests in controlling who enters (sees, uses, etc.) her property.

In these cases, there is a harm because there is an event wherein the subject's interests are wrongfully (or unjustifiably) set back. Now compare these two:

SEX: Jill has intercourse with a sleeping Frank, per their previous agreement.
VISIT: Per their previous agreement, Jill enters Frank's property and takes a nap before he returns home, when they will start their vacation together.

In *Sex* and *Visit*, there may be interests set back (Frank generally prefers not to have someone nap in his house when he is not present, etc.) but there are no harms.

The last four examples (*Rape, Sex, Trespass, Visit*) are useful for us as so-called "harmless trespass" cases seem to confound a variety of thinkers. A.P. Simester and Andrew von Hirsch,[28] for example, discuss Feinberg's answer (Feinberg 1984, 107) and claim it "tends to collapse the distinction between harms and wrongs, since individuals can always be said to have an interest in not being wronged." They go on to insist that the "very reason bare trespass is a difficult case is that the wrongdoer's action violates the landowner's right but causes no harm" (284). But Nancy's interest in *Trespass* is not an interest in not being harmed, nor an interest in not being wronged—it is an interest in not having others enter her property without her consent, wrongfully or not. Consider that

Bill would enter Nancy's property innocently if he did so solely to save the life of Nancy's dog, who, he could see through the window was stuck inside in the burning home. In that case, Nancy may still have her interest set back (as might Frank in *Visit*), but not wrongfully. By contrast, if he entered her home to smell all of the rooms, and then left—never having her permission to enter—the fact that he causes no damage to the home is simply irrelevant; he has wrongfully set back her interest in controlling who enters her home.[29] Consider also that taking Simester and Hirsch's line leads them to conclude that rape need not be a harm, though they agree it is a wrong that should be criminal.[30] The idea here is that as with so-called harmless trespass, there could be (so-called) harmless rape.

Consider that if Jackson entered your home while you were away and without your permission but leaves everything exactly as it was before you left, you would not be aware that he was ever present and would not suffer as a consequence of his trespass. He did not take anything of yours or dirty anything—indeed, he left it *exactly* as it was. His trespass is supposedly harmless, even if wrongful. Now consider a parallel instance of rape. Imagine that the rape victim is completely unaware of the rape—both during and after, perhaps through hypnosis or the use of some nefarious drug (and assume the rapist left his victim exactly as he found her). As she is unaware of the incident and has no remaining physical duress, she is not—on this mistaken view—harmed (though she would be wronged).

The idea that rape could fail to be a harm seems to me both conceptually mistaken and morally unacceptable. In normal parlance, I think the linguistic intuition is very clear: Any instance of nonconsensual sex is a harm. In terms I am using, it would be a wrongful setback of at least the victim's interests in bodily integrity and personal autonomy. While certain cases of rape may be completely undetected, they are nonetheless not only wrongful and punishable, but also harmful. Part of the problem is that Simester and Hirsch have a state-based account of harm and since there is no bad state after the supposedly harmless act, there seems to be no harm (see their 2002, 280–281). On my Feinbergian event-based account, by contrast, we get the proper conclusion that rape and trespass are always harmful. What distinguishes so-called "harmless trespass" cases from *Visit*, on this account, is that in the former but not the latter, there is a wrong (in addition to an event that is a setting back of the interest in controlling who enters one's property and when—which may or may not be present).

On my account, "harmless trespass" is impossible—it would be a "harmless harm." Similarly, what distinguishes so-called "harmless rape" from *Sex* is that in the former but not the latter, there is a wrong (in addition to an event that is a setting back of the interest in controlling who enters one's body, who can touch it, etc). "Harmless rape" is impossible—it too would be a "harmless harm." (Violent rape includes harms in addition to those present in so-called "harmless rape" cases.)

In none of these cases, are the harms involved states or conditions, though there are *harmed states*—states wherein one *has been harmed* and has not yet recovered. The harms themselves are the events: Nancy's murdering Bill, Nancy's stealing from Bill, Bill's raping of Nancy, Bill's trespassing in Nancy's home. In all of these events, there is a wrongful setting back of the other's interests.

Some may question what I have said previously, indicating that when they talk of "harmless trespass" or "harmless rape," they do not mean to belittle the wrongfulness of the acts in question, but adding that it makes little sense to call such things harms as they are not *experienced* and harms must be experienced. I think this is straightforwardly misguided. "Harmless trespass" may not result in the homeowner experiencing any physical harm, but there are other sorts of harms, including psychological harms. If Nancy finds out that Bill trespassed on her property a week after the fact, she may rightfully feel distressed and violated—and this setback to her interest in mental calm would have been wrongfully brought about by Bill's act. One might say "OK, but then she is experiencing the harm." Still, if we ask when the harm occurs, it seems clear to me (ignoring the debate in action theory) that the event occurs when Bill trespasses, not when Nancy finds out—i.e., not when it is experienced. Indeed, it seems reasonable to say that an *additional* harm occurs when she finds out. The first harm is the setback to Nancy's interest in in controlling who enters (sees, uses, etc.) her property; the second harm is the setback to her interest in mental calm. The first harm may, I should note, go forever undetected. (Remember that some harms will not be sufficient for interference.)

As a final response to the worry that one cannot suffer a harm without experiencing it, I should note that this is entirely obvious in other sorts of cases. Consider, for example, that if Lou has kidnapped Gary and thoroughly anesthetized Gary's leg—imagine Gary seated, unable to see his legs, and unaware that they have been anesthetized—Lou or his accomplice might stab Gary's leg without Gary knowing it. He would be harmed nonetheless. Perhaps they even show Gary a monitor with the action occurring, but tell him this is someone else's leg. He might cringe when he sees it and cry out "why are you doing that?" All without knowing it is his leg. The harm to him is still clear.[31]

Let's now consider the understanding of harm I am discussing against some problematic examples from the literature. The understanding of harm, again, is that *to undergo a harm is to be the subject of an event wherein one's interests are wrongfully set back and wherein the status of the undergoing of the harm derives from its being the sort of event that it is (namely, a setting back of interests), independently of the badness of any resulting state.*

Consider Thomson's example of *Gene-paraplegia*, wherein an individual is "genetically programmed to be paraplegic by about age 10" (2011, 446). We could ask if Jean, the agent with gene-paraplegia, is in a harmed state and we can ask if she has been harmed. Imagine that before her conception, Jean's potential parents have been told that if they conceive a child within the next month, it will be born with gene-paraplegia and that they then ask themselves if they should try to have such a child. They agree that they should, agreeing that it would be fun to have a child that they could tease about becoming paraplegic and that they could then torment as a paraplegic. As I described the case, it seems that these potential parents act wrongfully, but there is no subject of the event that has interests to be setback as a result of the gene-paraplegia until after the child is conceived.[32] As such, Jean is not harmed by the act of conception and so is not in a harmed state, though she is in a state that will cause her difficulty. Of course, should her parents carry through with their horrible plans for (what they consider) parenting, they would be harming the child, but that is a separate issue.

Now consider *Gene-paraplegia* with different, kinder, potential parents. These parents agree that it would be better if they could have a child without gene-paraplegia, but for other reasons, that is impossible. They seek to have a child to shower with love, knowing that their offspring will have significant difficulty after it is ten years old and becomes a paraplegic. Here, I think, there is no wrong—I won't try to defend that here—and there is, again, no subject with interests to be setback until after conception. The child is born, loved, and cared for. Perhaps these parents are research scientists and they use the ten years looking for a cure to paraplegia. They do no harm done to Jean; she is not put into a harmed state.

Some may think that intuitively, Jean is in a harmed state, but I see no benefit to saying that instead of simply saying, what seems more straightforward, that Jean is in an unfortunate state or that she would be better off if she were her without gene-paraplegia. In any case, we must remember that what matters is whether interference with the parents would be *pro tanto* permissible according to the harm principle. I think it clear that it would not. (Those that might think interference with them is permissible are more likely to seek support in some form of legal moralism.)

Consider now *Dim Vision*:

> Suppose villain C threw acid in A's eyes, to cause him to be blind. The acid began to affect A's eyes, but before it could complete the process of blinding A, bystander B intervened—he used a neutralizer on A's eyes, thereby causing A to be in a state short of blindness, namely [A] "has dim vision." We must surely accept that each of C and B caused A to be in "has dim vision," and yet that C harmed A but B did not. (Thomson 2011, 447–448)

Thomson correctly notes that while we would say that C harmed A, we would not say that B did so, even though both C and B caused A to have dim vision. On the account offered here, this is because whereas both B and C contribute to how the event resulting in dim vision unfolds, only C wronged A and only C acted in a way that brought about the event that set back A's interests in her vision. (B did no wrong and acted in a way to end that event.) Again, the real question here is whether interference is *pro tanto* permissible according to the harm principle and it seems clear that interference with C would be and interference with B would not. (We might think B should be rewarded!)

It's worth considering that when the child in *Gene-paraplegia* turns six years old, they will still have gene-paraplegia—that is, they will be in a state that will result in their being paraplegic in four years. Similarly, six years after the event, A in *Dim Vision* will have dim vision. In neither case, though, are the relevant parties now suffering a harm. In the first case, there was no harm; in the second case, there was. In both cases, though, the event is in the past. Despite Thomson's protestation to the contrary (2011, 456), this seems entirely right. A was harmed when C threw acid at her. A now has dim vision as a result of that harm, but she is not now being harmed or suffering a harm. Of course, she may be in what we call a *harmed state*—i.e., a state wherein she has not yet recovered from the harm—that likely depends on the seriousness, degree, and intensity of the harm as well as factors about A's life.[33] She likely suffers more if she were an art critic, for example, than if she was a singer.[34] Thomson seems to think A is still suffering the harm (2011, 456), but suffering the results of the harm and suffering the harm are clearly distinct. (Moreover, it seems plausible to say both are events rather than states.)

Consider now a rescue case.

> REVIVE: Rebecca gives CPR to unconscious Randy, saving his life, but in the process breaking one of his ribs.

I take it as obvious that in the normal variation of this story, Rebecca does not harm Randy even though what she does results in his having a broken rib. That is, there is no cause for interference with Rebecca according to the harm principle. She *hurts* him, but does so in the process of saving his life—neither setting back his (overall) interests nor wronging him. Sometimes, one hurts another in the process of helping them.[35] There is no reason to think of that hurt as a harm. Of course, the judgment may be different if Randy was known to have a *do not resuscitate* order; there it may well be that Rebecca wrongfully set back his interests.

Michael Rabenberg provides a more troublesome rescue (or quasi-rescue) case:

> *Broken Arm*. Jim breaks my arm, but if Jim had not broken my arm, then Joe would have torn it off at the exact same time.
>
> (Rabenberg 2015, 10)

Rabenberg thinks it is absurd to say that in this case I was benefited. He claims "My arm's getting broken is an instance of my getting harmed in Broken Arm, even if I ought to be somewhat glad that I am harmed in Broken Arm as I am" since having one's arm torn off is far worse than having one's arm broken (Rabenberg 2015, 10). This is somewhat unclear to me and depends, I think, on why Jim breaks my arm. Rabenberg provides this as an example of preemptive harm in the course of discussing the counterfactual view of harm (a state-based view of harm). If Jim breaks my arm at my request because we know that Joe will otherwise tear it off, I am inclined to think Jim does not wrong me and so, on my account, does not harm me (or, if I am harmed, it's by Joe, whose threat resulted in my arm being broken). Of course, if Jim breaks my arm maliciously, he at least wrongs me. Indeed, in that case, I think he harms me—he may not set my interests back as much as Joe otherwise would, but that has no bearing on my account since my account is event-based and not a state-based counterfactual account. (On a counterfactual state-based account, because I would be worse off if Jim did not break my arm, we cannot say he harms me.) Here, I think my account aligns with common sense; interference with Jim is permissible.

Consider another case from Rabenberg:

> *Sniffles*. Bob is sick with a cold. He will get well today unless I increase the temperature in the room by a few degrees, for in so doing I will prevent the cold germs in his body from dying for another day. I do so. However, it is not the case that, as a result of my action, Bob's cold germs get stronger or that his cold gets worse.
>
> (Rabenberg 2015, 18)

Rabenberg thinks that intuitively, I harm Bob. My account gives that result. One might think that what happens in *Sniffles* is that I *fail to harm* despite trying to. Certainly, If Bob got better despite my wrongful act, we would say I tried, but failed, to harm him. But Bob did not get better and his not getting better was due to my wrongful action. What we should say here, I think, is that I wrongfully set back Bob's interest in recovering quickly. This might be less of a setback to his interests than if I had managed to make him worse off (making the cold last longer or worsening the symptoms Bob manifests), but it is a setback nonetheless.

Finally, consider preventative harms, with an example from Seanna Shiffrin, similar to my drowning Sue case but with an additional party involved:

> Suppose I am drowning, Harry is about to save me, and you obstruct him. There I remain, drowning. I am not left in any worse a position than I was before, but still, I have been harmed by your action.
>
> (Shiffrin 2012, 368)

If I do not harm Sue when I decide to turn away from her, can you be doing harm here, as Shiffrin thinks? Had you merely decided not to help, you would not do her harm because you would not do anything to her. Shiffrin disagrees (see 369). This case, though, is different: You do something and arguably, do it to Shiffrin (in the example). If that is right, we can say you harm her: You wrongfully set back her interest in being saved by Harry. This is in agreement with Shiffrin's claim that "If efforts to remove me from harm are stymied, I think it is fair to say that I am harmed by the obstructions even if I am not made any worse off than I was" (368–369). The state she finds herself in after the obstruction may be no different than the state she was in before it, but there was nonetheless an event wherein her interests were set back. This is contingent, though, on the event being a wrong to her—as seems likely when you prevent Harry from saving her. (If Harry is prevented from saving her because he responds to Lucy's honest call for help in a nearer emergency, there would be no wrong and hence no harm. If you prevent Harry from saving her but do so without realizing she is in danger—you wish only to obstruct Harry from swimming, say—there would be a wrong, but not to Shiffrin. In this case, you harm Harry but not Shiffrin—alternatively, we might say you inadvertently cause Shiffrin a harm since you should have seen that she was in danger.)

Consider how our event based account handles these cases. On Hanser's view, preventative harms are derivative of ordinary harms, which are losses of some quantity of a basic good. When someone prevents you from gaining some quantity of that good, they derivatively cause you not to have the quantity of good in question and we say that person causes you a preventative harm (see, Hanser 2008, 240–241). On the Feinbergian event-based account, things are similar: When Harry interferes with your saving Shiffrin, he sets back her interest in your saving her. When Harry does this wrongfully, he harms Shiffrin.

Advantage: Feinbergian event-based account of harm.

By repeatedly hearkening back to John Stuart Mill's harm principle, I have shown that *to undergo a harm is to be the subject of an event wherein one's interests are wrongfully set back and wherein the status of the undergoing of the harm derives from its being the sort of event that it is (namely, a setting back of interests), independently of the badness of any resulting state*. This is a Feinbergian event-based account that seems to have advantages over Hanser's initial event-based accounts as well as state-based accounts.

While individuals can be harmed by speech—slander and libel are likely events that cause their victims to be subjects whose interests are wrongfully set back regardless of any resulting state (perhaps the victim is made more famous and wealthy by the attention after being harmed by the slander)—speech on college and university campuses that cause students to think, even if they are offended, is not harmful.[36] It may set back a student's interest in maintaining psychological comfort, but it does not do so wrongfully. It thus must be permitted.

Notes

1. This essay uses the argumentation in Chapter 3 of my *Toleration and Freedom From Harm* (New York: Routledge, 2018). I am grateful to Routledge for permission to use it here. I am also grateful to Chris Surprenant and Don Downs for the invitation to recast it for this volume.
2. See my 2018 and my *Toleration* (Cambridge: Polity Press, 2014).
3. The first volume is *Harm to Others* (New York: Oxford University Press, 1984).
4. I develop this argument further in my "Psychological Harm and Free Speech on Campus," *Society*, Vol. 54, No. 4 (2017): 320–325.
5. John Stuart Mill, *On Liberty* (Indianapolis, IN: Hackett Publishing, 1978; originally 1859).
6. Mary Warnock, "The Limits of Toleration," in *On Toleration*, ed. Susan Mendus and David Edwards (Oxford: Clarendon Press, 1987): 123.
7. We can understand interference to be any act that has the effect of impeding or preventing—even partially—an agent from doing as they wish, intend, or will. That is, it is hindrance or obstruction.
8. The Millian text concerns harm prevention rather than rectification. I nonetheless assume rectification is permissible. If we can interfere with John to stop him from going to harm Bill (e.g., getting his gun), to interrupt his harming Bill (e.g., pulling him off Bill whom he is sitting on and punching), it seems reasonable to think we can do something if he has succeeded in harming Bill. The timing of the interference seems irrelevant (within limits). Of course, who has jurisdiction is an open question. We might agree that anyone can act to prevent a harm or to stop a harm in process, but think that jurisdiction once a harm is completed is limited to the state or some specific organization.
9. Linguistic behavior can be coercive, but rational persuasion cannot. One only tries to rationally persuade another if one respects the other. Still, while Mill is concerned to allow demonstrations of moral disapprobation, he is opposed to many forms of social pressure—some of which may not be coercive.
10. Philip Selznick, "Personhood and Moral Obligation," in *New Communitarian Thinking: Persons, Virtues, Institutions, and Communities*, ed. A. Etzioni (Charlottesville, VA: University Press of Virginia, 1995): 125.
11. Again, some, but not all, pains are hurts. The pain of a good workout is not likely a hurt. Some, but not all, hurts are pains. A financial hurt is likely a pain only if the hurt party is aware of it. If Bob acts to prevent the raise I would have otherwise unexpectedly received, he hurts me, but causes no pain. Pains must be felt; hurts do not.
12. Seana Valentine Shiffrin, "Harm and Its Moral Significance," *Legal Theory*, Vol. 18 (2012): 371.
13. Shiffrin seems to think this does not make wrongful hurts more weighty than hurts; she also seems to think we ought not "commit[] to the more grand idea that the sufferer has a *stake* or *interest*, in the stressed senses, in not enduring pain" (Shiffrin, 371). I do not see why we should think this a "grand" idea nor why we should not accept it. It seems clear we have interests in not suffering pains.
14. See, for example, his 1984, p. 36. Some argue against Feinberg's understanding of harm being in Mill's work. See Dan Jacobson's "Mill on Liberty, Speech, and the Free Society," *Philosophy and Public Affairs*, Vol. 29, No. 3

(2000): 276–309, Dale Miller's *J. S. Mill* (Cambridge: Polity Press, 2010), and Piers Norris Turner's " 'Harm' and Mill's Harm Principle," *Ethics*, Vol. 124, No. 2 (2014): 299–326. I put this aside as I am not interpreting Mill. (Nor am I interpreting Feinberg.)

15. Feinberg identifies a third form of harm according to which *objects* can be harmed. Breaking a window harms the window's owner, but it can also be said that the window is harmed "in a derivative and extended sense" (1984, 32).
16. Some advocate legal requirements and/or inspections to prevent pain, but a branch may fall no matter how well maintained. Some advocate catastrophic medical insurance. Arguably, such would protect us from extreme suffering that would be a harmed state.
17. R. H. Dees, "The Justification of Tolerance," in *Values and Public Life: An Interdisciplinary Study*, ed. G. Magill and M. D. Hoff (Lanham, MD: University Press of America, 1995): 46.
18. John Horton, "Toleration, Morality and Harm," in *Aspects of Toleration: Philosophical Studies,* ed. J. Horton and S. Mendus (London, England: Methuen, 1985): 114.
19. Ben Bradley, "Doing Away with Harm," *Philosophy and Phenomenological Research*, Vol. 85, No. 2 (September 2012): 391. Bradley's treatment of Feinberg's definition is unsatisfying. In a footnote, he writes that "Like Feinberg," he is not concerned with the "alleged sense of 'harm' where 'x harms y iff x wrongs y' " (395, footnote 10). This, though, is only one sense of harm that Feinberg discusses (1984, 34–35) and he claims the relevant sense—the sense he is emphatically *most interested in*—is the sense that is the overlap of this with the sense of harm wherein it is a setback of interests. (It may be that Bradley meant "Unlike Feinberg," but this is not clear.)
20. T. M. Scanlon, "The Difficulty of Tolerance," in *Toleration: An Elusive Virtue*, ed. David Heyd (Princeton, NJ: Princeton University Press, 1996): 236.
21. Feinberg speaks of harmed and harmful states. He notes "the idea of a harmed condition seems more fundamental conceptually than an act of harming, since one must mention harm in the explanation of what it is for one person to harm another, whereas one can hope to analyze the idea of harm (harmed condition) without mentioning causally contributory actions" (1984, 31). As should be clear, I think this mistaken. Moreover, I doubt Feinberg is committed to it; the passage is very early in Feinberg's four volume work.
22. To be clear, this is not because of a counterfactual analysis. It's not that absent Buffet's contribution you would be worse off. It's rather that what I am doing is setting back your interests even though your interests are overall forwarded at the end of the week.
23. See Matthew Hanser's "The Metaphysics of Harm," *Philosophy and Phenomenological Research*, Vol. 77 (2008): 421–450. See also Judith Jarvis Thomson's "More on the Metaphysics of Harm," *Philosophy and Phenomenological Research*, Vol. 82 (2011): 436–458 for an argument against Hanser and, finally, Hanser's defense ("Still More on the Metaphysics of Harm," same volume, 459–469).
24. On my account, that is because there is no wrongfulness and hence no harm. Properly speaking, on my view, I hurt myself but do not harm myself. Absent that distinction—and it is absent from Hanser's definition—the harm principle would seem to indicate interference is permissible unless self-harm is ruled out on an ad hoc basis.
25. It's true that "familiar accounts portray harms and benefits as symmetrical" (Shiffrin 2012, 358), but such accounts work with harms as purely descriptive rather than normative. Shiffrin claims this is the dominant picture (366), but I am not sure it is. She seems to think Feinberg accepts it, saying that on

his interpretation "One is harmed if one's overall interest has been set back, and benefited if it is advanced," but it's clear that this refers only to one sense of the term he considers, while it's the overlap of that and wrongfulness (the other sense) that he takes to be relevant to the harm principle. Shiffrin recognizes this in her footnote 22, but follows Feinberg in his unnecessarily narrow concern solely with legally criminal harm.

26. Michael Rabenberg, "Harm," *Journal of Ethics and Social Philosophy*, Vol. 8 (2015): 22.
27. If I am murdered, my interests are wrongfully set back. It's true, I think, that once dead, I am not in a harmed condition. But the ante-mortem me was/is harmed. This is Feinberg's answer to the quandary; I accept it.
28. A. P. Simester and Andrew von Hirsch, "Rethinking the Offense Principle," *Legal Theory*, Vol. 8 (2002): 269–295. See also Victor Tadros' "Harm, Sovereignty, and Prohibition," *Legal Theory*, Vol. 17 (2011): 36–65, 46ff and James Edwards' "Harm Principles," *Legal Theory*, Vol. 20 (2014): 272 for better views about this (and so-called "pure" rape).
29. Some may worry that this allows for too much interference since anytime P has even a slight interest it could be wrongfully set back. I am not sympathetic to this concern. It's important that the harm principle provides only a necessary and not a sufficient condition for interference. *De minimis* harms are not likely such that there should be interference but that need not lead us to think they are not harms. Indeed, interference in the form of a prohibition regarding a type of *de minimis* harm designed to prevent their frequent occurrence may well be justifiable even if punishment for causing a specific token of that harm is not.
30. A. P. Simester and Andrew von Hirsch, "Remote Harms and Non-Constitutive Crimes," *Criminal Justice Ethics*, Vol. 28 (2009): 104. See also John Gardner and Stephen Shute, "The Wrongfulness of Rape," in *Oxford Essays in Jurisprudence*, ed. J. Horder (Oxford: Oxford University Press): 196.
31. (a) Hanser agrees (2008, 421). So does Thomson (2011, 436–437). (b) I may be eliding awareness and experience. My intuition—admittedly uncertain—is that Gary does not experience the stabbing. I tend to think one must be aware of X in order to experience X, but that one need not experience X in order to be aware of X.
32. Obviously, my account has implications for discussions of abortion—some abortions will be harms and some not. Whether any are harms to the potential child is an interesting question. In cases like gene-paraplegia, where there is an issue of wrongful life, it may be that the child has interests set back by the wrongful event that occurs before their birth. This may parallel Feinberg's discussion of anti-mortem harm. Call it *ante-vitam* harm.
33. When the harms take place is clear in these cases, but admittedly less clear in other cases.
34. Cf. Hanser's response in 2011 at 466–467.
35. Similarly, one may harm another in one way while benefiting them overall.
36. Of course, students can be slandered or libeled and I would not deny that there are other ways students might be harmed on a college campus by speech acts. This is not what occurs, though, with academic discourse, no matter how unsettling or offensive it might be.

Works Cited

Bradley, Ben. "Doing Away With Harm." *Philosophy and Phenomenological Research*, Vol. 85, No. 2 (September 2012): 390–412.

Cohen, Andrew. *Toleration*. Cambridge: Polity Press, 2014.
———. "Psychological Harm and Free Speech on Campus." *Society*, Vol. 54, No. 4 (2017): 320–325.
———. *Toleration and Freedom From Harm*. New York: Routledge, 2018.
Dees, R. H. "The Justification of Tolerance." In *Values and Public Life: An Interdisciplinary Study*, edited by G. Magill and M. D. Hoff. Lanham, MD: University Press of America, 1995: 29–56.
Edwards, James. "Harm Principles." *Legal Theory*, Vol. 20 (2014): 253–285.
Feinberg, Joel. *Harm to Others*. New York: Oxford University Press, 1984.
Gardner, John and Shute, Stephen. "The Wrongfulness of Rape." In *Oxford Essays in Jurisprudence*, edited by J. Horder. Oxford: Oxford University Press, 2000: 193–217.
Hanser, Matthew. "The Metaphysics of Harm." *Philosophy and Phenomenological Research*, Vol. 77 (2008): 421–450.
———. "Still More on the Metaphysics of Harm." *Philosophy and Phenomenological Research*, Vol. 82 (2011): 459–469.
Horton, John. "Toleration, Morality and Harm." In *Aspects of Toleration: Philosophical Studies*, edited by J. Horton and S. Mendus. London, England: Methuen, 1985: 113–135.
Jacobson, Dan. "Mill on Liberty, Speech, and the Free Society." *Philosophy and Public Affairs*, Vol. 29, No. 3 (2000): 276–309.
Mill, John Stuart. *On Liberty*. Indianapolis, IN: Hackett Publishing, 1978.
Miller, Dale. *J. S. Mill*. Cambridge: Polity Press, 2010.
Rabenberg, Michael. "Harm." *Journal of Ethics and Social Philosophy*, Vol. 8 (2015): 1–32.
Scanlon, T. M. "The Difficulty of Tolerance." In *Toleration: An Elusive Virtue*, edited by David Heyd. Princeton, NJ: Princeton University Press, 1996: 226–239.
Selznick, Philip. "Personhood and Moral Obligation." In *New Communitarian Thinking: Persons, Virtues, Institutions, and Communities*, edited by A. Etzioni. Charlottesville, VA: University Press of Virginia, 1995: 110–125.
Shiffrin, Seana Valentine. "Harm and Its Moral Significance." *Legal Theory*, Vol. 18 (2012): 357–398.
Simester, A. P. and von Hirsch, Andrew. "Rethinking the Offense Principle." *Legal Theory*, Vol. 8 (2002): 269–295.
———. "Remote Harms and Non-Constitutive Crimes." *Criminal Justice Ethics*, Vol. 28 (2009): 89–107.
Tadros, Victor. "Harm, Sovereignty, and Prohibition." *Legal Theory*, Vol. 17 (2011): 36–65.
Thomson, Judith Jarvis. "More on the Metaphysics of Harm." *Philosophy and Phenomenological Research*, Vol. 82 (2011): 436–458.
Turner, Piers Norris. "'Harm' and Mill's Harm Principle." *Ethics*, Vol. 124, No. 2 (2014): 299–326.
Warnock, Mary. "The Limits of Toleration." In *On Toleration*, edited by Susan Mendus and David Edwards. Oxford: Clarendon Press, 1987: 123–140.

8 The Difference Between Being Offended and Taking Offense[1]

Michael Joel Kessler

In a widely discussed letter, the Dean of Students at the University of Chicago advised incoming freshmen that the institution's commitment to freedom of thought meant it would not support the following three practices: (1) trigger warnings, (2) banning controversial speakers, and (3) the creation of intellectual safe spaces "where individuals can retreat from ideas and perspectives at odds with their own."[2] The letter presents the issue as a choice between defending freedom of expression and protecting students from discomfiting exposure. The framing assumption is that these goals cannot both be realized, and so universities must make an existential choice regarding their fundamental priorities. In Chicago's view these policies would be inimical to the mission of the university.

Some supporters of this letter and similar stances taken by other universities welcomed it as pushing back against a social trend that places too much importance on ensuring that no one is offended by the speech or conduct of others. They believe that students should not expect to be swaddled out in the real world and that university space provides the first opportunity to learn this lesson.

There are at least two objections at work in the arguments made by proponents of the Chicago model. The first is that universities cannot fulfill their intellectual objectives if they are constrained by worries about causing offense. A second, stronger, objection is that it is part of the role of the university to challenge a student's intellectual comfort zone. On this view, offense is just proof that it is doing its job. Both objections raise the question of what significance *the fact of offense* should have on university policy. The second objection treats offense as a goal, while the former sees it as a by-product that should not be a side-constraint. My aim in this paper is to show why the first objection is misguided. I will argue that the avoidance of offense can be a beneficial side-constraint on universities without threatening anything important. In advancing this view, I will be rejecting the second objection.

Is there a necessary tension between the intellectual mission of universities and offense? The debate about campus speech policies has focused mostly on what is and is not offensive. Beyond the issue of who gets to decide, this topic invites difficult questions about how to define offensive subject matter. The difficulty lies in evaluating the reasons people have for offense as the basis for drawing a line between acceptable and unacceptable speech. I will argue that by focusing on the *context* of offense rather than its *content*, it will be easier to find clear lines about what universities should do when offense is cited as an objection to campus speech. In many cases it will be possible to accommodate the fact of offense without compromising on a commitment to freedom of thought.

My argument depends on the premise that university space is not like the public square and it is also not like a conventional office space. Both sides of this debate have been importing norms from other domains and assuming they apply in the same way to university space. The first task is to show what makes academic space distinctive. Next, I will argue that, based on the intellectual mission of universities, they have specific duties both to students and to faculty. Each group occupies a certain role in the overarching institutional structure, and the relationship between the two provides guidance for how universities should regulate speech. On the basis of this account I will show: (1) that trigger warnings are a reasonable response to the interests of students and (2) that the banning of controversial speakers is in principle compatible with the intellectual mission of the university but not always the best way to advance that mission.

The Intellectual Mission of Universities

The debate surrounding campus speech policies rests on background assumptions about what a university is. Bringing these assumptions to the foreground is the first step in clarifying what is at issue. One helpful question to ask is how campus space differs from other kinds of spaces? In this section, I'll argue that one defining characteristic of universities is that they have an intellectual mission. This mission will be key in deciding on principles to use when determining whether to regulate speech on campus.

To see what makes universities distinctive it will be useful to compare them to other kinds of spaces where questions about freedom of expression arise. Consider first the town square or, as would be more common these days, the busy downtown street corner. This is public space in the sense that no one owns it. Since no one owns it, it follows that no one can exclude others from being there. The right to exclude is a prerogative that comes with private ownership. Since no one can be excluded from the town square, people should be free to speak their minds without fear of violence or censorship. Whether this means handing out flyers for a rally, or decrying the government's action, or warning others about the wages of sin, all speech belongs in public space regardless of its message. To single out some speech as not belonging would be incompatible with the equality of citizens.

Next, consider a typical office with a common break room. There is a sense in which the break room also belongs to no one, since all employees are entitled to go there to mingle or eat. But there is an important sense in which the break room is not public space. Non-workers of the company would not be allowed in, for example. Furthermore, the company retains the right to adopt various policies about break-room usage. These could include restrictions on the kinds of jokes that can be told, whether proselytizing is allowed, if you can play music from your phone's speaker, and other restrictions aimed at ensuring the break-room remains a welcoming space for all employees. Because this is public space within a private institution, the rules regarding allowable speech will be more restrictive.[3]

Where do universities fit relative to these two points of comparison? One way to answer this is to focus on whether there is an overarching intellectual purpose for each space. In the case of the street corner the answer is yes. The mission of public space is to remain neutral among the competing views that citizens hold. It is a core liberal value that the government should not be telling adults what to think but rather enabling individuals to express their thoughts to others. There should be no preference for any specific point of view, and steps should be taken to ensure that minority points of view are not drowned out. So while there is an intellectual mission, it is viewpoint-neutral.[4] In the case of the office there is no intellectual mission at all. A company, by the very nature of what it is, will have certain goals pertaining to financial outcomes or growth. But these aren't plausibly described as intellectual goals. As such, the company's policies for how workers behave in the workplace are not constrained by a prior commitment to any intellectual project.

This is where the university stands in a distinct place. As institutions of higher learning, their overarching goal is to expand knowledge. There are two main ways that universities expand knowledge. Research seeks to uncover new truths or to expose accepted truths as falsehoods. Teaching aims to convey truths to students, and to train them to distinguish truth from falsity and good ideas from bad ones. I won't belabour this point because it is fairly straightforward: A university has an intellectual mission that bears some important relationship to knowledge. This makes it different from public space by having a basis for valuing certain ideas over others. False ideas have less relevance to a university, given its overall aim. This also makes it different from conventional workplaces where creation and transfer of knowledge is not the direct goal. The fact that some workplace policy would inhibit intellectually productive debate is not a decisive reason against it. By contrast, given what universities are for, the same restrictive policy would be rejected as inconsistent with its mission.

What does this mean in practice? The intellectual goal of universities informs how professors are expected to teach. A faculty member who taught discredited research as if it were true would face sanctions either at the departmental or divisional level. The reason is that it is a basic expectation that courses expand the knowledge of students. This involves teaching things that are true. Faculty who use their institutional authority to teach false ideas are violating their duties both to the institution and also to students. This doesn't mean we can never discuss falsehoods. There is value in studying how false ideas take root, but this lesson itself requires clear framing by the instructor. Teaching false ideas without contextualization would, however, not be consistent with the intellectual mission of a university.

This is a small but ultimately important point. Contrary to popular discourse, university classrooms are not places where all ideas are on the table. There is at least one major constraint, namely that studying these ideas must advance knowledge. A syllabus reflects the expertise of the instructor with respect to the topic. This expertise manifests itself in the choice of readings, the content of the lectures, the assignments, and so on. All of these choices are made with the goal of teaching students some body of knowledge. These choices involve the judgment that some readings are better than others, some debates are more instructive than others, and so on. This also involves judgments that some ideas won't be useful and might actually detract from the overall goal of the course. Deploying this expertise is an intrinsic part of what faculty are hired to do.

It follows that universities value a kind of intellectual objective that meets a higher threshold than just encountering different viewpoints. Thus far we have been focusing on the substantive aspect of teaching: The content in question must actually count as knowledge. There is, in addition, a formal aspect to the goal of advancing knowledge. The knowledge in question must be conveyed in the right way so that it is successfully transferred from one party to the other. Faculty are under a professional obligation to teach in such a way that students will be able to grasp the material. If I succeed in getting you to believe something false, I have met the formal requirement but failed the substantive one, since what I have transferred is not knowledge. Likewise, I can try to teach you something that is true but if I present it in such a way that uptake is impossible, then knowledge will not occur.

Trigger warnings, as I'll argue in the third section, involve formal constraints aimed at enabling student learning. Offense is something that interferes with learning for some students. As such, the fact of offense is something that must be dealt with if classes are going to meet their objective. To see this, we first need to know a little more about how offense can be a barrier to learning.

Feinberg's Offense Principle

The language of offense is ambiguous and can be used express a range of reactions. To evaluate the merits of Chicago's rejection of offense we need to distinguish different ways that people can experience offense. The most systematic treatment of offense as a legal category comes from Joel Feinberg. He notes that some offensive speech is akin to loud noises and foul odors in terms of its effect on the audience. As Feinberg argues, we all have a reasonable objection to having our senses affected in this way, at least some of the time. He concludes that in a small number of circumstances the criminal law can legitimately intervene to protect people from this kind of offense. This argument can be applied in helpful ways to campus speech.

Feinberg writes within a liberal tradition, drawing primarily from John Stuart Mill, according to which we have strong reasons to oppose criminalizing speech. This means that we should tolerate many suboptimal consequences that arise from speech for the sake of protecting an important political value. These consequences include unpleasant mental states ranging from "affront to sense or sensibility, disgust, shock, shame, embarrassment, annoyance, boredom, anger, fear, or humiliation" (Feinberg, 5). When this takes place in public and we cannot easily escape, these mental states are "unwelcome demands on one's attention [and] a bother that must be coped with however inconvenient it may be at the time to do so" (Feinberg, 9). Offensive speech is therefore costly when it is uttered in public.[5] Rather than conclude that such costs are always ones we must pay for living in a free society, Feinberg argues that we can craft a principle to place a limit on how much offense liberals must tolerate.

Feinberg's Offense Principle involves a complicated balancing exercise that considers the seriousness of the offense on one hand and the reasonableness of the offending speech act on the other.[6] *Seriousness* of offense is a function of the intensity of the offense combined with a judgment about how easy it would be for unwilling audiences to anticipate and avoid it. Accordingly, unwanted exposure to images that would be shocking and hard to forget, like a rotting corpse, would rank as more serious than images that are more familiar, like a skeleton. *Reasonableness* of offending conduct is a function of the personal importance of the offending conduct, the social utility of this kind of action, the context in which it occurs, the availability of other times and places, and the motives behind the offending action. Conduct maliciously aimed at upsetting others would rank lower compared to conduct aimed at raising social awareness about some issue.

Courts must balance these two variables—seriousness and reasonableness—and determine whether there is greater value in prohibiting or protecting the offensive act.[7] Feinberg argues that defending the importance of freedom of expression is nevertheless compatible with countenancing some offenses as rising to the level of legal regulation. He models his argument by considering the kinds of public nuisances we should permit on a crowded city bus. Each of us accepts that when we leave our homes we will encounter conduct that offends us. This is just the cost of sharing public space. In general, so long as your offensive ways do not invade my body physically then I can avoid your annoying habits by turning away or sitting somewhere else. This general model runs into trouble when the offending conduct manages to invade my body via my senses. As sensate creatures, all of us can have our inner life derailed in the presence of certain sounds, smells, and sights. For example, some high-pitched sounds will cause serious headaches in almost all persons. Certain smells, like burning plastic or vomit, will induce gag reflexes in a large percentage of the population. The effect of these sounds and smells is rightly described as causing offense: They interact with our senses, without our consent, in ways that give rise to unpleasant physiological and psychological reactions. When this happens, we are deprived of the kind of privacy from others that our bodies usually provide. While I might be willing to sit on a bus with a loud talker, I would not be willing to do so with someone carrying a bucket of manure. It is reasonable to assume that most others on the bus share the same aversion.

We can take the same structure and apply it in other, less captive, contexts. A blinding flash of light from a billboard is an obvious example. The offense caused doesn't need any deep explanation: This bothers people passing by. Some will suffer headaches, others will bump into things as a result of the visual distraction, and this may even trigger epileptic seizures in those predisposed to such episodes. The offense created is real, and it will have a range of effects on individuals depending on their own physiologies and psychologies. In light of the nuisance created, it is reasonable to look for ways to mitigate the bad effects of the speech in question.

The foregoing establishes the basic point that individuals have a reasonable *prima facie* objection to being exposed to sensory input that invades their inner life through imposing unpleasant sensations. The nuisance component of these examples is that one party imposes significant burdens on others from which it is difficult or costly for them to escape. To accommodate the objection people have to these unpleasant sensations, the law of public nuisance prohibits certain actions because of the kinds of effects they create in space that we share with others.

The structure of these examples is such that the issue of censorship does not arise at all. When one appeals to a purely sensory notion of offense there is no message or point of view that is being silenced by the law. A loud noise and a gag-inducing smell don't have expressive content. Banning the person carrying the bag of manure from the bus is compatible with the strongest protections for freedom of expression because this is not a case of trying to communicate with others.

Censorship does enter the picture when we turn to a second category of offense. In the previous category, the offense just is the negative effect on one's senses. In other cases, what offends is specific to the message expressed—*what* one says rather than *how* one says it. Here it is the meaning of the expression that causes the offense. According to Feinberg in these cases the offense is to one's sensibilities in addition to one's senses. What he means is that there is some contribution by the agent that is "cognitively mediated" (Feinberg, 14) which in turn makes some experience a source of turmoil for that person. The distinction is nicely articulated by saying that an affront to sensibilities offends *us* rather than merely *our senses*.

Consider the example provided by Kurt Baier of the smell of pork to an Orthodox Jew.[8] The smell is not offensive in itself in the way that the smell of burning rubber is for most people. Rather the smell becomes offensive because of this person's religious standards with respect to food. "The standard which shapes our sensibilities determines whether we are offended" (Baier 1979, 621). The smell of pork means something to a Jewish person because of his or her values. The senses are still involved—that is how the offense gains access—but the explanation lies elsewhere. We tell our senses what they should register as offensive based on our own sensibilities. There is no such mediating step in cases of sensory offense.

The role of the criminal law in regulating offenses to sensibility is very complicated precisely because of this cognitive component. To recognize this kind of offense as a nuisance is to give legal priority to the values of some segment of the population.[9] This encodes their standards of sensibility into the law at the expense of those with different ones. He gives the example of flag burning to show that it would be wrong to ban expression just on the ground that it conflicts with some deeply held belief about sacred symbols (Feinberg 1985, 47). While the intensity of the negative experience will be strong for many citizens, this must give way to the competing value of freedom of expression. If offense at the desecration of sacred symbols could silence unpopular speech, then we would lose an important form of political dissent. This is a significant threat to the possibility of political protest, and so the reasonableness of the offending conduct would outweigh the seriousness of the offense caused (Feinberg, 53).

There are many more interesting details of Feinberg's view, but for present purposes all we need is the difference between offense to senses and offense to sensibilities. When the assault is directly on our senses, this is a place where we find near unanimity in the judgment that something is a nuisance. As human beings, our biology provides a shared standard for what counts as offensive smells and sounds. There is no such common ground once we move to sensibilities. This is part of the reason why many are suspicious of campus speech policies surrounding offense and take the Chicago model to be the right one. How could a university protect against offense given the diversity of things that offend people? As I'll argue in the next section, this worry imports a concern from the public domain that lacks weight in the campus context.

Triggers and Offense

We can now turn to the question of what significance offense should have on campus. Using Feinberg's model for balancing, I'll argue that in most cases involving trigger-warnings the seriousness of the offense justifies fairly extensive use of warnings by universities. Refusing to do so is unreasonable, given the role instructors play within the institution.

Feinberg's Offense Principle is crafted to answer questions about the justified use of the criminal law to prevent offensive expression in public, and in this way limit a person's ability to use public space for her purposes. Since the consequence of invoking the criminal law is the threat of coercive punishment, the standards for what counts as wrongful offense are quite high. There is an inherent neutrality with respect to how governments should approach offensive content within public space. The matter looks different once we move to university space. The university is decidedly not committed to remaining neutral regarding ideas. As argued in the first section, it is a core function of a university to advance knowledge. In the classroom this means, among other things, successfully conveying material to students. This overarching goal makes the fact of serious offense by students an object of professional concern for faculty.

The language of triggers as a psychological phenomenon comes from the treatment of Post Traumatic Stress Disorder (PTSD). One of the defining characteristics of PTSD is that the traumatic event is re-lived by the patient when exposed to certain experiences (sights, words, smells, etc.). For the triggered person with PTSD, this means suffering the trauma over again. Supposing this is an accurate description of the mechanism of triggering, the next question is whether students experience this effect while in the classroom. This is a place where investigation is not required. Many students will have experience as victims of physical and sexual assault. Others will have suffered psychological abuse at the hands of parents or partners. Whether their symptoms would warrant a clinical diagnosis is irrelevant. It is sufficient to acknowledge that the life experiences of some of our students will make them vulnerable in the presence of certain material. Recalling Feinberg's list, some members of the audience will experience shock, shame, embarrassment, fear, or humiliation. Notice that these are not the widely shared sense-based reactions, like being blinded by a flash of light. Rather, all of these negative responses are conditioned by the person's trauma. For these students, sudden exposure to certain ideas will be experienced as an assault on their senses.

The key point is that serious offense impairs the person's ability to be in the same room as the offending material. If we accept Feinberg's model, then we should recognize that this is a serious interference with their inner life. The offense has the same effect on their ability to learn as shrill sounds and noxious smells would for others. For the affected individual, this is a psychological state within which it can be impossible to do anything else. Framed in this way, it is reasonable to take their offense seriously even if one thinks the material in question is not offensive. If we accept that PTSD is a real psychological phenomenon, then we acknowledge that some content can trigger trauma. If this is true, it would be unreasonable not to investigate whether accommodations can be made to avoid this outcome.

We are now in a position to deal with the complaint that trigger warnings interfere with the mission of the university. Why do students want advance notice of potentially upsetting material? Things that shock our senses derail us from the kind of mental security that we need to pursue daily activities. All of us have the same interest in wanting to control whether we are putting ourselves into the path of shocking material.

The social recognition of the value of being protected from this kind of offense goes beyond universities. Television programs display warnings regarding what one is about to watch. This serves the interests of parents but also any person who wishes to decide in advance whether to expose himself to upsetting imagery. News programs will similarly display warnings when the footage they are about to show is graphic. By requiring that such images only be displayed with advance warning, we recognize the reasonable interest each person has in avoiding this kind of serious offense.

This solution to the fact of offense is equally available to universities. On this account, it is just as reasonable for people to want protection from emotional triggers as it is for them to want to avoid being exposed to a blinding flash of light or a smell that activates one's gag reflex. The difference between sense and sensibility should not matter because "[o]ffense is not disagreeable or unpleasant to a lesser extent for the fact that it has its source in some specific set of beliefs" (Archard 2014). The effect of serious offense is that in the presence of the offending material it is hard to continue with the task at hand. In the educational context, we know that someone experiencing serious offense will shut down rather than engage their intellectual powers.[10] Of course, some students might be able to power through the discomfort. Some people also have unusually tolerant gag reflexes and can endure smells most of us cannot. It does not follow from this that all others should be expected to. If one's pedagogical approach is incompatible with reaching some students then, given the purpose of classroom education, it is incumbent on universities to look for ways to mitigate the fact of offense. The mistake that opponents of trigger warnings make is to assume that the kind of offense in question is a mere annoyance. We all agree that there are offenses that annoy and disturb but not in a way that derails one from one's normal activities. This is not the same as serious offense.

My argument is that universities should approach trigger warnings the same way we approach accessibility accommodations. If there are accommodations that we can make to enable as many students as possible to learn, then we should do so. Like any accessibility accommodation, trigger warnings pertain to the way material is presented rather than the content of what is taught. This does not mean ceding control over syllabi. That would be an unreasonable expectation by students. After all, students cannot decide what they will be taught without undermining the expertise that makes faculty qualified to teach in the first place. Rather, the most students can rightfully demand is disclosure about what will be taught. This allows them to decide for themselves whether this class is compatible with their sensibilities or whether they should look for another one that doesn't involve subjectively risky material.

The reason I have framed this as an institutional duty rather than something faculty owe their students is that faculty are not experts in accessibility and should not be asked to evaluate the seriousness of offense their courses might create. Instead, this is a responsibility that should be outsourced to some other office that can provide the requisite disclosure. This is akin to the role that movie and television rating agencies provide. All universities publish course calendars, and adding some content disclosure information about the syllabus is trivial. The responsibility to inform students about course content is shared among the student, the institution, and faculty. The goal of each is the same, namely to enable learning.

It is hard to see why this issue has generated the kind of debate it has. Recall that the Chicago letter says that its commitment to academic freedom cannot be reconciled with adopting trigger warnings. This would only be the case if trigger warnings were conceived of as a veto power over the syllabus. I have argued this is not the case. Unfortunately, control over content is how many have chosen to frame the issue. For example, Purdue University's free speech statement reads: "concerns about civility and mutual respect can never be used as a justification for closing off discussion of ideas, however offensive or disagreeable those ideas may be to some members of our community."[11] As I have argued, the error in this approach is in thinking that trigger warnings "close off" discussion. On my account, the reason one wants not to be triggered is exactly the opposite of Purdue's interpretation. Rejecting trigger warnings is what closes off discussion because being triggered interferes with the possibility of engaging with offensive ideas. Faculty have a responsibility to teach students and students have a responsibility to learn. A triggered student cannot learn. A policy that allows students to know what they are getting in to gives them the best chance of making informed decision in light of their own sensibilities. By adopting policies that mitigate the debilitating effects of shocking exposure, the university does not impose objectionable constraints on either party.

When universities enact protective policies for students this does not mean they are putting hurt feelings ahead of the search after truth. Rather, this provides advanced notice that some students may experience visceral reactions to the material they will encounter. This is a policy about creating a context for learning. The goal of the warning is to enable students to engage critically with the offensive ideas rather than shutting down in their presence.

One objection to this argument is that disclosure will allow students to shy away from ideas that challenge their world view. While some students will heed the warnings and steel themselves for a difficult discussion, others will avoid the discussion altogether. This invokes the second objection to trigger warnings that I mentioned at the outset: The function of the university is to challenge specific comfort zones and students should not be able to opt out of the challenge. This seems to me to be a fight not worth having. A commitment to this view would mean prescribing specific courses for all students, regardless of major or area of study. Most universities have breadth requirements but allow students to pick and choose among courses that satisfy the requirements. So the objection would have far wider ranging implications for curriculum design. Perhaps some universities will take up the challenge of deciding on the specific ideas that all students must be taught, whether they like it or not. This goes beyond the stated aims of the Chicago approach, and also introduces very serious worries about indoctrination on campus.

Truth, Falsity, and the Marketplace

The argument of the first section leads to the conclusion that, unlike companies or governments, universities have a specific intellectual mandate, namely to advance knowledge. This implies that false ideas have limited value. This is at odds with John Stuart Mill's argument that false speech should enjoy the same protection as all other speech. Mill's argument provides support for the Chicago model, since it endorses the idea that restricting discussion is never a good option. In this section, I will consider, and reject, Mill's defense of the value of false speech. I'll then consider how universities should approach the issue of controversial speakers.

Since the publication of *On Liberty* it has become common to follow Mill in referring to realm of ideas as a "marketplace." The metaphor works like this: Individuals are like consumers and ideas are like goods. Consumers will gravitate towards good products over bad ones. People who purchase bad products will learn from that mistake and no longer support producers of these products in the future. In this way, simply by its own unmediated incentive structure, "the market" rewards good ideas and punishes bad ones. Speech acts, and expression more generally, are like bringing goods to the market. The proof of their value will be revealed by how well they resonate with the other ideas already on offer. Ideas that improve on others will thrive, while bad ones will fail to gain adherents and eventually be eliminated from the marketplace.

This is why Mill famously argues that there are no good reasons for banning false ideas from entering the marketplace. He offers two distinct arguments. First, we should always be open to the possibility that our currently accepted truths are in fact falsehoods. No matter how certain we are that an idea is false, we cannot ignore that some of our current truths were once held to be false. Discussion of a seemingly false idea may end up being a catalyst for the next Copernican revolution. The theoretical possibility that this may be the case is sufficient to allow all ideas to enter the marketplace.

Second, supposing that we could know with absolute certainty that an idea is false, whenever false ideas are expressed this provides an opportunity for us to sharpen our arguments against them. Mill worries that in the absence of false ideas to argue against we might become dogmatic with respect to our true beliefs, since we no longer need to defend them. In this way, false ideas provide a benefit, which adds to the reasons against censoring them.

When you put these two arguments together, according to Mill, there is a greater risk of harm in restricting the expression of what is thought to be false than there is in allowing it to be expressed and then repudiated.

> If there are any persons who contest a received opinion . . . let us thank them for it, open our minds to listen to them, and rejoice that there is some one to do for us what we otherwise ought, if we have any regard for either the certainty or the vitality of our convictions, to do with much greater labour for ourselves.
>
> (Mill, 122)

Despite its rhetorical appeal, Mill's argument is flawed. The flaw is that it fails to countenance the damage that false ideas can bring with them even if they are eventually repudiated. The clearest example of this is defamation. The reason this is a tort in civil law is that one's reputation can be materially harmed by false speech. A similar case can be seen with false advertising. In Canada, this can lead to criminal charges when the false or misleading expression was reckless and was intentionally targeted at vulnerable groups.[12] The reason this is in the criminal code is that when this speech is successful it means vulnerable groups will have been exposed to significant harms that threaten their liberty within society.

If we were to apply Mill's arguments here, we would say that the chance to defend one's reputation enlivens the truth of one's upstanding character. This is not compelling. It ignores the harms caused by defamatory speech even if one manages to vindicate one's reputation. So there is at least one category where the harms outweigh the value that the speech contributes. This significantly weakens Mill's defense of false ideas. At most, he has shown that we should not restrict false ideas that are benign.

At that point, it ceases to be an interesting claim since harmless false speech is rarely the subject of censorship.[13]

The case of defamation shows that some speech brings harm along with it, and the possibility that we would have been better off not allowing the speech in the first place. We can ask this same question about both true and false speech, and also with speech that has no truth-value per se, like drawings. Is there more harm in banning the speech or allowing it? Like all questions about utility, this will depend on the balancing. While Mill does not discuss harmful opinions in any detail he does acknowledge that some speech acts can lead to physical harms that are wrong.

> Even opinions lose their immunity when the circumstances in which they are expressed are such as to constitute their expression a positive instigation to some mischievous act. An opinion that corn-dealers are starvers of the poor, or that private property is robbery, ought to be unmolested when simply circulated through the press, but may justly incur punishment when delivered orally to an excited mob assembled before the house of a corn-dealer, or when handed about among the same mob in the form of a placard.
>
> (Mill, 131)

Mill acknowledges here that inflammatory speech can lead to harms, but he is only willing to interfere when it will indirectly bring about wrongful harm to another. Notice that the issue of truth or falsity is not Mill's main concern. The issue is whether the speech will cause harm, mediated through the actions of others, when uttered. This passage blocks interpreting *On Liberty* as saying that nothing is worse, all things considered, than censorship. This would be a highly problematic conclusion since it would place the value of unrestrained false speech above preventing foreseeable wrongful deaths.

The example of the corn-dealers opens up space within Mill's theory, and for those who follow it, for a distinction between inflammatory speech worth tolerating and inflammatory speech not worth tolerating. As he argues, one variable that affects the value of speech is its context. The very same opinion that should be banned when said to an assembled mob must be protected when expressed to the reading public. The image that Mill conjures up with the corn-dealers is not that a productive debate about fair pricing will ensue. Instead, the enraged mob will dish out mob justice. This reflects the merits of a distinction I drew at the outset, namely that contextual factors should be part of the analysis when thinking about the overall value of speech acts. Instead of saying that the opinion about the corn-dealers should not be uttered, Mill argues that by changing its context we can mitigate the harms inherent in such an opinion. This shows that Mill's theory does not support the conclusion that there is always greater harm in censorship. That determination depends on several factors, including whether the truth will have a chance to prevail. In some cases, the context won't allow for that. The enraged mob will not give the corn dealers a chance to be heard. The speech is dangerous in part because of its message and in part with how it is presented.

We can apply this account of inflammatory speech to the academic context when thinking about what value controversial speakers add when they come to campus.

Taking Offense as an Academic Responsibility

The previous discussion of Mill shows that it is a question of political morality how much harm we should allow people to create through the expression of opinions. This encompasses a huge range of speech acts with different content and motivations. We have to look at each speech act and weigh its positive and negative contributions. Maliciously false speech leading to harms to assignable persons provides one bright line for when speech can be restricted. These restrictions are compatible with valuing freedom of expression and the search after truth. We do not question the legislature's commitment to intellectual freedom when it bans criminally false advertising. Why not? The answer is that the speech in question can be banned without threatening the kind of discourse that we want to protect. Another bright line is incitement that threatens the life or property of some identifiable person or group. Whatever the independent merits of the expression are, we can still impose standards on how it can be expressed in order to enjoy the usual protections for speech.

Campus speech policies do not have the status of law but universities face an analogous question about campus morality: Would anything of value be lost if we restricted speech to mitigate campus disruption? This is a complex question for familiar reasons. The simplest way to shut down debate over some topic is to turn it into a riot. Once that threat is real, universities have no choice but to cancel the talk for the safety of the community. Is there a way to avoid granting all groups this "heckler's veto" over controversial speakers?

To answer this question, I will introduce a sense of offense that is not fully captured by Feinberg's account. Sometimes taking offense is a way of signaling that we find something to be morally wrong. Like offense to sensibilities, this involves a violation of standards that we endorse and adds to it the dimension of moral address to others. Indicating that one takes offense is different from the kind of emotional report one gives by saying "I'm offended." When I say, "That's offensive" I am attempting to engage in a form of moral dialogue with my community. The phrase both identifies something as wrong and involves others to share in this judgment. This is a speech act that invites dialectical engagement with the audience. In some cases, others will echo my judgment and together we will repudiate the offensive content. In other cases, my claim will be challenged and further debate will be required.

To return to Feinberg's thought-experiment, consider being on a crowded bus and witnessing someone shout racist slurs at another passenger. The morally right thing to do is to counter-speak. Standing up for the abused passenger both repudiates the racist claim that this person does not have equal standing in society and calls for endorsement by the wider community, in this case the rest of the passengers. Failure to do so is a moral failing by everyone on the bus. If no one speaks up two distinct wrongs will have occurred: (1) The victim has been wrongfully insulted and (2) the message that racism is acceptable has gone unchallenged. The first wrong is individual, since it involves the victim's moral rights. The second wrong is collective. The community has failed to live up to its own standards of civility and toleration. It would be appropriate for each person on the bus to feel guilt at not having spoken up.

The analogy to controversial speakers on campus is the following. As all parties to the debate agree, universities have intellectual missions. According to the view defended here, part of that mission involves taking an intellectual stand regarding which debates are worth having. As I have argued with the case of course content, not all debates are productive. Spending class time on these ideas simply because we can is a waste of faculty and student resources. More significantly, the institution is not advancing knowledge when it engages with ideas that fail to meet certain standards. These standards are up to faculty to determine. Their authority to make these determinations comes from the expertise they have with respect to the discipline.

The same principles should apply when it comes to controversial speakers, although there is a new variable that needs consideration. In addition to judgment about whether there is a productive intellectual debate to be had on some issue, the university should ask itself whether it would be morally criticizable for allowing certain ideas to enter its community. Hosting a speaker is a decision to lend institutional credibility to certain ideas. This is not a neutral act, and universities should give thought to whether they wish to take ownership of the message this conveys.

Consider the example of a speaker defending Holocaust denial. The university has two options when students put the name forth and try to book campus space. One option is to allow the speaker on the condition that there be an academically credible respondent. This is one way to ensure that morally offensive ideas are not left unchallenged. Another option is to deny the invitation and issue a statement explaining why the institution is declining to give a platform to this thesis. Both are instances of taking offense in the sense I have developed here. Both involve a decision to hold ideas to academic standards as a condition of entering the academic marketplace.

Notice that these options cannot be available to governments faced with the same offensive speech. The status that citizens have as equals entitles them to no less space than others just because they have offensive views.[14] This is a place where it is important not to confuse the neutrality that binds states with the norms that govern universities. States must protect unpopular speech even when that speech is morally offensive, though it can also take measures to limit its time, manner, and place. Universities don't have to protect unpopular speech to the same extent as governments do.

This argument supports rejecting speakers who are controversial because they adopt morally offensive positions. In addition to being a waste of resources, inviting such speakers is inimical to the creation of knowledge since their ideas have no credentials within academic debate. Hosting the Holocaust denier implies that there is value in hearing these ideas. However, no credible faculty would teach these same ideas as true, so there is no reason to change our standards simply because this takes place elsewhere on campus. The mission of the university to advance knowledge covers both contexts.

This is a relatively easy case and others will be much harder. In hard cases, the university should adopt the stance that debates are worth having. However, this does not imply that just any speaker should be allowed on campus. Faculty teach hard questions in classes, but we do not teach bad arguments just because they support defensible positions. We should not deviate from this approach just because a student group has invited a speaker. At most institutions, student groups require faculty sponsors and are accountable to the institution more generally with respect to how they spend their funds. This brings their activities under the aegis of the broader academic mission of the university. That mission should inform the selection of speakers. Faculty should apply their expertise in assisting students to see why certain speakers are better than others at advancing some controversial points of view. Many controversial speakers will fail to meet these standards.

The reason to have outside speakers on campus is to expand the range of views available to students. However, this is not a case of diversity for its own sake. Institutions must decide whether there is a productive debate to be had on this topic *with this person*. If the public lecture will turn into a circus of protests and counter-protests and end up being shut down due to safety concerns, then the answer is that this won't lead to anything productive. If the circus can be mitigated by requiring that the talk meet standards of academic rigour, the question remains whether seeing certain ideas debated contributes to the advancement of knowledge. Institutions should regard that as a genuinely open question that can be answered in either direction. The judgment that nothing of value will be gained by listening to racist ideas is a judgment they should be willing to make without fear that they are betraying a commitment to freedom of thought on campus. As with class time, campus resources are finite and the mission of a university should dictate how these are spent.

In conclusion, it is important to recall that the value universities place on freedom of expression is instrumental. As concerns the relationship between students and faculty, our commitment to allowing ideas on the table is conditional on a belief that this enhances learning. Faculty don't take themselves to be an under an obligation to engage in just any debate simply because the university has a commitment to freedom of thought. Some discussions are not worth having, and universities should have the authority to make that judgment.

The reason it is important to make this judgment is that both students and the general public think of universities as the places where debates can be had at the highest level. This identifies university space as a home for different caliber of conversations than can be found on the street corner, the newspaper, the Internet forum, and cable news. In order for that to remain true, universities should be mindful of whether they are enacting policies that enable meaningful exchange of the best ideas. Treating campus as an unregulated marketplace is not compatible with preserving what makes university space intellectually distinctive.

One aspect of this goal is, as I have argued, formal. In the trigger-warning case, this means giving advance notice so that all students can participate in the debate when difficult ideas are on the table. In the controversial speakers case, this means ensuring that ideas are presented in a way that allows for productive debate. When we have reason to think that unrestrained speech will not allow for meaningful exchange of ideas, then we should follow Mill in placing certain constraints on how that the speech is presented.

The other aspect is substantive. Universities should take up the responsibility that comes with expertise. We should teach debates that we think advance knowledge. And we should not waste our time hosting debates that fail to live up to academic standards. There are plenty of other forums where those discussions are already thriving.

Notes

1. I would like to thank Japa Pallikkathayil, John Duncan, and Jonathan Peterson for helpful discussions on early versions of this argument. I would also like to thank Nish Chankar for research assistance and for providing a student perspective on these issues.
2. The letter is reproduced at www.insidehighered.com/sites/default/server_files/media/acceptance_letter.jpg Accessed November 7, 2017.
3. For a discussion of the scope of employer rights over the speech of their employees see Volokh 1992.
4. Viewpoint neutrality is a species of content neutrality. The contrast to content-neutral policies is content-based policies. See Stone 1978.

5. Importantly, the different ways of being offended are distinct from being harmed by speech. There is such a thing as being harmed by the words of another—for example, when one is threatened or bullied into engaging in harmful acts—but in these cases the harm is distinct from the offense. See Feinberg 3.
6. For a different balancing account that focuses on the competing interests of speakers, audiences, and bystanders, see Scanlon 1979
7. One main objection is whether Feinberg's account is coherent without assessing the reasonableness of the offense. He tries to avoid this by discussing seriousness of offense instead, on the grounds that this is more objective and easier to quantify. For a discussion of that debate, see Simester and von Hirsch 2002 and Shoemaker 2000.
8. This example comes from Kurt Baier in response to an early version of Feinberg's Offense Principle. See Baier 1979.
9. Feinberg draws a distinction between higher and lower order sensibilities. See Feinberg 1985, 16. The cases where he thinks the Offense Principle should not apply pertain mostly to higher order sensibilities.
10. In the context of hate speech regulations on campus David Brink (2001) argues that racial slurs can have a similar shutting down effect on their audience.
11. www.purdue.edu/purdue/about/free-speech.html Accessed December 14, 2017.
12. See Canadian Competition Act 1985.
13. For a defense of Mill's position on infallibility see Haworth 2007.
14. This right will have a different shape in countries with hate speech laws. For example, in Canada no citizen may use public or private space to incite hatred towards identifiable groups. See Sumner 2004.

Works Cited

Archard, David. "Insults, Free Speech and Offensiveness." *Journal of Applied Philosophy*, Vol. 31, No. 2 (2014): 127–141.

Baier, Kurt. "Response: The Liberal Approach to Pornography." *University of Pittsburgh Law Review*, Vol. 40 (1979): 619–625.

Brink, David. "Millian Principles, Freedom of Expression, and Hate Speech." *Legal Theory*, Vol. 7 (2001): 119–157.

Canadian Competition Act R.S.C., 1985, c. C-34. http://laws.justice.gc.ca/eng/acts/C-34/index.html

Feinberg, Joel. *Offense to Others: The Moral Limits of the Criminal Law*. Oxford: Oxford University Press, 1985.

Haworth, Alan. "On Mill, Infallibility, and Freedom of Expression." *Res Publica*, Vol. 13 (2007): 77–100.

Mill, John Stuart. "On Liberty," in *Utilitarianism and On Liberty*. Oxford: Blackwell Publishing, 2003.

Scanlon, T. M. "Freedom of Expression and Categories of Expression." *University of Pittsburgh Law Review*, Vol. 40 (1979): 519–550.

Shoemaker, David W. "'Dirty Words' and the Offense Principle." *Law and Philosophy*, Vol. 19 (2000): 545–584.

Simester, A. P. and von Hirsch, A. "Rethinking the Offense Principle." *Legal Theory*, Vol. 8 (2002): 269–295.

Stone, Geoffrey R. "Restrictions of Speech Because of Its Content: The Peculiar Case of Subject-Matter Restrictions." *University of Chicago Law Review*, Vol. 46 (1978): 81–115.

Sumner, L. W. *The Hateful & the Obscene*. Toronto: University of Toronto Press, 2004.

Volokh, Eugene. "Freedom of Speech and Workplace Harassment." *UCLA Law Review*, Vol. 6 (1992): 1791–1872.

9 The Necessity of Offense[1]

Shane D. Courtland

In the now classic *Kindly Inquisitors*, Jonathan Rauch writes that, "knowledge is painful. . . . [It] does not come free to any of us; we have to suffer for it" (1993, 125). Often when educators try to shield students from this pain, they compromise the attainment of knowledge. In this chapter, I will examine the connection between offense (pain) and practical knowledge (e.g., knowledge regarding ethics, politics, public policy, etc.). With the assistance of Millian principles, I argue that it is not just empirically unlikely that one will possess practical knowledge by avoiding offense—rather, I advance a stronger conclusion—that it is conceptually impossible to both possess such knowledge and to avoid offense. To know something requires that one be familiar with, and perhaps even seriously entertain, falsehoods. With practical fields, not only must one entertain false propositions but one also *must* (conceptually) entertain value systems that one finds flawed/perverse. To fail to do so, would deny one practical knowledge, even including knowledge of values he/she currently endorses (via a Millian dead dogma).

The Set-Up

Over the last ten years there has been a palpable increase involving student resistance and protest due to the, purportedly, offensive content of an invited speaker's research and/or speech. Some of the more recent, and infamous, examples include Charles Murray's talk at Middlebury College, Laura Kipnis's talk at Wellesley College, Wendy McElroy's debate (with Jessica Valenti) at Brown University, and Milo Yiannopoulos's attempted talk at Berkeley. Students, alumni, faculty, and administrators have used various methods (open letters, protests, and the heckler's veto) to stop such events from occurring. And, in some cases (like Yiannopoulos and Murray) this has escalated to outright violence.

One of the reasons behind this resistance is that such controversial speakers seemingly offer particularly offensive viewpoints regarding sensitive topics. Take, for example, this email from CERE faculty (at Wellesley College) regarding Laura Kipnis's talk:

> We are especially concerned with the impact of speakers' presentations on Wellesley students, who often *feel the injury most acutely and invest time and energy in rebutting the speakers' arguments*. Students object in order to affirm their humanity. This work is not optional; students feel they would be unable to carry out their responsibilities as students without standing up for themselves. Furthermore, *we object to the notion that onlookers who are part of the faculty or administration are qualified to adjudicate the harm described by students*, especially when so many students have come forward. When dozens of students tell us they are in distress as a result of a speaker's words, we must take these complaints at face value.
>
> (Wellesley Statement 2017, emphasis added)

Similar concerns are echoed in other statements associated with this sort of resistance. A major goal is to shut down "intolerant or ignorant perspectives, . . . to curtail voices that are insensitive, or outright hostile, to their experiences on campus" (Groetzinger 2015). It is also claimed that listening to such speakers "is not an educational opportunity, but a threat." In particular, some add, "When you ask us to consider the other side of the argument, you are asking us to consider our assumed inferiority as a logical position. In no way does this consideration further our (or your) education" (Charles Murray at Middlebury 2017).

Unfortunately, a recent study seems to indicate that this sentiment may be widespread. In a 2017 Brooking's survey, students were asked to choose between two different types of learning environments. The first option was to "create a positive learning environment for all students by prohibiting certain speech or expression of viewpoints that are offensive or biased against certain groups of people." The second option, on the other hand, was to "create an open learning environment where students are exposed to all types of speech and viewpoints, even if it means allowing speech that is offensive or biased against certain groups of people." The majority of students (53 percent) favored the first option. That is, these students preferred a situation in which their school was expected "to create an environment that shelters them from offensive views" (Villasenor 2017).[2]

The purpose of this chapter is to show that the shutting down of speech, merely because it is offensive (via its content), necessarily undermines certain types of knowledge. In particular, it undermines practical knowledge. That is—knowledge centered upon value judgements. If we are to allow the banning of offensive discussions and/or speakers, then such policies are not, epistemologically, without their costs.

Before I engage in the central movements of this argument, there are certain presuppositions and caveats I must address. First, I will presuppose that the offended party(ies) have "landed upon" (they believe/assert) the true view. In other words, those seeking to shut down discussion because they are offended happen to have the correct view regarding that discussion. Not about it being shut down, per se, but about the truth conditions regarding the content of the speech/discussion. This essay will grant, for the sake of argument, that the offensive speakers came to the wrong conclusions—and, it just so happens, that those who are offended believe in the right conclusions.

Second, my use of the terms "offense" and "offended" are largely congruent with commonsense usage. As *Webster's Dictionary* defines it, offense is the "act of displeasing or affronting." And to be "offended" is "the state of being insulted or morally outraged" (Merriam-Webster n.d.). Joel Feinberg refers to this as the "general sense" of offense. He writes, "[It is] a miscellany of universally disliked mental states" (2008, 438). Later, he adds, "The offending conduct produces unpleasant or uncomfortable experiences—affronts to sense or sensibility, disgust, shock, shame, embarrassment, annoyance, boredom, anger, fear, or humiliation" (2008, 441). Additionally, I would suggest that to "be offended" is a subjective state[3] and it can vary over time and between individuals.[4]

Third, there are some caveats regarding my argument. Obviously, this chapter presupposes some moves within both epistemology and metaethics. While I hold that these moves are justifiable, it is, of course, beyond the scope of this essay to provide a sustained defense of them. For the sake of argument, I hope that the reader will view these moves as "plausible, though potentially contentious." Next, while this paper will exclusively focus upon moral knowledge, it could, *mutatis mutandis*, also apply to other value laden fields (e.g., public policy, political philosophy, aesthetics, etc.).

Mill's Dead Dogma

In Chapter Two of John Stuart Mill's *On Liberty*, he offers one of the most compelling arguments for allowing the free expression of ideas. Either the idea being expressed is right/true or it is wrong/false.[5] If it is the former, then to suppress that idea would rob humanity of an exchange of error for truth. If it is the latter, on the other hand, the suppression of the false idea robs humanity of a livelier impression of the truth. Without confronting falsehood, we might, then, be embracing a dead dogma (Mill 1989, 20).

Since a presupposition of this chapter is that we have already discovered the truth, we will entirely focus on the latter problem—dead dogma. Mill was optimistic, perhaps too optimistic, that as humanity progressed, we would likely discover the truth regarding many contested ideas. He lamented, however, that such discoveries would tend to dilute the "diversity of opinion." He writes:

> But though this gradual narrowing of the bounds of diversity of opinion is necessary in both senses of the term, being at once inevitable and indispensable, we are not therefore obliged to conclude that all its consequences must be beneficial. The loss of so important an aid to the intelligent and living apprehension of a truth, as is afforded by the necessity of explaining it to, or defending it against, opponents, though not sufficient to outweigh, is no trifling drawback from the benefit of its universal recognition.
>
> (Mill 1989, 45)

This narrowing of held opinions is such a problem "that if opponents of all important truths do not exist, it is indispensable to imagine them, and supply them with the strongest arguments which the most skillful devil's advocate can conjure up" (Mill 1989, 39). These heterodox and false views should be pressed upon "the learner's consciousness, as if they were pressed upon him by a dissentient champion, eager for his conversion" (Mill 1989, 45).

The reason that such advocates would be required, though the truth was already discovered, is that knowledge requires more than the mere holding of true beliefs. One also needs justification. And, justification requires that a person be pressured by diverse opinions. Mill writes:

> In the case of any person whose judgment is really deserving of confidence, how has it become so? Because he has kept his mind open to criticism of his opinions and conduct. Because it has been his practice to listen to all that could be said against him; to profit by as much of it as was just, and expound to himself, and upon occasion to others, the fallacy of what was fallacious. *Because he has felt, that the only way in which a human being can make some approach to knowing the whole of a subject, is by hearing what can be said about it by persons of every variety of opinion, and studying all modes in which it can be looked at by every character of mind.* No wise man ever acquired his wisdom in any mode but this; nor is it in the nature of human intellect to become wise in any other manner. *The steady habit of correcting and completing his own opinion by collating it with those of others, so far from causing doubt and hesitation in carrying it into practice, is the only stable foundation for a just reliance on it:* for, being cognisant of all that can, at least obviously, be said against him, and having taken up his position against all gainsayers—knowing that he has sought for objections and difficulties, instead of avoiding them, *and has shut out no light which can be*

> *thrown upon the subject from any quarter*—he has a right to think his judgment better than that of any person, or any multitude, who have not gone through a similar process.
>
> (Mill 1989, 23–24) (emphasis added)

Later, Mill adds:

> *On any other subject no one's opinions deserve the name of knowledge, except so far as he has either had forced upon him by others, or gone through of himself, the same mental process which would have been required of him in carrying on an active controversy with opponents.* That, therefore, which when absent, it is so indispensable, but so difficult, to create, how worse than absurd is it to forego, when spontaneously offering itself! If there are any persons who contest a received opinion, or who will do so if law or opinion will let them, let us thank them for it, open our minds to listen to them, and rejoice that there is some one to do for us what we otherwise ought, if we have any regard for either the certainty or the vitality of our convictions, to do with much greater labour for ourselves.
>
> (Mill 1989, 46–47, emphasis added)

To have a justified belief, according to Mill, requires encountering and defusing a belief that actively resists the one you assert to be true. That is why the advocacy of even false views is so important. Without this advocacy (by sincere believers or a talented devil's advocate) we lose the only justification/warrant that humans can attain. And without a claim to justification/warrant we, ipso facto, lose any claim to knowledge.

Not only will we lose out on knowledge, according to Mill, but the very meaning of our dogmas will be lost. He writes, "If the cultivation of the understanding consists in one thing more than in another, it is surely in learning the grounds of one's own opinions" (Mill 1989, 37). The justification for a view, then, is not merely an attendant element in the understating of that view; it is necessary. An essential part to truly understanding that "X is the case"—is to grasp the features of the world and of X that fund the truth conditions for that sentence.

That is why, for example, Mill claims that the Platonic dialogues provided more than mere justification; it demonstrated a real lack of understanding on the part of Socrates' interlocutors. Mill writes:

> The Socratic dialectics, so magnificently exemplified in the dialogues of Plato, were a contrivance of this description. They were essentially a negative discussion of the great questions of philosophy and life, directed with consummate skill to the purpose of convincing any one who had merely adopted the commonplaces of received opinion, *that he did not understand the subject—that he as yet attached no definite*

> *meaning to the doctrines he professed*; in order that, becoming aware of his ignorance, he might be put in the way to attain a stable belief, resting on a clear apprehension both of the meaning of doctrines and of their evidence . . . They were intended to make sure that the pupil understood his own opinion, *and (by necessary correlation) the opinion opposed to it*, and could enforce the grounds of the one and confute those of the other.
>
> (Mill 1989, 45–46, emphasis added)

In these dialogues, we see Socrates not only besting his interlocutors in argument—he outright embarrasses them. Their views are not merely without warrant; Socrates, in a sense, shows them to be without content. The only way to possess such content, according to Mill, is to have a firm grasp of "the opinion opposed to it." That's why, when praising Cicero earlier in *On Liberty*, Mill states that "[h]e who knows only his own side of the case, knows little of that" (Mill 1989, 38).

The core problem with preventing the open discussion of false ideas is two-fold, though interrelated. The only way we can justify our views is to offer "a standing invitation to the whole world to prove them unfounded" (Mill 1989, 24). To avoid such debate prevents one from attaining knowledge. Moreover, it undermines our understanding of our own views. As Mill writes, "Their conclusion may be true, but it might be false for anything they know: they have never thrown themselves into the mental position of those who think differently from them, and considered what such persons may have to say; and consequently they do not, in any proper sense of the word, know the doctrine which they themselves profess" (Mill 1989, 39).

Values and Knowledge

With some forms of knowledge (e.g., theoretical or factual) it is possible to affirm the truth of a proposition without, at the same time, possessing a positive valuation of that proposition. In other words, to say that "X is true" is not necessarily to say that I harbor a pro-attitude regarding X. This feature of this type of non-evaluative knowledge is ever present to our commonsense experience. First, there are many facts we dislike and wish were not true. Many things fall into this category. I might affirm the truth of my own mortality (when the doctor gives me a terminal diagnosis). Or, I might have to believe that my wife is guilty of spousal infidelity (when presented with pictures). The examples of such inconvenient truths are legion. Second, there are countless facts for which I am evaluatively indifferent. It does not matter to me that there are thirty teams in the NBA, that the Eiffel Tower is 312 meters high or that October comes after September. I might be surprised if these facts happen to be untrue, but I would not be upset.

On the other hand, there are forms of knowledge (e.g., practical) that are, at their core, evaluative. That means that when one asserts "X is the case" it is tied, unlike the forms of knowledge discussed previously, to a pro-attitude. For the remainder of this essay, I will discusses one particular kind of evaluative knowledge—moral knowledge.

In his 1937 essay, "The Emotive Meaning of Ethical Terms," C. L. Stevenson lays out three requirements to the "vital" sense of "good." For the sake of this argument, I will only explore Stevenson's second requirement—*magnetism*. He writes, "A person who recognizes X to be 'good' must *ipso facto* acquire a stronger tendency to act in its favour than he otherwise would have had" (Stevenson 1937, 16). To sincerely hold that something is morally "good" (e.g., "It is true that X is good") requires that the affirming person is, in some way, drawn to that thing, action, or whatever. If a person declares that "X is good" and is not-so-drawn, *ceteris paribus*, it is entirely appropriate to question either that person's sincerity and/or to claim that the person fails to grasp the meaning of "good."

Of course, some non-moral forms of the word "good" lack such magnetism (Stevenson limits his discussion to ethics). For example, I might sincerely say, "Y is a good knife." That does not mean that I am drawn to that knife. I may be completely indifferent to that knife. In this case, I understand the criteria for good vs. bad knives and I sincerely believe that Y meets that criteria. My affects never, *ceteris paribus*, come into play with this usage of "good."[6]

With morality, when one affirms that "X is good," one is not merely affirming the truth of a proposition. The sincere affirmation of the morally good thing/action also seems to require a pro-disposition. With the knife example, on the other hand, it can be strictly propositions all-the-way-down. There are propositions (the affirming of which does not require a pro-disposition) that constitute the criteria for excellency in knives and there are propositions (again, the affirming of which does not require a pro-disposition) regarding whether a particular knife, Y, meets that criteria.

Of course, at this point, a critic might claim that whatever I can do with the knife example he can do with the moral example. We can imagine a person that treats the claims of morality in a similar fashion to the claims associated with excellency in knives. There may be mere rules (or criteria) about what constitutes morally good behavior and that person could sincerely affirm that behavior X meets such criteria. Moreover, it seems that such a person could do this with warrant and without a pro-disposition.

Unfortunately, we don't have to use our imagination to envision such people. Psychopaths, arguably, can fulfill such a role. Gerald Gaus, in *Value and Justification*, mentions the "semantic dementia" suffered by psychopaths (1990, 297).[7] He writes, "The psychopath, we can say, often possesses sound beliefs as to what grounds a judgment that something is disgusting, exciting, benevolent, or horrible, but the intentional affective states to which these judgments refer are quite beyond him" (Gaus 1990, 297). Like the knife case, the psychopath can possess warranted beliefs regarding morality, but something is nonetheless missing.

To see what is missing, and why it is significant, I will refer to an analogy that Gaus offers in the same text. He writes:

> [C]onsider the ascription of amusingness to X. Amusingness, I take it, is a sort of valuableness, but, even should one be prone to deny this, we shall see that the analysis of amusingness casts light on serious types of value judgments. A person who believes a joke to be funny because he has been informed by an expert authority that it is so has a (true) belief that the joke is amusing, but his grasp or appreciation of its amusingness seems privative compared with he who believes it to be funny because he finds it to be so. The difference is not simply that the two have arrived at the belief by different epistemological paths; the purely testimonial credent seems to have a less complete or intimate grasp of the joke's amusingness. In absence of direct access to a joke's funniness, the testimonial credent knows *that* the joke is funny, but he is lacking, as it were, knowledge *of* its funniness. And if he does not "see" how it is funny, his asserting that "X is amusing" is a sort of puzzled, uncomprehending, assertion.
>
> (Gaus 1990, 149–150)

In a sense, then, the psychopath is in a similar boat to this completely humorless person. Indeed, Gaus seems to indicate as much. When discussing the psychopath's semantic dementia, Gaus writes, "His life can thus be understood on the model of a person with no sense of humor, who knows how to tell a joke in order to impress other guests at a party" (1990, 297). The semantic dementia of the psychopath is part-in-parcel of his being unable to possess knowledge *of* certain types of value. As Hervey Cleckley writes in *The Mask of Sanity*, "He is also indifferent to all these matters in life itself. Beauty and ugliness, except in a very superficial sense, goodness, evil, love, horror, and humor, have no actual meaning, no power to move him. . . . He can repeat the words and say glibly that he understands, and there is no way for him to realize that he does not understand" (2014, 61).[8]

The magnetism that I discussed previously is missing in the case of the psychopath. He has semantic dementia because he lacks the affects associated with valuing what is morally good. In order to have full knowledge[9] regarding whether some thing or action is morally good one must experience the pro-dispositions that constitute the magnetism of "good." Otherwise, the ascription of "good" (in the moral case) will, at best, be "a sort of puzzled, uncomprehending, assertion" (Gaus 1990, 150).

Offense and Moral Knowledge

It is time to put all of the pieces together. In *Kindly Inquisitors*, Jonathan Rauch offers a bold statement. He writes, "*It is not good to offend people, but it is necessary. A no offense society is a no knowledge society*" (1993, 126) (emphasis added). Now while Rauch's focus is different than what appears in this chapter, his statement neatly encapsulates the core intuition at the heart of my thesis.[10] There is a necessary tradeoff between offense and moral knowledge. To avoid offense is to undermine, at least in part, this type of knowledge.

For the sake of argument, say that we have landed upon the right moral views regarding some very contentious issues. All of our moral views regarding race and gender (from now on, R&G), for example, happen to be the correct views to hold. In other words, if we were all knowing we would affirm our conclusions regarding all moral issues associated with R&G. Our views are, then, in harmony with a God's eye view of the matter.

To have full knowledge of R&G requires that we have pro-dispositions. This is Stevenson's magnetism. We are not merely affirming propositions regarding R&G, it is an affective attachment—we are drawn to these views. If this attachment is not there, we would lack full knowledge regarding R&G. We would be suffering something akin to the semantic dementia that encumbers psychopaths. A lack of attachment would entail, in a sense, a failure to understand R&G.[11]

In addition, if Mill is correct regarding dead dogmas and the need for dispute, then that means that we will require the engaging of views, and perhaps even sincere individuals, that contradict the views we hold regarding R&G. If, however, we fail to engage and entertain those counter-views, then we lose full knowledge—*again*. As Mill argues, we would lose the only justification that mankind is capable of, the active collision between true and false views. At best, our views about R&G (though true) would only be another dogma. At worst, our views regarding them would be devoid of content.

By now we should see why offense is required. To have full knowledge of R&G requires that we actively encounter views that contradict positions in which we have a pro-disposition. Such an encounter, by the tension it brings, due to the affects involved, will lead to some uncomfortableness and disapprobation. It is this tension, then, that is offense. And, unfortunately, there is no way to avoid it without sacrificing moral knowledge. To stop the encounter leads to a dead dogma. To erase the affect leads to a variant of sematic dementia. Moral knowledge requires that one, to some degree, be offended.[12]

Concluding Thoughts

Before this chapter ends, I need to be careful that I am not "overselling" what the argument has accomplished. I have only claimed that someone must be offended, to some extent, in order to possess full moral knowledge. This does not entail that the offense experienced be large. In fact, if a person were to constantly engage in contentious debates regarding such ideas, the irritation should be rather benign and quite tolerable. That being said, this chapter is committed to there being at least some irritation while engaging views that forcefully argue against what one sincerely affirms to be good. In addition, I have not, in this argument, showed that the tradeoff between offense and knowledge should always favor the latter. There may be some cases in which the former is *so* harmful that it is not worth it to possess the attendant knowledge. I am skeptical that this is the case, but I admit that it is a possibility.

Notes

1. This essay has been improved by the thoughtful comments of Erica Ronning, Graham Peterson, Tyler England, Eric Webber, colloquium participants at UT-San Antonio, and the attendees at the 2017 Foundation for Individual Rights in Education (FIRE) faculty conference.
2. The study also found that 51 percent of students claimed that it was acceptable to disrupt a speech that proffered a viewpoint they disagreed with by "loudly and repeatedly shouting." In other words, the majority supported a heckler's veto.
3. There is no truth condition separate from your feeling. If you feel offended, *ceteris paribus*, then you are offended.
4. Person A may not be offended by X, though X is highly offensive to Person B. Moreover, A may find X offensive at Time T, but not find it offensive at Time T+1.
5. Of course, Mill acknowledges that it is more complicated than this. There can be partial truths and partial falsehoods.
6. For a more complete discussion regarding this sort of value judgment, see Gaus (1990, 157).
7. Gaus takes this term from Hervey Cleckley's famous work, *The Mask of Sanity*. In that work, Cleckley writes, "Semantic aphasia is, of course, a very different matter from the condition which we maintain exists in the so-called psychopath. It affords, however, an analogy which may help make clear the conception which we mean to offer as semantic dementia. Just as in semantic aphasia, meaning and the sense of things as a whole are lost in the circumscribed field of speech though the technical mimicry of language remains intact, in semantic dementia, the purposiveness, the significance of all life-striving and of all subjective experience are affected without obvious damage to the outer appearance of the personality" (2014, 269).
8. I should note that there have been more recent studies that seem to support Cleckley's claims regarding the semantic dementia of psychopaths. For example, a study by Williamson et al. had subjects sort words from non-words that flashed before their field of view. They found that nonpsychopaths responded quicker than psychopaths to the presence of emotional words, as opposed to emotional-neutral words (Williamson, Harpur, and Hare 1991, 263–264). Moreover, the authors wrote, "[W]hen confronted with a word and asked to judge its 'goodness,' psychopaths may be able to invoke alternative strategies, such as trying to guess how other people would judge the word, which could mask their inability to judge the word's affect for themselves" (Williamson,

Harpur and Hare 1991, 271). In another example, a study sought to "examine the psychopath's ability to interpret metaphors and to make decisions based on the emotional valence of such complex linguistic material" (Hervé, Hayes and Hare 2003, 1499). It found that psychopaths, unlike nonpsychopaths, "appeared to have considerable difficulty in sorting the metaphorical statements in terms of their emotional valence" (Hervé, Hayes and Hare 2003, 1504). The psychopaths, the authors conclude, "may have known what the sentence meant on a surface (semantic) level, but they appeared to ignore or miss its 'affective meaning' " (Hervé, Hayes and Hare 2003, 1505).

9. Gaus refers to this as *Weak Impersonality*:

    1. "X is V" always has a truth-value.
    2. This truth-value is nonrelative, that is, uniform across individuals. In particular, it is not relative to an individual's experience of X's value.
    3. For Alf to be entitled to assent to "X is V," it is not necessary that he has some personal experience of X's value.
    4. Those who rationally assent to "X is V" on the basis of personal experience have a fuller knowledge of X's value than do those who assent to "X is V" on other grounds.

    (1990, 149)

10. Of course, it is related. He is just not explaining, in detail, the phenomena regarding moral knowledge that I am describing.
11. One might suggest that *akrasia* would constitute a counterexample to the magnetism of "good." A person, for example, may claim that he fully knows that the right the thing to do is to get out of bed and exercise. His weak will, however, inclines him toward sleeping in. In response, I should note that I have not claimed that this magnetism is necessarily sufficient to fully determine a person's behavior. It is quite possible, and in many situations likely, that there will be countervailing impulses/drives to offset such magnetism. My argument only requires that the person feel some pull associated with "good." It does not require, however, that that pull fully determines an agent's behavior.
12. Of course, the degree to which each particular person feels "offended" will vary.

Works Cited

"Charles Murray at Middlebury: Unacceptable and Unethical, Say Over 500 Alumni." March 2, 2017. https://beyondthegreenmidd.wordpress.com/2017/03/02/charles-murray-at-middlebury-unacceptable-and-unethical-say-over-500-alumni/

Cleckley, Hervey M. *The Mask of Sanity: An Attempt to Clarify Some Issues About the So-Called Psychopathic Personality*. Whitefish, MT: Literary Licensing, 2014.

Feinberg, Joel. "Offense to Others, Selections." In *Philosophy of Law*, edited by Joel Feinberg and Jules Coleman. Belmont: Thomson Wadsworth, 2008: 438–455.

Gaus, Jerry. *Value and Justification*. Cambridge: Cambridge University Press, 1990.

Groetzinger, Kate. "Angry Student Activists Aren't a Problem, They're the Engine of Change." *Quartz*. November 19, 2015. https://qz.com/551802/guess-what-shouting-at-administrators-is-how-students-are-getting-things-done-at-brown/

Hervé, Hugues, Hayes, P. Justus and Hare, Robert. "Psychopathy and Sensitivity to the Emotional Polarity of Metaphorical Statements." *Personality and Individual Differences*, Vol. 35 (2003): 1497–1507.

Merriam-Webster. "Offense." *Merriam-Webster.com*. Accessed August 25, 2017. www.merriam-webster.com/dictionary/offense

Mill, John Stuart. *On Liberty and Other Writings*. Edited by Stefan Collini. Cambridge: Cambridge University Press, 1989.

Rauch, Jonathan. *Kindly Inquisitors*. Chicago: The University of Chicago Press, 1993.

Stevenson, C. L. "The Emotive Meaning of Ethical Terms." *Mind*, Vol. 46, No. 181 (1937): 14–31.

Villasenor, John. "Views Among College Students Regarding the First Amendment: Results From a New Survey." *Brookings*. September 18, 2017. www.brookings.edu/blog/fixgov/2017/09/18/views-among-college-students-regarding-the-first-amendment-results-from-a-new-survey/

"Wellesley Statement From CERE Faculty re: Laura Kipnis Freedom Project Visit and Aftermath." March 20, 2017. www.thefire.org/subject-facstaffdiscuss-statement-cere-faculty-re-laura-kipnis-freedom-project-visit-aftermath/

Williamson, Sherrie, Harpur, Timothy and Hare, Robert. "Abnormal Processing of Affective Words by Psychopaths." *Psychophysiology*, Vol. 28, No. 3 (1991): 260–273.

10 'Words that Wound' in the Classroom[1]

Should They Be Silenced or Discussed?

Christina Easton

Introduction

> During a debate on same-sex marriage, a student argues that homosexual acts are sinful and so they should not be endorsed by the state. At least one student in the room is homosexual.

Student speech like this will, at best, leave some students feeling uncomfortable and embarrassed. But there may be more destructive effects: The speech may reinforce negative social identities and damage the dignity and standing of some students in the class. As a consequence, some students may feel unable to participate fully in future classroom discussion, moving us further from an ideal of equal educational opportunity.

This example from my own teaching highlights that students' speech can deeply wound their peers, even whilst falling short of hate speech. I refer to such speech as "words that wound" (WtW)—speech that, given the context, is likely to cause harm.[2] Teachers have special responsibilities to care for the well-being of their students and promote equal educational opportunity. In light of this, how should teachers react to WtW?

This chapter discusses two possible ways that teachers might respond: *silencing* and *discussion*. (Later, I briefly discuss a third option, *advocacy*, where a teacher supports and justifies a particular view.) By "silencing," I mean the use of authority to curb any further expression or discussion of the offending speech.[3] This might be accompanied by sanctions, such as being "told off" by the teacher.[4] By "discussion," I mean critical dialogue, amongst students and facilitated by the teacher, about the claims underlying the speech. Whilst silencing is a narrow category, discussion is broad, since the level of teacher regulation of a discussion can vary. A teacher can steer discussion towards a certain outcome, to the extent that what *looks* like discussion is in fact closer to advocacy. Or, the teacher can stand back and leave it completely open as to where a discussion leads. When I talk about discussion, I am usually envisaging *open discussion*, where the teacher aims to be a neutral facilitator. However, I acknowledge that if discussion goes awry in relation to certain topics (such as the wrongness of racism), teachers will need to manipulate discussion more.

I refer to this sort of discussion as *steered discussion* and suggest in the section on "Guidance for Teachers" in what contexts this is appropriate.

Challenges

I argue that it is only in a small number of cases that teachers should silence their students' WtW. In most cases, the appropriate response is discussion. This is, perhaps, the common-sense view, but it nonetheless faces some important challenges.

Firstly, there is a challenge to provide a consistent defense of a position that advocates silencing for some cases but discussion for others. If we accept that there are cases where it is right that the teacher silence in order to protect students from harm, applying the same reasoning would appear to require silencing in other cases of harmful speech. Thus, there is a theoretical challenge to explain what is morally distinctive about the small number of cases where silencing is appropriate.

Secondly, having accepted that a relevant distinction exists, there is a challenge to provide a convincing case for discussion over silencing in the remaining cases. Given the costs of discussion, and the fact that it is often the most vulnerable students who bear these costs, how can we justify discussion as the right response?

Thirdly, there is a practical challenge to provide guidance for teachers on how to apply this theory in the classroom. Emma Arneback (2014) has argued that we should not give moral prescriptions to teachers other than that they attend to context. Her "Deweyan proposal" is that teachers must make use of "moral imagination" in deciding how to act in each individual case (269–270). But we can agree with Arneback on the importance of attending to context, without giving up on providing guidance altogether. The challenge is to be able to make some general statements about *how* context matters so as to enable *some* guidance.

Responding to the third challenge is important. Empirical studies in this area, alongside my own experiences of working with teachers at schools and universities, suggest that teachers generally lack confidence over how to respond to potentially harmful speech in the classroom.[5] As a result, some teachers try to minimize the chances of such speech occurring. For example, one study found that teachers at an integrated school in Northern Ireland deliberately avoided discussing issues over which Protestants and Catholics disagree, citing fear of "lots of rows" and "confrontation" (Donnelly 2004, 11). Similarly, a large, mixed-methods study of political discussions taking place in US high schools suggested that many of the teachers interviewed intentionally avoided discussion of controversial issues. This was justified by reasons of "safety, fairness or personal discomfort" (Hess and McAvoy 2015, 174).

Avoiding controversial issues in the classroom is concerning, since these will often be the same issues as those being debated in the democratic sphere. Thinking critically about these issues is therefore an important part of education for civic life. This adds urgency to the need for teacher guidance on how to identify and respond to wounding speech.

I begin by discussing what is distinctive about cases where the right response is silencing, adopting Eamonn Callan's (2011) distinction between "easy" and "hard" cases and offering my own interpretation of "hard" cases. I consider, and respond to, two of the strongest arguments for silencing in hard cases, and offer some positive arguments in favor of discussion. I identify one way in which Callan's defense of discussion is incomplete, noting that it cannot recommend discussion in what I call "harder" cases. To be able to defend discussion in these "harder" cases, more argument is required, and I sketch one such additional argument. I finish by addressing the practical challenge, by giving a four-part test to guide teachers in responding to WtW. This test sharpens Callan's distinction between cases where we should and should not silence, as well as providing guidance on when it is right for teachers to steer discussion towards a particular outcome.

Where examples are my own, they come from past experiences teaching children and young adults between eleven and eighteen years of age at English secondary schools. However, similar concerns appear at all levels of education, and what is said in this chapter applies to all age groups, from elementary to postgraduate level. Clearly, we need to adjust our responses according to the sensitivity of our students, their ability to engage in fruitful discussion, and other relevant factors that vary with age. However, age is partly accounted for in the guidance given below, since it will factor in how teachers answer each of the suggested questions in the flowchart.[6]

An Easy Case

Callan (2011, 4) gives the following as an example of an "easy" case:[7]

> *Easy Case:* A Political Science lesson is taking place on a topic unrelated to affirmative action. A Black student asks the teacher a question. A White student, unimpressed with the question, interrupts with "That's what you get with affirmative action."

Clearly, this interruption is likely to have negative effects on the black students in the class, especially on the student who is the target of this vilifying speech. Even the most charitable interpreter would struggle to see the speech as a well-intentioned contribution to the discussion, for it does not even relate to the lesson topic. Responding to such rudeness as if it were a legitimate academic contribution would lend undeserved acceptability and credibility to the speech and could exacerbate the negative impact on the targeted individual or group.

Here, and in comparable cases, it is right for the teacher to silence. For example, the teacher might reprimand the student for her rudeness and ask her to stay at the end of the class for a further dressing down.

A Hard Case

This is an adaptation of Callan's (2011, 4) "hard" case:[8]

> *Hard Case*: A Political Science lesson is taking place on affirmative action, in a mixed-race classroom that includes black students. During the discussion, Claire (a white student) puts her hand up and says that those who have benefited from affirmative action are academically weak. Their presence has diminished the standard of her education; they ask foolish questions and waste lesson time.

As in *Easy Case*, the speech in *Hard Case* is likely to cause hurt; these are undoubtedly WtW. Indeed, Callan suggests that the speech here may cause *more* offense, for it "cannot be so easily dismissed as mere oafish malice or stupidity which civilized people can be trusted to discount" (8). Since the immediate hurt caused by the speech is equal to or worse than in *Easy Case*, there is a prima facie case for responding in the same way here, namely, by silencing.

However, I side with Callan in arguing that discussion, rather than silencing, is the right response here.[9] The *Hard Case* is distinguished from the *Easy Case* by at least two features. Firstly, Claire's comment is *relevant* to the discussion taking place. This feature more easily allows the charitable interpreter to see the comment as being what Callan calls "made in good faith," that is, "sincerely expressed views intended to advance a common pursuit of truth" (7). Secondly and relatedly, the language used suggests an attempt at an academic contribution. It comments on subjects of affirmative action more generally, unlike the *ad hominem* swipe at a particular individual in *Easy Case*. Although this could be seen as worse since the scope for offense is wider, this same feature of "generality" makes the comment more easily interpretable as an academic claim.

Although Callan and I agree about the minimal use of silencing, we differ in our interpretation of hard cases. Callan deliberately sets up *Hard Case* as "an instance of serious incivility" (4). My category of hard cases is broader; even if the speech had been phrased more civilly, it would still count as a hard case because of negative effects brought about by the content of the speech. Callan comments on *Hard Case* that if the point had just been that affirmative action unjustly favors less meritorious students, there would be "no reason for anyone to be offended" (4). I disagree. Even civilly-phrased opinions about affirmative action easily result in offense. Indeed, Hess and McAvoy report that in *both* years that they observed a school tackle this topic, black students ended up in tears (2015, 123, 126). As should become clear when I discuss arguments in favor of silencing in hard cases, civilly-phrased speech will raise similar problems to uncivil speech.

Arguments for Silencing in Hard Cases

Silencing in hard cases involves curbing (at least purported) academic speech. Silencing could, over time, amount to censorship, since students may be afraid of making controversial comments. In light of this, powerful considerations need to be present in order to justify silencing. In this section, I discuss two of the strongest of these arguments.

Words as Harmful Acts

Catharine MacKinnon (1993) has famously argued that speech is not *just words*, for speech also *acts*. She gives the example of someone saying "kill" to an attack dog. Not only does the word indicate a viewpoint ("I want you dead"), its expression is also a performative act, "an act tantamount to someone's destruction" (12). Her analysis suggests that we should not see free speech as purely a matter of expression of opinions that may cause offense, but as potentially involving harmful *acts*. MacKinnon (13) argues that "social inequality is substantially created and enforced—that is, *done*—through words and images." Thus we could argue that the speech in *Hard Case* is not just expressing a viewpoint about affirmative action but is an act that reinforces existing social identities and re-asserts unequal power relations.

Clearly influenced by MacKinnon's ideas, Barbara Applebaum (2003) offers a defense of silencing WtW in the classroom. She discusses an example from her own teaching experience, where a student says that she accepts homosexuals because she "loves the sinner but hates the sin." We can view this example as a hard case, (roughly) comparable to our *Hard Case*. Applebaum argues that silencing is appropriate here and in comparable cases, because the student's speech is "an instrument of subordination as much as it is an expression of her viewpoint" (157). In Applebaum's view, WtW need silencing so that the classroom can be a "safe zone" for everyone's identity (161).

It is true that speech is often a form of action rather than "only words." However, this does not mean that the words spoken in hard cases are *instruments* of subordination. "Instrument" is suggestive of a user with an aim in mind, whereas in fact the negative effects (of subordination, of reinforcing stigmas and inequalities) may be present as an unintended side-effect of expressing an opinion. (This would be the charitable interpretation of the speech in *Hard Case*.) Additionally, regardless of whether the speech was intended as an "instrument of subordination," we should remember that such speech is at the same time expressing an opinion. Taken as an expression of a viewpoint (that exists regardless of whether it is voiced), such speech needs to be discussed rather than silenced, for the reasons set out in the next section.

We should also be careful not to overestimate the overall harm done to victims of WtW. In Hess and McAvoy's study, although some minority students reported finding particular discussions uncomfortable, they were nevertheless glad that the discussions took place. These students reported more confidence in their ability to discuss and "respond productively to offensive views" (2015, 175). The study observed discussion of many sensitive issues that were "extremely difficult for some students." Yet out of the hundreds of surveys and interviews, very few students thought that the issues should be stripped from the curriculum (179). This suggests that most students, including vulnerable minorities, felt that discussion of difficult issues was, on balance, worthwhile.

Stereotype Threat

The empirical literature on stereotype threat, beginning with the seminal study by Steele and Aronson (1995), suggests that WtW can also affect the *performance* of the subjects of such speech. Stereotype threat occurs when individuals feel at risk of performing in a way that confirms a negative stereotype. Victims of stereotype threat perform worse on relevant tasks than they do when the threat is not present. Even when unaware of stereotype threat, they show signs of a physical stress response, including elevated heart rate and blood pressure (Steele 2010, 119–120).

Stereotype threat is most likely to occur in situations where a group is negatively stigmatized in that particular context and where group membership is made salient. These are precisely the conditions brought about by the speech in *Hard Case* (and by extension, in *Easy Case*). The speech draws attention to an existing stereotype (that black students are less academically able) and makes black students hyper-aware of their race, potentially activating stereotype threat and leading to under-performance. It can therefore be argued that concern with equal educational opportunity should require silencing in *Hard Case*.

The argument from stereotype threat is particularly worrying for the defender of discussion, for it implies more than just that teachers should silence WtW in (at least some) hard cases. It also gives a reason for teachers to avoid *any* discussion of topics that draw attention to negative stereotypes. Discussing affirmative action will involve talk of (for example) accepting students with lower test scores. Simply by discussing the issue, race is made salient, potentially activating stereotype threat. So, perhaps the duty to promote equal educational opportunity requires that teachers steer clear of the topic of affirmative action altogether.

This worry can be alleviated by reflecting on the fact that many stereotypes can be *countered* via discussion. For example, arguments can be given that clear up the common misperceptions and errors of reasoning that lead to negative stereotypes. Where this is possible, discussion is less likely to undermine the confidence and performance of the subjects of such speech than is a negative stereotype being heard but not argued against. Indeed, such discussion may *improve* confidence and performance.[10] This intuitive suggestion is supported by a study by Spencer, Steele and Quinn (1999) which found that telling women that a maths test does *not* show gender differences improved their performance to the extent that they performed as well as men. Additionally, if the stereotype is discussed and argued against, over time opinions may change such that the stereotype gradually disappears, improving educational opportunity for future generations.[11]

The Positive Case for Discussion over Silencing

The literature has tended to emphasize the negative effects of WtW without justifying the assumption that silencing is the *best way* to mitigate the negative effects of such speech (see, for example, Applebaum 2003). In this section, I question this assumption by arguing that discussion has better long-term effects.

Silencing Does Not Address Underlying Viewpoints

In some, but not all cases, WtW will be evidence of hateful views lying behind the speech. If silenced, the view is left unaddressed and is left to linger, only to re-appear as speech and actions in other settings. An opportunity is lost to change the person's opinion by subjecting the view to rigorous discussion. Discussion has positive effects for vulnerable groups, as it corrects false stereotypes and helps contribute to *future* equal educational opportunity.

This optimism about the power of discussion to change false, hateful opinions is especially warranted in the case of young people, for often their views are taken unthinkingly from speech heard at home. In my experience, younger students will sometimes voice a viewpoint that they have heard their parents express but that they have not yet thought through for themselves. Once they realize that the viewpoint is debatable, and are presented with good reasons against their view by other students, they will often change their opinion (or at least temper it from its initial expression).

Rehearsing Arguments

We should also be concerned with the effects of silencing on students who hold views in opposition to the WtW. When a teacher silences rather than allows discussion, these students lose the opportunity to think through (or rehearse) the reasons for why they hold their views. This is important, for when opposing views surface in the world outside the classroom, students need to be able to provide arguments that defeat these views. This is, of course, a version of John Stuart Mill's "dead dogma" argument. Mill argued that we should allow false opinions to be heard and be the subject of discussion, for in silencing the opinion we lose the opportunity of "the clearer perception and livelier impression of truth produced by its collision with error" (2006, 23). I sometimes ask my students to defend their belief that "all races are equal." Their initial response is often silence. When I take up the role of devil's advocate, students are frequently unable to reply to the most basic of objections raised against racial equality. However, post discussion, they are able to do so, and leave armed with arguments to defeat racist views if they encounter them.

Silencing Models a Response Unavailable to Students

With the role of teacher comes the authority to silence. But in the ordinary spaces of daily life where WtW might be heard (pubs, staff kitchens, public transport, etc.), there is no authority to silence. It would therefore be unhelpful to use teacher authority to silence in situations like our *Hard Case*, for this would model a response that will usually be unavailable in the more everyday situations of harmful speech that occur *outside* the classroom. It would be like a rich Oxford don, tasked with educating undergraduates into college life, demonstrating how to tie his black tie by asking his valet to do it. To do so has little educational purpose, for it fails to model to the students a behavior that will be available to them. In contrast, if the teacher reacts to WtW by beginning a respectful exchange of arguments, the teacher models a response that students will have open to them in future.

Practicing the Virtues of Civic Discourse

Callan argues that excessive silencing will lead to an undesirable lack of candor in classroom discussions. Intellectual candor is "a cardinal virtue in a democratic culture of free speech" (2011, 13) because for discussions to be fruitful, we need our speech to reliably express what we stand for and who we are individually. Silencing would therefore come at great cost to free speech and the pursuit of truth (12).

We can build up Callan's case for discussion by seeing candor as one of a number of civic virtues that are developed via discussion of controversial issues (Easton 2018). Outside the classroom as much as inside the classroom, there is a requirement to carefully moderate one's speech and to find the right balance between candor and civility, especially when engaging with those with whom one disagrees. Learning the practical wisdom of treading the fine line between candor and incivility requires both modelling and practice. Silencing goes too far towards promoting civility and does so at the expense of candor, whereas discussion is a means by which we can teach students how to get the balance right.

Evaluating the Positive Case for Discussion Over Silencing

Why Discussion over Advocacy?

I have only considered the two options of silencing and discussion. An important option not considered here is advocacy, where the teacher supports and justifies a view. This omission is partly for simplicity, but there are also a number of reasons why advocacy should generally be avoided as a response to the sorts of situations considered in this chapter.

Firstly, this chapter focuses on speech that raises *political*, *ethical*, or *policy* questions.[12] Advocacy might be a valuable option in cases where the questions are *empirical* and *resolved within the academic community*. For example, if a student denies the Holocaust or climate change, it may be appropriate to respond simply by reporting the facts. Hess and McAvoy (2015, 163) consider a case where students were given an assignment to discuss whether the Holocaust happened. Unsurprisingly, this caused a great deal of controversy, and the authors conclude that "this is a clear example of why settled empirical questions should be taught as settled" (164). This case forms a useful contrast to hard cases for two reasons. Firstly, whether the Holocaust happened is an empirical question, and the academic community of historians are agreed on an answer. Secondly, the question was set by the teachers, implying that this is a question worthy of discussion. In our context, the *student* has brought up the viewpoint. Indeed, it is a feature of hard cases that these will often involve viewpoints that the teacher would not have chosen to bring into the discussion.

Secondly, there are pedagogical benefits to the teacher adopting a non-partisan stance on controversial matters and only *facilitating* discussion. In my experience, if the teacher takes a particular side, this has the effect of closing down discussion and pacifying students, either because they wait to be "instructed" about the correct way to think, or because they disagree with the teacher but feel that the imbalance in power means that there is no point trying to argue.

Moreover, there are plausible educational reasons for allowing students to reach conclusions via group discussion. Drawing on recent empirical research, Mercier and Sperber (2017) point to the epistemic gains that come from reasoning together. Reasoning as a group helps us correct flaws and formulate better, wiser beliefs. Students may also be more likely to hold onto viewpoints in the long-term if they arrive at these *by themselves*, because they have a sense of ownership. Mill (2006, 53) even seems to think that if beliefs are to constitute "knowledge" at all, we must understand their justification: "[N]o one's opinions deserve the name of knowledge, except so far as he has either had forced upon him by others, or gone through of himself, the same mental process which would have been required of him in carrying on an active controversy with opponents." We can take Mill's point that opinions have greater stability and resilience when they are reached via a reasoning process, without committing to his stringent understanding of knowledge. Moreover, beliefs arrived at in this way are more likely to be "living beliefs," "full of meaning and vitality," that will actually be acted upon (Mill 2006, 47). These are, of course, empirical claims that require testing, but they do fit with research pointing towards the positive effects of autonomy-supportive classrooms on learning (see, for example, Wang, Ng, Liu and Ryan 2016).

Thirdly, there are benefits to discussion that go beyond the concern with students leaving with a particular opinion. Discussion helps us better understand and empathize with each other, as well as contributing to the development of civic virtues required for active democratic citizenship. Although it might be possible to develop some of these virtues with only the help of a skilled teacher, other virtues need to be developed *in conversation with each other* over controversial issues, for it is this that teaches students how to respond appropriately to disagreement (Easton 2018).

Is Such Confidence in Discussion Justified?

I have not questioned the harms that come from WtW. Rather, the argument has been that discussion is less harmful in the long-run than silencing. An objector will question whether this confidence in the power of discussion is justified. Surely there is a real risk that discussion fails to address the harms caused by WtW; the victim's wounds are left undressed *and* any harmful beliefs that were present remain.

Callan considers a version of this objection and responds that the defender of discussion need not require that the speaker change their views. All that is required is that the discussion *mitigates* the negative effects of the WtW. Since the WtW have *already* been voiced, the harm is done, and "it would be foolish to suppose that silencing could simply cancel its effects any more than engagement would" (2011, 15). Discussion is the best way to blunt the potentially adverse effects of WtW.

Callan's reply does still require at least some optimism, however. He is still assuming that the outcome is not *worsened* by discussion. Yet this is a real possibility. Further instances of WtW may arise in the discussion that ensues, exacerbating the harm already caused to the victimized student(s). Even more worrying is the possibility that other students are "won over" by a speaker's arguments in favor of harmful views.

Callan's argument also relies on the fact that the WtW have *already* occurred. Since the harm is done, the question becomes one of how best to mitigate the harm, and this makes the job of defending discussion easier. However, teachers can easily engineer lessons to allow for the possibility of pre-emptive silencing. Here is an example from my own teaching:

> *Harder Case*: Students are working in pairs planning their contributions to a debate on the motion "Anyone should be allowed to have IVF." The teacher becomes aware that Rupal is going to put forward the point that being brought up by two lesbians is "not fair on the child, as they might also turn out a lesbian themselves." There is at least one "out" lesbian in the class. The teacher is easily able to avoid picking Rupal so that this contribution is not heard.

Not picking Rupal would have gone unnoticed by the class and would have avoided the negative effects on homosexual students. However, I did pick Rupal and her comment prompted a lively discussion.

This is not a rare situation; teachers can easily set up lesson activities in this way so as to minimize the chances of WtW being voiced. In these "harder cases," we cannot avoid the trade-off between the potential harms that will come from WtW and the potential benefits of discussion. So, if we want to argue for discussion over silencing in *Harder Case* (which I do, and I suspect Callan might too), we do not just need to show that the situation post discussion of WtW will be *the same or better* than where there has been WtW plus silencing. We must also show that the situation post discussion of WtW will be *the same or better* than where the WtW were *never heard at all*. This requires that discussion reap greater benefits than Callan assumes that he needs to argue for. Thus, we are back to where we began in the need to justify our confidence in the power of discussion.

This is a significant challenge, and the defender of discussion must take this worry seriously. If left unanswered, the challenge provides justification for shaping classroom activities so as to avoid WtW being spoken at all.

In response, we can once again rehearse the importance of engaging with harmful views rather than allowing them to linger and potentially reappear in less tightly controlled circumstances. Pre-emptive silencing in *Harder Case* allows no opportunity for correction or tempering of the view, even if just by the obvious questions "why would that make the child a lesbian?" and "what's so bad about the child being a lesbian anyway?" It remains a somewhat controversial question in society whether same-sex homes provide as good an upbringing for children as traditional homes, and so it is important that the next generation of citizens have discussed this issue.

We might also say the following as a last defense of discussion: The situation of *being in the classroom* (as compared to many other situations) supports confidence in the power of discussion.[13] The classroom is a controlled environment that should have clearly established rules for discussion. The group is united by an educative purpose, the pursuit of knowledge, and is guided towards this purpose by their teacher. Reason should rule here, rather than who can shout the loudest or who has most power. For these reasons, the classroom is the best place for discussion of controversial issues. If discussion goes awry and students are being led into unreasonable views, then in these "emergency circumstances" the teacher can guide discussion back "on track." A good teacher will have it within their capabilities to skillfully argue in support of the opposite view.

Guidance for Teachers

Arneback (2014, 270) claims that no prescriptions should be given to teachers on when to silence, beyond that they must attend to context. In this section, I respond to this challenge by showing *in what ways* context matters. Figure 10.1 gives a simplification of the thought process that a teacher might go through in making the difficult decision on when to silence.

In the remainder of this section, I discuss some new examples to exemplify each step in the flowchart.[14]

Amended Easy Case: A political science lesson is taking place on affirmative action. John, a white student, unimpressed with a contribution made by a black student, says "That's what you get with affirmative action."

Eugenics: A whole-class discussion is taking place amongst thirteen-year olds on the ethics of genetic engineering. Ajai (who has frequently exhibited disruptive behavior) suggests that "We could use it to get rid of Gingers."

Suicide: A discussion on euthanasia is taking place amongst eighteen-year olds. Simmy suggests that it may be rational for someone to commit suicide when there is nothing of value in their life. A fellow student's father recently committed suicide.

Nativity Play: A class of eleven-year olds are debating whether schools with high numbers of Muslim students should put on Nativity plays at Christmas. Laura suggests that schools should put on Nativity plays because if Muslims don't like it, they can "go home."

Amended Hard Case: A political science lesson is taking place on affirmative action, in a mixed-race classroom that includes black students. Charlie (a white student) argues that affirmative action schemes may not benefit the disadvantaged after all, because (for

Figure 10.1 Should this wounding speech be silenced?

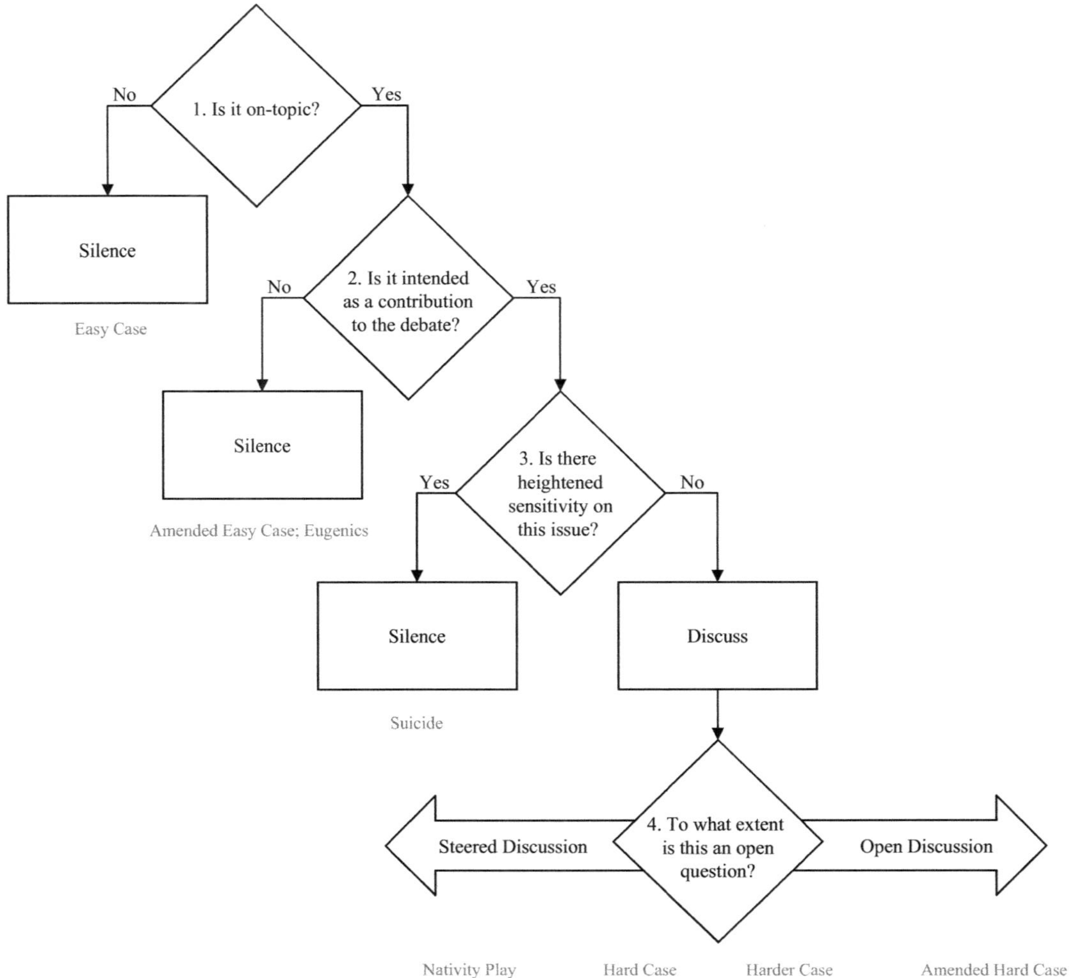

example) the beneficiaries of these schemes may struggle to meet the demands of university life.

A Pre-Condition for Discussion

An important pre-condition of discussion, which must be established before we start thinking through the steps in the flowchart, is that the classroom environment must allow for rational, sensitive discussion. The argument favoring discussion ended up hinging on the classroom as a place specially set up for fruitful discussion of controversial issues, yet this is not true of every classroom. A classroom lacking rules for discussion and led by a teacher with poor behavior management skills will not be the right environment for rigorous discussion. Nor will a classroom where (through no fault of the teacher) behavior is so challenging that the minimal level of order required for discussion cannot be achieved. We therefore need a proviso that the teacher has good control of the class and is capable of managing an organized, sensible discussion. He must also be reasonably competent on the subject, since he needs to be able to step in to defend certain views if the discussion goes awry.

Encompassed in "classroom environment" is the students' own abilities to engage in discussion. Mill (2006, 17) designated minors as falling below the line of "capable of being improved by free and equal discussion." My own experience suggests that students of at least eleven years old and above are capable of some "improvement" through discussion. However, the teacher must make a decision about whether their students can maturely and rationally discuss the particular instance of WtW.

If the right classroom environment is in place, the teacher is in a position to think through the steps in the flowchart. Each question in the flowchart allows for wide interpretation, and so the judgement and expertise of the teacher continue to be required throughout the decision-making process.

When to Silence

Step 1 asks whether the *content* of the speech relates to the lesson topic, allowing for silencing in cases of off-topic speech such as *Easy Case*. Off-topic speech cannot easily be seen as a "good faith" contribution aimed at furthering insight into the subject being discussed. So, being off-topic is a good indication that this speech will not pass through the next step.

Step 2 asks about the *intention* of the speech. Is the speech genuinely intended to be a contribution to the debate? Does the student really believe the view to be plausible? Working this out will depend on factors such as the tone of voice and body language. However, we can also look at the words themselves and ask whether there is a general, academic claim explicit in, or lying behind, the speech. Academic claims tend to make general statements rather than being aimed at specific members of the class. These claims may be reasonable or unreasonable; what is key is that the speech is not merely an *ad hominem* swipe.

Unlike in *Easy Case*, the comment in *Amended Easy Case* does relate to the lesson topic, but it is not intended to advance discussion on the legitimacy of affirmative action. Rather, John is making an *ad hominem* swipe with the intention of putting a fellow student down. His comment should therefore be silenced.

Similarly, *Eugenics* deserves a negative answer to Step 2. The charitable interpreter could try to see Ajai's remark as raising an academic question about the ethics of selecting for aesthetic features. However, this is a stretch. Given the context, it was clear that Ajai's comment was intended only to cause amusement and de-rail the lesson.

Whether a viewpoint is patently unreasonable or not may factor in your assessment of how to answer Step 2, for a view being utterly unreasonable should increase your skepticism about whether this is a genuine contribution to debate. However, the reasonableness of the viewpoint does not feature in the flowchart as an independent step in deciding whether to silence. This is because if a student *does* genuinely believe the view, then it is worth discussing. Such speech may raise issues that you would not *choose* to discuss if you were *selecting* topics for discussion, because they are not the subject of significant and reasonable disagreement. However, given that a student has spoken the words and genuinely believes them to be plausible, the view needs addressing through discussion.

On rare occasions, speech that it would *normally* be appropriate to discuss must be silenced, due to the heightened sensitivity of one or more students. This is the case in *Suicide*, which gets an affirmative answer to Step 3. Simmy's comment raises an interesting point, which is relevant to the topic and intended as a serious claim. However, in the current context, it is deeply insensitive to discuss it further, and so the right response is silencing. Unlike in the previous two cases, the silencing is not a rebuke. Rather, there is a quiet dismissal of the sub-topic and a redirection to other aspects of the less sensitive, wider topic.

Although both cases involve potential harm to fellow students, *Suicide* is unlike *Hard Case* (and other cases that should be discussed) because the sensitivity arises as a result of the specific timing of the speech. Discussion of Simmy's point can be delayed for another time when it will be less sensitive. In contrast, discussing affirmative action in a mixed-race classroom will always be sensitive, and yet it remains important for it to be discussed.

How to Discuss

All the remaining examples should be discussed, not silenced. But there are different ways to discuss a topic. *How* the teacher approaches a discussion should be affected by the extent to which the speech raises an open question. Here an open question is defined as one where there is both reasonable disagreement—where there are arguments on both sides that have a chance of convincing a rational person—*and* where there is significant disagreement in society over this issue.[15]

In *Amended Hard Case* the teacher can allow open discussion. The question of whether affirmative action benefits the disadvantaged is one where plausible arguments can be provided on both sides. There also exists a good deal of disagreement in society over the legitimacy of affirmative action.

The view voiced in *Nativity Play* has significant public support, but despite this, should not be seen as raising an open question. The Muslim children who Laura is referring to *are* (officially) home, and so the view expressed cannot be reasonably supported. The teacher should therefore be ready to engineer the discussion towards cultivating a more sympathetic approach to British Muslims who have already made their home in the UK.[16] The teacher may not need to intervene in order to achieve this aim, because Laura's view may be adequately addressed by the responses of other students. (This is in fact what happened in my classroom. The responses included a Muslim student objecting that "I am home.")

This example demonstrates that often there will be no difference in *practice* between a teacher's approach to open and closed questions, because the student discussion will often "put to bed" unreasonable views. The difference lies in the teacher's *aim*, for with closed questions the teacher is ready to steer discussion in a particular direction if necessary.

Much speech will be hard to place in the continuum between open and closed questions, and the teacher will have to make a difficult judgement over the extent to which discussion should have a predetermined outcome. In *Hard Case*, some steering may be necessary to correct any false views about standards in Claire's class and to point out the way that diversity might improve standards. However, there remains disagreement over this and related questions, and so the direction of discussion should not be entirely prescribed.

I have placed *Harder Case* in the middle. We might steer the discussion so as to bring out false assumptions underlying the view expressed about lesbians. But there remains significant disagreement in society over whether same-sex homes provide as good an upbringing for children as traditional homes. Some teachers will disagree with my positioning of *Harder Case*, arguing that it is wrong to present gay rights issues as open-ended.[17] Such disagreement is to be expected, as it is controversial whether there is "reasonable disagreement." Whether a question is open will also change over time; issues that were once open, such as whether women should have the vote, are no longer open. Teachers must therefore engage in continual critical reflection, as well as deliberation with colleagues, on how to approach these difficult issues.

Conclusion

The on-the-spot moral decisions that teachers must make when managing their classroom have high stakes attached. Student speech can wound other students, reinforcing social inequalities and taking us further from an ideal of equal respect and dignity for all. The phenomenon of stereotype threat shows that there is at least one reason to worry about the costs of WtW to equality of educational opportunity.

Whilst acknowledging this, I have endorsed the view that discussion is the best remedy for WtW. Although there may be costs that come when WtW are not silenced, in most cases these costs will be outweighed by the benefits of discussion. WtW can be symptomatic of harmful views, views which (left unaddressed) may influence behavior in the school corridors and other public spaces. Classroom discussion provides opportunities for the speaker of WtW to hear arguments against their view, as well as for students to rehearse or formulate arguments defending the opposite view. Additionally, students learn how to respond appropriately to WtW that might occur in public spaces in future. By participating in discussion of controversial issues, students develop important skills required for democratic participation. They practice the virtues needed to engage in fruitful, civil political discourse.

The classroom provides the right conditions for discussion to bear these fruits, for classroom discussion is guided by pre-established rules and is framed by the pursuit of knowledge. The discussion is facilitated by a teacher with the disciplinary and intellectual authority to influence the direction of discussion if this becomes necessary.

Not all cases of harmful speech are the same. My aim has been to show that although no simple formula can be given as to when we should silence, we can pin down at least some relevant considerations for making this judgement. In a small number of cases, the content and context of the speech means that we must silence in order to make clear that such speech is unacceptable or to protect the heightened sensitivities of our students. In the harder cases of WtW, there is an uncomfortable trade-off to navigate between the adverse effects of hearing such speech and the benefits that come from discussion.

The challenging decision on when to silence will require the professional judgement of the teacher, made in light of their specific context, including a deep knowledge of the individuals in their class. However, contrary to Arneback (2014), some guidance is possible. The flowchart provides a tool to guide teachers in identifying which features of student speech should be attended to when making this difficult decision.

Notes

1. I am grateful to Luc Bovens, Valerie Davis, Stuart Easton, Mike Otsuka, Robert Simpson, and participants in the LSE Philosophy Research Seminar for their comments on drafts of this chapter.

2. Speech can cause great upset and/or have highly immoral intentions without constituting hate speech. Since I allow that speech may qualify for silencing despite not constituting hate speech, "WtW" is a more useful category for the purposes of this chapter (see Callan 2011, 8). The expression "words that wound" originates in Delgado (1982).
3. Teachers may need to silence for other reasons, including off-topic speech, excessive speech, or speech that exhibits bad manners not because of its *content* but because of its manner of delivery (for example, it is an interruption). My claims about the limited use of silencing are intended to apply only to silencing *in response to WtW*.
4. I artificially treat silencing as a narrow, tightly-bounded category, when in fact there are different ways that a teacher might silence, and the right method of silencing will depend on the context. Sometimes it will be appropriate to silence in a way that includes the teacher making clear that the expressed viewpoint is wrong and/or abhorrent. This type of silencing is still different from what I call *advocacy*, which I take to involve more speech and a justification of the view being advocated.
5. For examples, see Ofsted (2010) and Oulton, Day, Dillon and Grace (2004).
6. Since I intend my discussion to be applicable to the "classroom" in this wide sense, rather than just to *children*, I do not discuss arguments appealing to the special vulnerability of children. Yet it does seem that where children are involved, more hangs on responding appropriately to WtW. Children are in a process of moral development and may be especially susceptible to picking up negative identity-prejudicial attitudes. Children may also be in a particularly malleable stage in their own identity-formation. For a discussion of arguments relating to the special harmfulness of hate speech when it comes to children, see Simpson (unpublished).
7. The example comes from Elizabeth Anderson (1995, 211), who describes it as an incident occurring at the University of Michigan.
8. I present the example slightly differently. For example, Callan has a black student speaking first, which I have removed so as to avoid readers assuming that the WtW are a direct retort to the black student's contribution. With Callan (2011, 19, n.3), I assume that the tone of voice, body language and volume of the speech indicate that this was not a comment deliberately aimed to denigrate other students.
9. Inviting discussion does not mean that the teacher should ignore that the point should have been better phrased. The teacher might take Claire aside to point out the hurt that her comment caused, and may even ask the whole class to reflect on how similar comments might be phrased in more civil language.
10. This coheres with the findings by Hess and McAvoy (2015, 175) described earlier in this section.
11. This response only works where the stereotype is a false one. If there are (for example) some unpalatable truths about gender or racial differences, then there is a distinct and difficult question to be answered about whether these views should be discussed or silenced. Discussion might have the effect of worsening performance due to activation of stereotype threat. However, honest and frank discussion might help those involved deal with the realities of difference.
12. Hess and McAvoy (2015, 161) draw a distinction firstly between empirical and political/policy questions and secondly between open and settled questions. They argue that when selecting issues for discussion in Social Studies, teachers should normally select open political/policy questions. Although

I largely agree with their conclusions, this chapter takes a more inclusive approach to what should be the subject of discussion, by allowing discussion of settled questions. This is because our question of how teachers should react to comments *made by students* is a different (though related) question to how teachers should decide which topics to put on the agenda for discussion.

13. Cf. Callan's (2011, 14) comment that "classrooms . . . are about as auspicious a setting for Brandeisian confidence as we could hope to find." However, note that what Callan describes as "open dialogue" is in fact closer to what I call "steered discussion" (2011, 13–14). As a result, his reasons for being confident about classroom discussion relate more to the authority and abilities of the teacher, who has the upper-hand in an argument, whereas my reasons relate more to wider considerations about the nature and purpose of the classroom.
14. With the exception of the amended easy and hard cases, these are real examples from past teaching.
15. My view on what makes a question "open" is influenced by Hess and McAvoy (2015, 168).
16. In this and other cases, the teacher may decide to redirect discussion onto a more open question. For example, Laura's comment could be seen to raise wider issues about immigration and/or the extent to which the more traditional culture should be prioritized.
17. Hess and McAvoy report that teachers were split on the issue of whether gay marriage should be framed as a controversial issue. Some saw it as "a human rights question for which there is a correct answer" (2015, 159) whereas others pointed to the ongoing political and legal controversies as evidence of its controversial nature.

Works Cited

Anderson, E. "The Democratic University: The Role of Justice in the Production of Knowledge." *Social Philosophy and Policy*, Vol. 12 (1995): 186–219.

Applebaum, B. "Social Justice, Democratic Education and the Silencing of Words That Wound." *Journal of Moral Education*, Vol. 32, No. 2 (2003): 151–162.

Arneback, E. "Moral Imagination in Education: A Deweyan Proposal for Teachers Responding to Hate Speech." *Journal of Moral Education*, Vol. 43, No. 3

Callan, E. "When to Shut Students Up: Civility, Silencing, and Free Speech." *Theory and Research in Education*, Vol. 9, No. 1 (2011): 3–22.

Delgado, R. "Words That Wound: A Tort Action for Racial Insults, Epithets and Name-Calling." *Harvard Civil Rights-Civil Liberties Law Review*, Vol. 17, No. 1 (1982): 133–182.

Donnelly, C. "What Price Harmony? Teachers' Methods of Delivering an Ethos of Tolerance and Respect for Diversity in an Integrated School in Northern Ireland." *Educational Research*, Vol. 46, No. 1 (2004): 3–16.

Easton, C. "Educating in Respect: Against Neutral Discourse as a Norm for Respectful Classroom Discussion." *Philosophy*, Vol. 93, No. 2 (2018).

Hess, D. E. and McAvoy, P. *The Political Classroom: Evidence and Ethics in Democratic Education*. New York: Routledge, 2015.

MacKinnon, C. A. *Only Words*. Cambridge, MA: Harvard University Press, 1993.

Mercier, H. and Sperber, D. *The Enigma of Reason*. London: Allen Lane, 2017.

Mill, J. S. *On Liberty and the Subjection of Women*. London: Penguin Classics, 2006.

Ofsted. "Transforming Religious Education." *The National Archives*. June 2010. Accessed November 22, 2017. http://webarchive.nationalarchives.gov.uk/20141105214525/www.ofsted.gov.uk/sites/default/files/documents/surveys-and-good-practice/t/Transforming%20religious%20education.pdf

Oulton, C., Day, V., Dillon, J. and Grace, M. "Controversial Issues: Teachers' Attitudes and Practices in the Context of Citizenship Education." *Oxford Review of Education*, Vol. 30, No. 4 (2004): 489–507.

Simpson, R. M. "'Won't Somebody Please Think of the Children?' Hate Speech, Harm and Childhood." Unpublished paper, University College London.

Spencer, S. J., Steele, C. M. and Quinn, D. M. "Stereotype Threat and Women's Math Performance." *Journal of Experimental Social Psychology*, Vol. 35 (1999): 4–28.

Steele, C. M. *Whistling Vivaldi and Other Clues to How Stereotypes Affect Us*. New York: Norton, 2010.

Steele, C. M. and Aronson, J. "Stereotype Threat and the Intellectual Test Performance of African-Americans." *Journal of Personality and Social Psychology*, Vol. 69 (1995): 797–811.

Wang, J. C. K., Ng, B. L. L., Liu, W. C. and Ryan, R. M. "Can Being Autonomy-Supportive in Teaching Improve Students' Self-Regulation and Performance?" In *Building Autonomous Learners: Perspectives From Research and Practice using Self-Determination Theory*, edited by W. C. Liu, J. C. K. Wang and R. M. Ryan. Singapore: Springer (2016): 227–243.

11 Speech and War

Rethinking the Ethics of Speech Restrictions[1]

Burkay T. Ozturk and Bob Fischer

Introduction

Universities regulate speech in various ways: They disinvite some speakers and invite others in their stead; they cancel events entirely; they make it financially impossible for students to organize events in the first place; they interpret speech as harassment, and then discipline the speaker; they develop speech codes against "offensive" speech; they discourage faculty from developing certain courses or covering certain material in existing courses.[2] How should we assess when such restrictions are justified, if they ever are?

Here, we propose an answer to this question. In short, we argue that we should think about speech restrictions as being like acts of war, and so should approach their justification using just war theory. We also make some suggestions about its implications. For instance, one of the *jus ad bellum* requirements for a just war is that you have a reasonable hope of success; you shouldn't enter or continue a war unless you've got good reason to think that your objectives are achievable. We offer some reasons to think that many speech restrictions fail to pass this test in our current political climate: We are too far from the kind of society that universities hope to create via speech restrictions, and in employing them, they only exacerbate the problems they're trying to solve.

The plan is as follows. First, we criticize the standard way of thinking about the ethics of speech restrictions—namely, one based on the "marketplace of ideas" metaphor. We contend that this approach is problematic because it overlooks the ways in which the aims of speech differ from the aims of market transactions. Second, we introduce just war theory, which we think is a more promising fit with the telos of speech than the ethics of the marketplace, and examine in some depth the just cause, necessity, and likelihood of success conditions it sets over just war. Based on this, we conclude that if we see speech restrictions as acts of war, there are good reasons to doubt that most speech restrictions on campuses today could satisfy these three conditions.

The Marketplace Metaphor and its Problems

We have two aims in this section. The first is to get a standard way of thinking about free speech on the table. The second is to suggest why it's inadequate for dealing with the question we want to pursue here—namely, how we ought to assess when speech restrictions are justified.

The Marketplace Metaphor

In 1919, Justice Holmes wrote this:

> [W]hen men have realized that time has upset many fighting faiths, they may come to believe even more than they believe the very foundations of their own conduct that the ultimate good desired is better reached by free trade in ideas—that the best test of truth is the power of the thought to get itself accepted in the competition of the market, and that truth is the only ground upon which their wishes safely can be carried out. That at any rate is the theory of our Constitution.
> (*Abrams v. United States*, 250 U.S. 616, 630 (1919))

This passage appears in Holmes's dissenting opinion in *Abrams v. United States*, the details of which aren't particularly important here. What does matter, however, is that his position has become central to our contemporary conception of speech. We now model the exchange of ideas on the exchange of goods, and insofar as we value free markets, the marketplace metaphor encourages us to value free speech. What's more, insofar as we see universities as institutions tasked with seeking and disseminating the truth, we have special reason to value free speech in that context.

There are, of course, some reasons to doubt that Holmes's view is correct. Consider, for instance, the enduring appeal of figures like Milo Yiannopoulos—a once-prominent figure in the alt-right movement and a former senior editor at Breitbart—who made a name for himself mocking Muslims, proponents of political correctness, fat people, and lesbians (among many others). For some time, Yiannopoulos was a popular figure on the college speaking circuit, despite remarkable resistance to his presence on various campuses. In February 2017, for example, Yiannopoulos was scheduled to appear at the University of California, Berkeley. He was prevented from speaking by protesters who injured at least six people and caused about $100,000 in property damage.[3] In August of that year, Yiannopoulos tried to come again. He was scheduled as part of *Free Speech Week*, an event organized by a conservative student group. However, the group decided to cancel the event at the last minute, citing obstruction by Berkeley's administration and credible threats from ANTIFA. Yiannopoulos insisted on coming anyway.[4] His speech was drowned out by protesters.[5]

Yiannopoulos is largely a provocateur, with little to offer in the way of intellectual rigor. Still, conservative student groups are attracted to his ideas, and they are willing to take on significant costs and risks to have him visit. So we might worry, with Aaron Hanlon (2017), that the marketplace of ideas isn't going to bring the truth to light. As he puts it:

> The problem . . . is that the "marketplace of ideas" is a misleading metaphor for what's really happening with campus speakers [like Yiannopoulos]. Such a "marketplace" does a poor job of signaling and rewarding quality speech and valuable ideas, exemplified by the enthusiasm with which students embrace controversy over substance. And unlike the marketplace for material goods—in which it's a boon, not a problem, for some loyal consumers to sustain Oreos cookies while others buy Hydrox—the "marketplace of ideas" metaphor promises something more than "to each her own."

Hanlon is correct in one respect and wrong in another. He's correct that we should worry about "markets" favoring intellectually cheap, cognitively sweet, and socially unhealthy ideas over their superior alternatives. Convenient fictions are always going to be tempting, and there is no guarantee that certain demographics—or even the majority—won't choose them. He's wrong, of course, in suggesting that this is a problem with the marketplace metaphor. To the contrary, Yiannopoulos's popularity validates the metaphor, just not Holmes's specific hope for the free trade of ideas. For decades now, there has been sustained demand for crystal meth and land mines in actual, real, concrete, 100-percent non-metaphorical markets. Problematic goods are always going to be desirable, and those who oversee markets have to find ways to deal with them.

At this juncture, we should note that in and of itself, the marketplace metaphor isn't incompatible with speech restrictions. Just as there may be various morally legitimate reasons for restricting the sale of specific goods—such as crystal meth and landmines—so there may be various morally legitimate reasons for restricting speech. Thus, although a completely free market in ideas may not achieve Holmes's vision, the hope is that a regulated one just may. However, we submit that there are good reasons not to approach speech restrictions on college campuses through the lens that the marketplace metaphor provides. These reasons concern the value and telos of speech.

The Value and Telos of Speech

The fundamental problem with the marketplace metaphor is that it rests on false assumptions about the value and ends of speech. Speech matters to us for many reasons, but that isn't obvious from the marketplace metaphor. Of particular relevance here is the fact that markets are based on the idea that we want to be able to interact with one another, that our goal is to have a shared space in which everyone can conduct transactions with everyone else. The restrictions serve to manage the competing interests of people who, ultimately, want to interact with one another in various ways—buying, selling, negotiating, and so on. And sometimes, of course, that's the goal of speech too: We want to be able to argue about matters of importance; we want to be able to protest perceived wrongdoing, especially when we don't see adequate remedies available from existing institutions; we want to be able to promote our respective visions of things. In these cases, we are looking for people with whom we disagree; we want there to be an exchange of ideas that resembles something like a market. However, the telos of speech isn't always—or perhaps even usually—"selling" one's views to others. We protect speech in part to allow people to set up their own communities, with values and ways of operating that aren't meant to be universally shared. Speech is often about opting out of one community to form a different one.

This idea should be familiar to the student of US political history. The fact that the Bill of Rights starts out by guaranteeing freedom of speech, religion, and assembly is highly suggestive; the US Constitution, and the socio-political order it established, prize the right of individuals and communities to pursue their lives quite independently of one another, at least in certain crucial respects. So perhaps, the Framers established a system of rights in which speech isn't just a tool for the dissemination of ideas: It's also way of telling the world who you are and for aligning yourself with like-minded people.

This constitutional interpretation, moreover, is in line with the practical reality on the ground. For both individuals and groups, speech is essential to marking boundaries between themselves and the rest of the world. Without speech, our ability to draw lines between our comprehensive doctrines and those of others—between our moral, metaphysical, and political outlooks—would be severely hampered. In this way, these three basic rights are linked. We have an interest in being able to associate with those with whom we disagree, at least in certain venues and at certain times, as we want the opportunity to persuade them. But we also have an interest in being able to associate with those with whom we agree, at least in certain venues and at certain times, so as not to need to engage with those with whom we are at odds, and to be able to organize our ideological lives as we see fit.

Someone might think that none of this is particularly relevant to campus speech restrictions, as the aim in that context is always dialogue across ideology, and never simply within an ideological perspective. However, the vision of the university as a completely open forum is clearly mistaken.

First, as Jacob Levy argues, the university is set up to create spaces where people can have conversations that build on shared assumptions, ignoring challenges to them for the time being. This is most obvious when challenges are incompetent. Geologists have no obligation to invite members of the Flat Earth Society to give colloquium talks, just like biologists have no duty to "teach the controversy" between evolution and creation "science." However, even competent objections can be excluded in the right context. For instance, physicists are quite right to go on doing their investigations even when philosophers think that their research begs various important questions; they don't need to spend all their time responding to our challenges, or even to include a philosopher to speak critically at their events. Likewise, no one blames sociologists when they proceed without worrying about the criticisms of economists, or literary theorists when they don't engage with arguments from anthropology. There's a time and a place for interdisciplinary investigation and the questioning of foundational assumptions, but it isn't every day and everywhere on campus. As experts, we justifiably spend most of our time working within certain ideological frameworks, and we don't have to constantly question the merits of those frameworks. So, insofar as the associative dimension of speech is aimed toward establishing communities of inquiry on campus, or contribute to existing ones, it's in line with what universities already permit—and, indeed, highly value.[6]

Second, it's worth remembering that in the context of the modern university, quite a lot of controversial speech really isn't directed toward those who most strenuously object to it. Ideological tribes are sufficiently well established that there is little reason to think that we are going to convert detractors with our arguments. Liberals are not suddenly going to be convinced—or even slowly be convinced—that it's a great idea to have fewer firearm restrictions, or that abortions should be more difficult to get, or that we should place substantially more emphasis on personal responsibility in our discussions of poverty. Similarly, conservatives are not suddenly going to be convinced—or even slowly be convinced—that we should push for mass disarmament, that we should have easily-accessible abortion on demand at all stages of pregnancy, or that we should place much more emphasis on the structural explanations of poverty. People are dug in on these issues. So, there's an important sense in which speech about them isn't really participating in the marketplace of ideas, insofar as there is one. Instead, it's largely a mixture of preaching to the choir and attempting to secure converts from the undecided—not actually engaging with those most suited to be critical interlocutors. We might not like this situation, but we shouldn't ignore it either. Ideological balkanization is real (and is growing).[7] And the result is that if we value free speech in contexts where we can't convince our interlocutors, not because our arguments are poor but because our tribal identities are getting in the way, then it's a mistake to frame the value of our speech in terms of a marketplace of ideas. Speech is, among other things, about building and maintaining communities, part of which involves protecting them from ideological attacks. Insofar as association matters, speech does—not because it's always about unity, but precisely because it often isn't.

Indeed, the world of ideas today resembles the fractured landscape of nation states, each maintaining its borders via military measures, more than it resembles any marketplace, whether fictional or real. And that's a reason for favoring a different normative framework for thinking about the ethics of speech restrictions.

An Alternative: Speech and War

Just war theory is an attempt to identify those conditions under which wars can be justly entered and justly fought. The *jus ad bellum* conditions specify the former; the *jus in bello* requirements, the latter. The standard *jus ad bellum* conditions include having a just cause, there being the likelihood of success, having legitimate authority to begin the conflict, waging war with the right intention, the proportionality of the war, and the necessity of violence—i.e., its being a last resort. The standard *jus in bello* requirements include discrimination (i.e., intentionally targeting only combatants and trying to avoid killing or injuring civilians), the proportionality of the force you employ, and the necessity of that particular military action. Unsurprisingly, there is a vast literature on the proper interpretation of these conditions; ample debate over whether each one is necessary and whether they are, jointly, sufficient for just engagement; and a range of debates about the complexities of institutionalizing particular versions of this moral framework in various political and historical contexts. We don't have space here to explore these issues in detail, and so our aim here is modest. We simply want to outline the way that we might approach the ethics of speech restrictions from this perspective, granting that if this approach is fruitful, it will be important, in future work, to refine what we say in light of theoretical details that simply can't concern us here.[8]

In any case, the appeal of employing just war theory should be clear: It's designed to provide an account of when actions that would normally be impermissible are, in fact, permissible. After all, its sole purpose is to answer the question: What makes it morally acceptable to engage in conduct—such as killing and maiming—that is normally wrong? In the present context, that helps us answer a parallel question: What makes it permissible to restrict speech, which would normally be a serious violation of a basic interest?

This way of thinking should be intuitive even given Holmes's approach to free speech. For Holmes, free speech wasn't valuable in and of itself. Instead, it was valuable because of the way that it might contribute to the goal of finding the truth. The idea, of course, was that the truth might emerge through the free exchange of ideas. Insofar as that hope has any basis at all, and insofar as universities are supposed to be institutions that create and transmit knowledge, we should regard as central to university life that people be given the liberty to explore, articulate, and defend a wide range of theses, whether popular or not, in their respective communities of inquiry. And since such activity is central to university life, there should be a high bar for restricting speech; it should be seen as among the weightiest decisions, if not the weightiest decision, ever made by members of the university community. And if that's right, then the attraction of just war theory—the *jus ad bellum* conditions in particular—is that it's designed to regulate such high-stakes decisions.

In what follows, we'll focus our attention on three *jus ad bellum* conditions—just cause, necessity, and likelihood of success—as they promise especially valuable insights into the ethics of many current speech restrictions.[9] And we should say that while we're focusing on the *jus ad bellum* conditions, the motivations for the two sets of conditions are often similar. For instance, the reasonable hope of success condition is motivated by the idea behind the proportionality condition, which is part of *jus in bello* as well. The goal of the proportionality condition is to ensure that the reasons in favor of fighting actually outweigh those against, lest we jeopardize lives and waste considerable resources without sufficient cause. (On this, see Suarez's *On War*, section IV, §10.) And, of course, one way to lack sufficient cause is to have success be so unlikely that it is irrational to bet on it, at least where other options are available. So because the proportionality condition applies both when deciding whether to begin a war and when engaged in one, and we could make similar points for the other conditions, very little turns on the choice to focus our attention on the *jus ad bellum* requirements—that is, we doubt that it makes much difference whether we frame speech restrictions as an initial act of war or as an act within an existing conflict. The same kinds of moral constraints obtain either way.

In any case, let's now consider a few conditions of just war and their implications for speech restrictions on campus.

Just Cause

Standard just war theory and international law recognizes only two legitimate reasons to start or enter a war: self-defense (properly understood) and humanitarian causes (which can usually be construed as third-party defense). In principle, such reasons could also justify restricting speech on campuses. Indeed, the proponents of speech restrictions use both self-defense (i.e., defending the university as a community of inquiry) and defense of others (i.e., defending the minorities on and outside the campus) as justification for restricting speech. When we examine these justifications however, it's hard to claim that they could constitute genuinely just causes.

Self-Defense as Just Cause

Let's first address the claim that speech restrictions are actions committed in defense of the university as a community of inquiry. Some proponents of this claim argue that certain conservative opinions aren't welcome at universities, as Oxford law professor Leslie Green put it recently and bluntly, "*because they are universities*."[10]

Here, the reasoning is based on the thought that, in addition to a general freedom of association, there is a specific corollary—a freedom of intellectual association. The freedom to associate with whomever you'd like is of obvious value: We are inherently social beings for whom the good life depends, in large part, on our being able to enjoy the company of particular people and exclude others, where "company" should be understood to include not only physical proximity but also intellectual affinity. Just like a nation state has a right to protect its borders from intrusion, by military action if necessary, an intellectual community also has a right to protect itself from outsiders.

This line of reasoning, however, is not applicable to universities, which are *special* intellectual communities. What makes them special is that they are built around the idea of free inquiry. It matters a great deal that we have conversations that advance our understanding, spur us on to appreciate new things, and challenge our ideas in ways we find constructive.

One worry, then, about disinviting, banning, or otherwise impeding the presence of a particular visitor—at least when that visitor aims to address the university community (or some part of it), and not simply use university facilities to speak to a largely independent audience—is that it might inhibit the kind of free association that's central to intellectual life. The same applies to restricting the speech of faculty members and students, insofar as it prevents them from having the kinds of conversations that they might like to have. Banning speech is a blow against these communities of inquiry, which is particularly objectionable when ideas are excluded because they may offend and without due consideration of their merits. Again, this is worrisome precisely because of the link between speech and the freedom of intellectual association: By restricting speech in this way, administrators make it impossible for faculty and students to maintain communities of inquiry one needs in order to do research, teach, and learn effectively.

Plainly, it's possible to take this line of thought too far. Universities aren't just venues for independent intellectual communities to gather and operate more or less independently. They are, as we've said, communities that produce knowledge. As a result, it's perfectly appropriate for them to have standards of intellectual rigor—indeed, they are central to their mission—and to consider whether the standards are being met when deciding whether to give a platform to particular people. So it doesn't follow from what we've said that every crank deserves a place in the classroom or in the lecture hall. Some people don't deserve a hearing, and that's due to what we know about the way they reach their conclusions.

However, we are not debating whether to let fortunetellers have access to the platform that universities can provide. Those are the kinds of cases that are easy to rule out by appealing to standards of intellectual rigor. The interesting cases are the ones that generally make the news: for example, disinviting Charles Murray or trying to restrict certain views about gender or gender identity from being explored. Here, we should be highly skeptical of arguments to the effect that the relevant speakers failed to live up to the standards of the university. After all, in the domains in question, the standards of the university are quite permissive. English departments tolerate a wide range of disagreements about what's true, how you might know, and how willing we should be to follow various intellectual trends; likewise for anthropology, psychology, history, and plenty of others. If many of our colleagues deserve tenure, then the conservative ideas that tend to be the objects of speech restrictions are likely to meet the going standard of rigor—whatever problems they may ultimately have. So, we can't defend anti-conservative speech restrictions based on the idea that doing so is necessary to defend the university itself.

We can reach the same conclusion via a different route. Consider Kuhn's distinction between normal and revolutionary science. There is a sense in which normal science is uncritical: Scientists operating in the normal mode somewhat dogmatically presuppose a central conceptual framework, which Kuhn called a "dominant paradigm," and focus their critical attention only on the periphery of that scheme. In the case of contemporary physics, the fundamentals of the atomic theory are part of the central framework. Thus, assuming that physics today is normal, physicists would not and should not question those fundamentals. Instead, they do and should focus on debates about the details of the atomic theory, concerning the exact half-life of a newly discovered isotope, or on controversies over different measurement methods.

Normal science, however, isn't all there is to science. Science, according to Kuhn, must also necessarily undergo a revolutionary phase when failed predictions and inexplicable phenomena start cluttering a discipline. This is a time of crisis when the relatively dogmatic approach of normal scientists should give way to criticism of the fundamentals. In such seasons, gadflies must not only be allowed but actively encouraged. So, when physics is in crisis, the physics department might want to bring over the otherwise-troublesome philosopher. When sociologists can't seem to predict much that's empirically meaningful, they should engage with their critics from economics.

As many[11] have rightly observed, though, Kuhn's model is only a rough approximation of what actually happens in science. Rarely, if ever, there is a clear temporal distinction between normal and revolutionary modes. Indeed, these two aren't successive phases of scientific inquiry as

Kuhn thought they were. Dogmatism of normal science and criticality of revolutionaries are two ways of proceeding that can—and often do work—hand in hand. They are two complementary approaches to solve puzzles, which differ mostly in how much risk they tolerate, and the best overall strategy in inquiry is a combination of risk-averse and risk-loving approaches. Indeed, it may well be the case that science is successful partly because it strikes the right balance between these two modes of investigation. And Kuhn's ideas are flexible enough to be applied not only to the sciences but also to other academic disciplines that busy themselves with solving puzzles, and there is no reason not to apply the same logic to the university as a whole. The university is a community that exists for inquiry, and if physicists need gadflies, so do universities. As a result, speech restrictions that aim to marginalize or exclude gadflies should be seen as counter to the aims of the very institution that implements them. This strongly suggest that many such restrictions lack a just cause in the form of the university defending its intellectual borders against attacks by conservative forces that are bent on harming it.

Prevention of Anticipated Threats as Just Cause

Periodically, we hear rhetoric to the effect that some conservative speech is a precursor to various great social harms and moral disasters: for example, mass deportations, the erosion of civil rights, and even genocide. If there were ample evidence for the claim that permitting such speech substantially increases the probability that, say, certain groups will be targeted for extermination, then speech could plausibly be curtailed on that basis.

However, there is a weighty burden of proof on anyone who would make such an argument. Too often, we suspect that the "argument" amounts to rhetoric about what is, admittedly, a terrifying possibility—but doesn't rise to the level of showing that this possibility is at all likely, and certainly not imminent. In any case, restricting speech on such grounds would be comparable to waging a preventive war, which is prohibited by international law and standard just war theory (Walzer 2006;[12] see also the discussions in Luban 2004, Shue and Rodin 2007).

This prohibition makes perfect sense for the following reason: When an anticipated threat is not imminent but temporally distant, you have to rely on dubious predictions about how the future will unfold to meet the high burden of proof that (a) the threat is real (as opposed to merely perceived) and (b) that violence is necessary to respond to it (another condition of *jus ad bellum*, and one to which we'll return in the next section). For the time being, however, let's focus on the first component of the evidentiary burden: establishing that the anticipated threat is real, rather than merely perceived.

Granted, regimes that have pursued totalitarian and genocidal ends in history have used dehumanizing rhetoric aimed at undermining the rights and interests of the people they wanted to subjugate or eliminate. However, people also use such rhetoric when they have absolutely no interest in establishing a totalitarian order or committing genocide, but a very strong interest in some other political, social, or religious goal, such as maintaining the borders of their moral and political communities. In other cases, the speakers might indeed intend to cause such harms but lack the means to do so. As a result, we can't draw a straight line from the presence of this rhetoric to any likely outcome.

Moreover, the epistemic bar seems particularly high when we think about the nature of the anticipated threat in question. Repeated failures to predict the rise of totalitarianism throughout history indicate that these events are black swans. They are easy to explain in retrospect but very hard to anticipate, in part because the public awareness of previous moral disasters lowers the likelihood that history will repeat itself in prediction-friendly ways. For instance, the living memory of Japanese internment camps is arguably the greatest obstacle for a similar program being deployed against Muslims in America. State-sanctioned genocide, if it ever returns to the West, probably isn't going march down the street wearing brown shirts and swastikas (or "Make America Great Again" hats).[13] If it ever arrives, it will arrive in a form that is utterly unrecognizable, since long before it could pose an imminent threat, its familiar forms will be neutralized by the moral sense of the general public.

One might object here that many of the genocides in the past had been predictable. For instance, one might wonder how much clearer the signs could get than forcing Jews to wear the Star of David. This objection, however, ignores the chronology. The "Star of David Decree" issued by Reinhard Heydrich in September 1941, which mandated all Jews of age six and up to wear it, came *after* the first deportations to Dachau and Auschwitz, not before. Although there were limited and local instances of such practices dating back to late 1939, the clear signs, whatever they were, came too late. This also explains why thousands of German Jewish families who would have otherwise left found themselves trapped. Moreover, the Nazi "yellow star" is not the first of its kind; Islamic and Medieval European history are full of examples of such mandates, many of which were not precursors to mass killings of Jews.

In any case, our claim here is not that genocides can never be predicted. Indeed, they can—for instance, the Kristallnacht and the formation of ghettos should have been clearer signs for the Holocaust—but this sort of thing happens only when genocide is *almost underway*. We take it that no reasonable person can claim that the US is currently on the verge of committing genocide. The threat, whether real or perceived, must be located at an arbitrarily distant future. As a result, it's implausible that speech restrictions we encounter on US campuses today can be justified based on considerations about preventing mass murder or the rise of a fascist theocracy.[14]

Necessity

The necessity condition asks us to consider whether war is the only way to achieve our aims. As pointed out earlier, when the purported just cause is defense against a threat, whether there's a genuine just cause depends on whether all other reasonable options have been exhausted. In the case of speech, this means whether or not there are alternative ways of defending universities as communities of inquiry or defending minorities against future threats.

Note, however, that there are many kinds of programs and related support structures that universities can implement to assist students and faculty who may otherwise feel vulnerable to speech they find objectionable. Universities can establish safe spaces;[15] they can pursue affirmative action campaigns to diversify their students and faculty; they can create extracurricular educational opportunities for both students and faculty concerning the best ways to discuss contentious topics; they can create first-year seminars that are designed to help students have fraught conversations, engage in self-care, and appreciate the value of a community that fosters difficult dialogue. We certainly aren't suggesting any of these options, or all of them jointly, are superior to restricting speech in all contexts. However, this is an area where the sheer range of options can make for productive exchanges about how best to achieve institutional goals: There are many potential proposals to study here, and many ways in which philosophers might be useful in clarifying the goods at stake in each one.

But if that's right, then we have good reason to doubt that the necessity condition is met by the typical speech restrictions we encounter on today's campuses. Therefore, the epistemic burden of proving that the anticipated threat to minorities is real and non-restrictive measures will not suffice to neutralize it is exceedingly high, and arguably hasn't been met.

Likelihood of Success

Finally, let's turn our attention to the likelihood of success condition. As mentioned earlier, the condition matters in the context of war because we don't want to throw away lives: If we are going to put our population at moral risk, then we had better have good reason to think that doing so is likely to achieve our aims (which, of course, themselves need to be morally justified). Here, the issue has a larger empirical component, and for that reason may be more tractable. We may consider whether particular restrictions actually limit the kind of speech we find objectionable or whether they simply drive it underground or outside the university entirely. In both cases, we have to consider the costs and benefits of those outcomes. Likewise, we may want to consider whether our long-term objectives are likely to be achieved by speech regulation. How does speech restriction affect the position of the university in public life more generally, with special attention to the degree to which it's seen as a valuable institution that's worth continued public subsidy?

We doubt that many speech restrictions meet the likelihood of success condition. Our suspicion is that, in the mid-to-long term, speech restrictions will greatly harm university budgets, leading to increased pressures, especially on the humanities and social sciences. What's more, they're likely to accelerate the corporatization of academia.

These are likely outcomes because excluding conservative opinions from campuses validates the idea that universities are propaganda centers to serve the liberal agenda. Take, for instance, the University of Oregon, which last year effectively banned certain conservative statements by its faculty and students as "discriminatory harassment" on issues such as race, gender, and sexual orientation, even when said speech takes place in private homes (Volokh 2016; Harnden, Le and Liebman 2016). It's probably only a matter of time before someone successfully sues the University of Oregon in a Federal Court on the grounds that it's violating the First Amendment.[16] Or consider President Trump, who tweeted after one of the dustups about Yiannopoulos, "If U.C. Berkeley does not allow free speech and practices violence on innocent people with a different point of view—NO FEDERAL FUNDS?" (Trump 2017). Add to that, of course, frustrated conservative voters, who have already shown their willingness to pressure their state representatives to teach universities a lesson.

It's hard to exaggerate the significance of the threat posed to public universities by this legislative-judicial pincer. A big part of our funding comes from public sources. Many conservatives, rightly or wrongly, see the university's mission as providing job skills to individuals—not pursuing the social good of making citizens—and object to funding private benefits with public dollars. What's more, they object to what they regard as indoctrination in progressive thought, and the growing resentment towards public universities and their employees is a testament to this perception. In fact, one might see the stunning electoral success of politicians such as Donald Trump and Scott Walker as a sign that this way of thinking is gaining traction in US politics (Cramer 2016). If universities keep giving ammunition to these populist conservatives by effectively banning their views from discussion, they will have all the more motivation to gut higher education and cut off the funding for the humanities and social sciences, which are seen as the greatest culprits in excluding conservatives from campus. This threat is real and imminent. The Republican tax bill that passed the House of Representatives in late 2017 treats graduate tuition waivers as taxable income. Had this bill survived the Senate vote in its original form and were it signed into law, who would have studied philosophy, sociology, political science, astronomy, history, or dance? Prestigious programs at private universities would have survived, but the prospects for the rest would have been grim, and it wouldn't have been surprising if most universities were slowly transformed into vocational schools.

What's more, we shouldn't think that these problems only affect public universities. Consider a bill proposed in California in 2016, SB 1146, which would have prevented religious schools that prohibit same-sex relationships from receiving state grants, and which would have made them subject to discrimination lawsuits. Given that so many such schools are tuition driven, threatening their funding would have amounted to rather serious pressure. The same is true of an earlier California initiative to limit the tax-exempt status of religious schools.

One might object that California is a relatively "blue" state (i.e., democrat/liberal/left-leaning), and these initiatives are supported by liberal voters. However, it isn't hard to imagine similar strategies being employed in red states against those private universities that restrict conservative speech. Moreover, recent trends suggest that some "blue" states, where many of the best private universities are located, are actually swing states with conservative-leaning rural populations—many of whom have more consistent voting records than their urban/liberal counterparts.[17] What's more, given a Republican-held Congress, we certainly can't rule out federal actions that would financially starve all but the wealthiest institutions.

In short, universities can't sway the public opinion against such attempts to scuttle higher education while also prohibiting conservative opinions from campus. If we keep fighting this battle to the bitter end, we won't just lose. We'll be wiped out. And insofar as that's the case, the likelihood of success condition isn't met, and many speech restrictions on campuses today are unjustified.

Conclusion

Many academics favor speech restrictions on campuses; they reason that speech can be harmful, and so should be regulated. After all, since the government regulates products and services to protect consumers, and the world of ideas is like a marketplace, administrations should place limits on campus speech to protect the faculty and students. We've argued that this is the wrong way to approach the ethics of speech restrictions. It's better to see that issue through the lens of just war theory rather than the ethics of the marketplace. This is, in part, due to a lack of fit between the marketplace and the world of ideas: Framing speech as a sales pitch is to get its telos wrong; speech doesn't just aim to convert, it also exists to mark boundaries between individuals and communities. What's more, just war theory is better equipped to answer the relevant moral question, *what makes it permissible to engage in conduct—such as speech restrictions—that would normally be impermissible?* If we take the war metaphor seriously, we should worry about speech restrictions. In particular, just cause, necessity, and likelihood of success conditions of *jus ad bellum* probably prohibit the kinds of speech restrictions we see on today's campuses.

Notes

1. We would like to thank Ivan Marquez, Eric Gilbertson and especially Adam Betz for their very valuable comments on several drafts of this paper.
2. The following is a selection of news articles sampling the kind of speech restrictions we have in mind: www.washingtonpost.com/news/grade-point/wp/2017/09/23/uc-berkeley-says-free-speech-week-is-canceled-milo-yiannopoulos-says-hes-still-coming-to-campus/?utm_term=.03b607422175
   http://time.com/4955245/milo-yiannopoulos-berkeley-free-speech-week/
   https://electronicintifada.net/blogs/nora-barrows-friedman/chicago-university-latest-investigate-students-over-palestine-activism
   www.breitbart.com/jerusalem/2017/10/18/palestinian-refugee-activist-claims-speech-at-gwu-was-nixed-by-students-for-justice-in-palestine-for-being-anti-semitic/
   www.newyorker.com/culture/persons-of-interest/laura-kipniss-battle-against-vulnerability
   www.insidehighered.com/news/2016/09/06/northwestern-bans-professor-campus-and-faculty-members-split-whether-move-justified
   www.theatlantic.com/politics/archive/2016/05/the-peril-of-writing-a-provocative-email-at-yale/484418/
   www.insidehighered.com/news/2017/07/24/debate-over-art-teaching-and-prejudice-school-art-institute-chicago
   www.algemeiner.com/2017/10/17/palestinian-activist-on-us-tour-says-event-cancelled-by-sjp-over-antisemitism-concerns/
   http://beta.latimes.com/local/lanow/la-me-ln-berkeley-milo-20170924-story.html
3. www.foxnews.com/politics/2017/04/25/berkeley-free-speech-protests-arrests-injuries-damages-since-february.html
4. www.washingtonpost.com/news/grade-point/wp/2017/09/23/uc-berkeley-says-free-speech-week-is-canceled-milo-yiannopoulos-says-hes-still-coming-to-campus/?utm_term=.03b607422175
5. http://time.com/4955245/milo-yiannopoulos-berkeley-free-speech-week/
6. As we will argue later, this associative dimension needs to be balanced with the requirement that the communities of inquiry in question should be free in some non-trivial sense.
7. www.people-press.org/2014/06/12/political-polarization-in-the-american-public/
8. For surveys of these issues, see Begby, Reichberg and Syse (2012a, 2012b).
9. The proportionality, right intention, and legitimate authority conditions raise important issues too, but we don't have room to pursue them in detail. In the case of legitimate authority, for instance, note that that condition is designed to ensure that only the appropriate bodies begin wars, on the

assumption that states have special duties and responsibilities that individual actors lack. There are various ways to defend this condition, perhaps the least controversial being that well-functioning states provide a system of checks and balances for such decisions, ensuring that no one can unleash violence unilaterally. In the context of speech restrictions, we might see this condition as bound up with larger concerns about the relationship between administrations and faculties. Since the latter has steadily been conceding power to the former, faculty members are now particularly vulnerable to administrators, who find themselves balancing academic freedom with worries about lawsuits and explicit and implicit threats from donors. Additionally, there are now-familiar concerns about the impact that Title IX has had on speech at universities, adding in complex issues about how to navigate the value of federal oversight, the importance of autonomy at the local level, and the broader project of social justice.

10. https://ljmgreen.com/2017/09/18/why-it-is-hard-to-be-a-campus-conservative/
11. For an early example, see Toulmin (1965).
12. Walzer offers a criticism of the international law and standard just war theory about the *pre-emption vs prevention* distinction on the grounds that choosing imminence of a threat as the demarcation line between justified and unjustified first-strikes is unreasonable. This is in part because imminence is a vague concept and in part because in some cases waiting until the threat is imminent would put an undue burden on the target of the threat (Walzer 2006, 81).

    However, in the ensuing discussion, he concedes the evidentiary burden we adopt here as a necessary condition for justifiability (82–85). In this regard, Walzer's criticism here is merely about whether there are *rare* exceptions to the way international law and standard just war theory handle the *pre-emption vs prevention* distinction. Wherever we end up drawing the line, clearly the burden of proof that the first-striker has for establishing the reality of the threat and the exhaustion of all reasonable alternatives will be very high for arbitrarily distant future threats.
13. This isn't meant to defend Trump and Trumpism against anything other than this specific charge.
14. Someone might argue that the epistemic bar shouldn't be so high when it comes to restricting speech, given the consequences of restricting speech aren't as serious as the consequences of waging a preventive war—after all, human lives aren't at stake. There are two ways to address this objection. First, you could take our discussion of the value of speech to be an argument for thinking that speech is especially valuable, given its links to other fundamental interests, such as freedoms of association and religion. Then, the line could be that it's easy to underestimate the harm of having speech restricted. Second, you could observe that we have a right to free speech, and that rights violations take priority over harms. So it's a mistake to think that we should balance the consequences for the people whose speech is restricted against the consequences for those who are affected by the unrestricted speech of others. Those in the latter group do, of course, have an interest in not being harmed, but unless the harms violate their rights, then those harms are an acceptable cost of not violating the rights of others. It's quite complex to assess whether anyone's rights are being violated by the unrestricted speech of others, and we can't settle the issue here. Our inclination, however, is to think that given what we say next about the likelihood of success condition, we should say that as long as none of the harms are physical, or stem from real threats of such harm, no one's rights are being violated by unrestricted speech.

15. Here we aren't recommending converting classrooms, academic or public lectures, or official functions of the university into safe spaces. Doing so would be restricting speech in the same problematic ways we criticize in this essay. Our claim is merely that universities can create safe spaces *in addition to* the "unsafe" spaces with which they are ordinarily furnished.
16. There is indeed legal precedent. See, for instance, *Saxe v. State College Area School District*, 240 F.3d 200 (2001), which found unconstitutional a similar speech code which prohibited unwanted and offensive comments about one's "race, religion, color, national origin, gender, sexual orientation, disability or other personal characteristics."
17. See The Pew Research Center's report, "Regular Voters, Intermittent Voters, and Those Who Don't: Who Votes, Who Doesn't, and Why?": 6.

Works Cited

Begby, E., Reichberg, G. and Syse, H. "The Ethics of War. Part I: Historical Trends." *Philosophy Compass*, Vo. 7 (2012): 316–327.

———. "The Ethics of War. Part II: Contemporary Authors and Issues." *Philosophy Compass*, Vol. 7 (2012): 328–347.

Cramer, K. *Politics of Resentment: Rural Consciousness in Wisconsin and the Rise of Scott Walker*. Chicago: University of Chicago Press, 2016.

Hanlon, A. "The Myth of the 'Marketplace of Ideas' on Campus." March 6, 2017. https://newrepublic.com/article/141150/myth-marketplace-ideas-campus-charles-murray-milo-yiannopoulos

Harnden, E., Le, S. and Liebman, B. "University of Oregon Investigative Report." November 30, 2016. https://provost.uoregon.edu/sites/provost1.uoregon.edu/files/final_investigative_report_redacted_-_final.pdf

Levy, J. "Safe Spaces, Academic Freedom, and the University as a Complex Association." March 28, 2016. http://bleedingheartlibertarians.com/2016/03/safe-spaces-academic-freedom-and-the-university-as-a-complex-association/

Luban, D. "Preventive War." *Philosophy and Public Affairs*, Vol. 32 (2004): 207–248.

"Regular Voters, Intermittent Voters, and Those Who Don't: Who Votes, Who Doesn't, and Why?" *Pew Research Center*. October 18, 2006. www.people-press.org/files/legacy-pdf/292.pdf

Shue, H. and Rodin, D. *Preemption: Military Action and Moral Justification*. Oxford: Oxford University Press, 2007.

Toulmin, S. "Does the Distinction Between Normal and Revolutionary Science Hold Water?" In *Criticism and the Growth of Knowledge: Proceedings of the International Colloquium in the Philosophy of Science*, edited by I. Lakatos and A. Musgrave. Cambridge: Cambridge University Press, 1965: 39–48.

Trump, Donald (@realDonaldTrump) "If U.C. Berkeley Does Not Allow Free Speech and Practices Violence on Innocent People With a Different Point of View—No Federal Funds?" February 2, 2017, 3:13 AM, Tweet. https://twitter.com/realDonaldTrump/status/827112633224544256?ref_src=twsrc%5Etfw&ref_url=http%3A%2F%2Fwww.mercurynews.com%2F2017%2F02%2F02%2Ftrump-tweets-at-uc-berkeley-no-free-speech-no-federal-funds%2F

Volokh, E. "At the University of Oregon, No More Free Speech for Professors on Subjects Such as Race, Religion, Sexual Orientation." *Washington Post*. December 26, 2016. www.washingtonpost.com/news/volokh-conspiracy/wp/2016/12/26/at-the-university-of-oregon-no-more-free-speech-for-professors-on-subjects-such-as-race-religion-sexual-orientation/?utm_term=.6a063d043aa7

Walzer, M. *Just and Unjust Wars: A Moral Argument with Historical Illustrations*. New York: Basic Books, 2006.

12 Growing-Up Disturbed

Frank Furedi

In recent decades, higher education has spawned a cohort of illiberal administrators and academics. It has also institutionalized numerous censorious practices and behaviors. However, the current illiberal climate on campuses does not emanate entirely from within the university. One reason why so many students are drawn towards the current intolerant regime of censoriousness is because they have been socialized to internalize the psychological sentiments associated with calls for trigger warnings, safe spaces, and linguistic policing. Unlike previous generations, who were often drawn towards risk-taking and the ideals of freedom, the current cohort of undergraduates were brought up on a diet that emphasized therapeutic values, such as caution, safety, and emotional security. From their perspectives, these values are far more relevant and important than those associated with the exercise of freedom.

A Different Cohort of Students

I have stopped counting the number of times that an academic colleague reminds me that "undergraduates are not what they used to be." In private conversations, a significant minority of academic teachers have raised the concern, that the age-old distinction between school children and university students was fast losing its meaning. At least some faculty members have gone so far as to draw the conclusion that the existing cohort of undergraduates are far less mature than previous generations of students. They assert that undergraduates need to be treated as biologically mature children rather than as young adults.

Numerous academics and educators have expressed concern with the capacity of new undergraduates to engage with the life of independent learning and living. "We know that the students experience can be overwhelming" wrote Norman Lamb, MP, in his foreword to a report on the subject by the UK's Higher Education Policy Institute.[1] The report presented the normal experiences of university life—hitherto perceived as unexceptional—as now constituting a serious challenge to the well-being of the current cohort of students. It noted that "students are vulnerable" because in most cases they are "living away from home for the first time." It also pointed to the "new challenges" they faced, such as "a different method of learning" and "living with people they have never met before."

Typically, the authors of this report did not pause to ask the question, "What has changed?" Universities have always constituted a serious challenge to new undergraduates. Students arriving on campuses in the 1950s or 1970s were confronted with an environment that was no less testing than today. However, whereas in the past the novelty of this experience was not perceived as a threat to the well-being of new students, today it is represented as a threat to their mental health.

The claim that students are likely to find their transition to university an arduous encounter is often supported by surveys that allege that twenty-first-century undergraduates suffer from unusually high levels of mental health problems. The HEPI report contends that "survey data repeatedly show that, on average, students are less happy and more anxious than non-students, including other young people."[2] Numerous surveys reinforce this point and convey the impression that studying at a university is highly toxic enterprise. In some instances, the scale of the alleged problem simply beggars belief. In April 2017, a report on an "epidemic of stressed students" in Australia suggested that more than 70 percent of students reported high or very high levels of psychological distress, and apparently more than a third of the respondents stated that they contemplated self- harm or suicide.[3] In Britain, a National Union of Students' survey in 2015 indicated that 78 percent of students had experienced mental health problems, and a third of the respondents claimed to have had suicidal thoughts.

The problems that eighteen- to twenty-year-old young people have in making the transition to higher education is often explained on the ground that this generation is far less mature and resilient than previous ones. Neil Howe and William Strauss, the authors of the study *Millennials Go To College*, advanced this thesis back in 2003. They noted that the millennial generation is far more "closely tied to their parents" than the students that preceded them. Apparently, millennials also insist on a "secure and regulated environment." Howe and Strauss concluded that consequently, students today find it difficult to flourish in the relatively unstructured environment of higher education. The assessment that the millennials find it more troublesome to make the transition to independent living on campuses than previous generations is widely endorsed by educators on both sides of the Atlantic.

A new ethos of benevolent paternalism directed at "supporting" the well being of the intake of fragile students has become institutionalized on campuses. Such paternalistic concern for the well being of students covers an extraordinary variety of problems that were until recently perceived as the normal stuff of life. For example, Bournemouth University offers the services of its wellbeing advisors, "who can offer practical help with issues such as stress, worry, homesickness, panic, sleeping and eating difficulties, lifestyle issues and low mood or anxiety."[4]

That university administrators depict worry, homesickness, or "lifestyle issues" as problems whose resolution requires professional intervention indicates that student's well being is rarely perceived as a normal state. Such paternalistic interventions assume that students lack the maturity and the emotional and moral resources required for independent learning in higher education. Such interventions send out the message that you, the student, is presumed to be unwell and in need of support. This orientation is explicitly endorsed by the mental well being service of the University of Leicester. To encourage its would-be clients to come forward and acknowledge their un-wellness, its website cites an anonymous student, saying:

> Everyone said University would be great, but, for me, it was torture. I felt miserably shy and alone, as if I was on one side of a glass wall and everyone else was on the other.[5]

The aim of citing the words of this troubled individual is to reassure distressed undergraduates that they are not alone. But the unintended message conveyed by the well being service is that you are unlikely to cope with the demands of university life on your own. Unfortunately, the system of student support institutionalized in higher education have the perverse effect of cultivating the vulnerability and insecurity of young people.

Treated as Children

One of the most significant, and yet rarely analyzed developments in campus culture has been its infantilization. Universities throughout the Anglo-American world portray the transition from secondary to higher education as a variant of the psychological upheaval that primary school pupils experience when they enter high school. Implicitly and increasingly explicitly the newly arriving undergraduate is perceived as a biologically mature child rather than as a young adult. A brochure targeting parents, published by the University of Tasmania is paradigmatic in this respect. It states that the "type of support you provided for your child during earlier transitions, such as from primary to high school, is still just as important in making decisions about going to university." The literature that American universities publish for parents echoes this outlook and often conveys the impression that their potential undergraduates are still just children.

Eric Posner, a leading legal scholar at the University of Chicago, has declared that "students today are more like children than adults and need protection."[6] Posner contends that today's university students are not ready for independence and require the moral guidance of their institutions. Posner expresses the paternalistic ethos of infantilization in an unusually unambiguous form. However, his premise of undergraduate immaturity is widely shared by university administrators.

In England a group educators have criticized universities for not treating their new intake of students as if they were children. One school principal, Richard Harman, warned that "we know" that school leavers "do not magically turn into fully fledged adults the minute they step out of the classroom into the lecture hall." His point was previously asserted by Sir Anthony Seldon, now head of Buckingham University, who stated that "there is a belief among Vice Chancellors that young people are adults and can fend for themselves," but "eighteen-year-olds today are a lot less robust and worldly wise."[7]

Amongst academics there is a widespread consensus that the recent cohorts of students appears to be more emotionally fragile and far less self sufficient than in the past. There is, however, little clarity about why the current generation of undergraduates appear less mature and more emotionally fragile than their predecessors. Marvin Krislov, president of Oberlin College, raises more questions than answers on this point, speculating:

> I don't know if it's related to the way we parent. I don't know if it's related to the media or the pervasive role of technology—I'm sure there are lot of different factors—but what I can tell you is that every campus I know is investing more resources in mental health. . . . Students are coming to campuses today with mental-health challenges that in some instances have been diagnosed and in some instances have not. Maybe, in previous eras, those students would not have been coming to college.[8]

Krislov's description of the current state of affairs is one that many administrators and academics recognize but also struggle to understand.

Many accounts of the unprecedented emotional fragility of university undergraduates claim that this development is the outcome of the expansion of student numbers. They suggest that many of these students come from diverse nontraditional backgrounds and lack the confidence and financial security of their more privileged predecessors. Catherine McAteer, the head of University College London's student psychological services observed that the reason why a growing number of students require mental health support is because "students are now coming to university" who previously "would not have come"[9]

Those concerned with the emotional fragility of university students frequently assert that the reason for their reaction is likely to be linked to the unprecedented economic insecurity that they face. University students are often portrayed as confronted with a wide range of exceptional problems. Advocates of this thesis claim that many undergraduates are constantly struggling to make ends meet. According to this argument, these difficulties are likely to have a corrosive impact on economically insecure students.

There is little doubt that many students face serious financial pressure and that they are often forced to juggle the conflicting demands of course work and economic survival. However, it is far from evident if there is a link between a precarious economic existence and emotional fragility. Students from well-to-do affluent backgrounds are no less likely than their poorer peers to talk the language of trauma and psychological distress. Indeed, some of the most privileged campuses—Oxford, Cambridge, Yale, Berkeley, Oberlin—have been in the forefront of campaigns that draw attention to the emotional harms suffered by activists and other students.

The most influential explanation used to account for the emotional fragility of students in higher education is to link it to the growing number of first-generation university students, who lack the parental, financial, and cultural support that was once enjoyed by undergraduates. Some argue that first-generation students—that is, undergraduates whose parents did not attend university—face unique problems attempting to fit in to what is an alien and high-pressure environment. It is also asserted that since a significant proportion of first-generation student come from minority and socially deprived backgrounds, they face a unique problem of fitting into the traditional white middle-class campus environment.

That the first-generation university students may well be at a disadvantage in comparison to their peers who have parents with a degree is not in doubt. The socially mobile often face such obstacles, as was the case with the large number of first generation students who entered higher education in the 1960s, 1970s, and 1980s. The principal problem faced by first-generation students is that their parents had little cultural capital to hand on to them and were therefore less prepared for university life then their more comfortably off peers. But unlike today, the problems they faced were not portrayed in psychological terms but in the language of culture and socio-economic depravation. It is only now that the experience of first-generation students has become thoroughly medicalized.

Unfortunately, when first-generation students arrive on campus today they are often treated as if they are likely to possess some emotional deficits. In the US, it is common for universities to organize special programs for integrating first-generation students. Diversity officers dealing with the first generation often operate under the theory that this group faces a unique problem of being torn between family and university. They frequently contend that first-generation students suffer from pangs of guilt for leaving their family behind. The upshot of these theories is the belief that first-generation students need special dedicated psychological support. As one expert on his subject advised: "the challenge of higher education is to recognise the psychological impact that first generation status has on students and to provide help."[10]

Regrettably, the focus on psychology distracts attention from more constructive ways of preparing students from disadvantaged backgrounds to deal with the pressures of academic learning. The provision of academic support to help students gain intellectual confidence is probably the most useful way of helping students to make their way in the university. Perversely, the provision of psychological support as the default solution for helping first-generation students is likely to intensify their quest for validation. Instead of developing their power of resilience, it may well heighten their sense of vulnerability. What universities need to do is not to cultivate the insecure identity of first-generation students but to provide them with the intellectual resources that will help them to gain confidence in their ability to achieve.

The assumption that university students are in fact insecure children has profound implications for the conduct of academic life. The premise of academic teaching and learning is that a student—unlike a school pupil—is capable of independent and self-directed learning. In order to promote the intellectual independence of undergraduates, the aim of an enlightened faculty is to stretch and challenge them. Exposing students to criticism and pressure are integral to a sound academic education. Such an orientation towards the pursuit of intellectual independence requires an atmosphere of freedom and directly contradicts the current tendency to shield students from uncertainty.

Why Does This Generation Appear To Behave So Different?

The reason why the current generation appears to behave different to their predecessor has little to do with their socio-economic background. Rather, the sense of emotional fragility expressed by some undergraduates is the outcome of the prevailing ethos of socialization that treats young people as children. What's different about the current generation of undergraduates is the way that they were raised and socialized by the adult world.

The socialization of young people has become increasingly reliant on therapeutic techniques that have the perverse effect of encouraging children and youth to interpret existential problems as psychological ones. Concern with children's emotions has fostered a climate where many young people are continually educated to understand the challenges they face through the language of mental health. Not surprisingly, they often find it difficult to acquire the habit of independence and make the transition to forms of behavior associated with the exercise of autonomy.

The complex emotional tensions that are integral to the process of growing up are now discussed as stressful events with which children and young people cannot be expected to cope. Yet is through dealing with such emotional upheavals that young people learn to manage risks and gain an understanding of their strengths and weaknesses. Instead of being encouraged to acquire an aspiration for independence, many youngsters are subject to influences that promote childish behavior. The infantilization of young people is the unintended outcome of parenting practices that rely on levels of support and supervision that are more suitable for much younger children. The relations of dependence that are nurtured through these practices serve to prolong adolescence to the point that many young people in their twenties do not perceive themselves as adults. Whereas in the past infantilization was classically associated with the phenomenon of maternal overprotection, today the prolongation of adolescence is culturally sanctioned. In the case of universities, it is institutionally enforced.

Several commentators have drawn attention to what they describe as "overparenting" or "helicopter parenting" and its tendency to diminish the capacity for independent and autonomous behavior of young people. Writing of his adolescent patients, the psychiatrist Abilash Gopal notes how "overly-involved parents have been impeding the development of autonomy in their child for years." Drawing on his experience, Gopal claims that the state of emotional dependency that parents impose on their children contributes to the outburst of the highly charged anxiety displayed by students activists. "I have noticed a parallel between the behavior and psychological distress I see in the overparented child and the growing number of college students protesting on campuses with sensitivities and demands that seem disproportionate to reality," he wrote.[11]

Though some commentators present over-parenting as the main driver of the infantilization of young people, it is important to note that risk-averse child rearing practices are based on cultural values and attitudes that prevail throughout society. Parents are merely adopting childrearing practices that are promoted and endorsed as more or less mandatory by agencies of socialization and child protection. In the present circumstances, many parents believe that they have little choice but to conform and adopt the practices associated with intensive childrearing.

Precautionary attitudes towards children and young people are also promoted in wider society—including by institutions of education. These attitudes have led to the emergence of the custom of interpreting the existential troubles and anxieties of childhood through the prism of mental health. Since the 1980s, the invention of child-related mental health pathologies has turned into a growth industry. Report after report insists that children are more stressed and depressed than in the past. Yet the constant proliferation of new medicalized categories with which to label school pupils says far more about the about the inventive powers of the therapeutic imagination than the conditions of childhood. Pupils who suffer from shyness are offered the diagnosis of social phobia. The diagnosis of school phobia can now be applied to label those children who really dislike going to school. The transformation of the negative and anxious attitudes towards examination into a standalone category of "exam stress" shows how age-old sentiments and reactions to pressure are today recycled in the language of mental health.

Anyone who has been a child is unlikely to be surprised by the discovery that many pupils are concerned about their performance in an impending exam. But as children's normal emotional upheavals have become medicalized, young people are trained to regard the challenges integral to growing up—such as sitting for exams or changing schools—as a source of psychological distress. In recent decades, the transition from primary school to secondary school has become presented as a potentially traumatic event. Instead of discussing children's arrival at "big school" as an exciting opportunity, experts offer transitional counselling for what was regarded, for decades, as a routine aspect of young people's lives.

The provision of transitional counselling does not end once the child goes to big school. Numerous universities offer the services of transitional counsellors on the grounds that many young students arriving on campus cannot cope on their own. "The counselling team are fully aware of the importance of managing transition and are here to help you find the way ahead," claims the University of Bath Counselling Service on its website. As illustrations of the kinds of the transitions that might require professional support, it mentions entering university as a first-year undergraduate, the move of second-year students from campus-based residence to living in town, final year students returning after being away on placement, and newly-arrived postgraduate students. "It could be that feelings of self-confidence are quite threatened by the unfamiliarity of new surroundings and new people," warns the service.[12]

Transitional counselling, like many forms of routine mental health intervention with children, has a habit of turning into a self-fulfilling prophecy. Once children pick up on the idea that going to secondary school is a traumatic experience, many of them may interpret their normal anxieties and insecurities through the idiom of mental health problems. Instead of gaining resilience, children who are instructed to interpret their life experiences in medicalized terms may well become disoriented. When they arrive on campus, many will expect to be looked after by their university—as well as by the continued oversight of their parents. Some commentators go so far as to suggest that the continuation of parental involvement in the life of university students is a positive development.

That the issue of transition to higher education is perceived as a mental health challenge was illustrated by the controversy surrounding the decision made by Johns Hopkins University to put a stop to the practice of concealing the first semester grades of new students from future employers and graduate schools. A group of students reacted by protesting against this decision and claimed that it undermined their mental health and put them at risk of worsening their depression and anxiety. "I can't be expected to do well in class if I'm depressed and have anxiety" argued one student.[13] The university's administration responded that it recognized that the students "need support in transitioning to the Hopkins environment." However, in this case it felt that the "best way to help them transition is to give them the study skills that help them to do well."[14] What this episode showed is that at least a minority of students arrive on campus convinced that they need to be immunized from the psychological harms of transitioning. As one student explained "I'm paying to have a support network, academically and mentally." Such sentiments are the outcome of their previous phase of socialization that disposes them to perceive the challenges they face through the idioms of mental health.

The attitudes that promote precautionary parenting and the medicalization of the existential problems facing young people directly influences policy in higher education. In the United States, the reintroduction of attitudes traditionally linked with in loco parentis have as their premise the continuous involvement of parents in their university education. With the help of the Family Educational Rights and Privacy Act, universities and colleges are able to disclose information to parents about their children's alcohol and drug violations.[15] Today, this Act is used that to help "enhance student achievement through greater parent involvement in their children's education,"[16] while special facilities and programs have mushroomed on US campuses to "encourage parents to become enmeshed . . . with their children's lives on campus."[17]

The assumption of the doctrine of in loco parentis by Anglo-American universities is the logical outcome of the reorganization of childrearing around the principle of caution. This doctrine, which charged universities to assume the role of standing "in place of the parents" influenced campus life in the first half of the twentieth century. Following in the wake of the turmoil of the 1960s and 1970s, this doctrine gave way to the assumption that university students were capable of making mature choices and living with their consequences. During this period, campus life was relatively unregulated and students regarded attempts by university authorities to regulate their social and political life as a violation of their autonomy. Since the 1980s there has been a reversal of this trend back towards the paternalistic regulation of campus life. However, in some respects the current version of in loco parentis is more paternalistic than in the past. It implicitly welcomes the continued involvement of parents in the academic life of students.

Studies indicate that the cumulative effect of current child-rearing and socialization practices is to foster positive attitudes towards parental involvement in higher education amongst undergraduates. Neil Howe and William Strauss predicted that in the future parental involvement in higher education would increase and would lead to an explicit partnership between students, parents, and university authorities.[18] In other words, a modified version of the type of parent involvement that characterizes high school would continue into university life

Failure of Socialization

The erosion of the line that divides secondary from higher education is a trend that contradicts the ethos of academic teaching and the vocation associated with it. In theory, the ideals associated with the university remain widely affirmed but in practice they are often tested by the introduction of conventions that were formerly confined to secondary or further education. The adoption of paternalistic practices and the wider tendency towards the infantilization of campus life can in part be understood as an outcome of the difficulties that society has encountered in the socialization of young people.

As David Walsh noted in his *The Growth of the Liberal Soul*, "more than anything else it has been the inability of liberal societies to develop any institutional means of transmitting its own virtues that has precipitated the crisis."[19] The failure to develop an institutional means for transmitting traditional virtues to the younger generations is closely linked to the erosion of adult authority. From the turn of the twentieth century onwards, a significant section of adult society became less and less able or willing to socialize children into the values upheld by the previous generations. This trend was particularly discernible in the school, where pedagogy diverted its emphasis from character education towards a more psychologically informed teaching style.

The estrangement of many adults from the values upheld by their parents was paralleled by a discernable reaction against traditional education by "modern" pedagogy. When at the outbreak of the Great War in 1914, the *Times Educational Supplement* noted that "every great war in the modern world has been followed by changes in education" it probably had little idea of the scale of the impending revolution in the classroom.

One of the most significant outcomes of World War One on schooling was to strengthen the influence of so-called progressive education. The progressive critique of traditional values resonated with the mood of revulsion and demoralization that prevailed in the post-World War One era. At this conjuncture, calls to break with the past possessed significant cultural appeal and many educators hoped that their progressive ethos could help create a brave new world through the influence they exerted on children. From their perspectives, the older generations were beyond redemption and they concluded that reform could only come through the efforts of the children. Their ideal of child-centered education flourished alongside the growth of post-war disenchantment with the moral status of adulthood.

The arguments supporting child-centered education expressed the sensibility of demoralization and disorientation of a significant section of the cultural elites. As one important study of this period explains "among many of the progressives can be detected the feeling that modern Western civilization, and especially that part of it which was industrial and urban, had become corrupt."[20] One significant manifestation of this sensibility was hostility to the prevailing forms of authority—including that of the adult over the lives of children.

The clearest expression of the waning of confidence in adult authority was a perceptible hesitancy and reluctance to take responsibility for the socialization of the younger generations. This reluctance to transmit the experience and legacy of the past to the young was particularly widespread among progressive educators in inter-war era. As R. J. W. Selleck noted in his study *English Primary Education and the Progressives: 1914–1939*, this group of educators were "distressed and alienated" by the values that prevailed at the time and "they shied away from imprinting the future generation with the marks of the present." J. H. Nicholson, a professor of education at Newcastle University, forcefully articulated this sentiment. He lamented that "we are an uneasy generation, most of us to some extent ill-adjusted to present conditions" and "should therefore beware of passing on our own prejudices and maladjustments to those we educate."[21]

Skepticism about the moral status of the prevailing values had important implications about the conduct of inter-generational relations. It had a particularly direct impact on education. Similar trends were evident in the sphere of child rearing, where parents looked to new experts to instruct them in the science of parenting. In his 1953 sociological classic, *The Lonely Crowd: A Study of the Changing American Character*, David Riesman drew attention to the erosion of adult authority and the changing relationship between parents and children. Riesman noted that as adults felt less and less certain about "how to bring up children" they opted to retain control through adopting techniques of psychological manipulation.[22]

At the time, it was the political philosopher, Hannah Arendt, who made the most important statement on the implication of the loss of adult authority. She informed a 1956 meeting of the American Society for Political and Legal Philosophy that "authority has vanished from the modern world, and that if we raise the question what authority is, we can no longer fall back upon authentic and undisputable experiences common to all."[23] To emphasize the dimension of the issues at stake, Arendt drew attention to an unprecedented development, which was the "gradual breakdown of the one form of authority" which existed in "all historically known societies, the authority of parents over children, of teachers over pupils and, generally of the elders over the young."[24] She observed that this form of authority "required as much by natural needs, the helplessness of the child, as by political necessity" was always accepted by society. However, she added "ours is the first century in which this argument no longer carries an overwhelming weight of plausibility and it announced its anti-authoritarian spirit more radically when it promised the emancipation of youth as an oppressed class and called itself the 'century of the child.'"[25] Although Arendt did not directly touch on the implications her reflection on the loss of adult authority on the process of socialization, she provided an important contribution for understanding the radical revision of the relationship between the elder generation and the young.

The hesitant and defensive manner with which the task of socialization is pursued has created a demand for new ways of influencing children. A lack of clarity about the exercise of adult authority and regarding the transmission of values has led to a search for alternatives. The adoption of psychologically informed practices of behavior management served as one influential approach towards solving the problem of socialization.[26] These psychological techniques of expert-directed behavior management have had an important influence on childrearing, especially from the 1960s onwards. From this standpoint, the role of parents is not so much to transmit values but to validate the feelings, attitudes, and accomplishment of their children.

Though parents still do their best to transmit their beliefs and ideals to their children, there is a perceptible shift from instilling values to the provision of validation. Affirming children and raising their self-esteem is a project that is actively promoted by parents as well as schools. This emphasis on validation has run in tandem with the custom of a risk-averse regime of child-rearing. The (unintended) consequence of this regime of parenting has been to limit opportunities for the cultivation of independence and to extend the phase of dependence of young people on adult society. Protecting the infantilized child from harm has become the main responsibility of the modern parent. Steven Mintz, in his study of adulthood *The Prime of Life*, claims that "separation from parents is critical for maturation, and for a growing number of the young, psychological independence is achieved more slowly than in previous generations."[27]

One consequence of the delay in the achievement of psychological independence is that many undergraduates except and on occasions even welcome the paternalistic practices of their universities. Such paternalistic practices and support systems are advocated on the grounds that it helps students feel comfortable and safe. Ensuring that undergraduates do not feel uncomfortable during the journey to adulthood has become one of the unstated missions of higher education.

University as an Institute of Socialization

During the past century, responsibility for socialization has gradually shifted from the parent to the school. In recent decades, this activity has seamlessly extended into the sphere of higher education. Higher education now plays an important role in the socialization of an ever-increasing proportion of the younger generation. As Steven Mintz argued, the aim of "universalizing post secondary education" is to significant extent influenced by the objective of assisting the process of socialization.[28]

The trend towards the extension of the role of socialization into the sphere of higher education was well observed by the American sociologist Alvin Gouldner as early as 1979. Gouldner drew attention to the difficulties that parents faced in the carrying out of the task of socializing their children. He stated that "parental, particularly paternal, authority is increasingly vulnerable and is thus less able to insist that children respect societal or political authority outside the home."[29] He claimed that teachers in higher education were increasingly involved in socializing their students into its values. Gouldner described "colleges and universities" as "the finishing schools" for socializing students into the values promote in higher education.

Gouldner's reflections on the difficulty that society had in reproducing its values through the socialization of young people is if anything more apposite today than back in the late 1970s. For some time now, it has been evident that parents and schools have been struggling with the transmission of values and rules of behavior to young people. In part, this problem was caused by the lack confidence of older generations in the values into which it was socialized. More broadly, Western society has become estranged from the values that used to inspire it in the past and found it difficult to provide its adult members with a compelling narrative for socialization.

The absence of a consensus on the narrative of adulthood enhances the difficulty for young people to adopt "grown-up" attitudes to life. Unprepared for a more grown-up independent life, many students regard universities as merely a more difficult and challenging version of a school. What some of them expect is more of the same rather than a qualitatively different experience where they are far more likely to be tested than validated. Under pressure from students, parents, and wider society to share responsibility for the socialization of young people, universities have responded positively to carrying out this task. Unfortunately, this, paternalistic turn of the university has been rarely contested by either its academic staff or its students.

Protecting Students from Pressure

In all but name the imperative of validation has been institutionalized in higher education. In numerous instances the demands of validation have directly contradicted the ethos associated with the exercise of academic freedom and of free speech. Protecting students from the confusion, distress, and pain caused by criticism and academic pressure is often presented as a medical or psychological necessity. The right not to be offended is frequently promoted as a legitimate argument against the exercise of free speech. The call to immunize students from distress and pain underlines the call for trigger warnings and safe spaces. From this perspective, security and safety constitute first-order values, which clearly trump the value of free speech and academic freedom. This transformation of freedom into a second order value in campuses is the inexorable consequence of the psychological turn of socialization.

The devaluation of the ideal of freedom is closely paralleled by the hostility directed at the practice of judgment. Institutes of higher education continually avow the value of non-judgementalism. The act of judgment is often decried as an unpleasant practice that is likely to make its targets feel insecure and emotionally disoriented. Criticism and judgment, which were once seen as essential components of academic teaching, learning, and argument are often condemned as a threat to people's sense of self.[30] In order to assuage the fear of judgment, students are offered safe space and speech codes that aim to criminalize "hurtful" words. Universities celebrate non-judgmentalism as a core value and implicitly regard intellectual pressure and criticism as a health risk

The current claim that students should not have to deal with judgment is based on the proposition that they are too fragile to be expected to deal with its threatening effects, and the advice is to avoid judgment altogether. In recent times, the harms caused by criticism and judgment have become medicalized, and offensive words are condemned as vehicles of a psychological disease. The claim that language offends is not new; what has altered is the manner in which the state of being offended is portrayed. According to the paradigm that informs university guidelines on speech, offensive language does not merely insult but also constitutes a risk to the wellbeing of people. "We always knew that words could hurt our *feelings*, but it turns out that words have a profound effect on our *bodies* as well" claims life coach Linda Pucci in her discussion of "toxic words."[31] Fearful attitudes towards words indicates that in our institutions of higher education, the regulation of language becomes essential for the maintenance of public health.

That many university students are emotionally drawn towards practices that promise to protect them from judgment is not surprising. From an early age, school children are socialized into the commanding pedagogic values of empathy, self-esteem, and unconditionally respecting the view of others. With so much time and resources devoted to affirming the identities of young people, it is not surprising that they believe that they have a right to be validated. So when they arrive at university, they regard an ideal classroom environment as one where their selves and their views are accepted and affirmed. Many undergraduates may have never heard of a safe space, but their socialization has disposed them to expect their institutions to validate their identity. Conversely, many undergraduates regard serious criticism and debate as an unacceptable challenge to their personas.

Many observers are bemused about the rapid escalation of the demand for safe space. Some of those who find the safe space idea melodramatic or incomprehensible dismiss it as a temporary fad that will soon give way to a different target of campus protest. That may well be the case. But so long as the powerful animosity directed at the act of judgment continues to dominate the campus landscape, it will continue to demand protection from free speech and criticism.[32] The spirit of freedom, which has for so long animated academic inquiry, is now directly challenged by the illiberal impulses unleashed by the therapeutic turn of higher education.

The problem afflicting many university undergraduates originates in the cradle. The inability or reluctance of the adult world to socialize the younger generations and educate them to acquire the habit of independence and freedom has created an environment where illiberal and censorious values will continue to flourish. Challenging the current model of psychologically-driven socialization is the precondition for inspiring the younger generations to take freedom really seriously.

Notes

1. Rt Hon. Norman Lamb M. P., "The Invisible Problem? Improving Students' Mental Health," *Higher Education Policy Institute*, September 22, 2016, www.hepi.ac.uk/2016/09/22/3592/
2. See Executive Summary, *ibid.*
3. Julie Hare, "Epidemic of Stressed University Students," *The Australian*, April 6, 2017.
4. "Student Well-Being," *Bournemouth University*. Accessed 8 February, 2016, https://www1.bournemouth.ac.uk/students/health-wellbeing/student-wellbeing
5. "Mental Wellbeing Service," University of Leicester. Accessed 16 February, 2014, http://www2.le.ac.uk/offices/mental-wellbeing
6. Eric Posner, "Universities Are Right—and Within Their Rights—to Crack Down on Speech and Behavior," *Slate*, February 12, 2015.
7. Cited in Jonathan Brown, "Universities Ignoring Binge Drinking Culture and Failing to Protect Students' Wellbeing, Say Teachers," *Independent*, March 6, 2013, www.independent.co.uk/news/education/education-news/universities-ignoring-binge-drinking-culture-and-failing-to-protect-students-wellbeing-say-teachers-8523254.html
8. Cited in Nathan Heller, "The Big Uneasy," *The New Yorker*, May 30, 2016, www.newyorker.com/magazine/2016/05/30/the-new-activism-of-liberal-arts-colleges
9. Cited in Peter Yeung, Sally Weale and Frances Perraudin, "University Mental Health Services Face Strain as Demand Rises 50%," *The Guardian*, September 23, 2016, www.theguardian.com/education/2016/sep/23/university-mental-health-services-face-strain-as-demand-rises-50

10. Linda Banks-Santili, "The Unique Challenges of a First-Generation College Student," *Quartz*, June 3, 2015, http://qz.com/418695/the-unique-challenges-of-a-first-generation-college-student/
11. Abilash Gopal, "Helicopter Parenting Has Given Birth to a Generation of Entitled Victims," *Huffington Post*, April 12, 2016, www.huffingtonpost.com/abilash-gopal-md/helicopter-parenting-has-_b_9657534.html
12. "Help for Common Problems," University of Bath, www.bath.ac.uk/counselling/cshelp
13. See Carrie Wells, "Grading Policy Change Draws Protest at Johns Hopkins," *The Baltimore Sun*, June 1, 2016.
14. *Ibid.*
15. See B. White, "Student Rights: From in Loco Parentis to Sine Parentibus and Back Again-Understanding the Family Educational Rights and Privacy Act in Higher Education," *Brigham Young University Education and Law Journal*, Vol. 2007, No. 2 (2007): 350.
16. See *ibid.*, 331.
17. See Helen E. Johnson, "Educating Parents About College Life," *Chronicle of Higher Education*, January 9, 2004.
18. See N. Howe and W. Strauss, *Millennials Go to College* (Washington, DC: American Association of Collegiate Registrars and Admissions Officers, 2003).
19. David Walsh, *The Growth of the Liberal Soul* (Columbia: University of Missouri Press, 1997): 89.
20. R. J. W Selleck, *English Primary Education and the Progressives: 1914–1939* (London: Routledge & Kegan Paul, 1972): 87.
21. See *ibid.*, 94, 118–119.
22. D. Riesman, *The Lonely Crowd: A Study of the Changing American Character* (New York: Doubleday, 1953): 49, 51, 57.
23. H. Arendt, "What Is Authority," in H. Arendt, *Between Past and Future* (London: Penguin Books, 2006): 81.
24. H. Arendt, "Authority in the Twentieth Century," *The Review of Politics*, Vol. 18, No. 4 (1956): 403.
25. *Ibid.*, 404.
26. These problems are discussed in Chapter 4 of F. Furedi, *Wasted: Why Education Isn't Educating* (London: Continuum Press, 2009).
27. S. Mintz, *The Prime of Life* (Cambridge, MA: Harvard University Press, 2015): 21.
28. See chapter "The Tangled transition to Adulthood" in Mintz 2015.
29. A. W. Gouldner, *The Future of Intellectuals and the Rise of the New Class* (London: The Macmillan Press, 1979): 44.
30. See F. Furedi, *What's Happened to the University?* (Abingdon-on-Thames: Routledge, 2016), Chapter 4.
31. See Linda Pucci, "Toxic Words—Verbal Abuse Can Hurt You," *Ezine Articles*, July 23, 2008, http://ezinearticles.com/?Toxic-Words—-Verbal-Abuse-Can-Hurt-You&id=1350602
32. See my chapter on verbal purification in Furedi, *What's Happened to the University?* 2016.

Works Cited

Arendt, H. "Authority in the Twentieth Century." *The Review of Politics*, Vol. 18, No. 4 (1956): 403–417.

———. "What Is Authority." In *Between Past and Future*, by H. Arendt. London: Penguin Books, 2006.

Banks-Santili, Linda. "The Unique Challenges of a First-Generation College Student." *Quartz*. June 3, 2015. http://qz.com/418695/the-unique-challenges-of-a-first-generation-college-student/

Brown, Jonathan. "Universities Ignoring Binge Drinking Culture and Failing to Protect Students' Wellbeing, Say Teachers." *Independent*. March 6, 2013.

Furedi, Frank. *Wasted: Why Education Isn't Educating*. London: Continuum Press, 2009.

———. *What's Happened to the University?* Abingdon-on-Thames: Routledge, 2016.

Gopal, Abilash. "Helicopter Parenting Has Given Birth to a Generation of Entitled Victims." *Huffington Post*. April 12, 2016. www.huffingtonpost.com/abilash-gopal-md/helicopter-parenting-has-_b_9657534.html

Gouldner, A. W. *The Future of Intellectuals and the Rise of the New Class*. London: The Macmillan Press, 1979.

Hare, Julie. "Epidemic of Stressed University Students." *The Australian*. April 6, 2017.

Heller, Nathan. "The Big Uneasy." *The New Yorker*. May 30, 2016. www.newyorker.com/magazine/2016/05/30/the-new-activism-of-liberal-arts-colleges

"Help for Common Problems." *University of Bath*. www.bath.ac.uk/counselling/cshelp

Howe, N. and Strauss, W. *Millennials go to College*. Washington, DC: American Association of Collegiate Registrars and Admissions Officers, 2003.

Johnson, Helen E. "Educating Parents About College Life." *Chronicle of Higher Education*. January 9, 2004.

Lamb, M. P., Rt Hon. Norman. "The Invisible Problem? Improving Students' Mental Health." *Higher Education Policy Institute*. September 22, 2016. www.hepi.ac.uk/2016/09/22/3592/

"Mental Wellbeing Service." *University of Leicester*. Accessed February 16, 2014. http://www2.le.ac.uk/offices/mental-wellbeing

Mintz, S. *The Prime of Life*. Cambridge, MA: Harvard University Press, 2015.

Posner, Eric. "Universities Are Right—and Within Their Rights—to Crack Down on Speech and Behavior." *Slate*. February 12, 2015.

Pucci, Linda. "Toxic Words—Verbal Abuse Can Hurt You." *Ezine Articles*. July 23, 2008. http://ezinearticles.com/?Toxic-Words---Verbal-Abuse-Can-Hurt-You&id=1350602

Riesman, D. *The Lonely Crowd: A Study of the Changing American Character*. New York: Doubleday, 1953.

Selleck, R. J. W. *English Primary Education and the Progressives: 1914–1939*. London: Routledge & Kegan Paul, 1972.

"Student Well-Being." *Bournemouth University*. Accessed February 8, 2016. https://www1.bournemouth.ac.uk/students/health-wellbeing/student-wellbeing

Walsh, David. *The Growth of the Liberal Soul*. Columbia: University of Missouri Press, 1997.

Wells, Carrie. "Grading Policy Change Draws Protest at Johns Hopkins." *The Baltimore Sun*. June 1, 2016.

White, B. "Student Rights: From in Loco Parentis to Sine Parentibus and Back Again-Understanding the Family Educational Rights and Privacy Act in Higher Education." *Brigham Young University Education and Law Journal*, Vol. 2007, No. 2 (2007): 321–350.

Yeung, P., Weale, S. and Perraudin, F. "University Mental Health Services Face Strain as Demand Rises 50%." *The Guardian*. September 23, 2016.

13 Don't Make Me Laugh

Speech Codes and the Humorless Campus

Edward Johnson

Major comedians such as Chris Rock and Jerry Seinfeld have stopped performing on college campuses, "because the audiences are too easily offended." A report in the *Wall Street Journal* (Belkin 2015) notes a general trend, among those comedians who must still rely on the college circuit, toward self-censorship and the substitution of less challenging material. Anne Libera, director of comedy studies in the theater department at Columbia College in Chicago, points out that a gradual shift, over the past couple decades, "has been sped up by the Internet and social media . . . if they push too far now, they risk being recorded and shamed." Journalist Douglas Belkin adds, "Many comedians find it ironic that the venues that gave birth to social movements and comedy legends such as George Carlin are becoming too squeamish for their material."

Campus audiences that are quick to take offense at comic jibes are filled with students who seem to their critics to be self-centered, thin-skinned, and litigious, lacking an ability to laugh at themselves, in universities that are increasingly rule-bound ("procedural"), bureaucratic ("managerial"), and crassly utilitarian ("results oriented"), obsessed with "effectiveness" and liability. Leftist faculty lament the influence of corporations, and right-wing faculty complain about "political correctness" (see Johnson 1997).

The effect of this drift towards a humorless campus leads not only to the treatment of particular words and even topics as taboo and to the use of speech codes, trigger warnings, and other impediments to spontaneity. It extends to the placing of unspecifiable limits on communication and, in aim, thought itself. As sociologist Frank Furedi observes, "the battle against inappropriate language can never end. In such circumstances, even the most unlikely words can become a target of a mini moral crusade" (Furedi 2017, 96). This is where the well-intentioned objections (by Negroes/blacks/African Americans) to "boy" and (by feminists) to "girl," seem to have led us, half a century later: to the quest for "microaggression" behind every word chosen, or even omitted, and to the conviction (from a University of Melbourne guidebook, cited in Furedi 2017, 98) that "we discriminate through assuming the normality and neutrality of our own identity group."

The point of law is to protect individuals from unreasonable harm and provide adequate redress. The traditional liberal position, exemplified in John Stuart Mill, distinguishes "harm" from "offense," offering little comfort for the latter (for the philosophical complexities involved see Feinberg 1984, 1985; for the legal complexities see Greenawalt 1989, 1995). The line between harm and offense may be difficult to draw, but that is why we need philosophers (in theory) and judges (in practice). Journalist David K. Shipler, in his recent history, *Freedom of Speech: Mightier than the Sword*, espouses this traditional position in straightforward terms: "I am as close to being an absolutist on the First Amendment as possible without quite being one. I can accept the Supreme Court's differentiation between cross burning as symbolic speech in an empty field and cross burning as intimidation on a family's lawn." As for offense, Shipler adopts the traditional liberal view there as well: "the real answer to offensive speech is more speech, not retribution" (Shipler 2015, 10). In a similar spirit, after concluding that "campus speech codes . . . have serious formulation and enforcement problems," Martin Golding adds that "demeaning assertions should be combated by counterargument, not by punitive sanctions" (Goldman 2000, 64; see also Rauch, 1993).

One might have thought that the contemporary world of electronic communication—with which the college campus, in complex ways, overlaps—would fulfill the liberal dream of "more speech." More people can promulgate their views more widely and more quickly, and with less limitation, than ever before. And yet all of that seems only to have intensified the problem—in part, because the Internet has tended to diminish, or even erase, the difference between the near and the far, between the lawn and the empty field. The baleful effects of disinformation, misinformation, and even truth can be omnipresent ("viral") in an instant. Ideas spread, but context is optional, which provides a perfect environment for misunderstanding, even absent manipulative intent.

The idea that "more speech" is the solution has been under attack for some time. The quondam feminist critique of pornography, for example, viewed the pervasiveness of exploitative images of women as at least constituting intimidation, and probably being harmful in more direct ways (see Johnson 1995). The feminist-inspired critique of sexual harassment (currently radically transforming American society) has encouraged us to perceive (sufficiently) unfriendly environments as harmful. The creation of the category of "hate speech" aims (often successfully) to disqualify certain viewpoints from participation in public conversation. (Even as the Internet breaks down the distinction between public and private comment—as does the pervasiveness of surveillance.)

One of the most influential theorists on hate speech has been Stanley Fish, whose work derives in substantial measure from his career-long reflection on a passage in John Milton's famous defense of unregulated publication, *Areopagitica*, in which the poet makes it clear that he does not mean to include Catholics: "I mean not tolerated popery, and open superstition . . . [And] that also which is impious or evil absolutely against faith and manners no law can possibly permit that intends not to unlaw itself" (Fish, 103). Generalizing from Milton, Fish argues that the communities in which speech occurs are not abstract but concrete and based on some taken-for-granted good or purpose. Accordingly, "in some circumstances, freedom of expression may pose a threat to that purpose, and at that point it may be necessary to discipline or regulate speech, lest, to paraphrase Milton, the institution sacrifice itself to one of its *accidental* features." Moreover,

> free expression could only be a primary value if what you are valuing is the right to make noise; but if you are engaged in some purposive activity in the course of which speech happens to be produced, sooner or later you will come to a point when you decide that some forms of speech do not further but endanger that purpose.
>
> (Fish 1994, 107)

Fish argues that there is no nonpartisan way to separate speech from action, and that therefore every attempt to do so ultimately boils down to a political decision about which consequences of action are acceptable and which are not. "The question of whether or not to regulate will always be a local one, and we can not [*sic*] rely on abstractions that are either empty of content or filled with the content of some partisan agenda to generate a 'principled' answer" (111). We should not sacrifice substantive local concerns for vague and uncertain results down the line: "when it happens that the present shape of truth is compelling beyond a reasonable doubt, it is our moral obligation to act on it and not defer action in the name of an interpretative future that may never arrive" (113). Though there are no guarantees, says Fish, "right now [sc., 1994] the risk of not attending to hate speech is greater than the risk that by regulating it we will deprive ourselves of valuable voices and insights or slide down the slippery slope toward tyranny" (115).

In the end, Fish makes it clear that his argument is really against the role of regulative ideals:

> the strategy of saying, "Well, we can't get beyond or around ideology, but at least we can make a good faith try"—won't work either. In what cleared and ideology-free space will the "try" be made? One must ask, and, if the answer is . . . that there is no such cleared space, the notion of "trying" can have no real content. . . . I would expand this point into an argument for the emptiness of any gesture that invokes a regulative ideal.
>
> (116)

It would be possible to agree with Fish's account of the partisan character of free-speech rhetoric, and yet disagree with his judgment (of a quarter-century ago) that regulating hate speech is, here and now, more important that protecting it. Perhaps the pendulum has swung too far. "In Canada," as David Bernstein notes, "academics are beginning to learn firsthand what it's like to have their own censorship vehicles used against them" (Bernstein 2003, 71). But such variability is doubtless what Fish would expect, given the "local" nature of the question of speech regulation.

Accordingly, one looks for a more fundamental response to Fish's argument. Despite the large number of attacks in recent years on the "silencing" of academic discussion by "the left" (see, e.g., Lukianoff 2014; Ham and Benson 2015; Powers 2015; Strassel 2016). Fish's underlying point has rarely been addressed. Bernstein, taking up the subject briefly, argues that Fish "ignores the role played by psychology and social norms in shaping judicial behavior" (Bernstein 2003, 20), citing the importance of the norm of judicial objectivity in protecting minority rights in periods when members of such groups were culturally oppressed. Bernstein also suggests that Fish's view has an underlying inconsistency. "Those who argue that purportedly illusory notions of freedom of speech should be sacrificed to equalitarian commitments that are based on notions at least as delusive cannot possibly explain why" (21). In response to Bernstein's criticisms, Fish would presumably reply (like Nietzsche) that his emphasis on the political character of fundamental commitments applies to whatever normative vocabulary one deploys, and that his aim is to keep us from being distracted from those commitments by supposedly objective arguments for so-called objectivity.

A deeper critique of Fish depends on taking up the issue of regulative ideals. Not only do judges draw upon the ideal of judicial objectivity, as Bernstein emphasizes, and scientists draw upon the ideal of scientific objectivity, as Bernard Williams urges against Richard Rorty's pragmatism (Williams 1985), so that effectiveness in these fields is affected by the serious use of these ideals in practice—"trying" to do what may be strictly impossible. In addition, the presence of ideals of objectivity in our culture influences deliberation, as does its absence. While some may see these ideals as mystifications (Fish's own use of that concept is limited by his unapologetic relativism), it is hard to see how a pragmatist analysis can reject whatever efficacy they have. (If one substitutes "belief in X" as the cause of the effects one used to attribute to X, and that destroys belief in X—what then?)

In addition, the notion of a community as defined by a purpose does not make clear that we live in many communities, with many purposes, overlapping and conflicting. What predominates may be determined by power, force, or violence, in lieu of the partially manipulative, but partially sincere, rhetoric that makes peace, in its variegated forms and degrees, achievable.

I remember lecturing, some years ago, on Mark Twain's *Huckleberry Finn* to a mixed-race honors class, and addressing the delicate question of how to weigh bowdlerization against racial sensitivity. Years earlier, in my dissertation, *Species and Morality* (1976), I had quoted the passage in which Huck, responding to his aunt's question about whether an exploding boiler had injured anybody, says: "No'm. Killed a nigger." Obviously, "killed an N-word" would not do. It not only fails the gravity of the occasion, but it introduces an inappropriately comic note. More importantly, such jiggery-pokery encourages what philosophers call a use/mention confusion.

I heard a conservative political pundit on the radio recently (Paris Dennard, on NPR) commenting on a fraternity that "didn't want N words"—only to realize, after a moment's confusion, that what he meant was that the fraternity was discouraging, not use of the *word* "nigger," but rather black membership itself. This raises the use/mention confusion to a new level, weirdly pluralizing the mention as a way of pluralizing the tacit use. Let that serve as a reminder of the snares of self-censorship.

Comedian Louis C.K. (now among the growing number of famous men disgraced because of their sexual harassment) jokes (but, you know, seriously) that using "the N-word" (not the word "nigger," but the expression "the N-word") is just a sneaky way of making listeners hear in their heads what the speaker affects not to say. (For more on the epithet, see Kennedy 2002, Asim 2007, Larkin 2004, Allan and Burridge 2006, and Neu 2008; for more on the philosophical sophistication of Louis C.K.'s comedy, see Ralkowski 2016).

And yet . . . does it do no harm to hear one's (white) professor using (well, *mentioning*) that word? Obviously, if the employment of words produced direct, immediate, and serious harm, the case for restriction would be obvious. I am not free to say a word (through sound amplification) at a decibel-level that will injure your eardrums. What if the mere *hearing* of the (unamplified) word produced harm? Sci-fi thought experiment (*pace* Hilary Putnam): On the N planet, if someone hears another person say "nigger," the hearer immediately drops dead. Plainly, there would be a need for laws (and, perhaps, ear plugs). Now what if the harm is less immediate, less extreme, less certain? What if it depends on *who* says it?

The ongoing salience of this issue is evidenced by an event at Princeton University in February 2018, as this volume was in press. Anthropologist Lawrence Rosen announced the cancellation of his course on Cultural Freedoms—Hate Speech, Blasphemy, and Pornography—after some students walked out of class because his use of the word "nigger" in several examples. The campus controversy was reflected in letters to the *Daily Princetonian*. The Chair of the Anthropology Department defended her colleague (Rouse 2018). The paper's Editor-in-Chief explained why she "won't publish the word 'n****r'" (Brown 2018), though, in a philosophical irony, she did thereby publish "n****r." Timothy Haupt, another anthropologist, who teaches a course entitled "The Social and Political Lives of Humor," defended the students: "As regards to the N-word and other instances of hate speech, it may be the case that we cannot fully avoid or silence the performantive dimension of the terms even when we use them as Rosen did in his . . . question about a hypothetical situation in which the N-word was used performatively to humiliate another" (Haupt 2018).

Throughout most of his career, Richard Pryor used the word "nigger" prominently in his comedy, but towards the end he gave up the word after a transformational trip to Africa where, as he told audiences later, he saw no niggers. Comedian and civil rights activist Dick Gregory prefaced his 1964 autobiography, *Nigger*, with a touching dedication: "Dear Momma—Wherever you are, if ever you hear the word 'nigger' again, remember they are advertising my book" (Gregory 1964). Maybe, as with epithets, what matters is not (just) who is being laughed at (or with), but who is doing the laughing. Maybe "laughter out of place" can be a weapon of empowerment for the victim (see Goldstein 2003). That is certainly the leftist position.

One reason for the split between leftists and classical liberals turns on the question of how to understand harm. Meira Levinson, arguing for a pedagogy that empowers students, even in secondary school, to challenge the power relationships found in society, describes the challenge she faced in dealing with a Jewish student who wanted to do a project critiquing same-sex marriage. "Gay marriage was clearly a controversial public issue on which well-intentioned people disagreed," she concedes (Levinson 2012, 201). However:

> tolerance lies at the heart of having an open classroom climate, and frankly also at the heart of educating as opposed to indoctrinating. But not all positions are permissible, even in a public school classroom: we don't need to entertain pro-Nazi ideology, or wistfulness about the days of Jim Crow. So where did opposition to same-sex marriage fall? If gay rights are human rights, was it really appropriate to allow their civil, even human rights, to be married in the eyes of the state to be challenged in our classroom?
>
> (202)

Not every topic of conversation, apparently, is "a controversial public issue on which well-intentioned people" can disagree. Indeed, an important feature of the leftist position is that certain moral questions are settled, and so steps should be taken to keep them from falsely appearing to be controversial. Scholars such as Deborah Lipstadt decline to debate holocaust deniers because they don't want to support the impression that it is a serious view worth debating (Lipstadt 1994, 200–201, 221).

Deliberation is influenced, says Fish, "by whatever notions are current in the culture," and when David Duke appeared in prominent media forums, "these appearances legitimized him and put his views into national circulation in a way that made them an unavoidable component of the nation's thinking" (Fish 1994, 118; for Duke's deft exploitation of the media, see Esolen 1992). The creation of the category of "hate speech" aims to disqualify certain viewpoints from participation in public conversation (see Delgado and Stefancic 2004; Shiell 2007). Ultimately, the point is not just that some *language*, such as ethnic slurs, is demeaning or offensive—the point is that some *thought* is unacceptable, beyond discussion.

Levinson also explains why she is unconvinced by John Rawls's arguments about the priority of public reason over private considerations (which is just another version of the defining distinction liberalism tries to draw between the values that we share and the values that separate us). "I am suspicious of the hegemonic character of public reason, which too easily tends to elevate majoritarian cultural norms and perspectives into the 'public' category and reject minority norms and perspectives as 'nonpublic,'" she says (Levinson 2012, 205–206). Hence the perspective represented in the University of Melbourne guidebook cited at the beginning of this paper, that "we discriminate through assuming the normality and neutrality of our own identity group" (Furedi 2017, 98).

Even as I was finishing this paper, a profile by Richard Fausset, in the *New York Times*, of Tony Hovater, a white nationalist from Ohio who had marched in Charlottesville, was met with howls of outrage online claiming that the newspaper was "normalizing" (i.e., legitimizing) a Nazi sympathizer (Fausset 2017. Shane Bauer, a reporter at *Mother Jones* magazine, made a sensible suggestion: "People mad about this article want to believe that Nazis are monsters we cannot relate to. White supremacists are normal ass white people and it's been that way in America since 1776. We will continue to be in trouble till we understand that" (Lacey 2017). Indeed, the very premise of Fausset's story was to find out, "Why did this man—intelligent, socially adroit and raised middle class amid the relatively well-integrated environments of United States military bases—gravitate toward the furthest extremes of American political discourse?" Would one ask that question about . . . a Republican? Like his critics, Fausset assumed that pro-Nazi ideology does not need to be—should not be—entertained, but needs instead to be explained: It is not something about which well-intentioned people might just disagree. Hence the need to view the extremist as a case to be explained away, rather than as a (potential) partner in a political conversation. And similarly, *mutatis mutandis*, for all of the other settled moral issues.

One of the advantages of comedy is that it allows us to explore delicate subjects without committing ourselves. We can feel others out, and if we find we have gone too far, we can pull back, and be "only joking." And yet the flip side of that is that one can only pretend to be only joking, while really being cruel (see Johnson 2006; for "joking relationships" in anthropology, see Apte 1985). As James Poniewozik writes in the *New York Times* about public figures hiding behind their "jokes":

> The candidate who successfully merges entertainment and politics is potent, because you can claim to be joking to one audience while another sees you as a truth teller. . . . The idea that comedy is a protected space for testing boundaries—that it requires the freedom to take risks and say what forbidden elsewhere—is an old one. After the comedian Louis C.K. admitted to sexual misconduct . . . that idea sounds, at least in some cases, like an excuse.
>
> (Poniewozik 2017)

Though Voltaire himself appears not to have said the exact words, what we might reasonably call "the Voltairean ideal" is best captured by the sentiment ascribed to him by his biographer Evelyn Beatrice Hall (writing under the pseudonym S. G. Tallentyre): "I disapprove of what you say but I will defend to the death your right to say it" (see Boller and George 1989, 125; Keyes 1992, 44, 193). The same ideal is captured in what Supreme Court Justice Oliver Wendell Holmes Jr. characterized as "freedom for the thought that we hate" (see Lewis 2007; Strum 1999; Stern 1996).

Two decades ago, in concluding an article analyzing "Political Correctness," I cited the 1996 case of Keshia Thomas, a young black woman who intervened with her body to shield a Ku Klux Klan member who was being assaulted by anti-Klan demonstrators at a rally in Ann Arbor, Michigan. "Just because you beat somebody doesn't mean you are going to change his mind," she explained afterwards. "I was just doing what my parents taught me to do—just doing what's right" (Johnson 1997). Stanley Fish served as a referee for that article, and dismissed this case as merely a "feel good" story.

Three months ago, in Berkeley, California, at a large left-wing counter-protest against white supremacy, some anti-fascists ("antifa") began beating a right-wing man who fell to the ground. Al Letson, host of the investigative-reporting radio program *Reveal*, jumped in and put his body on top of the man to ward off blows. This not only exposed him to serious danger but also required him to set aside his journalistic reservations about becoming part of the story. "What came to me was that he was a human being," Letson said later. "It doesn't matter if he doesn't see my humanity, what matters to me is that I see his." He remembered once hearing Father Greg Boyle tell radio interviewer Terry Gross, " I want to live like the truth is true, and go where love has not been found" (McEvers 2017).

Fish's demystification of regulative ideals and reduction of praxis to politics is part of the Enlightenment project to make the world a better place through rational analysis, planning, and control. But part of what makes the world work is ambiguity. Both parties to a treaty may be able to agree they want a just and lasting peace, though they have quite different ideas about what all those terms mean. In *What's Happened to the University?* (2017), Frank Furedi rightly sees the managerial bureaucracy of higher education as the flip side of rules regulating speech:

> The imposition of learning outcomes . . . serves to diminish what would otherwise be an open-ended experience for student and teacher alike. Those who advocate them do so with the aim of abolishing such experiences, which is why they target anything that smacks of ambiguity. . . . Hostility to ambiguity speaks to a pedagogic ethos that has become estranged from the open-ended pursuit of ideas. . . . In demanding that the outcome of learning should be stated in advance, this technique undermines the freedom that is required for intellectual exploration.
>
> (174)

Irish Nobel laureate Seamus Heaney's response to Plato's doubts about the poets, in *The Redress of Poetry* (1995), invokes such open-endedness, which he calls "surprise," with a striking image:

> I want to profess the surprise of poetry as well as its reliability; I want to celebrate its given, unforeseeable thereness, the way it enters our field of vision and animates our physical and intelligent being in much the same way as those bird-shapes stencilled on the transparent surfaces of glass walls or windows must suddenly enter the vision and change the direction of the real birds' flight. In a flash the shapes register and transmit their unmistakable presence, so the birds veer off instinctively. An image of the living creatures has induced a totally salubrious swerve in the creatures themselves.
>
> (Heaney, 15)

In figuring what is possible, poetry (and art, and all the cultural forms that help us to understand one another) offers ideals that make possible such a "salubrious swerve"—make it possible to trust, after all, and to go where love has never been.

In "Nice Day for a Lynching," poet Kenneth Patchen contemplates the scene (in a photograph, presumably), identifying both with the black man who is being hanged and with "these honorable men who laugh" in the white crowd below (Patchen 1957, 52):

> One part of me is being strangled,
> While another part horribly laughs.

Does bad laughter deserve indulgence in a democracy? Does it have any place on a university campus? Beyond the offense of being laughed at, there is the (presumably, psychological) harm of being laughed at. And beyond that there is, as Levinson suggests, a kind of civic harm. (Unless being laughed at, in the rough and tumble of joking relationships, is part of being treated as an equal. Is the laughter inclusive, even if cruel, or exclusive, even if kind?)

We might insist that something is "not funny." But if "part of me" laughs at it, then, as comedians like to say, funny is funny. Then again, one might say that it is "not a laughing matter"—meaning that laughter is not proper or appropriate. The question is not whether one *does* laugh at something, but whether one *ought* to. Of course, the application of "ought" in the context of comedy is fraught with difficulty. (As new vaudevillian Bill Irwin remarks, tongue-in-cheek, in the 1997 documentary *Vaudeville*, "If you had read as much as I have, you would find this very funny.") What are the limits of humor? (See Lockyer and Pickering 2009).

If rape is wrong not just because it inflicts a harm but because it violates consent, or if violating consent is part of what makes it a harm (on the philosophical complexities here, see Werthheimer 2003), then what about making people feel (without their consent) what they don't want to feel, laugh at what they don't want to laugh at? Harry Frankfurt pointed out that we not only have first-order desires, but second-order desires about what we desire, and perhaps yet higher-order desires—indeed, he located what he viewed as distinctive about human persons in this capacity for higher-order desires (Frankfurt 1988). In this complex structure of desires, the possibilities of seducing, suborning, coercing, or otherwise interfering invite closer scrutiny (for more on the role of "metapreferences," see Epstein 2003).

Laughing *with* unites, and laughing *at* separates—but what does laughing at oneself do? If Aristotle is right in suggesting that pain is the mother of tragedy, and laughter is the mother of comedy, what do we have when we laugh at pain? There is a difference, some (e.g., Siegel 1987) would say, between laughing at the pain of others (satire) and laughing at our own pain (humor). To laugh at the pain of others is cruelty; to laugh at our own pain is irony, Richard Rorty might suggest (Rorty 1989). At the limit, Dionysus affronts Apollo, the god of moral judgment, by saying, "It's all good"—mercy and forgiveness trumping punishment and responsibility. It is saving *both* thieves. Because we *are* both. One side says: Don't take yourself so seriously, it's all a joke. The other side replies: Don't make me laugh.

Works Cited

Allan, Keith, and Burridge, Kate. *Forbidden Words: Taboo and the Censoring of Language*. Cambridge: Cambridge University Press, 2006.

Apte, Mahadev L. *Humor and Laughter: An Anthropological Approach*. Ithaca, NY: Cornell University Press, 1985.

Asim, Jabari. *The N Word: Who Can Say It, Who Shouldn't, and Why*. New York: Houghton Mifflin, 2007.

Belkin, Douglas. "For Stand-Up Comedians, Shows on Campus Are Often No Joke." *Wall Street Journal*. November 16, 2015.

Bernstein, David E. *You Can't Say That! The Growing Threat to Civil Liberties From Antidiscrimination Laws*. Washington, DC: Cato Institute, 2003.

Boller, Paul F., Jr. and George, John. *They Never Said It: A Book of Fake Quotes, Misquotes, and Misleading Attributions*. Oxford: Oxford University Press, 1989.

Brown, Marcia. "Letter from the Editor: Why I Won't Publish the Word 'N****R'," *Daily Princetonian*, February, 13, 2018.

Delgado, Richard, and Stefancic, Jean. *Understanding Words that Wound*. Boulder, CO: Westview Press, 2004.

Epstein, Richard. *Skepticism and Freedom: A Modern Case for Classical Liberalism*. Chicago: University of Chicago Press, 2003.

Esolen, Gary. "More than a Pretty Face: David Duke's Use of Television as a Political Tool." In *The Emergence of David Duke and the Politics of Race*, edited by Douglas Rose. Chapel Hill, NC: University of North Carolina Press, 136–155.

Fausset, Richard. "A Voice of Hate in America's Heartland." *New York Times*. November 25, 2017.

Feinberg, Joel. *The Moral Limits of the Criminal Law*, Vol. 1: *Harm to Others*. Oxford: Oxford University Press, 1984.

———. *The Moral Limits of the Criminal Law*, Vol. 2: *Offense to Others*. Oxford: Oxford University Press, 1985.

Fish, Stanley. *There's No Such Thing as Free Speech: And It's a Good Thing, Too*. Oxford: Oxford University Press, 1994.

Frankfurt, Harry. *The Importance of What We Care About*. Cambridge: Cambridge University Press, 1988.

Furedi, Frank. *What's Happened to the University? A Sociological Exploration of Its Infantilisation*. London: Routledge, 2017.

Golding, Martin. *Free Speech on Campus*. Lanham, MD: Rowman and Littlefield, 2000.

Goldstein, Donna M. *Laughter Out of Place: Race. Class Violence and Sexuality in a Rio Shantytown*. Berkeley, CA: University of California Press, 2003.

Greenawalt, Kent. *Speech, Crime, and the Use of Language*. Oxford: Oxford University Press, 1989.

———. *Fighting Words: Individuals, Communities, and Liberties of Speech*. Princeton, NJ: Princeton University Press, 1995.

Gregory, Dick. *Nigger*. New York: E. P. Dutton, 1964.

Ham, Mary Katharine and Benson, Guy. *End of Discussion: How the Left's Outrage Industry Shuts Down Debate, Manipulates Voters, and Makes America Less Free (and Fun)*. New York: Crown Forum, 2015.

Haupt, Timothy. "Letter to the Editor: In Defense of Students Who Walked Out on Rosen," *Daily Princetonian*, February 12, 2018.

Heaney, Seamus. *The Redress of Poetry*. New York: Farrar, Straus, and Giroux, 1995.

Johnson, Edward. "Beauty's Punishment: How Feminists Look at Pornography." In *Nagging Questions: Feminist Ethics in Everyday Life*, edited by Dana Bushnell. Lanham, MD: Rowman and Littlefield, 1995: 335–360.

———. "Political Correctness." In *Encyclopedia of Applied Ethics*, Vol. 3, edited by Ruth Chadwick. New York: Academic Press, 1997: 565–579.

———. "Humor." In *Sex From Plato to Paglia: A Philosophical Encyclopedia*, edited by Alan Soble. Westport, CT: Greenwood Press, 2006: 480–486.

Kennedy, Randall. *Nigger: The Strange Career of a Troublesome Word*. New York: Pantheon Books, 2002.

Keyes, Ralph. *"Nice Guys Finish Seventh": False Phrases, Spurious Sayings, and Familiar Misquotations*. New York: Harper Collins, 1992.

Lacey, Marc. "Readers Accuse Us of Normalizing a Nazi Sympathizer; We Respond." *New York Times*, online. November 26, 2017.

Larkin, Todd. *The N Word* (documentary film). 2004.

Levinson, Meira. *No Citizen Left Behind*. Cambridge, MA: Harvard University Press, 2012.

Lewis, Anthony. *Freedom for the Thought That We Hate: A Biography of the First Amendment*. New York: Basic Books, 2007.

Lipstadt, Debroah. *Denying the Holocaust: The Growing Assault on Truth and Memory*. New York: Free Press, 1994.

Lockyer, Sharon and Pickering, Michael. *Beyond a Joke: The Limits of Humour*. London: Palgrave Macmillan, 2009.

Lukianoff, Greg. *Unlearning Liberty: Campus Censorship and the End of American Debate*. New York: Encounter Books, 2014.

McEvers, Kelly. "I Saw His Humanity: 'Reveal' Host on Protecting Right-Wing Protester." National Public Radio. August 28, 2017.

Neu, Jerome. *Sticks and Stones: The Philosophy of Insults*. Oxford: Oxford University Press, 2008.

Patchen, Kenneth. *Selected Poems*. New York: New Directions, 1957.

Poniewozik, James. "Hiding Behind Their 'Jokes.'" *New York Times*. November 21, 2017.

Powers, Kirsten. *The Silencing: How the Left Is Killing Free Speech*. Washington, DC: Regnery, 2015.

Ralkowski, Mark. *Louis C.K. and Philosophy: You Don't Get to Be Bored*. Chicago: Open Court, 2016.

Rouse, Carolyn. "Letter to the Editor: In Defense of Rosen," *Daily Princetonian*, February 8, 2018.

Rorty, Richard. *Contingency, Irony, and Solidarity*. Cambridge: Cambridge University Press, 1989.

Shiell, Timothy. *Campus Hate Speech on Trial*. Lawrence, KS: University Press of Kansas, 2009.

Shipler, David K. *Freedom of Speech: Mightier Than the Sword*. New York: Alfred A. Knopf, 2015.

Siegel, Lee. *Laughing Matters: Comic Tradition in India*. Chicago: University of Chicago Press, 1987.

Strassel, Kimberley. *The Intimidation Game: How the Left Is Silencing Free Speech*. New York: Twelve, 2016.

Strum, Philippa. *When the Nazis Came to Skokie: Freedom for Speech We Hate*. Lawrence, KS: University Press of Kansas, 1999.

Werthheimer, Alan. *Consent to Sexual Relations*. Cambridge: Cambridge University Press, 2003.

Williams, Bernard. *Ethics and the Limits of Philosophy*. Cambridge, MA: Harvard University Press, 1985.

14 Sex, Liberty, and Freedom of Expression at the American University

Evan Gerstmann

The Rapid Rise of Affirmative Consent Regimes

In the fall of 2014, California Governor Jerry Brown signed the nation's first mandatory "affirmative consent" legislation regulating sexual activity among college students. It applies to all schools, public or private, receiving state funds. The law states:

> An affirmative consent standard in the determination of whether consent was given by both parties to sexual activity. "Affirmative consent" means affirmative, conscious, and voluntary agreement to engage in sexual activity. It is the responsibility of each person involved in the sexual activity to ensure that he or she has the affirmative consent of the other or others to engage in the sexual activity. Lack of protest or resistance does not mean consent, nor does silence mean consent. Affirmative consent must be ongoing throughout a sexual activity and can be revoked at any time. The existence of a dating relationship between the persons involved, or the fact of past sexual relations between them, should never by itself be assumed to be an indicator of consent.
>
> (State of California 2014)

New York State followed with its own legislation:

> Affirmative consent is a knowing, voluntary, and mutual decision among all participants to engage in sexual activity. Consent can be given by words or actions, as long as those words or actions create clear permission regarding willingness to engage in the sexual activity. Silence or lack of resistance, in and of itself, does not demonstrate consent. The definition of consent does not vary based upon a participant's sex, sexual orientation, gender identity, or gender expression.
>
> (State of New York 2015)

In addition, between 1,000 and 2,000 colleges across the country, both public and private, have adopted affirmative consent rules. In the United

States, affirmative consent is well on its way to becoming the norm for higher education. They vary in their exact wording and specificity. For example, Ohio State University, one of the nation's largest schools, specifies that "Previous relationships or prior consent cannot imply consent to future sexual acts . . . this includes 'blanket' consent (i.e., permission in advance for any/all actions at a later time/place)." Other universities go further, stating that "Consent is a voluntary, sober, imaginative, enthusiastic, creative, wanted, informed, mutual, honest, and verbal agreement." (Gersen and Suk 2016, 925).

Many advocates for rape victims applaud this development. They hope that such rules will encourage reporting by victims of sexual assault, make it easier for colleges to hold sexual assailants responsible for their actions, and encourage male students to always ensure that they have a person's consent before they touch them in a sexual manner.

Affirmative consent laws and policies are surely well-intentioned. After all, sexual contact without consent is by definition sexual assault, so these rules can be seen as a commonsense way to ensure that this does not happen.

This chapter argues that despite these good intentions, affirmative consent regimes violate students' rights to sexual autonomy. They mandate a government-approved way of engaging in and communicating about sex. It is important to understand that affirmative consent regimes go beyond merely requiring consent. They regulate how students express that consent and do so in a manner that is contrary to how most people actually engage in sexual activity. They turn many, if not most students, into expellable perpetrators of sexual assault.

Research shows that most people signal their consent by simply not objecting to what their partner is doing. For example, a recent study of college students showed: "The behaviors used most frequently to communicate consent were behaviors loading on the No Resistance factor: not stopping their partner from kissing or touching them, not resisting their partner's advances, and not saying no." (Muehlenhard et al. 2016, 468). Other studies conclude that "consent is often communicated and interpreted using ambiguous, nonverbal cues" (Jozkowski and Peterson 2013, 520).

In other words, when two people are being sexually passionate, they generally do not ask one another permission before touching the other person. They progress from one stage of sexual touching to the next and if one person feels that the other has gone too far, then they will indicate that verbally or in some other way. Under affirmative consent regimes, all of this typical, consensual sexual activity constitutes an expellable offense.

The scope of these rules are often breathtaking. They make no exceptions for couples in long-term relationships, or even married couples who develop over time their own understandings of what the rules of sexual contact are. Kimberly Kessler Ferzan, the Harrison Robertson Professor of Law at the University of Virginia, writes: "Moreover, there are reasons to be skeptical of whether affirmative consent standards can be successful even on campus. First, these provisions are absurdly sweeping. They bar not only sex but sexual contacts. They cover not only students but also [sometimes] faculty. They include not just first encounters but also married couples" (Kessler Ferzan 2016).

Outside of affirmative consent regimes, the law defines "consent" as a state of mind, not a set of actions. People are free to consent in advance, or to consent passively. According to the most recent draft of the *Restatement (Third) of Torts*, consent is defined as follows:

> § 112. Actual Consent A person actually consents to an actor's otherwise tortious conduct if the person is subjectively willing for that conduct to occur. *Actual consent need not be communicated to the actor to be effective.* It can be express or can be inferred from the facts.
>
> (Kessler Ferzan 2016, 407 [emphasis added])

The Model Penal Code also defines "consent" as a subjective mental state. So affirmative consent regimes are more radical than they might appear at first. They are contrary to the generally-accepted legal understanding of what consent means and they do so regarding the most personal and private of human behaviors. They also transform the types of sexual interaction that occurs every day among college students into expellable offenses.

When commonly engaged-in behavior becomes punishable, it is of course impossible to punish all transgressors. So who is it that is most likely to be singled out for punishment? This nation has a long and sorry history of singling out African American men for sexual transgressions, especially where white women were also involved. Therefore, one would think that the federal government, which requires that colleges and universities keep a wide variety of racial statistics, would be very interested in tracking whether African American men are being disproportionately accused of sexual assault. Remarkably, the federal government does not require colleges to keep a record of this information and it does not appear that many colleges maintain this data. However, as Emily Yoffe has written in *The Atlantic*, when the Office of Civil Right investigated Colgate University for racial bias, the results were concerning:

> Colgate University was recently investigated by the Office for Civil Rights for potential race discrimination, a Title VI violation, in its sexual-assault adjudication process. The university was cleared in April, on the grounds that the numbers did not allow OCR to conclude that race was a statistically significant factor in Colgate's

> adjudications—in any given year the number of men of any race referred for formal hearings was in the single digits. (The investigation does not appear to have examined any individual cases or otherwise reach beyond this statistical analysis.) But the report did bring those statistics to light, a rarity. In the 2013–14 academic year, 4.2 percent of Colgate's students were black. According to the university's records, in that year black male students were accused of 50 percent of the sexual violations reported to the university, and they made up 40 percent of the students formally adjudicated.
>
> During the three academic years from 2012–13 to 2014–15, black students were accused of 25 percent of the sexual misconduct reported to the university, and made up 21 percent of the students referred for formal hearings. Fifteen percent of the students found responsible for assault in those years were black. During that same three-year period, Asian students, who constituted a little more than 3 percent of Colgate's student body in 2013, were more than 13 percent of the accused, 21 percent of those referred for hearings, and 23 percent of those found responsible. (The rest were white; no Hispanic students were accused.)
>
> (Yoffe 2017)

One might be tempted to defend affirmative consent laws by arguing that consenting students are unaffected and that students are only punished when one of them files charges. However, that it is not necessarily the case. There has also been an expansion of the number of university officials who are "mandatory reporters"—people who must report to the university when they have reason to believe that sexual assault has occurred. Depending upon the school, mandatory reporters might include student resident advisors, professors, coaches, and supervisors. So if a mandatory reporter hears, say, a student complaining about how her roommate's boyfriend touches her roommate without advance, overt permission, that reporter *must* report this to campus authorities.

Even apart from third-party reporting, knowing that the way one engages in sexual activity might be an expellable offense is no small matter. Laws should not be passed on the premise that people will not follow them. If state law requires overt permission for each new level of sexual touching, it is no defense to say that most people will get away with secretly violating the law.

The legislators and college administrators who have mandated affirmative consent regimes surely must have been aware of how overreaching and unrealistic these laws are because they chose to apply these rules to college students but not to themselves. If affirmative consent is nothing more than the codification of common sense and decency, then why is it only applied to students? Surely in an era of Trumps and Weinsteins, Cosby's and Wieners, and so many other callous and powerful men in the world of business, politics, and entertainment we cannot believe that sexual assault is only a serious problem within the ivory-covered walls of academia. As the Supreme Court long ago cautioned us:

> The framers of the Constitution knew, and we should not forget today, that there is no more effective practical guaranty against arbitrary and unreasonable government than to require that the principles of law which officials would impose upon a minority must be imposed generally. Conversely, nothing opens the door to arbitrary action so effectively as to allow those officials to pick and choose only a few to whom they will apply legislation, and thus to escape the political retribution that might be visited upon them if larger numbers were affected. Courts can take no better measure to ensure that laws will be just than to require that laws be equal in operation.
> (*Railway Express Agency v. New York*, 336 U. S. 106, 336 U. S. 112–113 (1949))

Justifying Affirmative Consent

This double standard for college students is sometimes justified by citing alarming statistics about the very high rates of sexual assault in colleges. The numbers "1 in 5" have frequently been invoked. Vice President Joe Biden cited the "1 in 5" statistic in defending the Obama administration's aggressive approach to combating college sexual assault. Ezra Klein, in remarkably honestly titled article, "Yes Means Yes is a Terrible Bill and I Completely Support it," also leans hard on the "1 in 5" number: "Every discussion of the Yes Means Yes law needs to begin with a simple number: A *2007 study* by the Department of Justice found that one in five women is the victim of an attempted or completed sexual assault while in college. . . . One. In. Five." (Klein 2014).

Klein readily admits that affirmative consent will result in unjust punishments, but he argues that the "1 in 5" justifies this: "Because for one in five women to report an attempted or completed sexual assault means that everyday sexual practices on college campuses need to be upended, and men need to feel a cold spike of fear when they begin a sexual encounter" (Klein 2014).

The "1 in 5" statistic has been heavily politicized. The 2007 study referenced by Klein, "The Campus Sexual Assault (CSA) Study," has also been cited by President Obama and Vice President Biden as justification for various federal policies (Lombardi 2015). This is despite the fact that the principal author of the CSA, Christopher Krebs, has clearly stated that the "1 in 5" statistic is "not a nationally representative statistic" (Crocker 2017). In fact, the CSA survey was limited to two large universities, neither of which are particular representative of the broader range of American universities.

A number of other studies have also estimated the rate of college sexual assault to be in the "1 in 5" range. The page limits of a single chapter do not allow a lengthy analysis of the all problems with these studies. Briefly though, these numbers are based on surveys that do not ask students if they have been sexually assaulted or raped. Surveys that use those terms report vastly lower numbers of sexual assault or rape, both completed and attempted. The surveys that report "1 in 5" students have been sexually assaulted ask students if they ever been subjected to certain behaviors. The surveys vary in their exact wording, but they generally cover an extremely wide variety of behaviors including threatening to end a relationship if it does not include sex. They also tend to include questions about whether students have had sex while intoxicated or drunk without defining how what those terms means. Students who answer "yes" to these questions are defined as victims of sexual assault.

There is certainly an important and meaningful discussion to be had about all of this. Perhaps we should be teaching our children that it is not morally acceptable to break up with someone because they refuse to have sex with you. Perhaps we should be teaching our children that it is a terrible idea to engage in sexual activity while even a little bit drunk. Reasonable people can disagree about these things. However, it is entirely a different matter to simply report all of this sexual activity as "sexual assault" and use that to justify a set of restrictions on college students that do not apply to anybody else. This is especially indefensible given that popular perception of college students as teenagers and those barely older than teenagers is well out of date. About one quarter of college students are over 25 years of age, and about one quarter of students are single parents. The sexual lives that are being regulated are largely those of adults.

Finally, it is worth noting that the studies that conclude that "1 in 5" students have been sexually assaulted only survey college students and therefore cannot serve as a basis of comparison for sexual assault rates regarding college students and non-students. In fact, when the same survey questions are put to college students and similarly-aged non students, we find that college students are actually at significantly *less* risk of sexual assault than their peers who do not attend college (Sinozich and Langton 1995–2013).

Sometimes affirmative consent regimes are justified on the basis that they are necessary to catch "predators" on college campuses. Amanda Taub writes: "When we pretend that determining consent is some sort of complex sorcery that mere mortals cannot be expected to manage, we implicitly condone the behavior of sexual predators who ignore their partners' clear signals" (Taub 2014). The image of a "predator" has been oft-used by both sides of the political aisle to justify harsh punishment regimes. Hillary Clinton used the term to build support for laws that led to mass incarceration of mostly minority young men (Alexander 2016).

The leading exponent of the theory that most college sexual assaults are committed by serial predators is the researcher David Lisak, whose work is frequently cited by government officials and others arguing for a "get tough," approach to sexual assault on campuses:

> At a meeting last fall of several hundred university administrators who were gathered to discuss campus sexual assault, *a Department of Justice official repeated a frightening statistic.* "We know that the majority of rapes are committed by serial rapists, and those folks are very unlikely to be reached by any prevention messages that we're going to be sending out, or education about rape," said Bea Hanson, who works in the DOJ's Office of Violence Against Women and served on a White House task force on the issue of campus rape.
>
> Hanson was referring to an influential study, published in 2002 by David Lisak, then a professor of psychology at the University of Massachusetts Boston, and Paul Miller, then a clinical psychologist at Brown University School of Medicine. . . . Over the past few years, the data from Lisak and Miller's 2002 study has become ubiquitous, cited in countless news reports and advocacy briefs, and even appearing in a report by the White House Council on Women and Girls. Recently, it has been used to argue for harsher punishments—and even jail time—for student rapists, whose cases have traditionally been handled through university judicial systems.
>
> (Thomson-DeVeaux 2015)

The image of the "serial predator" is a frightening one and, as indicated previously, it has been cited by sources as high as the White House and Justice Department and by countless media reports. It has also been at the center of much of the student-organized anti-rape movement. At the "heart of the movement" is the belief that "No one should talk the way activists did in the '90s—no more date rape. Focus on college men as serial predators, and cite a study that claimed that 6 percent commit three or more undetected rapes and attempted rapes each" (Grigoriadis 2014).

The study referred to in this quotation is from the aforementioned 2002 article by David Lisak and Paul M. Miller. However, there is surprisingly little research on this important question and the Lisak and Miller study is generally the only study cited in support of it. But that study has extremely serious methodological problems and in a less charged environment would be unlikely to be as influential as it currently is. To begin with, the entire sample for the study is taken from a single university. To quote from the study itself:

> Participants in this study were 1,882 students at a mid-sized, urban commuter university where students are diverse both in age and

> ethnicity. The mean age of the sample was 26.5 years (SD = 8.28), with a range of 18 to 71. More than 20% were over age 30, and nearly 8% were over 40.
>
> (Lisak and Miller, 76)

Given the highly diverse nature of the student bodies at various American universities, there is no possibility that a sample from a single school can provide nationally representative results. Furthermore, the study did not rely upon its own sampling or survey data. Rather it combined the results of four different studies, taken during different years over a seven-year period, all with sample sizes too small themselves to produce statistically significant results on questions of sexual assault:

> The total sample consisted of four separate studies (n = 576; n = 587; n = 123; n = 596), conducted between 1991 and 1998. The three largest samples each represented 10% to 12% of the total male student population of the university at the time. The four samples were combined to provide a large enough subsample of rapists to permit the proposed analyses. Although the percentage of rapists within the samples varied from 4% to 9.8%, X2(3, N = 1,881) = 11.57, $p < .05$, there were no significant differences among the samples on any of the variables used in the analyses. The mean number of rapes per rapist, the mean number of other violent acts committed, and the proportion of rapists who used physical force versus intoxication was consistent across the samples. Although the samples were gathered at two- to four-year intervals, a careful set of analyses were conducted to ensure that there were no duplicates among the participants in the combined sample.
>
> (Lisak and Miller, 76)

Further, these four studies were not principally concerned with the issue of sexual assault on university campuses and the questions were not oriented toward ascertaining the specific information that would be necessary to draw reliable conclusions about the nature of sexual assault on college campuses. Since this was a commuter campus consisting of largely part-time, adult students, there is no way to tell how many of the sexual assaults admitted to in the survey data were committed while the survey subjects were college students or whether they victimized other college students or whether they occurred on or near the college campus or at college events. These are extremely serious problems for a study that has been so influential.

Finally, it should be noted that a 2015 study published in the prestigious journal *JAMA* (Journal of the American Medical Association) *Pediatrics* directly contradicts the Lisak and Miller study: “Although a small group of men perpetrated rape across multiple college years, they constituted a significant minority of those who committed college rape and did not compose the group at highest risk of perpetrating rape when entering college."

In sum, there is no real justification for imposing special rules on the sexual behavior of college students. It is merely the latest iteration of one generation bemoaning the lax morality of "kids these days." The next section argues that affirmative consent laws are not merely bad ideas. When imposed by state law or by state institutions, they violate the constitutional rights of college students.

Another justification for affirmative consent regimes is that they will increase reporting of sexual assaults. It is certainly true that sexual assault on university campuses is probably underreported. For example, the vast majority of colleges reported that there were zero sexual assaults on their campus during the 2014–2015 academic year. That seems highly unlikely regardless of how loosely or strictly one defines sexual assault. Yet there is no evidence that affirmative consent laws will improve this situation. According to the oft-cited Campus Sexual Assault Study: "Of the victims who did not report the incident (of sexual assault) to law enforcement, the most commonly reported reasons for non-reporting were that they did not think it was serious enough to report [endorsed by 56% of physically forced sexual assault victims and 67% of incapacitated sexual assault victims]" (Krebs, 18). Another very common reason for non-reporting was "that they did not want anyone to know about the incident." (Krebs, 18). Affirmative consent will not affect either of these reasons.

In sum, there is no good reason to create a special, exceptionally broad definition of sexual assault that applies only to college students. It is easy for middle-aged and older administrators and legislators to impose rules on students that they are not willing to live by themselves. But the reasons for a two-tiered system cannot withstand scrutiny. The evidence that sexual assault takes place in massive numbers on campuses depends upon definitions of sexual assault that are far outside of the common understanding of that term. Indeed, when the same terminology is used to compare groups, college students are *less* likely to be sexually assaulted than their non-college student cohorts. Nor is there real evidence that serial predators are roaming college campuses or that affirmative consent laws are the key to curing the problem of underreporting.

So affirmative consent arguably fails on policy grounds. The next section argues that affirmative consent regimes, when imposed by state actors, also violate the constitutional rights of students.

Affirmative Consent and the Constitution

It is well known that the Constitution explicitly protects a variety of constitutional rights. Many of these are found in The Bill of Rights—the first 10 amendments to the Constitution. These rights include freedom of speech, religion, assembly, the right to bear arms and the right to refuse to house soldiers in one's home. They also include the right against unreasonable searches and seizures, the right against self-incrimination, and against cruel and unusual punishment. These are all, of course, important rights.

In addition, the Constitution also protects other rights that are not explicitly mentioned therein. These are sometimes called implied or unenumerated rights. Their textual basis in the Constitution is the Due Process Clause, which is contained in both the Fifth Amendment (and applied to the federal government) and the Fourteenth Amendment (and applies to state and local governments). The Due Process Clause prevents the government from depriving any person of liberty without due process of law.

Importantly, this has long been understood to protect various substantive rights irrespective of procedural issues. A well-known example is the right to an abortion. Except under very limited circumstances, the government may not prevent a woman from having a pre-viability abortion no matter what sort of process is provided to her. This is called substantive due process. It covers a wide variety of rights in addition to abortion. It includes the right to travel from state to state, to live in a house with your relatives even if you and they are not considered a "family" pursuant to a city's single-family zoning laws, and to refuse unwanted life-saving medical treatment. Among these unenumerated rights is the right to sexual "privacy" or "autonomy." The government may not interfere with as personal a decision as how we make love to one another.

The sexual autonomy line of cases began with *Griswold v. Connecticut* in 1965. Considering a statute that prohibited the use of "any drug, medicinal article or instrument for the purpose of preventing conception," the Court struck down the law, emphasizing that it "operate[d] directly on the intimate relation of husband and wife."

While *Griswold* could have been viewed as a case that is primarily concerned about marital rights, the Court corrected any such misimpression a few years later. In *Eisenstadt v. Baird*, the Supreme Court held that unmarried couples have the exact same rights to acquire and to use contraception: "whatever the rights of the individual to access to contraceptives may be, the rights must be the same for unmarried and the married alike" (453).

In the infamous, and now overruled case *Bowers v. Hardwick*, a five Justice majority of the Supreme Court averred that contraception cases, along with the abortion rights cases, really just protected reproductive freedom and therefore gave no protection to same-sex couples who practice sodomy. However, in 2003, the Court corrected its course and overruled *Bowers*, in *Lawrence v. Texas*. In that case the Court held that "that liberty gives substantial protection to adult persons in deciding how to conduct their private lives in matters pertaining to sex" (572). In

2015, in *Obergefell v. Hodges*, the same-sex marriage case, the Supreme Court clearly referred to intimacy as a "fundamental right."

It is certainly true that not all college sexual encounters involve "intimacy" as we would ideally like to define that term. A "hook-up" is not something that seems particularly intimate. It is worth noting though, the notion of college as a "hook-up" culture is quite likely exaggerated (Monto and Carey 2014). But more importantly, it is very unlikely that the *Lawrence* Court meant that only emotionally intimate sexual conduct is constitutionally protected. Indeed, the two men arrested in the *Lawrence* case were not at all intimate in that sense. In fact, one of them was cheating on his boyfriend, who jealously called the police, which is how the case got into the court system in the first place (Rosenbury and Rothman 2010).

By invoking "intimacy" the *Lawrence* Court was merely distinguishing between consensual sexual relations among adults and other types of sexual contact such as prostitution, child molestation, and bestiality. Any other interpretation of *Lawrence* would put courts in the position of serving as case-by-case adjudicators of how deeply sexual partners care about one another or may come to care about one another. It is difficult to imagine that this is what the Court had in mind.

Affirmative consent regimes are clear violations of this constitutional right to sexual intimacy. If someone wishes to allow their boyfriend or girlfriend (or spouse, in the case of married students) to touch them spontaneously, they have the right to do so. Affirmative consent regimes fail to distinguish between strangers and the most intimate of couples. This negates the power of intimacy itself by making the closest of lovers treat each other as sexual strangers every time they touch each other intimately. Under the Constitution, there can be no government-approved way of having sex. The government may, of course, forbid and punish sexual contact without consent, but, as we have seen, affirmative consent regimes go well beyond this.

Conclusion

Affirmative consent laws and policies are no doubt well-intentioned. Although the amount of sexual assault on college campuses has been exaggerated, it is equally true that every sexual assault that does occur is a serious crime and the government has the right and the duty to take steps to prevent that. But concern for liberty should not be confused for lack of seriousness about crime prevention. There are many steps that can be taken to address sexual assault on campus that have nothing to do with affirmative consent. These include more effective enforcement of no-contact orders, pro-active measures to address binge drinking, decreasing barriers to reporting, augmenting by-stander prevention programs, and removing investigation of sexual assault accusations against college athletes from the jurisdiction of athletic departments. Further, efforts against sexual assault should not be confined to college campuses. Non-students deserve the same protection against sexual violence as students receive. Funding should be found to clear the backlog of unexamined rape kits and legislatures should re-examine overly-narrow rape laws. There is much to be done to help create a safer and less predatory society. Affirmative consent is not the answer.

Works Cited

Alexander, Michelle. "Why Hillary Clinton Doesn't Deserve the Black Vote." February 10, 2016. www.thenation.com/article/hillary-clinton-does-not-deserve-black-peoples-votes/

Crocker, Lizzie. "There's Been a Huge Increase in Campus Sex Assaults. Why?" May 16, 2017. www.thedailybeast.com/theres-been-a-huge-increase-in-campus-sex-assaults-why

Ferzan, K. Kimberly. "Consent, Culpability, and the Law of Rape." *Ohio State Journal of Criminal Law*, Vol. 13, No. 2 (2016): 397–439.

Gersen, Jacob and Suk, Jeannie. "The Sex Bureaucracy." *California Law Review*, Vol. 104 (2016): 881–948.

Grigoriadis, Vanessa. "Meet the College Women Who Are Starting a Revolution Against Campus Sexual Assault." *New York Magazine*. 2014. https://www.thecut.com/2014/09/emma-sulkowicz-campus-sexual-assault-activism.html?mid=twitter_nymag

Jozkowski, N. Kristen and Peterson, Zoë D. "College Students and Sexual Consent: Unique Insights." *The Journal of Sex Research*, Vol. 50 (2013): 517–523.

Klein, Ezra. " 'Yes Means Yes' Is a Terrible Law, and I Completely Support It." *Vox*. October 13, 2014. www.vox.com/2014/10/13/6966847/yes-means-yes-is-a-terrible-bill-and-i-completely-support-it.

Krebs, Christopher P.; Christine H. Lindquist; Tara D. Warner; Bonnie S. Fisher.; Sandra L. Martin. "Campus Sexual Assault Study: Final Report." (2007).

Lombardi, Kristen. "Biden Cites Progress on Campus Sexual Assault, But Says There's 'so Much Farther to Go.' " *Center for Public Integrity*. April 24, 2015. www.publicintegrity.org/2015/04/24/17232/biden-cites-progress-campus-sexual-assault-says-theres-so-much-farther-go.

Monto, A. Martin and Carey, Anna G. "A New Standard of Sexual Behavior? Are Claims Associated With the 'Hookup Culture' Supported by General Social Survey Data?" *The Journal of Sex Research*, Vol. 51, No. 6 (2014): 605–615.

Muehlenhard, Charlene L., Humphreys,Terry P., Jozkowski, Kristen N., Peterson, Zoe D. "The Complexities of Sexual Consent among College Students: A Conceptual and Empirical Review," The Journal of Sex Research, Vol. 53 No.4–5 (2016): 457–487.

Rosenbury, Laura A. and Rothman, Jennifer E. "Sex in and out of Intimacy," 59 Emory L.J., No.59 (2010): 809–868.

Sinozich, Sofi and Langton, Lynn. "Rape and Sexual Assault Victimization Among College-Age Females, 1995–2013." *Bureau of Justice Statistics*. 2014. www.bjs.gov/content/pub/pdf/rsavcaf9513.pdf

State of California. "SB-967 Student safety: sexual assault." California State Legislature, 2014. https://leginfo.legislature.ca.gov/faces/billNavClient.xhtml?bill_id=201320140SB967

State of New York. "S. 5965." New York State Legislature, 2015. http://legislation.nysenate.gov/pdf/bills/2015/S5965

Taub, Amanda. "'Yes Means Yes' Is About Much More Than Rape." *Vox*. October 10, 2014. www.vox.com/2014/10/10/6952227/rape-culture-is-a-tax-on-women-CA-yes-means-yes-dierks-katz.

Thomson-DeVeaux, Amelia. "What If Most Campus Rapes Aren't Committed By Serial Rapists?" *FiveThirtyEight*. July 30, 2015. https://fivethirtyeight.com/features/what-if-most-campus-rapes-arent-committed-by-serial-rapists/.

Yoffe, Emily. "The Question of Race in Campus Sexual Assault Cases." *The Atlantic*. 2017. https://www.theatlantic.com/education/archive/2017/09/the-question-of-race-in-campus-sexual-assault-cases/539361/

Cases Cited

Bowers v. Hardwick 478 U.S. 186 (1986)
Eisenstadt v. Baird 405 U.S. 438 (1972)
Griswold v. Connecticut 381 U.S. 479 (1965)
Lawrence v. Texas 539 U.S. 558 (2003)
Obergefell v. Hodges 576 U.S. (2015)

15 Skepticism About Title IX Culture

J.K. Miles

A title as provocative as mine requires explanation. I am not skeptical about Title IX as an important piece of civil rights legislation. I agree with the conclusion of the American Association of University Professors, "There is no necessary contradiction between effectively addressing problems of sexual harassment . . . and fully protecting academic freedom" (AAUP 2016, 92).

I am concerned with how a culture has risen up around Title IX and how it clashes with a culture of free speech. This new culture has confidence that we can safely distinguish the merely offensive from the hateful, abusive, and dangerous. It is also profoundly skeptical of the tolerance that undergirds America's older free speech culture.[1] This older free speech culture emerged from First Amendment jurisprudence but is not identical with it. To distinguish the informal norms of free speech from First Amendment jurisprudence (and for aesthetic symmetry) I will call it "1A culture."

"Culture" is a loaded word of course. I'm after something like the informal norms (attitudes, behaviors etc.) that develop around aspects of society—in this case, legislation.[2] I'm very much after the same sort of analysis that gets applied to terms like "rape culture." Rape culture, Ariel Levy (2013) writes, is "a value system in which women are currency, and sex is something that men get—or take—from them." "Rape culture" might apply to attitudes about women's dress—the despicable "she was asking for it." A TV show might highlight it (e.g., *Mad Men*). A celebrity comment could represent the assumption of rape culture as could a college or university that does not investigate allegations of assault and discrimination.[3]

The campus speech conflicts represent a clash of cultures. This is not just a species of the larger culture war in America, but it emerges from the First Amendment and Title IX legislation. Title IX is not at necessarily at odds with the First Amendment. Title IX culture—the informal norms of attitude and behavior, however, deeply conflict with 1A culture. 1A culture is profoundly skeptical about regulating viewpoints and is confident that principled tolerance is better than even careful regulation because authorities might overreach. By contrast, Title IX culture is much more confident that authorities can discern the difference between hateful viewpoints and the merely offensive. This is coupled with a profound skepticism of tolerance which marginalizes some voices and protects others.

My neat division of Title IX culture from 1A culture is idealized to be sure. Cultures and movements are not neat and idealized. I use this heuristic only as a way of contrasting the sorts of arguments and behaviors we see on campuses. My claim is that there is a very real ideological divide between these two traditions.

Skepticism about Title IX culture is morally and epistemically justified. This skepticism is moderate. It is stronger than "I'm personally justified in my skepticism." I think everyone should be skeptical of Title IX culture. Skepticism should translate into wariness of legislation borne of Title IX culture. It is moderate however in that I am not willing to go so far as to say, "there is no evidence that would temper this skepticism." There may be empirical data that could undermine my claim.

There is a practical worry, however. The costs of Title IX noncompliance are more immediate and severe than the costs of violating the First Amendment. As such, universities have a strong incentive to comply with Title IX norms over First Amendment considerations. If a university student, a faculty member, or staff complains to the Office of Civil Rights (hereafter OCR) of the Department of Education that the university did not perform due diligence with regard to their Title IX complaint, the university could lose its federal funding. This includes not only public universities where the First Amendment applies strongly but *any* educational institution that receives student aid.

If a university violates a student or faculty member's First Amendment rights, the cost is less immediate and far less severe. There may be a reversal of the university's judgment if someone is punished but rarely would there be in any monetary loss. It is perfectly rational for universities to defer to Title IX over the First Amendment. As one Title IX administrator put it, "Title IX is a federal compliance policy. Those policies supersede anything else" (AAUP 2016, 87).[4]

Students are aware of what Title IX investigations can do—as Laura Kipnis, a professor at Northwestern found out in 2015. A Title IX complaint was lodged against her by student activists for an article she published in the *Chronicle of Higher Education* (Kipnis 2015). The students complained that Kipnis created a hostile environment because her article criticizing campus sexual politics could persuade people not to report sexual assault. Kipnis was investigated and ultimately cleared. She wrote about her ordeal in *Unwanted Advances*, and again she was investigated for creating a hostile environment on campus (Kipnis 2017). In an interview (Thomason 2017) Kipnis said, "These complaints seem like an attempt to bend the campus judicial system to punish someone whose work involves questioning the campus judicial system, just as bringing Title IX complaints over my first *Chronicle* essay attempted to do two years ago."

How did we get from a law ostensibly to prevent gender discrimination to this? Without going into a recitation of the history of Title IX or sexual discrimination law, I want to sketch a picture of the progression from the sexual discrimination mandate of Title IX to the process that got Kipnis investigated. It is a slippery slope that we should have seen coming.

Sexual discrimination includes sexual harassment and rightfully so. Sexual harassment includes not only inappropriate conduct but also a hostile environment. The hostile environment inclusion again seems reasonable if not more subjective. Why do we hear anecdotes of students or university employees facing investigations like Kipnis's but not the same sorts of anecdotes in the workplace? The OCR expanded the definition of "hostile environment" beyond that of the Equal Employment Opportunity Commission definition.

In a Supreme Court decision, *Davis v. Monroe County Board of Education*, the Court defined an educational hostile environment as one that is "severe and pervasive," but the OCR informed the University of Montana in a letter that the standard was "severe *or* pervasive."[5] It is a small but significant difference. When the standard is "severe and pervasive" it could imply that the contaminating element (e.g., sexual comment, speech) is both abusive and permeates the environment. Kipnis's article is neither abusive (directed at any one person) or so frequent or ubiquitous as to permeate the environment. Only students at Kipnis's university lodged a complaint. If the standard is "severe or pervasive" we are left with a subjective account of "severe" as opposed to a more objective account of "pervasive" (see AAUP 2016). This allows student activists to claim that any exposure to Kipnis's article is severe enough to cause a hostile environment.

Clearly Title IX is a powerful piece of legislation and an emergent culture has used it to justify and in some cases enforce norms of what is acceptable in public discourse and it clashes without another culture and its norms. We should look closely both of these.

Title IX Culture

The process of Title IX investigation and its interpretation of a hostile environment, create informal norms among students and faculty in our American universities. Again, for simplicity and aesthetics I will describe the informal norms that make up Title IX culture as made up of activities, attitudes, and assumptions.

Activities: Title IX culture is first and foremost an activist culture. It is no coincidence that the rise of current student activism coincides with the expanding series of "Dear Colleague Letters" issued from the OCR to clarify and interpret the thirty-seven words of Title IX. This is not sufficient to explain the surge in student activism. There are certainly other forces at work including a revitalized anti-fascist movement in the United States (Bray 2017). To use the vernacular, Title IX "woke" students to the concept of a hostile environment brought by racism, sexism, and the oppression of minorities. Contrary to the narrative, these student activists are not "snowflakes." Their use of the Title IX process is a very rational response to the institution of a hostile environment policy they have been taught as Laura Kipnis's story illustrates. As Chermerinsky and Gillman (2017) put it, "At the very least, it [OCR's interpretation of Title IX] has provided students with a rights-based vocabulary for demanding formal investigations of speakers on the grounds that their politically controversial speech creates 'discriminatory learning environment.'"

Attitudes: Title IX culture is infused with a confidence in regulating viewpoints. Surveys of college students, both incoming freshman and beyond, show a substantive break from the past. Three high profile studies indicate students value the First Amendment and when asked if colleges should protect speech that is offensive, the response is a solid "yes." One student survey indicates this confidence in the First Amendment is actually higher in college students (73 percent) than in the entire adult population (56 percent) (Knight Foundation 2016). In the same survey, over two-thirds of students (78 percent) agreed that colleges should "should expose students to all types of speech and viewpoints" which is 12 percentage points higher than the adult population as a whole.

However, the picture changes dramatically when asked about hate speech. All three major surveys show that students make a strong distinction between offensive speech and hate speech. Only half of the students in one survey (McLaughlin 2017) thought that the First Amendment protects hate speech. If the student could not correctly identify the First Amendment, they were more likely to think hate speech was not protected (McLaughlin 2017). In another survey, students affirmed their commitment to tolerating offensive messages (78 percent) but those same students said universities should restrict "slurs and other language that is intentionally offensive to certain groups" (Knight Foundation 2016).

This seems to imply that students are confident that those empowered to regulate campus speech can draw a bright line between offensive speech and speech intended to offend certain protected groups.[6] Students raised on Title IX are uncomfortable, for the most part, with censoring messages that are offensive but they are quite comfortable that authorities can distinguish between those political messages and hate speech.

This confidence in drawing lines makes sense when you consider that students draw these lines every day on campus. In one of the most comprehensive surveys to date, the Foundation for Individual Rights in Education (FIRE 2016) found that half of the 2,500 students surveyed have self-censored their own expression in class. Almost a third of them have self-censored outside of class.

Assumptions: These attitudes feed into a set of assumptions that function as norms for students confronted with messages they find abusive, hateful, or discriminating. As Jonathan Zimmerman, professor of history of education at the University of Pennsylvania notes, "Prior generations wanted less authority. This generation wants more" (McMurtrie 2017). They are not worried about these authorities "getting it wrong" or chilling valuable speech. Perhaps more concerning, is that about a third of those polled believe speech can be a form of violence and a very small minority (4 percent) believe that violence is justified in response (FIRE 2016).

In 2013, a campus group invited a former New York City police chief to speak on his controversial stop and frisk policy. Student activists made Kelly's talk impossible disrupting the event. One student was quoted in a documentary about the incident, "They didn't respond to our demand to cancel the lecture, so we canceled it for them" (Montz 2016). We could say that the assumption of Title IX culture is that authorities will regulate speech and if authorities will not, students will do it for them through disruption, shouting down, or even retaliating.

1A Culture

We can now consider the 1A culture and why it cannot coexist with Title IX culture even though it can coexist with Title IX itself.[7] The moral norm in 1A culture is the conviction that authorities should be neutral between viewpoints in any speech regulation. As Justice Robert Jackson put it in *West Virginia Board of Education v. Barnette*:

> If there is any fixed star in our constitutional constellation, it is that no official, high or petty, can prescribe what shall be orthodox in politics, nationalism, religion, or other matters of opinion, or force citizens to confess by word or act.[8]

In the context of college campuses, 1A culture says that while there may be time, place, and manner restrictions, there should never be a viewpoint or sentiment that cannot be expressed. J.S. Mill expressed this same viewpoint neutrality when he said, it is not the purpose of education to mold viewpoints but rather to give us the ability to develop our own capacities.

Activities: 1A culture's primary activity is a principled tolerance of speech. One might think that tolerance is not really an activity but a refraining from interference. This is mistaken. As Andrew Cohen (2014) notes, principled tolerance is not mere indifference. Those who tolerate offensive, even hateful speech do so as a conscious activity.

Attitudes: The overwhelming attitude of 1A culture is a profound skepticism about regulating viewpoints. This is what Justice Jackson refers to. While there have been many inconsistencies with First Amendment jurisprudence, The Court has been more skeptical about restrictions on content (no political flyers at work) and consistently against restrictions on speech that target specific viewpoints (e.g., no *Communist* propaganda, no *racist* demonstrations). These require the strictest scrutiny of all.

This attitude that no one should decide between viewpoints is very much in conflict with Title IX culture's confidence in regulation. This attitude is not just a product of American jurisprudence. It goes back to the classical liberal tradition of John Stuart Mill and his defense of free speech in *On Liberty*. Mill allowed for time, place, and manner restrictions but he was very specific that the essence of liberty was unregulated sentiment and opinion, and no society that did not have such freedom was not worthy of the name.[9] Mill applied this skepticism of viewpoint regulation to education as well. To prevent the State an "improper influence over opinion" even in "higher classes of examinations" curriculum on disputed topics should "not turn on the truth or falsehood of opinions" (Mill 1991, 120–121).

Why the skepticism about regulating viewpoints? Those familiar with J.S. Mill's defense of free speech will recall Mill's concerns about truth being threatened by speech regulation. Even if the viewpoint being regulated is widely believed to be false and useless—even pernicious—it might be true and to assume there is no value in it, would be to assume a kind *ex cathedra* infallibility. Even if false, the viewpoint may have some truth to it. And even if completely false, interaction with this false, utterly useless viewpoint, may yet keep true and good viewpoints from becoming stale and "dead dogma."

Assumptions: In 1A culture, the assumptions about the way the world ought to be follow logically from the activities and attitudes. They are embodied in the institution of the Agora. In ancient Greece, the agora was the marketplace where things were bought and sold but it was also where one would expect to be confronted with every kind of message and idea on offer. While Mill never spoke of a "marketplace of ideas" (it was Oliver Wendell Holmes) it is not far off from the truth of what a 1A culture would look like. In fact, to use an image readily available from campus life, the agora of 1A culture is much like the day when the university lawn is full of clubs and organizations all trying to persuade the students to get involved with this activity or that. Another image familiar to those in London is Speaker's Corner in Hyde Park where anyone can bring their own soapbox and hold forth to the passersby.

For 1A culture, life outside of our private spheres is one where we can be confronted at anytime by people trying to persuade us to buy into their viewpoint or just to acknowledge their viewpoint exists. It is, then by nature, chaotic and diverse. A certain order exists. Adherents cannot harass us or shout their viewpoints in a manner that is too disruptive of people who just want to go about their day. But notice any restrictions on the agora would have to neutral between viewpoints. It is wrong for any viewpoint to be expressed with a bullhorn, not just neo-Nazi ones.

In 1A culture we should assume that, in the agora, we will run into people who hold viewpoints we find offensive, repugnant, even sinful. Here the activities of principled tolerance are readily available. If some knucklehead is expressing a viewpoint we find distasteful, even evil, we can tolerate him by ignoring him or, if in the open air, we can remonstrate him, debate him, or try to show bystanders how awful his viewpoint is. All of these count as tolerating. There is a norm of reciprocity at work here. If we wish to remonstrate others or debate them, then we must be willing to have our own views subject to remonstrance or criticism.

A Clash of Norms: The Case of University of Washington Mary

To illustrate this disconnect of attitudes, assumptions, and activities, consider the clash between Feminists United on Campus (hereafter Feminists United) and the president of University of Mary Washington (UMW). The OCR opened an investigation because Feminists United alleged that the university did not ban the social media app Yik Yak, which allows people to post anonymously and others to view posts within a certain geographical radius. A feminist group on campus pressured UMW because as a result of protest against misogynistic chant from the rugby team, the Feminists United was lambasted on Yik Yak with comments like "Feminists need to calm the hell down" and should "Chill their tits" (Amended Administrative Complaint, 2015).

From the point of view of the Feminists United, the complaint was about women being attacked such that they felt unsafe. This created a hostile environment even if the speech did not violate the First Amendment. Toleration of Yik Yak meant female voices were being drowned out by vitriol. It wasn't just fear of violence, however. Throughout the complaint filed, there is language that apart from actual threats to individual members, which I should remark are not protected and should be investigated, the comments on Yik Yak were the equivalent of violence. Feminists United and other activists *as a group* were "attacked," "assaulted," and made to feel unsafe.

When the president, Richard Hurley, defended the university's policy of tolerating Yik Yak, he did so from the 1A cultural script. He first sent an email to the entire campus addressing the problem. UMW was a public university and was bound by the First Amendment more so than private universities. He argued that banning Yik Yak would be content-based and thus a violation of the First Amendment. He encouraged students to take measures to shut out Yik Yak and sought to dialogue with Feminists United.

The Feminists United, supported by Feminist Majority Foundation (FMF), amended their Title IX complaint accusing the president of violating Title IX because he wrote a "disparaging letter" to the FMF in order to explain why the university did not have the authority to restrict Yik Yak. The complaint shows the skepticism of tolerance. Feminists United's amended complaint makes clear that Hurley's appeal for principled tolerance and avoidance was tantamount to doing nothing. Furthermore, Hurley's inaction further made UMW unsafe. After the letter was published in the media, there were generalized threats and vitriol leveled at Feminists United through Yik Yak. In the amended complaint, Hurley's letter is characterized as retaliation.

As Eugene Volokh (2015) notes, "the claims are that Hurley 'retaliated' against the students by (1) expressing his opinions about the severity of the initial allegations and (2) publicizing those opinions widely, which led anonymous parties to further criticize Feminists United." Hurley, however, was acting within the accepted norms of 1A culture. He sought to make his argument in a reasonable manner (a letter) to his accusers. The alternative, notes Volokh would be to "just shut up and let the charges against them spread without response."

The clash between Title IX culture and 1A culture should be clear. What's interesting is that the *activities* of both cultures are compatible. Activism for marginalized voices and principled tolerance for all speech are not fundamentally at odds. The conflict is between the attitudes and assumptions. Title IX culture is confident about regulation and skeptical of tolerance. 1A culture, however, is skeptical of regulation and confident about tolerance. As I indicated, I want to make the case that skepticism about regulation and confidence in tolerance is the justified position. I will consider two of the strongest argument in favor of Title IX culture. Jeremy Waldron provides a reason to be confident about speech regulation. Herbert Marcuse provides a reason to be skeptical about tolerance. I will argue, however, that both arguments are ultimately unsuccessful.

Waldron's Confidence in Regulation

Jeremy Waldron's *Harm in Hate Speech* (2012) is the strongest argument in favor of regulating viewpoints. Waldron bravely does what others are reluctant to do. He defines hate speech as viewpoints, "that express profound disrespect, hatred, and vilification for the members of minority groups," (27). Waldron goes further by differentiating the disrespect of hate speech as messages that vilify a group as less than equal in society. He draws on a distinction between appraisal respect and recognition respect from Stephen Darwall (1977). The former is what is violated when I malign your character or offend you. The latter is what hate speech targets: one's very recognition as an equal member of society.

In Waldron's ideal society, hateful, bigoted, and vilifying viewpoints would be isolated and subject to punishment through a fine or some other punitive measure. He points with confidence to the human rights commissions in various countries that monitor and punish hate speech.

The harm of hate speech is the harm to a group's standing as equal citizens in a social order. Hate speech, in fact, is a kind of group libel. Just as an individual can have their reputation maligned so that others think falsely about them, so can minority groups as when someone says all Mexicans are lazy or that illegal immigrants are rapists and murderers.

Waldron finds legal precedent for group libel in the case of *Beauharnais v. Illinois*.[10] Beauharnais was a white supremacist who passed out leaflets for the White Circle League calling on the mayor of Chicago "to halt the further encroachment, harassment and invasion of White people, their property, neighborhoods and persons, by the Negro." He was arrested and convicted of an Illinois law prohibiting anyone to "publish or exhibit any writing or picture portraying the 'depravity, criminality, unchastity, or lack of virtue of a class of citizens of any race, color, creed or religion.'" The Supreme Court upheld Beauharnais's conviction for which he was fined 200 dollars.

Waldron sees in *Beauharnais* a way of regulating speech without violating the First Amendment. Waldron's group libel is viewpoint specific, however. The burden of proof is on anyone who would defend America's devotion to free speech absolutism. He finds Mill's arguments for truth to be misguided and largely irrelevant to the question of hate speech.

Waldron challenges free speech advocates to provide a reason to override the harm in group libel. Most of the world makes content-specific restrictions and the burden of proof is on those who would protect hate speech. Since the title of this paper is "Skepticism About Title IX Culture," it will be enough for me if I can raise serious doubts about Waldron's regulation of hate speech.

I will not rehearse all of Waldron's objections to 1A culture. I will instead zero in on an objection he almost considers in passing. What if the government censors some viewpoints but "gets it wrong"? Waldron responds:

> As I understand it, the idea is that governmental interference is always likely to be motivated by officials' lust for power, or their vanity, or their misguided insecurity or their undue responsiveness to majoritarian prejudice, anger or panic. They may not always get it wrong, but there is a standing danger that they will.
>
> (Waldron, 201)

For Waldron, the concern seems primarily to be official overreach that is motivated by their self-aware vices (i.e., lust for power) or majoritarian pressure from unwarranted fear. Government will inevitably get it wrong solely because of its moral failings. I think this is a mistake that allows him to give a cursory response to this objection. After all, this objection applies to any group in power. "Why this is felt particularly in the area of speech (as opposed to government actions generally), and in the even more particularized area of content-based restriction on speech, I am not quite sure." (201). He doesn't really consider that any regulatory body could get it wrong due to *epistemic* rather than moral failings.

When Frederick Schauer gave a version of this epistemic objection (Schauer 1984), he considered it the strongest argument for a free speech principle. "The desire to suppress . . . may be stronger in reference to speech than in reference to other forms of conduct" (83). This is because freedom for other kinds of conduct does not confront us. Speech, however, does confront in ways private conduct does not.

In recent years, we have seen an upsurge of social psychology literature that gives us reasons to be skeptical of the judgment of any group of people. Nobel laureate, Daniel Kahneman gives ample evidence that human beings have epistemic biases toward their own established beliefs (Kahneman 2011). Without exploring this literature in detail, I want to consider two elements of social psychology that justify skepticism and restraint rather than confidence in regulation: motivated reasoning and concept creep.

In the arena of politics and religion, psychologist Jonathan Haidt has documented particular biases related to motivated reasoning (Haidt 2012). When we want to believe something, our thinking is "Can I believe this?" Whereas if we are motivated not to believe something, our internal thinking is rather "Must I believe this?"[11] Haidt points out this does not bode well for groups who have to make judgments: "These processes—which are usually studied in individuals acting on self-serving motives—often become much stronger when individuals are embedded in groups that are locked into combat with other groups." (Haidt 2016)

I am not suggesting this social psychology data is a defeater for any speech regulation. I am suggesting this data is reason to be skeptical.

Another significant reason for skepticism is the psychological theories about "concept creep." The term is coined by Nick Haslam (Haslam 2016) to describe the tendency of negative psychological concepts to expand horizontally (new kinds of cases) and vertically, (treat old cases more severely). Haslam identifies six psychological concepts that have "stretched" to include new and inevitably milder infractions.

This stretching is evident in definitions of abuse that can count angry arguments as instances of emotional abuse, definitions of bullying that can include once-off displays of office tyranny, relaxed diagnostic criteria for mental disorders such as depression, the recognition of nonconscious forms of prejudice, and definitions of trauma that allow vicarious experiences to be counted as traumatic (2).

According to Haslam, these concepts start out as definitions of specific acts. Abuse is an act. Bullying is an act. However, the data indicates that these concepts expand to include omissions, not just acts. Instead of having two distinct terms, bullying elides to physical acts *and* emotional exclusion. Prejudice begins as acting on racist assumptions but rather than find a different term for the omission or non-interference, the same term is stretched to include *not* acting when one should. Evil may triumph if good men do nothing, but doing nothing is not the same morally or epistemically as doing evil.

Haslam also observes that in the evolution of psychological concepts, they tend to evolve toward the subjective:

Emotional abuse may be claimed if one party feels abused rather than by a set of objective abusive behaviors, bullying if employees perceives that their work has been criticized too harshly, prejudice if its target perceives it despite the sincere protestations of the perpetrator. (Haslam 2016, 11)

With those worries in mind, consider several kinds of judgments regulators need to render by Waldron's lights:

- Is a speech act a violation of recognition respect rather than appraisal respect?
- Are other less hateful ways that this same sentiment could be expressed (there may not be)?
- Is the speech racially motivated or religious?[12]
- Is the speech threatening, abusive, or merely offensive?
- Is it the viewpoint that is harmful or merely the mode or manner that is?

Given these fine-grained discernments: Is it possible that peremptory regulation will make serious and damaging mistakes? Is it also possible that *a posteriori* punishment (human rights commissions, fines, etc.) could also make serious and damaging mistakes?

For precisely the reasons Waldron mentions, one should fear regulation. The justified horror of speech that vilifies minorities might affect our ability to discern the proper manner and mode of viewpoint regulation. Indeed, it is our self-evident fury at the mistreatment of minorities that should give us pause—the pause not to legislate in our passion precisely because we might overreach in our good intentions for marginalized voices.

The "government will get it wrong" objection is usually considered one of the weakest objections to speech regulation. Waldron's argument reinvigorates it. The wealth of social psychology literature should make us wary of letting any group of people draw the lines between offensive and hateful speech. By extension, we should be skeptical of Title IX culture's confidence in distinguishing between them as well.

Marcuse's Skepticism of Tolerance

Title IX culture is skeptical of free speech because its commitment to tolerance often protects the status quo of injustice. Manne and Stanley (2015) explain that expressing oneself freely is an entirely different experience depending on one's status in society. If one's status is privileged, then one can expect public deference. If one is marginalized, free expression is seen as unruly. "When people lower down in social and institutional hierarchies criticize the speech acts of those higher up, it often reads as insubordination, defiance, or insolence. When things go the other way, it tends to read as business as usual."

Stanley and Manne also argue that freedom of expression is a co-opting of space. When someone speaks, others will have to wait their turn. And this norm also is dictated by social status. "The notion of freedom of speech is being co-opted by dominant social groups, distorted to serve their interests, and used to silence those who are oppressed and marginalized. All too often, when people depict others as threats to freedom of speech, what they really mean is, 'Quiet!' "

Herbert Marcuse gave the outline for this critique in his "Repressive Tolerance" (1965). It is pragmatic but over-simplified to characterize the clash between 1A and Title IX culture as a clash between J.S. Mill and Herbert Marcuse (Kors and Silverglate 1998), but I find in Marcuse the strongest critique of 1A tolerance. Marcuse explicitly abandons 1A culture's commitment to viewpoint neutrality. "Liberating tolerance, then, would mean intolerance against movements from the Right and toleration of movements from the Left" (109). All the way back in 1965 he argued this repressive tolerance would inevitably take place in academia. "This means that previously neutral, value-free, formal aspects of learning and teaching now become . . . in their own right, political" (112).

Marcuse's essay is also especially relevant as a critique of Mill's *On Liberty*. Mill was worried about the tyranny of the majority. Marcuse begins by acknowledging and critiquing Mill's argument from truth. "The telos of tolerance is truth. John Stuart Mill speaks of truth . . . which does not triumph over persecution by virtue of its 'inherent power' " (90). If truth is to flourish, it will need help. Marcuse interprets Mill's discussion of how the majority has suppressed heretics and concludes that tolerance is "first and foremost for the sake of heretics" (90).

This is a big leap, but it serves Marcuse's purposes because the left are the heretics—the rebels fighting the empire. This allows Marcuse to argue that some viewpoints can and should be suppressed for the sake of the rebels. 1A tolerance is fine for "harmless debates" and "academic discussions," "scientific enterprise," and "private religion" but when the stakes are foundational:

> Society cannot be indiscriminate where the pacification of existence, where freedom and happiness themselves are at stake: here, certain things cannot be said, certain ideas cannot be expressed, certain policies cannot be permitted without making tolerance an instrument for the continuation of servitude.
>
> (88)

There is both an epistemic and moral assumption nestled in Marcuse's statement. There is epistemic confidence that the revolutionaries can know accurately what we need to break off the chains of servitude and have a moral duty to do so. Since the "skepticism" in the title is an epistemic skepticism, I will only deal with the moral claim briefly. Isn't Marcuse's moral claim about freeing tolerance undermined by Marcuse's political commitments? In order to buy into Marcuse's repressive tolerance, we must not only stand *against* racism, sexism, patriarchy in society but must also adopt an economic and political philosophy that is by no means self-evident.

The sheer breadth and vagueness of Marcuse's list of ideas that would need to be repressed is breathtaking: "aggressive policies, armament, chauvinism, discrimination on the grounds of race and religion, or which oppose the extension of public services, social security, medical care, etc." Is it reasonable, given the data about confirmation bias and concept creep, to be skeptical that regulators can repress "chauvinism" without chilling too much speech? To buy into Marcuse's skepticism about tolerance we also must buy into the political program of the left and if we dare to suggest any of these social programs are faulty on scientific grounds, he reminds us science too will need to be regulated (100). The same goes for education: "The restoration of freedom of thought may necessitate new and rigid restrictions on teachings and practices in the educational institutions which . . . serve to enclose the mind within the established universe of discourse and behavior" (100–101).

Since I'm after a moderate skepticism, is there any reason for the unconverted to be skeptical of Marcuse's critique of 1A tolerance? I've already noted that one could divide Mill's arguments for unregulated sentiment and opinion into arguments for truth and arguments for self-development.[13] Mill says something very curious that makes one think he himself was not as interested in truth as much as how unregulated sentiment and opinion makes us better people. The peculiar evil of silencing opinions and sentiments is worse for those who dissent than for those who express the opinion that is silenced (37). If Mill is primarily interested in truth-will-out, then this is a curious claim to make. What does the world lose if bigots cannot talk of minorities as inferior races? What does the world lose if fascists cannot fill the air waves with false claims about nationalism and fallacious arguments about white separatism? Surely the injury must be to bigoted speakers who are silenced.

Yet Mill says it is the *dissenters* who suffer this peculiar evil when we decide to silence some pernicious viewpoint. What we lose when we silence neo-Nazis is the justification in our own opinions of neo-Nazis and their doctrines. The same goes for fascists, Holocaust deniers, and talking heads on pseudo-news programs.

In perhaps one of his strongest claims in *On Liberty*, Mill says that the only way anyone ever develops justified opinions is by keeping oneself open to arguments from viewpoints contrary to one's own, adjusting one's opinions when convinced the other side has a point, and expounding to one's self and on occasion others what is fallacious about the opposing viewpoints (55).[14]

As Jacobson (2000) argues, Mill seems to be saying that the sort of arguing and testing that goes on when we debate politics, religion, etc., is a kind of thinking out loud. We must be able to entertain pernicious and evil viewpoints in order to justify our hatred of them. This is Mill's strongest argument for unregulated thought and opinion. If we regulate opinions so that some viewpoints are never expressed in public, then our assessment, our criticism, of those viewpoints is what will be epistemically unjustified—the very "disapprobation" (to use Mill's words) that we need to have for fascists, neo-Nazis, and bigots.

I am sympathetic to Stanley and Manne's concerns about how free expression is perceived by different classes, though we might wish for some empirical data to back them up. However, beyond these claims I must confess Title IX culture's infallible attitude toward censoring viewpoints and its lack of concern for overreach is not only baffling, but it's hard to see what evidence would could falsify the claim.

Consider this example by Marcuse: "When a magazine prints side by side a negative and a positive report on the FBI, it fulfills honestly the requirements of objectivity: however, the chances are that the positive wins because the image of the institution is deeply engraved in the mind of the people." How would one even begin to test this claim? It is so amorphous that if the stakes were small, the rhetoric could be excused as artistic license. But the stakes, as Marcuse makes clear, are not small. If some sociological data were to refute the claim, that people are not so deferential or that even if they are it does not render critical judgment impossible without institutional repression, can we imagine Marcuse acquiescing?

I think not. Here's the reason why: "For the facts are never given immediately and never accessible immediately: they are established, 'mediated' by those who made them; the truth, 'the whole truth' surpasses these facts and requires the rupture with their appearance," (98–99). Any data is always contextual and thus suspect.

It is hard for me to square this claim with his earlier assurances, "there *is* an objective truth which can be discovered" (89–90). In this latter quote he goes on to say that, admittedly, this truth is not evident. It has to be uncovered by "separating right and wrong, good and bad, correct and incorrect." I can only conclude that Marcuse is skeptical of "mediated" facts except the facts about who are the good revolutionaries and who is the bad status quo. But why are these facts not mediated and thus suspect?

Marcuse's claims seem unfalsifiable (since any evidence that would count against it, can be dismissed as contextual). My skepticism would be hypocritical if I did not offer ways my own claims could be falsified. In the wake of Kahneman and Tversky's work on biases, a small literature has emerged about how to correct for our biases (e.g., Soll, Milkman and Payne 2015 and Kawakami, Dovidio, Moll, Hermsen and Russin 2000). If debiasing strategies could be shown to counter the effects of motivated reasoning and concept creep in groups, those in 1A culture would have to temper skepticism considerably.

Conclusion: Skepticism and Restraint

We should be skeptical of Title IX culture's confidence that viewpoints can be regulated by critiquing the strongest argument for viewpoint specific regulation. A great deal of data suggest that any group of humans will get it wrong if they have to make judgments about which viewpoints are acceptable as Title IX culture would ask campus administrators and investigators to do. We should also be skeptical of Title IX culture's critique of free speech tolerance. It may be true that speech co-opts spaces, and that marginalized and privileged experience free speech differently. This does not justify regulating speech as many universities have done by stretching Title IX and hostile environment until it snaps.

The fundamental difference between 1A culture and Title IX culture is what F. A. Hayek (2011) called the "fatal conceit." Hayek was speaking of those officials who think they can plan the economy so that the right goods are distributed in the right way to the right people. This sort of confidence is doomed, according to Hayek, because there is no group of philosopher-kings who can know enough about conditions and effects of market norms. Knowledge in a market is too diffuse. He said, "The curious task of economics is to demonstrate to men how little they really know about what they imagine they can design."

I cannot help but see a parallel in the attempt to design the modern-day agora. This agora has an order to be sure. There are norms of when, where, and in what manner people may speak. These norms can be policed, but what cannot be regulated without hubris toward the content of the myriad of opinions and sentiments that make up our various ways of life is the viewpoints themselves. Indeed, 1A culture could be described as a spontaneous order. This does not mean that individually we can't recognize evil when it speaks. Tolerance and counter-speech are the remedy, however—not because we neutral between evil and good but rather because all our data indicates humans are tribal, biased, and think best surrounded by people who disagree with them. We should be skeptical of anyone who simply asserts any group of authorities can miraculously overcome this reality.

Notes

1. I could just as easily have called this culture Title VII culture since Title IX of the Civil Rights Act of 1964 is restricted to gender discrimination and Title VII is restricted to race and national origin. However, I call it Title IX culture because, as I will show, Title IX (and the investigation process it engendered) is the catalyst for the student and faculty activism that is at odds with what I call 1A culture that grew up around the First Amendment of the United States Constitution.
2. *Merriam Webster Dictionary* (2014) named "culture" the word of the year. Joshua Rothman (2014) defines culture in three different ways. The first definition is a process of individual enrichment as when we say, "You need to be a bit more cultured. Less *Game of Thrones*. More *Masterpiece Theater*." The second definition of "culture" is "a particular group's way of life." The third definition involves the institutions that solidify a groups way of life. The kind of culture I'm interested in is a combination of the second and third definition.
3. I won't address in this essay concerns about the term "rape" in "rape culture" that seems to elide sexual assault with the objectification of women. See McElroy 2016 for criticism of the term. See Valenti 2014 for a defense.
4. I'm indebted to Ilya Somin and Greg Lukianoff for this point.
5. 526 U.S. 629 (1999) See (AAUP 2016) for University of Montana letter and the wording of the Davis decision.
6. Thus far refrained from using the word "censorship." The word conjures up images of government documents redacted with opaque black ink so that the words are blocked from view. It would be a mistake to think of regulating viewpoints in this way. An idea is a formidable thing and it is nearly impossible to get rid of completely. We can drive it underground and punish its expression but as anyone from the former Soviet bloc countries can attest, ideas do not die. This is the reason I use the term "regulation" rather than censorship.
7. Once again, 1A culture is not the same thing as the First Amendment. 1A culture consists of the activities, attitudes, and assumptions surrounding the concept of free speech embodied in the institution of tolerance for all opinions and the remedy of counter-speech. For my purposes it does not matter than the First Amendment only applies to government restrictions on speech, not private interactions, nor does it matter that the First Amendment obligations are stronger on public college campuses than private ones.
8. 319 U.S. 624 (1943)
9. "No society in which these liberties are not, on the whole, respected, is free, whatever may be its form of government; and none is completely free in which they do not exist absolute and unqualified." (Mill, 33)
10. 343 U.S. 250 (1952)
11. My favorite story that Haidt recounts is of a study about motivated reasoning done with psychology graduate students. The students were asked to evaluate

a series of research studies about the link between breast cancer and caffeine. The students were supposed to evaluate the studies based on method, data collection, etc. Which people do you think rate the studies the lowest? Women who drank coffee. Motivated reasoning biases is just one of many social biases that should make us concerned about any body of regulators making the decisions about what counts as hate speech and what doesn't.
12. Waldron says that we may have to distinguish between words that attack religious believers *qua* believers and words that attack religious beliefs themselves (118–120).
13. My thanks to Robert Taylor for this heuristic.
14. For more on this argument see Miles 2012.

Works Cited

"Amended Administrative Complaint University of Mary Washington." *U.S. Department of Education Office of Civil Rights*. 2015. www.washingtonpost.com/news/volokh-conspiracy/wp-content/uploads/sites/14/2015/10/UMWAmendedComplaint.pdf?tid=a_inl

Bray, Mark. *Antifa: The Anti-Fascist Handbook*. Brooklyn: Melville House, 2017.

Chemerinsky, Erwin, and Gillman, Howard. *Free Speech on Campus*. New Haven, CT: Yale University Press, 2017.

Cohen, Andrew Jason. *Toleration*. Malden, MA: Polity Press, 2014.

Darwall, Stephen. "Two Concepts of Respect." *Ethics*, Vol. 88 (1977): 36–49.

"Free Speech on Campus." *Knight Foundation*. April 4, 2016. https://knightfoundation.org/reports/free-speech-campus

Haidt, Jonathan. *The Righteous Mind: Why Good People Are Divided by Religion and Politics*. New York: Vintage, 2012.

———. "Why Concepts Creep Left." *Psychological Inquiry*, Vol. 27 (2016): 40–45. DOI: 10.1080/1047840X.2016.1115713

Haslam, Nick. "Concept Creep: Psychology's Expanding Concepts of Harm and Pathology." *Psychological Inquiry*, Vol. 27 (2016): 1–17. DOI: 10.1080/1047840X.2016.1082418

Hayek, F. A. *The Fatal Conceit: The Errors of Socialism*. Chicago: University of Chicago Press, 2011.

"The History, Uses, and Abuses of Title IX." *American Association of University Professors*. 2016.

Jacobson, Daniel. "Mill on Liberty, Speech, and the Free Society." *Philosophy & Public Affairs*, Vol. 29 (2000): 276–309.

Kahneman, Daniel. *Thinking Fast and Slow*. New York: Farrar, Straus and Giroux, 2011.

Kawakami, Kerry, Dovidio, John F., Moll, Jasper, Hermsen, Sander and Russin, Abby. "Just Say No (to Stereotyping): Effects of Training in the Negation of Stereotypic Associations on Stereotype Activation." *Journal of Personality and Social Psychology*, Vol. 78 (2000): 871–888.

Kipnis, Laura. "Sexual Paranoia Strikes Academia." *The Chronicle of Higher Education*. February 27, 2015. http://laurakipnis.com/wp-content/uploads/2010/08/Sexual-Paranoia-Strikes-Academe.pdf

———. *Unwanted Advances: Sexual Paranoia Comes to Campus*. New York: Harper, 2017.

Kors, Alan Charles and Silverglate, Harvey. *The Shadow University: The Betrayal of Liberty on America's Campuses*. New York: HarperCollins, 1998.

Levy, Ariel. "Trial by Twitter." *The New Yorker*. August 5, 2013. www.newyorker.com/magazine/2013/08/05/trial-by-twitter

Manne, Kate and Stanley, Jason. "When Free Speech Becomes a Political Weapon." *Chronicle of Higher Education*. November 13, 2015. www.chronicle.com/article/When-Free-Speech-Becomes-a/234207

Marcuse, Herbert. "Repressive Tolerance." In *The Critique of Pure Tolerance*, edited by Robert Paul Wolff, Barrington Moore, Jr. and Herbert Marcuse. Boston, MA: Beacon Press, 1965: 95–137.

McElroy, Wendy. *Rape Culture Hysteria: Fixing the Damage to Men and Women*. CreateSpace, 2016.

Mclaughlin Group Survey. "National Undergraduate Study." October 26, 2017. www.dropbox.com/s/sfmpoeytvqc3cl2/NATL%20College%2010-25-15%20Presentation.pdf?dl=0

McMurtrie, Beth. "A Free Speech Divide: Why Students and Professors May Think Differently About Free Expression." *Chronicle of Higher Education*. September 17, 2017. www.chronicle.com/article/The-Free-Speech-Divide-Is-a/241187

Merriam Webster Dictionary. "Word of the Year 2014." www.merriam-webster.com/words-at-play/2014-word-of-the-year/culture

Miles, J. K. "A Perfectionist Defense of Free Speech." *Social Theory and Practice*, Vol. 38 (2012): 213–229.

Mill, John Stuart. *On Liberty in Focus*. London and New York: Routledge, 1991.

Montz, Rob. "Silence U: Is the University Killing Free Speech and Open Debate?" *We the Internet*. July 14, 2016. https://www.youtube.com/watch?v=x5uaVFfX3AQ

Rothman, Joshua. "The Meaning of 'Culture.'" *The New Yorker*. December 26, 2014. www.newyorker.com/books/joshua-rothman/meaning-culture

Schauer, Frederick. *Free Speech: A Philosophical Inquiry*. Cambridge: Cambridge University Press, 1984.

Soll, Jack B., Milkman, Katherine L. and Payne, John W. "A User's Guide to Debiasing." In *Wiley-Blackwell Handbook of Judgment and Decision Making*. Hoboken, NJ: Wiley-Blackwell, 2015.

"Speaking Freely: What Students Think About Expression at America's Colleges." *FIRE* (Foundation for Individual Rights in Education). 2016. https://d28htnjz2elwuj.cloudfront.net/wp-content/uploads/2017/10/11091747/survey-2017-speaking-freely.pdf

Thomason, Andy. "Laura Kipnis Says She Faced Another Title IX Investigation, This Time for Her Book." *Chronicle of Higher Education*. September 20, 2017. www.chronicle.com/blogs/ticker/laura-kipnis-says-she-faced-another-title-ix-investigation-this-time-for-her-book/120210

Valenti, Jessica. *Full Frontal Feminism: A Young Woman's Guide to Why Feminism Matters*. Berkeley, CA: Seal Press, 2014.

Volokh, Eugene. "Feminist Majority Foundation (publisher of Ms. Magazine) and Others Call for Restricting Campus Speech." *Washington Post*. October 27, 2017. www.washingtonpost.com/news/volokh-conspiracy/wp/2015/10/27/feminist-majority-foundation-publisher-of-ms-magazine-and-others-call-for-restricting-campus-speech/?utm_term=.87eb8af485fd

Waldron, Jeremy. *The Harm in Hate Speech*. Cambridge, MA: Harvard University Press, 2012.

16 From Academic Freedom to Academic Responsibility

Privileges and Responsibilities Regarding Speech on Campus

Arianne Shahvisi

Introduction

If one paid attention only to the popular press (see e.g., Harding 2015; O'Neill 2014; Grayling 2015), it would be forgivable to infer that universities are in a moment of intellectual crisis, held hostage to the whims of militant, overly-sensitive students, and no longer able to foment innovative ideas or play host to fierce debate. Free speech is widely declared to be endangered, and we are told that students and sympathetic academics are responsible for its demise. Yet on the ground, things feel much the same as ever. Lively debates *do* continue to happen, and students are generally polite, deferential, and heterogeneous in their views. Eruptions of protest concerning permissible speech are rare. Where they do occur, it is difficult to argue that they are inconsistent with the ideals of the university: They are generally democratic, peaceful, and principled.

In this chapter, I counter a widespread misrepresentation of the trend towards more rigorous gate-keeping of knowledge-exchange in academic communities. In particular, I am interested in the duties of academics to (a) themselves speak responsibly and (b) provide equitable learning opportunities to an increasingly diverse student body (Blades 2017).

The chapter is structured as follows. I start by arguing that academics are uniquely situated within the epistemic community, since they experience "credibility excess" and "platform privilege." I assert that these epistemic privileges should lead to the uptake of additional responsibilities towards producing a more equitable epistemic community. I then explore the role academics might play in delivering on this responsibility by producing "safe spaces" within their classrooms, and engaging with the practice of "no-platforming." I address the threat of "concept creep" in relation to these practices, and conclude that the moral panic around freedom of speech in universities is unfounded. Provided these important regulatory devices are *themselves* properly defined and held to rigorous standards, I assert that academics should support them as a way of optimizing the quality and diversity of our collective epistemic resources.

Credibility Excess

Particular groups are denied full citizenship within our shared epistemic community, a situation which philosopher Miranda Fricker refers to as "epistemic injustice" (2007). Knowledge is generated by processing first-hand experience and is transmitted through testimony. Fricker asserts that opportunities to contribute to knowledge-generation and knowledge-transmission are not fairly distributed. Rather, those who belong to privileged social groups are better able, by virtue of that group membership, to contribute to knowledge creation and exchange, while others, by virtue of their membership of marginalized social groups, are less able to do so.

Fricker describes two varieties of epistemic injustice. The first is "hermeneutical injustice," which refers to inequalities in knowledge *production*. Less socially privileged groups have less authorship over the means of knowledge production—the words and concepts that are required to interpret our experiences in the world. Those groups are therefore sometimes unable to articulate and thereby process their social experiences, because the interpretational resources are generally devised by more powerful groups who have had no need to articulate those particular experiences. Less socially powerful groups are therefore sometimes unable to introduce their experiences into collective knowledge circulation, which also inhibits their ability to enact or motivate change if those experiences are negative, as they are too often liable to be.

The second injustice, "testimonial injustice," relates to knowledge *transmission*. Members of marginalized groups are not able to share their knowledge as readily as those within privileged groups. Successful transmission of knowledge relies on being *believed*. Being believed relies on being judged to be credible. In principle, our judgements of credibility are contingent on evidence of reliable knowledge, such as having verified the quality of a person's knowledge in the past (e.g., the mechanic who repaired your bicycle will thereafter be considered to be credible in matters relating to bicycles) or knowing that a particular person has had experiences which render them a good source of a particular kind of knowledge.

Only some of the time are we able to (or do we bother to) carefully adjudicate the credibility of a particular person. The rest of the time, we take short-cuts, and most of the time, it is reasonable to do so. We are attentive to "clues" of a given person's credibility. Those clues are invariably based on stereotypes, and they can go wrong. A person wearing a suit, or a person with a "respectable" accent, might be deemed to be more authoritative than a person wearing a tracksuit or a person with a working-class accent. Men are invariably deemed to be more credible than women; white people are deemed to be more credible than people of color; middle-class people are deemed to be more credible than working-class people. Our assessments of credibility are in many cases erroneous or disproportionate. Overall, people from certain social groups are more likely to have their actual credibility deflated, while those from other social groups are liable to have their credibility inflated.

All professions trade on the specific credibility of their workers, yet none trades on credibility more than academia, whose purpose is to create and confer knowledge. Academics are generally assigned high assessments of credibility, and these are, for the most part, defensible.[1] Yet in many cases, the credibility of an academic will be erroneously over-estimated. Fricker calls this "credibility excess" (*ibid.* 17).

In what follows, I consider three common cases of epistemic miscalculation with respect to academics which tends to result in credibility excess: credibility inflation, credibility over-spill, and virtue inflation.

I refer to the first variety of credibility excess as "credibility inflation." While academics are necessarily credible within their areas of specialism, the reliability or extent of their knowledge is easily over-estimated. Fricker's (*ibid.* 18) example serves as a useful comparator. She considers a general practitioner whose patients expect answers to their medical questions even where the required knowledge lies beyond the doctor's competence. This is a common conundrum for doctors, and academics will note similarities with students expecting their teachers to have a ready answer to every question within their field.

Some of this credibility inflation derives from the mystique of the academy, where esoteric language, overbearing architecture, and unique traditions contribute to a separation from local communities which renders universities and academics distant from, and elevated above, the general public. Academics are then cast as omniscient.

The second concern is that of "credibility over-spill." Views which academics express outside of their fields of expertise are more likely to be taken seriously than those of non-academics, regardless of their actual value. Consider that theoretical physicist Stephen Hawking has this year been given a platform in the *Guardian*, in which he has offered his reflections on the leader of the UK Labour Party (Elgot 2017) and the future of the National Health Service (Campbell 2017). Because of his status as a celebrity academic, his views on these topics, which inarguably lie far outside of his field of expertise, are taken as valuable additions to these conversations. This is an example of credibility inflation, in which the credibility of an academic spills beyond their disciplinary expertise. One might argue that Hawking is no more *automatically* qualified as an interlocutor within debates on these issues than a London taxi driver is to comment on the politics of the Middle-East.

This kind of credibility over-spill does not generally occur amongst academics themselves, who are acutely aware of the disciplinary limits of their own and their peers' knowledge, but students and the general public are likely to conceive of academics as credible in a broad sense.

The credibility of academics also extends into the moral domain. I call this "virtue inflation." Academics are invariably deemed to be virtuous as well as knowledgeable. Research shows that university lecturers are generally well-regarded and score favorably in public opinion ratings for "ethics and honesty" (see, e.g., Roy Morgan Research 2017). This bears on the authority of academics because it implies that the positions they adopt in relation to particular issues are liable to not only be factually correct but also morally superior. Academics may alter the moral landscape for their students, who often admire their teachers and may be easily persuaded by their personal moral or political views.

It is important to note that one might make compelling arguments for academics being credible beyond their areas of specialism and having greater potential moral credibility than non-academics. Academics are, after all, thinkers. Many of us use our research skills to educate ourselves beyond our disciplines. It is relatively easy for us to do so, since we are trained to seek and adjudicate knowledge. Many of us also spend time thinking through moral problems and are skilled at forming arguments and spotting inconsistencies. Again, the ability to digest and analyze large amounts of information makes it easier for us to be well-informed, which may be taken as a prerequisite for holding a justified moral stance. I do not mean to dispute any of this but rather to motivate the concern that there is considerable *risk* of a genuine over-estimation of an academic's credibility, which presents the potential for inflated harm as a result of our speech.

Platform Privilege

A minority of individuals are regularly invited, or permitted, to speak or write in public fora. Those to whom platforms are extended are generally supposed to be authoritative in some sense, so that their speech or writing is deemed to meet particular standards of quality.

Academics have regular access to a variety of platforms for both written and spoken communication, within which they are generally given free rein to discuss their ideas. Further, these platforms reach large audiences. Nominally, academics have a captive audience in the students they teach. Many academics address hundreds of students every week; some of us also reach hundreds or even thousands of people a year through public engagement events. In addition, there are now a plethora of print and online platforms that actively seek the commentary of academics. Websites such as the *Atlantic*, the *Conversation*, and *Aeon* publish academics almost exclusively, while mainstream newspapers regularly print the views of academics within their commentary sections. Academics dominate *TED Talks*, whose reach is considerable, and are frequently invited to contribute to radio and television broadcasts.

Often there is a genuine desire to engage with audiences outside of academia and offer one's work to a broader audience. Academics may also strategically seek out these public engagement opportunities as a way of evidencing their "impact" in the world outside of the academy. Many use these more informal outlets as a way of giving voice to views which would not be appropriate within academic journals. Sometimes this is because the tone of the work does not fit the staid, impersonal style that is common in academic writing, or because the essay really is *commentary* on a given topic, and does not make the substantial, novel contribution to the literature that is required of academic publications. In other cases, it may be because the topic falls outside of the writer's area of academic expertise. To return to the example in the previous section, Stephen Hawking's views on the health service would not be published in a public policy journal, but he nonetheless has access to other platforms (which in fact have a much wider circulation).

There is nothing obviously illicit in using non-academic channels in these ways, but of course the availability of these platforms collaborates with the credibility excess described in the previous section to increase the risk that academics could cause harm as a result of their speech if they were to misuse those platforms. The cost of academics professing falsehoods or misrepresentations (either maliciously or accidentally), reinforcing harmful stereotypes, or using insensitive language is very high. Since academics have access to large audiences, and are very likely to be believed, the possibility of causing harm through speech that is marginalizing or false is more pronounced than for a non-academic.[2]

In the next section, I consider the responsibilities that academics should shoulder, both as a protection against the risks of harm which are a consequence of being so readily afforded high credibility assessments and a range of platforms, but also as a way of ensuring that their own epistemic privileges are deployed in producing a more equitable knowledge community. This second point is key, since the same trends which lend epistemic privileges to academics deny epistemic opportunities to others. It is therefore primarily a matter of justice, but importantly, it is also a matter of optimizing epistemic outcomes, since inclusivity is most likely to facilitate more accurate forms of knowledge by giving voice to unheard perspectives.

Modulating Speech: Academic Responsibility, Safe Spaces, and No-Platforming

Within discourses on free speech on campus, there is a false dichotomy at work which pits considerations of student welfare against the possibility of healthy academic discourse (e.g., Fox 2016). It is believed that measures to permit particular student groups to engage optimally within educational settings preclude the possibility of challenging discursive exchanges. Yet it is precisely the opposite outcome that is being sought. In enabling the participation of groups with a broader range of identities, the discursive landscape ought to become *more*, not less, varied for all. More voices will be heard, more perspectives will need to be factored into each person's eventual position, greater challenges will be posed. To assume (without evidence) that measures to increase the participation of marginalized groups is antithetical to good epistemic outcomes is to proclaim that optimal knowledge production can be reached *without* optimal contributions from *all* social groups, which seems as implausible as it is objectionable.

Another important point to note is that universities are unique in that they are homes for students as well as places of learning. While academics conceive of the university as a workplace and use separate spaces for privacy, relaxation, and identity formation, many students are resident on campus or in institutional accommodation. As such, their relationship to the university is significantly determinative of their wellbeing. Nor is that relationship necessarily a straightforward one, since students are critically dependent on universities to confer the degrees which secure their independent futures. Universities have duties towards their students which transcend their nominal educational responsibilities.

In the previous section, I described credibility excess and platform privilege, which may be seen as being constitutive of the privilege better known as "academic freedom." As I have noted, with this privilege comes the potential for harm, and in this section I will argue that academics must be held to particular standards in their speech in order to ensure that any potential harm as a result of their epistemic position is minimized.[3] The potential consequences of misused academic freedom are tremendous, both inside and outside the classroom. As such, it seems reasonable that academic freedom should be tempered by "academic responsibility," which goes beyond the ordinary constraints on speech and makes additional demands on those with epistemic privileges. One such demand, which I develop here, is that academics speak so as to create educational environments (whether, in the physical classroom, in extra-curricular settings, or online) within which all learners can thrive, and within which a diversity of views is heard. Or, to put it another way, that academics *refrain* from speaking in ways that prevent learners from particular (marginalized) groups from being able to participate equitably in the epistemic community.

Within current debates on free speech and the academy, no concepts have been as strongly criticized as that of a "safe space," and the idea of "no-platforming" speakers.[4] In the following two subsections, I make my notion of "academic responsibility" more concrete by describing one possible facet of the duty: the responsibilities of academics towards their students in relation to "safe spaces" and "no-platforming." I suggest ways in which academics can usefully participate in an emerging campus culture in which speech is regulated in the service of generating more diverse bodies of knowledge, and thereby put their epistemic privilege to work in facilitating those who are marginalized by the very same epistemic trends.

Safe Spaces: In Search of Dignity

Eighteen months ago, I was invited to speak at a conference themed on academic freedom. In the first morning panel, a speaker finished his talk by decrying the demand for safe spaces within universities, to nods of assent from a few audience members. During the discussion, I asked him to outline what he understood by a "safe space." Discomfited, he responded that a safe space is used as a way of evading conversations that make you uncomfortable. Of course, that doesn't qualify as a definition of a safe space, but is rather an interpretation of its function. On further interrogation, he had nothing more detailed to offer. This kind of gloss is common in popular conceptions of safe spaces, and is the foundation of a moral panic around their assumed erosion of free speech and promotion of intellectual conformity. Commentators (see, e.g., Davis 2016) complain that safe spaces allow students to escape the "real world," and academics have complained that they feel "muzzled" by students' demands for safe spaces (Steinfeld 2017). In what follows, I will show that these views often stem from a mischaracterization of safe spaces.

Distinguishing between the definition and function of "safe spaces" (or, synonymously, "autonomous spaces") is important. In all my experiences, as a student, activist, and academic, safe spaces have meant either or both of two things. The first is a space (either online or offline) in which particular groups of *people* are deliberately excluded. The second is a space (either online or offline) in which particular kinds of *language* or *behavior* are excluded. The idea in both cases is that those present in the eventual conversation will experience a discursive space in which particular discussions will be facilitated by other distracting features having been pre-emptively subtracted away. Consider that a group of philosophers of physics might reasonably decide to exclude an ethicist from a workshop on the grounds that it would be distracting to have to explain quantum mechanics to them. In the same way, safe spaces often have an epistemic function: They aspire to include interlocutors who already possess particular forms of knowledge, often acquired via personal experiences (of, say, ableism, or homophobia). Or consider that if one belongs to a group of Jewish colleagues wishing to discuss ways to respond to anti-Semitic micro-aggressions in the workplace, the presence of a non-Jewish colleague might be distracting or upsetting (she might keep asking why such-and-such is anti-Semitic, or she may even have perpetrated some of the incidents under discussion). As in the previous point, safe spaces allow discussions to stay focused, but they also allow discussants to proceed with the matter in hand—invariably discussing something that is understandably upsetting or hurtful—without worrying that they are going to be insulted within that discussion. Rather, the atmosphere is more likely to be a supportive one, and discussions are invariably more productive when discussants feel supported.

Those creating safe spaces exclude members of groups who do not possess particular knowledge that will likely be taken as axiomatic within the intended discussion. That knowledge is generally the product of experience. Excluding men, or white people, is usually a way of excluding those who do not have first-hand experience of sexism or racism. Within the resulting space, discussion of sexism and racism will usually be high on the agenda, which is why the suggestion that those using safe spaces are *avoiding* difficult discussions is a misnomer. They are simply creating an epistemically optimal environment for a nuanced discussion. Normative critiques of safe spaces invariably ignore the fact that their primary function is an epistemic one.

In the first case, in which safe spaces are created by excluding *groups of people*, there is a basic heuristic in operation: The excluded group has greater social privilege than the included group. As such, comparisons with segregation, or claims of discrimination, are not apposite. In the second case, in which safe spaces are produced by excluding specific *language or behaviors*, there is generally another heuristic at work: The disqualified language or behaviors will be those that serve to exclude particular groups of people with less social privilege. This includes language or behaviors that are derogatory or humiliating, or that reinforce stereotypes.

What does all this mean for academics? There is an increasing trend towards ensuring that learning environments are safe spaces in the second sense, i.e., spaces in which particular *views*, rather than particular groups, are excluded. (Hereafter, I use "safe space" to denote this sense of the term only.) The purpose of establishing a safe space within a classroom is to create an educational environment in which all students feel able to participate equitably in intellectual exchange. This is generally achieved by ensuring that marginalizing speech or behaviors are not accepted within the classroom. Students are variably situated in the world outside the classroom; without carefully designed interventions, that social positioning is replicated within the classroom. Groups that are accustomed to epistemic injustice will continue to be subject to that injustice within the classroom.

There are countless studies which evidence the link between negative stereotypes of people of color (Massey and Fischer 2005; Rovai, Gallien and Wighting 2005) and/or women (O'Brien et al. 2015; Logel et al. 2009) and educational under-performance in higher education settings.

Students' underperformance affects their future opportunities. It also impacts on the quality of the discursive space that is created within the classroom. The absence of interventions to undermine background inequalities affects contributions to discussions in class, rendering certain voices quiet or silent, which impoverishes the learning environment for the group as a whole, since particular experiences and perspectives are likely to be absent from discussions. Yet we also know that by creating an "identity safe" environment, the effects of stereotype threat can be eliminated (Davies, Spencer and Steele 2005). An "identity safe" learning context is one in which the differential effects of identity are first of all *recognized*, and second, mitigated by evidenced-based interventions to offset any negative identity contingencies. The guiding insight is that heterogeneity of knowledge and experience is academically valuable, so that there is an epistemic, as well as a moral, motivation (Purdie-Vaughns and Walton 2011).

Unfortunately, the term "safe" seems to invite precisely the misunderstanding that the speaker at the start of this subsection typifies. This mischaracterization may be one source of the moral panic, or at least, a facilitating factor. "Safe" is read as "sheltered," when really what is more distinctive is that the space is *manufactured* to be more securely able to achieve a particular end, i.e., to facilitate a particular kind of discussion. This is not to claim that the term "safe" in its conventional sense is doing no work. A trans-woman would likely not feel safe or comfortable in a class in which a teacher denied that trans-women are women; a Muslim student would likely not feel safe or comfortable in a class in which the teacher did not problematize other students' Islamophobia. Yet even "comfortable" is open to misinterpretation, since there are senses in which we *hope* to make our students *un*comfortable, just as we want them to experience the lack of safety which comes of destabilizing one's assumptions. Safety from humiliation, and the comfort to be able to participate equitably, are presumably objectives within any classroom, yet the terms need to be demarcated more carefully.

On the basis of these misunderstandings, Callan (2016) distinguishes between "dignity safety" and "intellectual safety." Being "dignity safe" requires that one is "free of any reasonable anxiety that others will treat one as having an inferior social rank to theirs" (65). Being "intellectually unsafe" involves existing in a culture of antagonism, as "settled beliefs and values are subject to critique that some students will find distressing or exhilarating, or both at the same time" (*ibid.*). Callan argues that while dignity safety is a defensible aim within educational settings, intellectual safety should never be defended. And there is no compelling evidence that the two are mutually exclusive: Protecting dignity safety does not force one to settle for intellectual safety. It very likely has the opposite effect; protecting the dignity safety of a group whose dignity is threatened (i.e., black students) might trouble the intellectual safety of other (i.e., non-black) students, in ways that are morally and educationally productive.

Perhaps, then, being academically responsible involves creating "spaces of dignity" within our classrooms, and contributing to broader spaces of dignity within public discourse by ensuring that our epistemic privilege, while it may sometimes be used to speak in ways that are *intellectually* unsafe, is always directed towards protecting the dignity-safety of epistemically-marginalized groups.

No-Platforming: Exclusion as Discretion

As I write from Brighton in the United Kingdom, an event in the nearby town of Lewes, featuring fired newspaper columnist Katie Hopkins (who once compared refugees to cockroaches; see, e.g., Jones 2015) has just been cancelled (Ruddick 2017). Activists protested her invitation, claiming that Hopkins's propensity to hate speech means that she should not be given additional opportunities to voice her harmful views. This is an archetypal case of no-platforming.

No-platforming is the denial of a platform—i.e., a public-speaking opportunity—to a set of ideas, or a person who represents or espouses those ideas, on the grounds that the articulation of those ideas is likely to cause harm. Generally, no-platforming efforts begin once the speaker has already been invited and the event promoted. Members of the community then protest the invitation with the hope that the invitation will be withdrawn by the institution or declined by the speaker. No-platforming is therefore a form of protest whose desired outcome is a speaker being denied a platform, i.e., an opportunity to speak.

In some literal sense, then, no-platforming is a form of censorship. However, it is a form of censorship which lacks the sting that makes censorship so worrying; it is not censorship by bodies of power. Far from it. No-platforming is sometimes decided upon as a democratic policy of an organization (e.g., the National Union of Students in the United Kingdom) or it emerges more informally in response to protest action. The decision to deny a platform to a speaker is rarely, if ever, the flexing of institutional power, except perhaps in cases for which the physical safety of the speaker or members of the campus community is considered to be at risk. Even where organizers feel compelled to cancel an event against their will, there is generally no instruction from "above," so to speak, but rather an urgent discontent from below which may lead to complications (if the event is picketed) or embarrassment (in the form of bad press).

In any case, as O'Keefe (2016, 86) points out, there is an important difference between the right to free speech and the right to an audience. No-platforming denies the speaker an audience, it does not deny the person the right to speak; no-one has the *right* to speak at a particular institution or event. Returning to my discussion in the third section, no-platforming challenges the individual's *platform privilege*, rather than their right to freedom of speech.

Further, no-platforming is not always the denial of a platform to another person. In many cases the protest takes the form of not *sharing* a platform (see, e.g., Ahmed 2016), which is to say, relinquishing one's own platform, or, in other words, no-platforming oneself.[5] The purpose of not sharing a platform is not to avoid debate but to refuse to legitimize positions which are considered to be morally illegitimate. I would not share a platform with a person who claimed that colonialism was acceptable, because colonialism relies on a belief in the inferiority of particular groups, and I do not wish to elevate such a false and harmful claim to the level of academic debate. Equally, since my work discusses abortion from a pro-choice stance, I would not be surprised or outraged if a person who considers abortion to be equivalent to murder refused to share a platform with me. Ahmed (2016) describes her refusal to share a platform with a racist person, since this would be tantamount to presenting racism as "just another viewpoint that can be expressed at the happy table of diversity."

The rise of no-platforming has been accompanied by a new market for deliberately pugnacious views outside of their traditional home in the tabloid press. In order to capture and hold the attention of an increasingly distracted public, a "so-called controversialist must put these received opinions in a ruder, more priggish manner than his or her more mainstream counterparts do" (Dunbar 2017). (Katie Hopkins is one such controversialist.) Being no-platformed attracts attention in ways that typically result in the person being more likely to be offered platforms in the future. Their status as a controversial figure is substantiated, and for event committees seeking notorious names who will draw a crowd, they may become a more attractive option. This has two corollaries. First, it means that effect of no-platforming is often counter-productive if the aim is to limit the harms incurred as a result of that person's speech. Second, it contradicts the claim that no-platforming always equates to censorship. The first consequence does not undermine no-platforming, since an important function is for a particular group or institution (generally a university) to distance itself from the speaker in question. No-platforming is performative as well as being strategic; it makes a moral statement, and it asserts the importance of upholding the dignity of marginalized groups within a particular context.

As with safe spaces, it is important for academics to consider their relationship to no-platforming. First, because academics belong to a campus culture within which students are in some cases no-platforming external speakers, and in which academics may use their own platforms to speak out in opposition to, or in defense of, this practice. Second, because academics themselves, or their colleagues, may find themselves being no-platformed.

For those unmoved by considerations of harm, philosophers Simpson and Srinivasan (forthcoming) make the compelling suggestion that no-platforming can instead be justified by noting that within the academy, speech may be legitimately excluded for *content*-based reasons. They assert that "good teaching and research requires that communicative privileges be given to some and not others, based on people's disciplinary competence" (12). In other words, we should exclude particular speakers simply because they do not meet the methodological and/or epistemic norms of academia. After all, we exercise gate-keeping elsewhere in the academy in terms of, e.g., the students who are admitted, the grades they receive, the faculty who are hired, and the research that is funded and published. To return to the concept of platform privilege, it may be fruitful for academics to consider whether they are always *deserving* of their communicative privileges.

Simpson and Srinivasan's content-based framework easily supports the no-platforming of, say, Katie Hopkins, but would not (so easily) rule in favor of no-platforming writer Germaine Greer, who is nonetheless frequently no-platformed due to her transphobia. While Hopkins is not an academic and does not formulate arguments or summon evidence to support her views, Greer is an academic and is certainly capable of describing her views in terms that would be considered by many to meet the standards of academia. In fact, as Simpson and Srinivasan themselves concede, their framework would permit a variety of themes to be discussed which some would likely wish to see no-platformed.[6] One might undertake an ethical analysis of whether slavery is defensible, say, and still feel entitled to a platform because the arguments demonstrated disciplinary competence. Philosophers, in particular, have a habit of viewing more or less every topic as apt for analysis (*ibid.*, 19–20), and philosophical analysis invariably consists of unflinchingly interrogating our most cherished assumptions. Not all philosophers practice the same level of discretion in which assumptions they see as *morally* apposite for interrogation, which means that assumptions about the existence or rights of marginalized groups, or the justifiability of genocide, may also end up under the microscope. While some might argue that this is prerogative of the discipline, perhaps Simpson and Srinivasan's account could be strengthened by noting that attention to context is *methodologically* important when one's work deals with real-world issues. Wondering which assumptions are morally apposite for interrogation, is, of course, none other than a philosophical question, so those arguing for the "purity" of academia are hoist by their own petard. I think if this view is taken, Simpson and Srinivasan's filter can be made to uphold many more cases of no-platforming than they anticipate.

One of the challenges of no-platforming is the question of its legitimate boundaries. It is not clear whether sincere apologies for past harmful speech should revoke a speaker's no-platform status, or whether speakers should be permitted to address topics entirely orthogonal to the context in which they have previously caused harm or demonstrated disciplinary incompetence. What further guidelines might we devise in order to distinguish legitimate no-platforming from illegitimate no-platforming? I do not have answers to these questions here but suggest that if no-platforming is more carefully-defined, and more judiciously embraced by its current opponents, academics can join students in developing heuristics which protect dignity safety and adhere to the highest content-based standards, while allowing intellectual safety to be violated, and for there to be equitable participation in those violations, and the knowledge they yield.

Considering "Concept Creep"

While it is hyperbolic to suggest that safe spaces and no-platforming are tantamount to censorship in their current forms, it is reasonable to worry about the potential for misuse. One particular concern is that, even without any explicit intention, the concepts may be applied increasingly broadly, until they encompass a growing field of people and ideas, and become progressively distant from their original justification. The term "concept creep" is borrowed from psychology (Haslam 2016) where it is used to describe the gradual expansion of psychological concepts (e.g., bullying, trauma, abuse) to capture "ordinary" interactions, resulting in the pathologization of much of our social experience. In the case of safe spaces and no-platforming, the worry seems to be that proponents of these concepts may start to classify "new kinds of experience as harmful and new classes of people as harmed and . . . as needful of care and protection" (Haidt 2016, 40).

Opponents of regulation will obviously find the possibility of concept creep objectionable, but so too should proponents of regulation. No-platforming and safe spaces must be as rigorously defined as the injustices they intend to protect against. Failures to properly demarcate them not only jeopardize their ability to serve their intended purposes but could in turn threaten the credibility of the concepts, which may undermine their applications entirely.

Yet before entertaining these concerns, several points must be made. First, there is no evidence that concept creep is currently underway with regard to regulating speech on campus. Those who claim that regulation has already "gone too far" are liable to be those who did not at the time support the cases they now consider to be clear-cut and legitimate. Our social world changes; behavior that is now considered to be sexual harassment (say) was once widely accepted. So we need a way of distinguishing concept creep from the fact that our collective conceptions of what is acceptable do, in fact, change with time: Some "creep" is to be expected.

In other words, if our regulatory tools need clear definition, so too will our understanding of concept creep. While those on the ideological right might argue that the concepts at the heart of regulation creep *outwards*, those on the ideological left might respond that claims of concept creep themselves creep *inwards*. Perhaps it will be more fruitful to move away from these generalizations altogether, and instead focus on resolving concrete boundary cases.

Second, concept creep is an instance of the broader category of logical devices known as "slippery slope" (or "thin edge of the wedge") arguments. The standard form of these arguments is to claim that allowing a particular action will likely result in negative unintended effects. These concerns are legitimate only when one can demonstrate the mechanism by which the unintended consequences are approached. In the absence of such a mechanism, slippery slope arguments may face the charge of fear-mongering. In the case of no-platforming and safe spaces, this charge might be apt. Both regulatory tools seek to exclude marginalizing speech, i.e., speech that targets particular marginalized groups in ways that undermine the dignity of their members. In clearer terms, that means that racism, sexism, ableism, transphobia, classism, and homophobia (amongst others) are regulated against. The possibility of concept creep then depends on the extent to which one can reasonably argue that these forms of marginalization are not well-defined. Since a good deal of legislation depends on these definitions being practical and properly demarcated (e.g., in the UK, the Equality Act 2010), the charge of concept creep is not well-founded.

That said, I think there *are* reasons to be concerned. Losing a platform, or even one's job, because students deem certain views to violate the dignity of a particular marginalized group is one matter. Losing one's job because senior administration wish to unseat a troublemaker or because funding bodies object to one's ideological commitments, is another matter entirely.[3] This is less a question of concept creep and more a question of the outright misuse of these methods of regulation. Academics can best guard against these misuses by joining students in proactively protecting discourses on campus against violations of free speech, whether that be by ensuring the dignity of all groups, so they may more fully enjoy the right to free speech, or by ensuring that dissent can flourish, by being wary of misuses of power. Should concept creep become a genuine problem, academics would then be better positioned to avert it.

Conclusion: Raising the Regulatory Standards

Within this chapter I have described the epistemic positioning of academics as exceptional due to credibility inflation and platform privilege. I have argued that this exceptional positioning incurs additional responsibilities. Amongst these, the responsibility to promote honest, rigorous intellectual exchange which students may access equitably. This involves acting to create spaces within our classrooms which ensure that the dignity of all groups is taken as axiomatic, and supporting students as they lead in the development of a new culture of epistemic gate-keeping, in the service of curating more diverse knowledge communities.

Academic responsibility, which includes paying due regard to the rightful use of safe spaces and no-platforming, need not be an ill-defined set of limitations. Rather, if skeptical academics can take a moment from their scoffing, they might see this shifting culture as a moment in which they can work alongside students in defining the limits of these instruments in enhancing education and debate on campus. It would be naïve indeed to think that universities have automatically and adventitiously achieved the status of optimal sites for freedom of speech and that university demographics can change without cultures and methodologies also changing.

It is concerning that some academics resent students taking a more active interest in gate-keeping conversations on campus in order to promote epistemically-valuable (and morally-defensible) diversity. If students are deemed to hold more collective power than ever before, and are using that power to shape campus policy, it is not obvious that this should be viewed negatively. Unfortunately, I suspect that this misguided critique is gaining more prominence than that of the substantial new command students *do* hold as a consequence of the commercialization of the higher education sector. This is evidenced not through a greater propensity to engage in intellectual gate-keeping, but rather a demand for higher grades and more individualized contact time. In short, I think the concern amongst some administrators and academics about safe spaces and no-platforming has served as convenient cover for the changing understanding of learning as consumption, and the desire for better "value for money" within the new marketplace of education (Nixon, Scullion and Hearn 2016; Naidoo and Williams 2015).

With this in mind, we as scholars should be amenable to regulatory trends that are emerging from the bottom-up, conceived of by students, rather than senior administrators, and enacted for moral and epistemic, rather than financial, reasons. It is a sign of a healthy culture that those at the base of the edifice are able to assert enough power over those a little further up that they have caused many to worry and pine for a more familiar past. Instead of vilifying our students, perhaps it is time for academics to follow their example and remind senior administrators that we too deserve healthy, inclusive, equitable workplaces, and that the epistemic vigor of the profession will be better off for attending to all our diverse needs.

Notes

1. There has been a recent trend towards anti-intellectualism and distrust of experts, which amounts to a reduction in the perceived credibility of academics (Motta 2017). I bracket this detail here, since much of what I discuss concerns the way in which students, and interested members of the public, estimate the credibility of academics. I take it that neither of these self-selecting groups is significantly affected by the delegitimising of experts.
2. Though of course journalists, politicians, and to some extent, celebrities, are similarly positioned.
3. Of course, there is room for constraints on the speech of academics to be misused, and that is a serious concern. In 2014, Steven Salaita was fired from his position as professor of indigenous studies at the University of Illinois at Urbana Champaign because the tone of his online Twitter commentary of Israel's military bombardment of Gaza that summer was deemed to be "uncivil" (see e.g., Shahvisi [2014]). Then chancellor, Phyllis Wise, in a public statement, assured readers that her decision "was not influenced in any way by his positions on the conflict in the Middle East nor his criticism of Israel." Rather, she contended that the university would not tolerate "personal and disrespectful words or actions that demean and abuse either viewpoints themselves or those who express them. We have a particular duty to our students to ensure that they live in a community of scholarship that challenges their assumptions about the world but that also respects their rights as individuals" (2014). It later transpired that Wise had been pressured by pro-Israel donors to the university (Abraham 2015, 10). Yet even taking Wise's words at face value, as Greenwald (2015) points out, there is no "equal opportunity" trend when it comes to offending. There was widespread support for a presumed right to publish Islamophobic cartoons at Charlie Hebdo, yet it is little known that in 2009 the satirical magazine fired one of its writers for writing a sentence that was considered to be anti-Semitic (the writer later won a legal case for unfair dismissal).
4. I have opted to set aside "trigger warnings" or "content warnings" here, though they are often targets of the same critique. A lot can be said both in favor of trigger warnings (Godderis and Root 2016), but also cautioning against their use or over-use (Halberstam 2017; McNally 2014). I will note that what is often lost in the furor over trigger warnings is the fact that the material about which the students are being warned is emphatically not being censored, rather, it is being signaled as potentially emotionally-charged. This strikes me as no different to offering a prospectus to a talk or a paper. One does so in order that the audience may have some idea of what is to come, both for reasons of signposting and to allow for people to tune in/out according to their interests. The same is true of trigger warnings.
5. One common context in which this happens is in the Boycott, Divestment, Sanctions (BDS) movement (Barghouti 2011; McCarthy 2016), which aims to put economic and political pressure on the state of Israel to urge its adherence to international law in its treatment of the Palestinian people, in a similar vein to the anti-apartheid boycotts of South Africa. Those adhering to BDS may refuse to share platforms with representatives of the Israeli governments, and may refuse invitations to speak in Israel, thereby depriving themselves of platforms.
6. Consider two controversies this year: Bruce Gilley's "The Case for Colonialism" and Rebecca Tuvel's "In Defence of Transracialism" (see e.g., Ngo 2017). Their titles are self-explanatory. It is likely that these authors will both be denied platforms in the future, while according to Simpson and Srinivasan's filter, they should presumably be permitted to speak.

Works Cited

Abraham, M. "Conceptualizing Academic Freedom After the Salaita Affair." *First Amendment Studies*, Vol. 49 (2015): 8–12.

Ahmed, S. "You Are Oppressing Me." *feministkilljoys*. February 17, 2016. https://feministkilljoys.com/2016/02/17/you-are-oppressing-me/

Barghouti, O. *BDS: Boycott, Divestment, Sanctions: The Global Struggle for Palestinian Rights*. Chicago: Haymarket books, 2011.

Blades, L. A. "Colleges and Universities Are Becoming Less White, and Republicans Like Them Less." *Teen Vogue*. July 20, 2017. www.teenvogue.com/story/colleges-and-universities-are-becoming-less-white-and-republicans-like-them-less

Callan, E. "Education in Safe and Unsafe Spaces." *Philosophical Inquiry in Education*, Vol. 24 (2016): 64–78.

Campbell, D. "Stephen Hawking Blames Tory Politicians for Damaging NHS." *The Guardian*. August 18, 2017. www.theguardian.com/science/2017/aug/18/stephen-hawking-blames-tory-politicians-for-damaging-nhs

Davies, P. G., Spencer, S. J. and Steele, C. M. "Clearing the Air: Identity Safety Moderates the Effects of Stereotype Threat on Women's Leadership Aspirations." *Journal of Personality and Social Psychology*, Vol. 88 (2005): 276.

Davis, A. "Safe Spaces Rule 'Is Cutting Students Off From the Real World.'" *Evening Standard*. April 7, 2016. www.standard.co.uk/news/education/safe-spaces-rule-is-cutting-students-off-from-the-real-world-a3219911.html

Dunbar, M. "Choosing Your Fight." *The Humanist*, Vol. 77 (2017): 9.

Elgot, J. "Stephen Hawking: Jeremy Corbyn Is a Disaster for Labour." *The Guardian*. March 7, 2017. www.theguardian.com/politics/2017/mar/07/stephen-hawking-jeremy-corbyn-disastrous-labour-resign

Fox, C. *I Find That Offensive!* London: Biteback Publishing, 2016.

Fricker, M. *Epistemic Injustice: Power and the Ethics of Knowing*. Oxford: Oxford University Press, 2007.

Godderis, R. and Root, J. "Trigger Warnings: Compassion Is Not Censorship." *Radical Pedagogy*, Vol. 13 (2016): 130–138.

Grayling, A. C. "Whimpering Students Need to Grow Up or Get Out of University." *The Telegraph*. December 4, 2015. www.telegraph.co.uk/education/educationopinion/12034288/Wimpering-students-need-to-grow-up-or-get-out-ofuniversity.html

Greenwald, G. "In Solidarity With a Free Press: Some More Blasphemous Cartoons." *The Intercept*. January 9, 2015. https://theintercept.com/2015/01/09/solidarity-charlie-hebdo-cartoons/

Haidt, J. "Why Concepts Creep to the Left." *Psychological Inquiry*, Vol. 27 (2016): 40–45.

Halberstam, J. "Trigger Happy: From Content Warning to Censorship." *Signs: Journal of Women in Culture and Society*, Vol. 42 (2017): 535–542.

Harding, E. "Universities 'Dominated by Left-Wing Hate Mobs.'" *Daily Mail*. November 30, 2015. www.dailymail.co.uk/news/article-3338867/Universities-dominated-Left-wing-hate-mobs-Professor-says-free-speech-stifled-challenging views-shouted-down.html

Haslam, N. "Concept Creep: Psychology's Expanding Concepts of Harm and Pathology." *Psychological Inquiry*, Vol. 27 (2016): 1–17.

Jones, S. "UN Human Rights Chief Denounces Sun Over Katie Hopkins 'Cockroach' Column." *The Guardian*. April 24, 2015. www.theguardian.com/global-development/2015/apr/24/katie-hopkins-cockroach-migrants-denounced-united-nations-human-rights-commissioner

Logel, C., Walton, G. M., Spencer, S. J., Iserman, E. C., von Hippel, W. and Bell, A. E. "Interacting With Sexist Men Triggers Social Identity Threat Among Female Engineers." *Journal of Personality and Social Psychology*, Vol. 96 (2009):1089.

Massey, D. S. and Fischer, M. J. "Stereotype Threat and Academic Performance: New Findings From a Racially Diverse Sample of College Freshmen." *Du bois Review: Social Science Research on Race*, Vol. 2 (2005): 45–67.

McCarthy, C. "Academic Freedom and the Boycott of Israeli Universities: On the Necessity of Angry Knowledge." *College Literature*, Vol. 43 (2016): 264–274.

McNally, R. J. "Hazards Ahead: The Problem With Trigger Warnings, According to the Research: Five Studies You Should Read Before You Deploy a Trigger Warning." *Pacific Standard*. May 20, 2014. https://psmag.com/education/hazards-ahead-problem-trigger-warnings-according-research-81946

Motta, M. "The Dynamics and Political Implications of Anti-Intellectualism in the United States." *American Politics Research*. July 11, 2017. http://journals.sagepub.com/doi/abs/10.1177/1532673X17719507

Naidoo, R. and Williams, J. "The Neoliberal Regime in English Higher Education: Charters, Consumers and the Erosion of the Public Good." *Critical Studies in Education*, Vol. 56 (2015): 208–223.

Ngo, A. "Academic Article Withdrawn Following 'Serious and Credible' Threats of Violence." *Quillette*. October 11, 2017. http://quillette.com/2017/10/11/academic-article-withdrawn-following-serious-credible-threats-violence/

Nixon, E., Scullion, R. and Hearn, R. "Her Majesty the Student: Marketised Higher Education and the Narcissistic (Dis)satisfactions of the Student-Consumer." *Studies in Higher Education* (June 28, 2016): 1–21.

O'Brien, L. T., Garcia, D. M., Adams, G., Villalobos, J. G., Hammer, E. and Gilbert, P. "The Threat of Sexism in a STEM Educational Setting: The Moderating Impacts of Ethnicity and Legitimacy Beliefs on Test Performance." *Social Psychology of Education*, Vol. 18 (2015): 667–684.

O'Keefe, T. "Making Feminist Sense of No-Platforming." *Feminist Review*, Vol. 113 (2016): 85–92.

O'Neill, B. "Free Speech Is So Last Century. Today's Students Want the 'Right to Be Comfortable.'" *The Spectator*. November 22, 2014. www.spectator.co.uk/2014/11/free-speech-is-so-last-century-todays-students-want-the-right-to-becomfortable/

Purdie-Vaughns, V. and Walton, G. M. "Is Multiculturalism Bad for African Americans? Redefining Inclusion Through the Lens of Identity Safety." In *Moving Beyond Prejudice Reduction: Pathways to Positive Intergroup Relations*, edited by Linda R. Tropp and Robyn K. Mallett. Washington, DC: American Psychological Association, 2011: 159–177.

Rovai, A. P., Gallien Jr, L. B. and Wighting, M. J. "Cultural and Interpersonal Factors Affecting African American Academic Performance in Higher Education: A Review and Synthesis of the Research Literature." *The Journal of Negro Education*, Vol. 74 (2005): 359–370.

Roy Morgan Research. "Roy Morgan Image of Professions Survey 2017: Health Professionals Continue Domination With Nurses Most Highly Regarded Again; Followed by Doctors and Pharmacists." *RoyMorgan.com*. June 7, 2017. www.roymorgan.com/findings/7244-roy-morgan-image-of-professions-may-2017-201706051543

Ruddick, G. "Katie Hopkins' Mail Online Contract Ends 'by Mutual Consent.'" *The Guardian*. November 27, 2017. www.theguardian.com/media/2017/nov/27/katie-hopkins-mail-online-column-contract-ends

Shahvisi, A. "Money Where Your Mouth Is: Salaita, Freedom of Speech, and the New Market of Education." *Open Democracy*. October 3, 2014. www.opendemocracy.net/north-africa-west-asia/arianne-shahvisi/money-where-your-mouth-is-salaita-freedom-of-speech-and-new-market-o

Simpson, R. and Srinivasan, A. "No Platforming." In *Academic Freedom*, edited by J. Lackey. Oxford: Oxford University Press, forthcoming.

Steinfeld, J. "Universities Should Be Environments of Robust Debate, Not 'Safe Spaces.'" *Times Higher Education*. April 9, 2017. www.timeshighereducation.com/blog/universities-should-be-environments-robust-debate-not-safe-spaces

Wise, P. M. "The Principles on Which We Stand." *University of Illinois at Urbana-Champaign Chancellor's Blog*. August 22, 2014. https://chicagotonight.wttw.com/sites/default/files/article/ . . . /PhyllisWiseStatement.pdf

17 Campus Speech, Diverse Perspectives, and the Distribution of Burdens

Ryan Muldoon

Introduction

Mill's defense of free speech rests on the idea of a competition amongst arguments and ideas. We should avoid censoring speech, Mill argues, because we might find that unpopular ideas are in fact true, and even if they are wrong, they may help us come up with better arguments for better ideas. This is a compelling model of speech, both because it offers an interesting procedural account for how we might expand the stock of knowledge and arguments, and it provides an optimistic account of progress through opposition.

However, there is an important implicit assumption in the background of Mill's account: that the population participating in free speech is fixed, or at least unaffected, by the content of debates. However, this is at the very least a contentious assumption: It might be accurate for, say, debates in developmental biology or physics and other areas where there is a strong distinction between the subject of the speech and the participants, but there are reasons to think that this is false where the subject of the speech and the participants start to overlap—this is most notably the case in areas of social science and value theory in philosophy where normative status itself can be up for debate. Indeed, Langton (1993), Fricker (2007), and others have argued that certain forms of speech can serve to undermine the ability of others to fully participate in the marketplace of ideas. While they both identify particular ways in which disadvantaged groups can lose their ability to contribute to broader discussion, we might think that they are well-worked-out special cases of a more general phenomenon—that the content of debates can either serve to draw more people in or drive people away. In this paper, I develop the argument that we have epistemic reasons for wanting to create more inclusive debates, and that may give us reason to shape discussion in a way that serves to create a more robust exchange of ideas. This may require us to place some topics out of bounds for reasonable discussion. However, placing too many things outside of the realm of discussion has its own problems, as it can undermine robust deliberation. As such, we need to look for a compromise between inclusion of ideas and inclusion of people as a deliberative principle.

Because of this need for a compromise between maximalist inclusion of ideas and a maximalist inclusion of people, we have reason to look for a reasonable principle for distributing the burdens imposed by a more robust marketplace of ideas. However, this distribution is made more complex by the fact that different parties may hold different epistemic perspectives (as defined in Muldoon 2016) and as a result disagree on what might constitute a burden. As such, this distributive principle must be able to deal with deep disagreements on the kinds of burdens that participants recognize.

While this may initially seem to be an overly complex picture of free speech, I will argue that it offers a much richer picture of why campus speech has become such a sensitive issue and how it might be addressed in a way that both respects the importance of free speech and recognizes that the Millian defense of free speech depends on enough people willing to participate in the marketplace of ideas in the first place.

Mill's Defense of Free Speech

One of the powerful features of Mill's defense of free speech is that it has to overcome the naïve utilitarian objection to free speech: If some bit of speech creates more unhappiness than happiness, then the utility calculus would indicate that we should restrict that speech. This objection would cause us to restrict a great deal of speech, as plenty of speech generates more unhappiness than happiness.

Mill overcame this objection by arguing that the naïve analysis is not the full picture. Instead, we should consider the space of possibilities and think of the dynamic effects of speech, rather than just the first-order effects on people's emotions. Mill considered two main classes of speech: cases where the speaker was right, and cases where the speaker was wrong. In the first case, we can imagine someone like Galileo, generating significant unhappiness with his scientific claims, despite them being true. Mill takes this to be the easy case—while people may not like to hear the truth at first, society benefits in myriad ways from the truth. In the scientific case, this is readily apparent, as we can build on that knowledge to produce more science and technology, and gain greater predictive and causal power over the world. These accumulated benefits significantly outweigh the costs of truths uttered by a speaker, even if the costs are mostly frontloaded.

While this is easiest to see in the case of scientific case, this is meant to hold true in a variety of contexts. For instance, hearing an unpleasant truth about yourself or a loved one may be painful at first, but it could be necessary for future growth and maturation. Confronting hard truths is unpleasant. But doing so can enable us to move on and improve ourselves, our peer group, or society as a whole.

In the second case, Mill makes the more philosophically interesting argument. Mill argues that we should still allow people the ability to speak freely, even when they say false things that are upsetting to others. In this case, Mill can't leverage the downstream benefits of the truth as he could in the previous case, as society has already accepted the truth.[1] Instead, Mill has to offer a different argument for why false speech can be broadly socially beneficial. Here he suggests that false speech helps us because we are forced to develop arguments against it, and in favor of our (true) beliefs. Mill argues that this is important because simply *holding* true beliefs is not good enough. We have to understand what makes the true beliefs true. We need to understand the reasons that support those beliefs and why incorrect beliefs are based on bad arguments.

This is all part of a process that helps individuals—and society at large—develop judgment. This better captures the value of the rough and tumble of the marketplace of ideas. Contentious speech is valuable, whether right or wrong, because it demands a critical response, and in making those critical responses, we come to better understand the contours of the truth, the circumstances under which the truth holds, and what makes a true belief true. This helps us not merely have true beliefs, but have knowledge. And having *knowledge* rather than merely true beliefs helps us understand how to use what we know to develop new ideas, and the judgment to know when previously-true ideas no longer hold true. Free speech is then not merely valuable for improving the stock of knowledge but for improving the deliberative capacities of the agents who participate in the marketplace of ideas.

Mill's defense of free speech, then, offers two mechanisms for the value of speech—first in helping us to discover and disseminate more true beliefs, and second in helping us to better understand why those true beliefs are true. Both of these mechanisms rely on a background of what has come to be called the marketplace of ideas—a potentially confrontational environment where the currency is arguments. In this oppositional environment, we can suppose that with a long enough timescale, bad arguments will be discovered and discarded, and better arguments will rise to the top. As Mill shows, there would be real costs to try and smooth over this rough-and-tumble exchange of ideas. If we block unpleasant speech, we run the risk of biasing the processes that weed out bad ideas and select for good ones. This would leave us worse off in the long run, even if it would buy us more happiness in the moment. We suffer both for having lost out on an improved knowledge base but also for having lost out on further development to our capacity for judgment.

The Problem of Variable Participation

Mill's defense of free speech is a powerful one. However, there are reasons to think that the picture he offers is incomplete. Most notably, Mill fails to consider the possibility that the participants in the marketplace of ideas may well be a function of the content of those ideas. In a way, this is a little surprising. Mill sets up his defense of free speech as a solution to a puzzle. After all, why would a Utilitarian defend speech that generates a great deal of unhappiness? A simple utility calculus would suggest that this unhappiness should be reason to regulate speech. But Mill points out that in the longer run, happiness is increased by a free flow of ideas that can be subject to challenge. This is a convincing argument; however, it has a key premise that we have reason to weaken. Mill supposes that the participants in the marketplace of ideas are more or less fixed. Either it is everyone in a society participating, or at least a well-defined subset who participates.

This is an important premise. After all, let's consider the two reasons that Mill proposes speech can generate unhappiness: The speech is wrong, or the speech is true but counter to existing wrong beliefs. The true speech is valuable for being true, and the wrong speech is valuable for eliciting rebuttals that help people better understand the reasons for what they already believe. Let's consider that first category of wrong speech. Mill is right to say that wrong ideas can be proven to be wrong, even if it might take a while. But wrong ideas can take hold for quite a while, and they can do so especially effectively if they help to drive down opposing speech. That is, the content of some ideas can help shape their own environments to make it more likely that they persist than they would had they not altered the environment in their favor. More explicitly, I suggest that some speech may have the effect of reducing the number of participants in the marketplace of ideas. This reduction of participation is not uniform across the poles of discussion, but instead is directional.

I suggest that there are at least two mechanisms that can cause a reduction in participation: a silencing effect such as that outlined by Langton (1993), and a discouraging effect. Let's consider each mechanism in turn.

The first mechanism—one of silencing one's opponents by means of undermining their epistemic authority—was first articulated in the case of pornography by Langton (1993) and made much more general by Fricker (2007). The core idea is that some speech, given the presence of appropriate background conditions to the speech, can serve to reduce the illocutionary force of some agents' words. For instance, arguing that some group is untrustworthy can make it difficult for that group (or its allies) to provide an effective counter, as their words will be more immediately treated with suspicion. Likewise, declaring some agent or group to be unserious, or overly emotional, or lacking in cognitive capacity can lead us to treat the targets of such claims as we might treat children. Their mouths might form words, but not words that the larger epistemic community takes seriously. Langton argued that under background conditions of a patriarchal society, pornography serves to undermine the status of women by presenting them as objects of sexual gratification rather than full moral agents with their own considerations. Depictions of women who initially say no to sexual contact who actually consent to it in particular can undermine the illocutionary force of "no" for women. More generally, if women are primarily understood as sources of sexual gratification, their opinions on politics or civic life might be discounted.

This mechanism works by using speech to de-legitimize a group of potential contributors to the marketplace of ideas. Their speech becomes discounted or altogether dismissed, despite their interest in countering the wrong speech from the original speaker. As Jacobson (1995) noted, sometimes we want to reduce the illocutionary force of certain speakers. We don't take stock tips from eight year olds and we don't let foreigners vote, and we think that this is perfectly appropriate. One might extend Jacobson's argument to suggest that we would have reason to reduce the illocutionary force of the proclamations of a Chicken Little. Or, as Frankfurt (1986) suggests, there may be some speakers who attempt to persuade without regard for truth. Reducing the illocutionary force of such speakers may in fact improve the epistemic community, since it is not clear that such speakers are reasons-responsive or engaged in argumentative give and take at all. Instead, they may simply be muddying the epistemic waters. So while there may be good reasons to remove some participants from the broader epistemic community, this first mechanism can remove *legitimate* participants from the epistemic community, merely through engaging in free speech.

The second mechanism—discouraging one's opponents—relies on participants exiting the epistemic community of their own accord. While the first mechanism relied on shifts in illocutionary force for different agents or groups, this second mechanism is not so direct. Rather than a speech act itself impacting a third party's ability to respond, here we have the case where the content of someone's speech just causes another party to despair in continuing the discussion and exit the conversation. This mechanism is admittedly less like a direct functional relationship as found in the first case, but clearly has some explanatory power for changing sizes of epistemic communities.

In this set of cases, agents exit the epistemic community when they decide that the personal costs of participating outweigh the expected social gains that their participation would generate. This relies on an important aspect of Mill's account of free speech. Recall that he agreed that wrong speech can generate unhappiness, but that this would be outweighed by the eventual triumph of the truth and the gains to our understanding of how the arguments for the truth work. While this long-run argument is surely correct, it does not account for incentives *in the short run*. If it's too emotionally taxing, exhausting, or potentially dangerous to participate in a debate, agents will reasonably exit the debate even if they could offer useful arguments to counter the relevant speech.

Here one can imagine someone who is simply tired of arguing against Holocaust deniers. If Holocaust deniers aren't particularly reasons-responsive, it is simply restating the same arguments over and over, and especially for someone who has a personal connection to that tragedy, it may well be simply too emotionally exhausting to continue. Further, there may be a personal calculation that engaging the Holocaust denier in debate at all is granting their arguments a level of credibility they don't deserve. As a result, it may be simply not worth the effort. Conspiracy theorists of various sorts—whether it is "9/11 truthers" or flat-earthers or people who are convinced NASA faked the moon landing, can simply wear out their opposition. While their ideas are unlikely to ever become dominant, they don't go away, and they may be prominent enough in some sub-communities to be epistemically worrisome.

If we consider instances of campus speech, this sort of concern is widespread across the political spectrum. Conservatives, for instance, have claimed that the hostility to their views is such that they feel uncomfortable raising them for fear of being labeled a racist or a sexist or a homophobe. They have further argued that this helps to explain why campuses are so liberal compared to the general population—the speech environment is such that conservatives think it is too personally costly to participate. Likewise, various minority groups have voiced concerns that it is simply too exhausting to rebut what they feel is a steady stream of animus and mischaracterization of their views.

The discussion around "safe spaces" can indeed be understood in terms of this view of the personal costs of speech. While the Millian idea of the marketplace of ideas is clearly a *social good*, individuals have good reason to not want to argue all day long. A perfectly reasonable interpretation of a safe space is just an environment where one is not called on to constantly defend their beliefs and instead be in an environment with like-minded individuals at least some of the time. Those with minority views can feel this need more acutely simply because there are fewer of them. People whose views are more in line with the majority don't feel the same need for a safe space, simply because the relative burden of speech is lower for them in general. That epistemic minorities have highlighted the need for a space where they don't have to defend themselves suggests that this burden is sufficiently high that they would plausibly seek ways to at least partially exit the broader marketplace of ideas.

These two mechanisms highlight two features of the marketplace of ideas that are worth thinking about in more detail. First, that the broader epistemic environment may favor certain contributions over others, and second, that participants in the marketplace of ideas may exit given those details of the epistemic environment. The first concept here—that the epistemic environment may favor some ideas over others, is something that Mill would surely have agreed with. Often, this is a good thing. Some ideas really are just better than others, and the broader environment ought to favor better ideas. But this works best in areas where the content of speech is suitably removed from the features of the participants. There may be aggressive academic debates in physics or chemistry or geology, and indeed those epistemic environments may well be shaped such that they favor some ideas and are far more skeptical of other ideas. Kuhn's work on paradigms suggests as much. But the costs of the rough and tumble of those debates are at least mitigated by the fact that those debates don't hinge on personal qualities of the participants.[2] In other areas, though, there is a relationship between the content of the discussion and features of the participants, such that the burdens of speech can become more apparent.

Because of the potential burdens of this differential epistemic environment, we should expect that the more burdened participants have a greater likelihood of exiting the marketplace of ideas. This is sometimes a good thing. After all, not only do we want to drive bad ideas out of our epistemic environment, we'd like to drive out those participants who aren't reasons-responsive and seek to pollute the epistemic environment. If the costs of their speech are high enough, they will withdraw without further need of regulation. However, this can often be a problem. Minority views, or views that have fallen out of favor, still should have some place in the broader discussion, if only to help reveal what makes them wrong. Likewise, people who hold these views, provided that they are at least somewhat reasons-responsive, ought to have a place in the discussion.

Just as there are mechanisms that drive people out of discussions, there are mechanisms that can help draw them in. I will focus on just one. Beaman, Chattopadhyay, Duflo, Pande and Topalova (2009, 2010, 2012) present evidence drawn from an RCT in India that exposure to women in positions of political authority boosted female participation in town meetings, boosted perceptions of women's competence, and increased investment in schooling for girls. While this particular study did not find evidence that as a result of exposure people thought that women were peers with men in terms of judgment or political competence, it did significantly boost their perceptions of women compared to the control group.

This is in line with Bell, Chetty, Jaravel, Petkova and Reenen (2017), who find that amongst high-skill children, the best prediction of future innovation is early exposure to innovators who are from the same social group. Since the existing stock of innovators (as defined as patent holders) is heavily white and male, this favors exposure for white boys, while leaving girls and minorities out. Where there are opportunities for exposure, there are more resultant women and minority innovators.

In both of these cases, we find that some measure of representation helps all social groups, and even fairly constrained exposure to role models leads to significant increases in participation in the epistemic community. This representation approach can plausibly act to counter both of the mechanisms that drove exit: Having successful role models may undermine efforts to silence minority groups by changing the broader epistemic environment, and greater representation may lower the perceived personal costs of participation.

If we take these mechanisms for exit and entry seriously, this suggests that Mill's argument for free speech needs to be expanded upon. Maximizing speech is no longer merely minimizing the regulations that we place on the content of speech, but instead is a function both of the amount of speech any given participant makes, and the total number of participants. Most importantly, however, if we wish the marketplace of ideas to function in the way that Mill argues, we have reason to worry at least about the *composition* of speech, and therefore the composition of the participants, which I will discuss in the next section.

Composition Matters

In the previous section, we saw that the content of speech can serve to cause some people to exit from the marketplace of ideas. We also saw that people may enter into it if they perceive the costs to be low enough and the threat of silencing low enough that it is worth it to engage with others in debate. Once we have the possibility of variable participation, there are two things that we need to be worried about that Mill himself did not consider: the total number of participants, and the composition of those participants.

As we have already seen, total size of the epistemic community matters if our goal is to maximize speech. As should be intuitive, it is easier to generate more speech (and thus have more productive clashes of arguments and reasons) when there are more speakers—at least if we hold other things equal. We have at least a prima facie reason for doing what we can to increase the number of speakers if we are to make the marketplace of ideas more robust. Obviously, this would be undercut if the means by which we increased the number of speakers was to ban most content of speech, but we now have a reason to think not just the scope of speech but also the impact of the content of speech on the number of speakers.

The size of the epistemic community by itself isn't a satisfactory metric, however. After all, the marketplace of ideas isn't much improved if instead of one person offering a particular argument, we have 10,000 people offering the same argument. The more similar two agents are in the way they approach a debate, the less value the second agent brings to the marketplace of ideas. There may be some benefit from this redundancy in terms of correcting "trembling hand" errors—where someone merely fails to correctly carry out the epistemic procedure they rely on—but this redundancy won't help better evaluate the quality of the epistemic procedure or its outputs. Instead, the marketplace of ideas benefits from a diversity of arguments and approaches.[3] Mill, of course, recognized this—his argument for free speech depends on a variety of views engaging with each other. But he took it for granted that contentious speech would draw out more speech. I've suggested that at least some contentious speech can drive down opposing speech.

Our challenge, then, is to buttress the Millian idea of speech drawing out more speech by ensuring that we maintain a diverse set of participants in the marketplace of ideas. As we have already seen, one approach is by means of ensuring adequate representation of various positions and perspectives, such that the personal cost of participating is low enough to help draw people into the discussion. Another way of doing so is by attempting to balance the burdens of speech.

Distributing the Burdens of Speech

So far, I've argued that expanding the scope of free speech depends not only on the scope of allowable speech but the scope of participation in speech. However, to maximize one of these components may serve to reduce the other. If we allow any and all speech come what may, we are likely to drive down the rate of participation in the epistemic community; and what's worse, we would be driving down the participation rate of the people whose responses are most important for the Millian argument in favor of free speech to function. This loss of participation cannot be mitigated by adding more people who agree with the controversial speech, as mere numbers in support of an argument do not do any real epistemic work. The composition of the total population matters, precisely because a larger, more diverse epistemic community is one that is more primed to ensure that contentious speech draws out more speech, rather than diminishes it.

As we have seen, the content of some speech can function to drive down participation for two reasons: First, it may generate a silencing effect, in which people attempt to reply but their responses are discounted or ignored, and second, it might discourage participation by driving up the personal costs for some potential participants such that they do not respond at all. So, if we are to try and create a large and diverse epistemic community, we must find tools to address these issues.

One approach would be to simply ban any speech that silences or discourages participation in the marketplace of ideas. This would impose a fairly stringent regulation on speech in order to drive up participation. On a number of college campuses, we see demands for versions of this approach—that speakers should be denied a platform to speak they have previously expressed views that (liberal) protesters deem to be silencing or discouraging. Likewise, we have seen demands for some courses or professors be removed from campuses for teaching material that conservatives find denigrating. Over the past year, there have been several high-profile demands for retraction of peer-reviewed articles for being sufficiently silencing or discouraging for some audience. I believe this approach is ill-advised, for two reasons. First, and most importantly, it is simply too powerful a weapon to wield against an epistemic (or political) opponent. This would lead to victory by default in the marketplace of ideas. Second, it might serve to discourage participation more than encourage it. Let's consider each reason in turn.

While there are no doubt important cases of silencing and discouragement that it is important to address, this approach makes it too easy to reject speech that may be merely contentious or disagreeable. It may achieve a quick victory against one's opponents, but the victory is somewhat hollow. Adherents of the rejected view may well foster a belief that the larger society isn't willing to deal with the truth, and has therefore suppressed it. Neither the rejected view or the views that oppose it face the rigors of debate, so society would never learn to make better judgments, or better understand the reasons to support or reject either view. The epistemic benefits of Millian free speech would be drastically curtailed, such that it would likely be difficult to recover much of the original argument.

The second reason to reject this approach is that it has no guarantee that participation would increase. It may well fully address a silencing concern, but likely at the expense of perceived personal costs going up. For example, we may find that certain topics are sufficiently politically charged that well-intentioned people will avoid them simply because the risks of being construed as engaging in silencing becomes too great. Indeed, there are enough topics that are important, complex, and controversial that people run the risk of having their (well-meaning) errors interpreted as intentional slights. More worryingly, this may not discourage people whose aim it is to further poison the epistemic well, and so controversial topics could simply become toxic rather than areas where people may productively and respectfully disagree. So, the worry is that even beyond the people who are explicitly banned from the marketplace of ideas, there will be a significant reduction in who will participate in the discussion because this policy approach simply raises costs rather dramatically, causing people to opt out of the discussion.

What, then, can we do in place of the fairly straightforward approach of banning burdensome speech? I suggest that we instead focus on balancing the burdens of speech across groups. Silencing, for instance, is largely made possible by the background conditions of particular instances of speech. Langton argues that pornography is harmful given a patriarchal background, not just by itself. So, the question is, how can we ensure that the burdens of free speech are not *directional*—that is, how can we ensure that it isn't only particular minority groups that bear the burdens, while those in the majority garner the benefits?

As if this problem were not challenging enough, there is an extra wrinkle worth considering. In a suitably diverse population, there will not merely be different arguments but different assessments of what counts as a burden. The very perspectival diversity that makes the Millian approach to free speech so valuable makes it much more difficult for communities to agree on what kinds of speech impose particular burdens on others. As I discuss in Muldoon (2017), this creates a challenge in that we cannot by ourselves assess the potential burdens we may place on others, even if we can assess the burdens they place on us. One important consequence of this is that case-by-case assessments of burdens imposed by speech may be difficult to conduct.

However, if we accept that the scorched-earth approach of simply banning any speech that someone finds burdensome is not going to be an acceptable principle, we can instead rely on an idea of attempting a way for groups to balance how much burden they are willing to accept against how much they can potentially burden others. In this way, we can create a bargaining situation that can be assessed in two ways: first, by the volume of speech generated, so as to work to satisfy our commitment to a wide-ranging commitment to free speech, and second, by the degree to which different participants in speech have distributed the very real burdens and benefits that can be generated from free speech. We should aim for the largest marketplace of ideas that is consistent with relatively equal burden-sharing.

One might protest that this may seem to favor non-speech considerations over the widest extent of speech possible, but I think that this argument is wrong for an important reason. What I propose is meant to capture the conditions under which contentious speech draws out more speech, rather than less. If we allow for disproportionate burdens in the population, that primes the conditions for speech that can silence, and as the composition of speakers moves away from a diverse representation of a variety of views, it is more likely to increase the costs of participation for epistemic minorities. If we instead balance these burdens, we can maintain adequate representation, minimize the conditions under which a silencing mechanism could work, and increase the scope of participation.

My proposed approach to dealing with burden-sharing is meant to demonstrate that our epistemic interests in fact line up rather well with our broader ethical interests in providing conditions of mutual respect. For contentious speech to work to invite more speech, it must be the case that there is an expectation that the response will be considered by the wider epistemic community. Without such expectations, we lack the preconditions for productive epistemic exchange.

What might this look like in practice? In the campus context, it might require that campus communities do more to coordinate speakers across distinct epistemic groups, such that the community finds the total composition of those speakers to be broadly balanced, rather than fixating on any one speaker. Likewise, there may need to be more emphasis on greater epistemic diversity in other areas of campus life, including in the classroom. The metric for success is not whether every last opportunity for speech is seized but rather whether any given epistemic perspective has found a balance between its ability to impose burdens on others, and its willingness to take on burdens from others' speech.

Keeping the Soil Fertile for Millian Free Speech

Mill's defense of free speech is not simply that everyone should say whatever they want. Instead, Mill offers an account of how seemingly problematic speech can be socially useful. His defense of free speech depends on his ability to demonstrate that in the long run it generates more social welfare than speech restrictions. I have argued that the conditions under which this will occur are constrained by the need to maintain a sufficiently large and diverse epistemic community such that the give and take of speech can be rewarding in the way that Mill envisioned.

The picture that I've presented itself relies on an implicit premise: that there is at least a broad consensus that what we're trying to do in our debates with each other is to find out the truth, or at least find views of how society should be organized that we all have reasons to endorse. While the marketplace of ideas is broadly set up to be adversarial, in the sense that the different parties are at least partially motivated by a desire to win the argument, it is constrained by norms that encourage honesty, engaging with one's opponents with a recognition that while they are adversaries they are not enemies.

Efforts to balance the benefits and burdens of speech across groups who perceive those benefits and burdens differently is made much easier if everyone accepts that everyone is trying to find ways of accommodating the other. The more people perceive each other to be untrustworthy, the more efforts there will be to seek out epistemic advantages and impose disadvantages on others.

Sadly, we are increasingly likely to find ourselves in situations where interlocutors are not acting in good faith. Free speech remains valuable in these context, and instances of bad faith ought not be used as excuses for serious infringements on speech rights, but the mechanisms that make free speech so epistemically and democratically important break down when one or more parties in effect declares total war on another. We should be able to make distinctions between contentious speech whose purpose is to provoke thought and invite response, and contentious speech whose purpose is to undermine the conditions for the possibility of reasoned debate.

As much as we might like to think otherwise, most single instances of speech are not terribly profound or impactful. Our model of free speech shouldn't be the single great truth-teller who sets society straight.

Instead, free speech works as a bigger enterprise. Single bits of speech might not change society very often, but a well-functioning speech environment changes society regularly. The give and take of ideas as a broad system is what we need to protect, more than any individual bit of speech or single speaker. To do that, we need to ensure that we maintain the preconditions to a marketplace of ideas. A large, diverse set of speakers and hearers that are all willing to accept some burdens as hearers in exchange for the ability to burden others as speakers. A recognition that while we may disagree about particular claims or arguments, we agree on the constraints to speech so that we can allow the broader enterprise of a well-functioning free speech environment to persist.

Notes

1. Mill does not consider the case where the speaker and society at large could both be wrong, but I do not think that this weakens his argument. The relevant argumentative resources to handle this case are found in the two that he does consider.
2. Of course, natural science isn't immune to exit based on speech itself. Overly aggressive argument can drive people out who favor more collaborative environments, and sexism and other biases can cause people to favor evidence from one party over another. I contend only here that there is a less intimate connection between what is at issue epistemically with the conditions under which people may wish to participate in the debate.
3. I elaborate this argument in much more detail in Muldoon (2016), Chapters 2 and 3.

Works Cited

Beaman, Lori, Duflo, Esther, Pande, Rohini and Topalova, Petia. "Political Reservation and Substantive Representation: Evidence From Indian Village Councils." In *India Policy Forum 2010–11*, Vol. 7, edited by Suman Berry, Barry Bosworth and Arvind Panagariya. Thousand Oaks, CA: SAGE Publications, 2010.

———. "Female Leadership Raises Aspirations and Educational Attainment for Girls: A Policy Experiment in India." *Science*, Vol. 335 (2012): 582–586.

Beaman, Lori, Chattopadhyay, Raghabendra, Duflo, Esther, Pande, Rohini and Topalova, Petia. "Powerful Women: Does Exposure Reduce Bias?" *The Quarterly Journal of Economics*, Vol. 124 (2009): 1497–1540.

Bell, Alex, Chetty, Raj, Jaravel, Xavier, Petkova, Neviana and Reenen, John Van. "Who Becomes an Inventor in America? The Importance of Exposure to Innovation." *NBER Working Paper No. 24062*. December 2017.

Fricker, Miranda. *Epistemic Injustice: Power and the Ethics of Knowing*. Oxford: Oxford University Press, 2007.

Frankfurt, Harry. "On Bullshit." *Raritan*, Vol. 6 (1986): 81–100.

Jacobson, Daniel. "Freedom of Speech Acts? A Response to Langton." *Philosophy & Public Affairs*, Vol. 24 (1995): 64–79.

Langton, Rae. "Speech Acts and Unspeakable Acts." *Philosophy and Public Affairs*, Vol 22 (1993): 305–330.

Muldoon, Ryan. *Social Contract Theory for a Diverse World: Beyond Tolerance.* Abingdon-on-Thames: Routledge, 2016.

———. "Exploring Tradeoffs in Accommodating Moral Diversity." *Philosophical Studies*, Vol. 174 (2017): 1871–1883.

18 When Free Speech Is False Speech

Sarah Conly

Truth and Falsity Are Not the Same

Recently, PEN America published a plea for free speech on campus. In "Why Diversity Doesn't Trump Free Speech on Campus," the message was, as the title suggests, that speakers should not be forbidden simply because they make some people uncomfortable, even if those people are from traditionally oppressed groups for whom the university is actively trying to create an inclusive atmosphere (Nossel 2016). While it is certainly more difficult for students to feel at home on campuses from which they were traditionally excluded, and while university attempts to reach out to those in such groups is laudable, this should not come at the price of free speech, according to PEN America. In their "Principles on Campus Free Speech," they write:

> While some degree of caution and forethought in speech is healthy, college should be a place where ideas can range free, dissent is welcomed, and settled wisdom is reconsidered. . . . A critical function of the university is to expose students to a diversity of viewpoints, including those with which some may vehemently disagree.
>
> (2016, 65)

Discomfort may indeed be created by the messages some speakers send, and indeed by the fact that those speakers were invited to begin with, but in the long run such discomfort should be accepted as part of the price for the freedom of speech that will benefit all concerned, including those who object to the speaker. But, according to the same author, "Unfortunately, respect for divergent viewpoints has not been a consistent hallmark of recent debates on matters of diversity and inclusion on campus" (2016, 64). Thus, institutions fail in their education mission.

This is one of those cases where the argument is good, but the conclusion is nonetheless false. Or, to put it in a way more consistent with the rules of logic, this a good argument for a different conclusion. Speech should not be banned merely because it contributes to feelings of discomfort and exclusion, even though those are truly bad things both in the short and the long terms. Some speech should, however, be banned. Speech should be banned because some speech simply is not educational: It's false, obviously false, and too obviously false to serve as a useful focus for intellectual criticism. The limited time students spend in educational institutions should be geared to teaching them as much as we can of what is both important and true.

Diversity in Students vs. Diversity of Ideas

The position PEN America opposes, that institutions should avoid speakers whose message would alienate some students, is not unreasonable, even if in the long run it is mistaken. The most common situation is that campuses, which tend to be socially and politically liberal, might want to ban speakers from the conservative end of the spectrum. Colleges and universities have been making real efforts to reach out to underrepresented populations: to racial minorities, to ethnic minorities, to those who are not affluent. They have discovered, though, that creating a diverse campus society does not end at admissions—for students to fully benefit from their education, they need to feel accepted by their faculty and peers as they progress through their years of education. And for them to benefit their academic peers through intellectual and social participation, they need to feel respected as members of the community. What should be done to promote this sense of inclusion and respect is subject to a great deal of debate, but there is a sense that one important step is to avoid inviting speakers whose views seem to insult the status of these students.

So far so good. The response to this, though, is also reasonable. First, there is the worry that any well-defined view might make someone uncomfortable. A socialist speaker who decries capitalists as robber barons might rightly make the economics majors feel that their aspiration to be corporate bankers has been subjected to scorn; a speaker who promotes LGBTQ rights might seem to attack the religious faith of traditionalists, or to subject them to categorization as hateful bigots. It is natural to respond that these are not groups that have been historically underrepresented, and thus that they are much less likely to suffer from a sense that they don't belong in the school, but some will demur: While such beliefs and aspirations have not been traditionally underrepresented, they might still be at odds with the prevailing campus culture, and thus prone to sensing rejection by their peers when speakers are invited who deprecate their values. Conservatives on some campuses report that they are already afraid to express their political views for fear of backlash from both students and faculty, and to have speakers who reinforce condemnation of such views makes their position even more uncomfortable. Either we ban a wide range of speakers, to promote a sense of belonging for all concerned, or we ban only the more conservative speakers, which makes the more conservative students feel that, however well they well represented they may once have been on campuses, they are now pariahs. And, of course, those who oppose choosing speakers according to student comfort will argue that the avoidance of alienation can extend even more widely: Meat-eaters will be condemned by those who argue against factory farming, football enthusiasts by speakers on CTE, and those with more idiosyncratic views by almost anything. None of this posits irrationality on the part of the student—we aren't talking about students who are unpredictably triggered by innocuous words or phrases. These are views rational students can and do have, so offense is easily predictable.

Second, some can argue that while a sense of alienation is bad, it is, alas, something minority students need to learn to deal with. It is a fact that the world is not equally open to all, and if people let that bring them to disengage from society they themselves will suffer. Maybe there won't always be people around who are unaware of their own privilege, or who are insensitive to implicit bias, or who, without meaning any harm, still do harm, but there will be such people for the foreseeable future. So, the argument goes, the best thing for those who will suffer from such slights is to learn to deal with them in what is a relatively supportive atmosphere, a place where, after all, faculty and staff are there to help them learn what they need and to leave as successful graduates. Thus, free speech can actually benefit those who feel most insulted by it on particular occasions: They will learn skills at negotiating a too-often hostile world without debilitating anger or depression.

Lastly, there is the general response that discomfort isn't as important as intellectual stimulation when we are talking about an educational institution. Education, after all, is our goal, and designing curricula or campus speakers to augment comfort undercuts the educational mission. It's not that being comfortable doesn't help you learn, but it is not the primary condition of learning: The primary condition is exposure to views that arouse the intellect and prompt the exercise the critical faculties. We are moved to action by physical discomfort, and we may similarly be moved to action by intellectual discomfort: to confront and disarm the view we deplore. Of course, in some cases of physical discomfort, we may simply move away instead of acting to address the cause of our pain, and this might happen in the intellectual area as well: We may simply not think about the things we don't like, the way some people to refuse to think about climate change. Ideally, though, an educational institution can make such avoidance very difficult, by making exposure to inconvenient truths too pervasive to escape. While we can't guarantee that discomfort will be compensated for in each case by the rewards of intellectual insight, that is generally the goal at which educational institutions want to aim.

There are, then, arguments that even acute discomfort, including such discomfort in those who have been unfairly marginalized, does not justify any censorship of views that can and should stimulate the intellect. That, however, doesn't mean that the expression of any and all ideas should be permitted, much less encouraged. Since education is schools' mission, speech can and should be avoided when it is not educational. It should especially be avoided if it doesn't merely fail to educate but actually promotes the acceptance of false views. This is the standard we use in the classroom, and it is the standard we should use outside the classroom as well.

How Do We Educate?

In the Classroom

One obvious fact about education is that it is always selective. The semester is finite; even four years is not enough time to teach all that we would like to. Thus, we naturally choose what courses to offer, and within those which things to assign and what things to present. Is our goal to present the widest possible diversity of ideas? Of course not. Our goal is to present the ideas, factual claims, interpretations, theories, and methodologies that we think are most plausible. Who wants a physics professor who presents outmoded theories of cosmology as if they were accepted fact? No one. While a given physics theory may turn out to be false, at the time the professor teaches it, she believes it to be correct. In a case where there is no consensus among the informed on what is correct, a professor presents the major contending theories. Anything else is a waste of the students' time, and not what justifies the costs of tuition. What if the professor teaches the true theory and the false one as well, just to represent diversity of opinion? Most teachers will say that they barely have time to teach all the correct stuff they need to in the course of a semester, and to spend any considerable time on rejected theories would be a waste. One could, of course, where it is a useful exercise, look at a rejected theory and explain why it was once believed and why it is now seen to be false. Simply teaching both true and false theories and leaving it up the student to choose for herself is not, even when she is encouraged to use her critical faculties, the best education. For one thing, as said, it limits the time available to teach correct theories. For another, an undergraduate, even a talented one, may well not yet have the intellectual tools required for assessing theories and determining which is well-founded.

As noted previously, there are sometimes questions as to which of several relatively plausible theories is correct in a given case. While some theories have been definitively rejected, others vie for acceptance even among the experts who are well able to evaluate them. These theories address complex issues, and often it takes time to see which theory makes the best sense. Indeed, time may not be enough in some cases where the decision must be made by reasoning alone, in the absence of corroborative evidence. This may be more of an issue in fields that don't lend themselves to empirical evidence, such as philosophy. In these cases, it is perfectly reasonable to present different views, be it differing theories about black holes, empiricism, or the true causes of the Reformation. We do this with the understanding not simply that either of two conflicting theories might possibly be right, but because both are views supported by good arguments. There are some good reasons to believe either one, and neither is definitively ruled out. Thus, since both are contenders, it is a good idea to expose students to both. They may then use their critical skills to choose between them, given the understanding that the truth is so far unknown.

Outside of the Classroom

So, we don't teach things we are certain are false, while we do allow assessment of competing theories when any one of the theories concerned is plausible. Why should talks that occur outside the classroom be different? Why would an academic institution whose goal is education invite speakers whose opinions are clearly wrong? Richard Spencer, for example, is a racist: His views are clearly wrong. What would be the point of allowing him on a campus whose goal is education? If anyone argues that we can never know if a view is clearly wrong, they should review the criteria for in-class teaching—that views must be at least very plausible to be worth discussing, and that we do feel confident in declaring that some are not worth our time. It is probably true that for any clearly wrong view there is presumably some very remote possibility of its actually being true, if it is at least internally consistent, but such remote possibilities don't justify inclusion in a classroom curriculum intended to educate. Why should campus venues outside the classroom be open to the propagation of falsehood?

One might argue any that talks outside the classroom should be allowed according to a different standard from those in the classroom for at least any of four reasons: (1) Many controversial speakers are arguing about values, not about facts, and there is no way of assessing the plausibility of moral beliefs. It's not like physics. Decisions to ban certain speakers because of their moral opinions can only arise from prejudice. (2) Outside speakers are often invited by student groups, and it is good for student groups to exercise their autonomy in deciding whom to invite. Just as institutions give students the liberty to work on lab assignments or write papers, where they may make mistakes, we should give student groups the liberty to make their own organizational decisions. Even, or perhaps especially, a bad decision will turn out to be a learning experience, and the reason to sponsor student clubs is so that students may learn how to make decisions, even if only through trial and error. (3) The fact that a talk is given outside of the classroom means different standards apply—students know they shouldn't give to invited speakers the same credence as to their professors. They will accordingly be more skeptical of the message the outside speaker expresses. (Not that they aren't, or shouldn't be, skeptical about what a professor says—that is actually a good idea. The point is that we might expect them to be even more skeptical about some outsider passing through.) They don't even need to remember what the speaker said, since they won't have an exam on it. Thus, a speaker with fringe views can't do any harm, and might, in some sociological or psychological sense, be enlightening as to the forces that drive some people to accept obviously false opinions. (4) Even if a theory is wrong, it is good, as John Stuart Mill argued in *On Liberty*, for us to be exposed to it: Addressing the opposing theory reminds of us of the reasons we have the correct belief we do, so that that remains a living idea instead of mere dogma: "however true it may be, if it is not fully, frequently, and fearlessly discussed, it will be held as a dead dogma, not a living truth" (2003, 114). Listening to a false view, then, will not convince us that that false view is correct; on the contrary, the true beliefs we hold in contradistinction to the messages of racists and other purveyors of false opinion will become all the more salient.

These are not obviously false claims. While not obviously false, they are, however, false in the main, and thus don't serve to justify inviting speakers whose only virtue lies in their denial of correct theories.

(1) The first objection stems from a general about the justification for moral beliefs. The idea is that people in the sciences can offer empirical evidence for their beliefs, and thus are able to show which theories are or aren't right as they predict those empirical outcomes. When it comes to morality, though, who is to say? All opinions are equal and have an equal right to be heard.

It is true that justifications for moral theories, or for particular moral positions, are different from those typically offered in the sciences. This doesn't mean there are no standards of justification at all, however. (And if there were no standards, there would be no obvious reason to bring in a diverse point of view, since it could have no greater claim to be justified.) People who argue well for moral positions may differ in their conclusions, and in some cases there is no obvious way to show to the satisfaction of all that one conclusion is definitively better than another. People who argue well, though, are indeed offering arguments. They give reasoned expositions of what premises they rely on to reach a conclusion, why these premises are plausible, and more plausible than the denial of those premises. They show why their conclusions follow from their premises. This may not be sufficient for arguing well, but it is at least necessary. And they offer well-defended premises, which strengthens the plausibility of their conclusions. Alt-right racists don't do this. "You will not replace us!" is not an argument. And if an actual factual claim is made—say, "black people are inferior" or "non-white people are trying to dispossess white people"—no plausible premises are presented to justify these conclusions, because there aren't any. There just isn't any good reasoning going on, and in moral debates we can and do differentiate when reasoning is good and when it is not. Listening to someone like Richard Spencer is as intellectually stimulating as listening to a dog bark.

One may argue that these criteria are themselves the product of a particular elite's set of beliefs about education, justification, and the standards for good argument. Thus, I am recommending using criteria which by their nature don't allow equal status to messages that are expressed a different way. The gate is barred when it comes to allowing entry to alternative ways of thinking. This is true, of course. The university uses university criteria for evaluating speech. What standards would they be expected to use? Saying it is close-minded for educational institutions to use their own standards for evaluating who should speak on campus is like saying horse racing is close-minded in insisting that the prize goes to the fastest horse. These rules are what constitute this institution. You want to speak in a different institution, then the criteria at that institution should be invoked. The Hyde Park Speakers' Corner has its rules and conventions and educational institutions have theirs. These are what we use in the classroom, with, most agree, good effect. Extending them to the rest of campus is only reasonable.

(2) Student groups do have some latitude in how to run their groups—that's part of what makes it a student group, rather than a faculty-led class. However, student groups typically get funding from the college or university to which they are attached, rather than from their own pockets. That's also part of what makes it a student group. And, their speakers will appear in college- or university-provided venues. And, the students are acting under the aegis of their college or university, lending its name and implicitly its imprimatur to the guest speaker. Thus, the actions of the group reflect on the college and are supported by the college. Given this, it is hardly unreasonable to suppose that the college may set standards for the activities such groups participate in or sponsor. This is why sports teams often have to adhere to dress codes when they travel to away games—they are taken to represent the school in some sense, not just themselves as a set of independent football players. That's why a college can punish a club for hazing new team members, where it would have no authority over non-campus organizations. Colleges and universities can and do step in and require student groups to amend their behavior because such groups are never entirely independent. Should a university do this when it comes to the groups' inviting outside speakers?

Yes—this would be entirely consistent. Again, the reason for student groups is fundamentally educational—such groups are allowed to exist in order to contribute something to the college as a whole as well as to benefit individual members through the practice of running an organization. While it might be of some benefit to those who are organizing the club's event to invite a speaker whose extreme views will garner attention, that is not enough to justify such an invitation. The harm it does is too great. There is harm to the reputation of the school, and harm to other students, and in many cases harm to the surrounding community, without sufficient offsetting educational benefit. To say we should allow student autonomy in such a case would be like saying that since it is educational for students to do chemistry labs we should never intervene even when a particular student's mistake could blow the building up. Even if the student's error is only likely to make a few other students sick for a few weeks any lab instructor would step in—mistakes are often educational to the student in question, but may not be worth the price paid by others, whose education will be interrupted. There is an educational reason for these student organizations to exist, and if they stop being sufficiently educational, that is time to interfere.

(3) and (4) I am putting these two objections together because they may both be answered the same way. (3) says that hearing false messages won't do any harm, because students are relatively disinclined to believe them. (4) says that indeed, such messages might even do some good, since they can stimulate us to think why they are wrong, and to become better informed as to why our own belief in, e.g., human equality are correct. My answer to both these is that, sadly, they do not square with the empirical evidence. Students may well be more skeptical about messages they hear outside than about those they hear in the classroom, but we cannot assume they will be skeptical enough. If we were purely rational beings, we could be relied on to properly assess unargued conclusions and poor arguments on their merits, and reject them 100 percent of the time. That is what Mill seems to think will happen, at least if we are sufficiently educated, and students are more trained than many in critical thinking. It is good to be trained in critical thinking because in many instances it does help us to distinguish between better and worse arguments.

However, as we know, we are not entirely rational, and this means we don't reliably reach rational conclusions. Long before cognitive bias became a commonly known phenomenon, psychologists had attested to human irrationality. They demonstrated our tendency to believe what (we think) our group believes (Sherif 1936). They showed, too, our tendency to think better of our own group and to underestimate the intelligence and virtue of other groups without any evidence for our supposed superiority (Sherif, Harvey, White, Hood, and Sherif 1961). At present, we know that behavioral economists and others have made something of an industry of identifying biases, and we know that they are pervasive. A bias is a tendency to think less than rationally, and that means in the long run to believe conclusions that are not derived from plausible premises. While some biases may be relatively harmless, some can have very bad effects both on the individual and society. Among the latter are those that make us more prone to believe reasoning that purports to yield conclusions, that, if true, would be in our interests but which are, nonetheless, false. It is this tendency that makes some people believe that climate change is not real, despite all the evidence: We have a tendency to believe that things will turn out as we want them to, a tendency to select evidence according to what we want to be true rather than according to its objective strength, a tendency to believe whatever confirms our preconceptions, etc.

The optimism bias, wishful thinking, the confirmation bias, neglect of probability—all of these and many more make it hard for us to judge objectively what arguments are true. The fact that we can be and are influenced by these failures in rational thought may explain in part the fact that people like Richard Spencer or Milo Yiannopoulos are popular in the first place. Some who are enthusiastic about the views of racists, sexists, religious bigots, etc. may not be prey to bias—they may simply be self-interested people who think that propagating a myth of injury will help them achieve greater social advantages. Others, however, come to believe unjustified claims that white people are somehow being used unfairly, or that men are victimized by feminists, not because there is any evidence for this but because it is, in the long run, something they would like to believe. The fact that such views are being given a hearing in a place of education gives them an added respectability that makes it easier to distort our thinking. We identify arguments from authority as fallacious in part because we are prone to accept them and need to remind ourselves that we should not, and a speaker who has been invited to a university to speak will naturally appear authoritative: By and large, an invitation to speak is an endorsement, if not of your view, of the fact that you have an important message that is worth listening to. There's no way to put an asterisk next to a speaker's name saying, "not this guy, he's just here because we wanted someone to give a false opinion." Using educational institutions to propagate views that are both wrong and harmful is a perversion of their purpose. Education is a good thing, and institutions dedicated to it should not be used to spread views that are as opposed to the purpose of education as they could possibly be.

Problems with Selectivity

There are many, to be sure. How do we tell the difference between the definitively false and the plausible but unconfirmed?

This is sometimes a judgment call, meaning that it calls on our powers of discrimination, and that even we use those powers it may difficult to discern what is clearly true and what clearly false. In such cases, colleges and universities may decide to err on the side of liberality, and allow the controversial speaker. On the other hand, this is not always the case. There are views that are definitively false. This doesn't mean that everyone agrees about their falsity. There are still flat-earthers, after all. When there is a consensus among those who are rational and informed that the claims for such views are without justification, we may take it that the view as false. As Mill himself said, with progress issues where once there was doubt come to be resolved: "As Mankind improve, the number of doctrines which are no longer disputed or doubted will be constantly on the increase; and the well-being of mankind may almost be measured by the number and gravity which have reached the point of being uncontested" (2003, 121). Climate change is real, and those who believe it is not are simply incorrect. Homosexuality is not morally wrong. All races deserve equal consideration. All sexes deserve equal consideration. White people are not suffering from oppression relative to other races. Feminists are not oppressing men. Muslims are not all terrorists and do not all hate liberty. These are truths, and it is not difficult at this point in time for a reasonable person to see that they are true. They rank with "the earth is round" and "the earth orbits around the sun, not the reverse."

But what if we *are* wrong about what seems to be obviously false? This could happen: Sometimes, even if not very often, what we believe to be obviously false turns out to be true. If we disallow the expression of all obviously false opinions, we might suppress the very minority opinion that is in fact correct. This is fair enough, but not relevant to the present discussion. We are not talking about banning the expression of opinions, but about not having them expressed on educational campuses. That does not entail support for government censorship, which would be a move to keep an opinion being expressed anywhere. That would be a bad idea, for any number of reasons. A non-benevolent government might obviously use its powers of censorship to suppress criticism or the expression of truths that would lead to criticism. Even assuming the entire benevolence and altruism of the government, the opinion might conceivably turn out to be right, so not letting it survive in some venues is probably a mistake. And, it is important that people want to express themselves, without fear of reprisals. No one believes people have a right to express themselves in just any venue that they might prefer, but government suppression that outlaws certain speech anywhere at all is excessive. The argument here is that the expression of what we reasonably take to be an obviously false view is inappropriate in an institution of learning. Institutions of learning have specific goals, and it is not only permissible but obligatory for them to take necessary steps to further that goal. The role of the government is not simply to educate its citizens. Education is important, of course, and we do expect government to provide support for educational institutions, but government needs to do other things as well. It needs protect citizens in many pursuits, including self-expression. We apparently don't think the government has a duty to *provide* equal opportunities of self-expression—some private individuals can afford to own newspapers and television and radio stations, or to run ads through others' media, while most of us are limited to talking to our neighbors or the occasional letter to the editor. Still, we don't think the government's job is to shut opinions down. Its job is to protect individuals in many ways, and protecting their ability to express their opinions is one of those.

Conclusion

Many support diversity of opinion on the grounds that it is educational. That means, though, that we want diversity of opinion where that is educational. It doesn't follow from this that any and all opinions are worth hearing. The point of diversity of opinion is not just so we can have false opinions leavening our diet of dull facts and reasonable points of view. The point of diversity is to help us learn what is right. We face many complex, difficult issues and in some cases different approaches to these may in fact be just what we need. Contrasting reasonable opinions provoke thought, and even views that ultimately turn out to be false can give rise to insights as we consider them. This isn't true of any and every false view, though. We don't expect scientists to include the views of flat-earthers in their curriculum, or creationism, or astrology. Even though some people believe these, they are false, and while sociologists may be interested those support such theories, considering the views on their merits is not fruitful because they have no merits—no rational basis. We don't want to take the fact that many of us are eager to accept racism as evidence that the equality of the races is a complex, difficult question. We can be eager to accept beliefs that are both simplistic and false. Educational institutions exist to aid in enlightenment. Where there is ambiguity, this involves the use of critical evaluation of arguments on all sides. Where there is no ambiguity, it does not. Campuses are different from the public street precisely because they have this mission. Colleges and universities should, then, be a haven from nonsense.

Works Cited

Mill, John Stuart. "On Liberty." In *Utilitarianism and On Liberty*. Oxford: Blackwell Publishing, 2003.

Nossel, Suzanne. "Why Diversity Doesn't Trump Free Speech on Campus." https://pen.org/press-clip/why-diversity-doesnt-trump-speech-on-campus/. Originally published in *Huffington Post*. October 18, 2016. https://pen.org/press-clip/why-diversity-doesnt-trump-speech-on-campus/

Pen America. "And Campus for All: Diversity, Inclusion, and Freedom of Speech at US Universities." *Pen.org, 2016. https://pen.org/sites/default/files/PEN_campus_report_final_online_2.pdf*

Sherif, Muzafer. *The Psychology of Social Norms*. New York: Harper & Brothers, 1936.

Sherif, Muzafer, Harvey, O. J., White, B. Jack, Hood, William R. and Sherif, Carolyn W. *Intergroup Conflict and Cooperation: The Robbers Cave Experiment*. Norman, OK: University Book Exchange, 1961.

19 The Plausibility of Abhorrent Views, and Why it Matters

Calum Miller

> Discussing infanticide is not the best way to win friends or secure admiring book reviews.

So says Jeff McMahan (2007, 132), one of the foremost academic defenders of the permissibility of infanticide. He is not wrong: In a book review of *The Ethics of Killing* (2002), wherein McMahan defends the permissibility of infanticide, Stephen Mulhall (2002, 16) appears to accuse him of "thinking evil thoughts," of the kind Anscombe (1958, 17) once described as showing "a corrupt mind."

As an empirical point, it is hard to disagree with McMahan's evaluation here. And, while I think that McMahan is a most gentlemanly and kind person, I think what he defends is indeed truly evil.[1] But *ought* the defense of evil positions elicit contempt in all cases? More radically, should we suppose, with Anscombe and Mulhall, that the mere entertainment of evil thoughts is morally objectionable? I shall argue to the contrary. Not only must we think seriously about evil suggestions as individuals, we should do so as a community, and therefore should do so publicly.

There are various pragmatic reasons for allowing freedom of speech, including in academic contexts. One such reason is to allow wicked views to be publicly "shown up" and thereby rendered incredible in the fair light of open debate. Such views could not, in that case, be held by proponents to have been unduly or sinisterly quashed by an authoritarian regime scared of letting out the truth. And this would help to give an accurate picture of the number of adherents: Movements based on such views would have less need for secrecy and could not as plausibly claim artificially inflated numbers among their ranks.

Another reason for preserving academic freedom of speech is to minimize the risk of applying limits wrongly. Even if it were the case that some views ought not be discussed, why think that the actual authorities would accurately recognize and employ the relevant boundaries? Could a precedent for such boundaries not be exploited to stifle genuinely needed discussion on the grounds that the "right" answer had already been reached by the relevant authorities? The history of governments and zeitgeists, and the moral heterogeneity evident across and within times and cultures—not least our own—do not constitute cause for great optimism about the results of such restrictions. Indeed, most of our views about who counts as human, along with other core moral beliefs, have at some point been doubted or even deemed anathema. As McMahan (2016) himself puts it:

> It is salutary to recall that the early efforts of those we now recognize as having been in the vanguard of moral progress—abolitionists, campaigners for women's rights and female suffrage, vegetarians and opponents of vivisection—have always been fiercely resisted and ridiculed by those to whom it was inconceivable that the common sense view at the time might be mistaken.

There is thus at least some inductive reason to suppose these are not the lucky few decades in history where we have finally achieved moral equilibrium. We have set no such precedent.[2]

One might, alternatively, support academic freedom of speech on more theoretical grounds. One might think it a simple matter of liberty or autonomy that academic freedom be preserved. Perhaps a restriction on academic free speech would contravene certain human rights. Or perhaps it is simply part of the purpose and nature of universities to allow a completely open exchange of ideas.[3]

I do not pursue any of these lines of argument here (though they link closely to my main argument). Rather, I suggest that the character of moral epistemology itself suggests no clear connection between the (apparent) heinousness of a view and its obvious falsehood—at the very least, there is no reason to think that wicked views will always be obviously false.

This, I suggest, has a number of implications: First, that generally decent people can have wicked views and that having a wicked view should not automatically provoke contempt for the holder. Relatedly, having wicked views is not always culpable, and we should in certain respects and in certain cases be more sympathetic to those advocating them.

The second main set of implications concerns not the holders of seemingly wicked views but the extent to which we should entertain such views. The most obvious implication is that some wicked views may be somewhat plausible. I suggest that this—along with sympathy for their proponents—gives some reason to entertain at least some wicked views in academic settings.

While I do not go so far as to say that all views should be allowed extensive coverage in academic settings, I suggest that ostensible wickedness alone cannot be grounds for academic censorship, and that the considerations adduced herein lend support to considerably expanded limits of academic freedom. Moreover, alternative criteria for academic restrictions—such as plausibility—do not clearly generate the sorts of academic restrictions often thought plausible by some within academia. While the conclusion I reach may appear radical—and I certainly do not intend to thereby license the intellectual or moral legitimacy of any wicked positions—it is, I suggest, supported by the considerations I adduce here.

I understand academic freedom as a broadly negative freedom: the freedoms not to be fired on the basis of arguing for a particular view, not to be disinvited after, e.g., a student group invitation, not to have work otherwise involuntarily retracted (e.g., because of complaints to a journal).[4] My argument varies in strength for each of these conclusions, and may also support other conclusions. I do not intend here to give a principled argument for unrestricted academic freedom of every variety: I merely offer an argument which lends substantial support to various academic freedoms. Importantly, I note here that the academic freedom I defend does not involve unrestricted teaching freedom: Teachers—at least in more objective fields—must be capable of, and willing to, reflect to their students consensuses within their fields. So, for example, a science educator who deceives their students about scientific consensus (including by withholding information) will not, in most cases, be doing their job properly, and so may be liable to a termination of their contract. There are important academic freedoms other than teaching a radical opinion as mainstream, and it is those which concern me here. The arguments I give do lend some support to more liberal teaching freedom as well; but my primary target—especially as this is the domain most under threat at present—is the more liberal marketplace of ideas in university talks, journals, and so on.

A Case

Let us attend to some concrete cases to begin to illustrate the argument. Suppose that there are two competing views, both of similar plausibility, but both of which entail that the other view is not only wrong but utterly wickedly so—or, at least, has wicked consequences. It is not difficult to find real-life approximations, given some mutually agreed background information and values. Let us say that Daisy is accused of murdering Tobias, though in fact she is innocent. Nevertheless, the evidence against Daisy is very strong—Tobias's own family, known to be honest and reliable, saw Daisy's uncanny doppelganger Philippa murder Tobias in broad daylight, not knowing Philippa existed. They have no reason to doubt Daisy's guilt, and so it seems clear that their belief is justified. And let us say that another witness wants to bring important evidence to the table—that Philippa exists, looks identical to Daisy, and is, in fact, the killer. Or suppose that someone—also knowing this—defends Daisy's innocence publicly in the media.

Now imagine what Tobias's family might say: They have every reason to believe that Daisy is guilty and that those trying to defend Daisy are perverting justice, denying the gravity of the crime Daisy has committed, being insensitive to their loss as a family, and perhaps even facilitating future murders. To allow the new evidence to be heard might therefore be to take it more seriously than it deserves, to give dangerous and dehumanizing speech a platform, and so on. From their perspective, the case is clear: Murderers should not be defended, Daisy is very probably a murderer, and so should not be defended.[5]

What should be done in this case? Of course, we have artificially constructed this scenario so that the family are simply wrong, but it is not implausible to suppose that this form of case approximates at least some real cases. And when it comes to deciding innocence or guilt for this sort of crime, the intuitions of most people are clear: Everyone has the right to a fair trial—because only when the best case, with all the evidence, is presented for both sides are we most capable of reaching an appropriate judgment.

So it is curious that outside the courtroom these sorts of principles are frequently rejected. When a heinous view is espoused in the popular sphere or, sometimes, in the academy, it is frequently met with precisely these kinds of objections: Allowing the view a platform is insensitive or offensive or dangerous, helps to defend heinous people or actions, or gives the view the appearance of more legitimacy than it deserves. Even *true* positions are sometimes barred from discussion on similar grounds: Just this week of writing, a UK university barred research into transgender people "detransitioning," seemingly partly on the grounds that it might cause offense, despite there being no concern that the results or conclusions themselves might be false (BBC 2017). And, of course, given the enormous number of views which have been banned from universities over their history, it is virtually certain on probabilistic grounds that at least some of them have been true.

Are there relevant differences between the courtroom case and university cases? On inspection, it appears not. One might think that while in a fair court trial both sides have the best possible case presented for them, so that truth is likely to win out, this might not be the case in a university due to lack of resources, making deceit more likely to win than if no discussion were permitted at all. But this is not a very strong reason: In the first place, it is hardly plausible that lawyers always present the case for their defendant well. But, equally pressingly, there is every reason to think that universities should already have at least *someone* available to represent the side of truth relatively well—at least, if it is a widely recognized truth, which we are assuming is the case if the issue is whether or not to ban its negation. Indeed, if there is no one on campus available and capable of presenting the case for the widely recognized truth at least reasonably well, one wonders whether such a view *deserves* its widespread acceptance and a platform hegemony.

Another relevant difference might be that lawyers tend to debate empirical facts, while perhaps agreeing about the evaluative facts. They don't disagree that murder is wrong or on the appropriate punishment: They just dispute whether Daisy committed murder. Could one not say that the disputants should consider each other doxastically mistaken but not thereby culpable? Perhaps they agree on the core values and it is only the secondary prescriptive views (based partly on different empirical views) which differ—with terribly unfortunate consequences.

But nor is this as incisive as it might seem. For those who think that some academic answers should be off-limits will surely include some empirical disputes which are clearly politically charged: whether the Holocaust happened, whether some races are better on average at some things than others, or (in the Bath Spa case) how many post-op transgender persons regret their decision and decide to "detransition" afterwards. In any case, it will not always be clear in advance that any given dispute does not turn, in part, on an empirical matter. In advance of giving the opposing view a detailed hearing, then, there can be no reliable way of ensuring that the dispute is entirely evaluative. On the other hand, there are surely some legal (or otherwise accepted) cases where evaluative facts are in question: whether or not a certain consideration should be deemed exculpating, for example. So this factor is not going to satisfactorily account for our discrepant judgments.

Take an academic example—in particular, an example where the heinousness runs both ways. The abortion debate is one of the best examples of this. There are those who think that fetuses have the same moral value and rights as adult humans, and who are thereby inclined to think that abortion is tantamount to murder.[6] On the other hand, there are those who think that fetuses have significantly fewer and less pressing rights than adult humans, such that abortion is permissible. In particular, it has been argued persuasively that the most plausible position in support of abortion rights also entails an extreme view—the permissibility of infanticide (McMahan 2002; Giubilini and Minerva 2013; Singer 1993; Tooley 1972). As Tooley (1972, 38) puts it, "One of the interesting ways in which the abortion issue differs from most other moral issues is that the plausible positions on abortion appear to be extreme positions." Dworkin (1993, 10, as quoted in Greasley 2017, 15) similarly comments, "Self-respecting people who give opposite answers to whether the fetus is a person can no more compromise, or agree to live together allowing others to make their own decisions, than people can compromise about slavery or apartheid or rape." Finally, although she neither takes a pro-life view nor endorses infanticide, Kate Greasley (2017) has recently argued compellingly that *if* the fetus is granted personhood, there can be no plausible defense of abortion's legality except in the most extreme of circumstances (e.g., if *both* the pregnant woman and fetus are already destined to die, and abortion is likely to save the woman).

What can we say about this sort of case? In the first place, it seems that both sides are likely to act heinously (even if not culpably) if they are wrong: If the abortion opponents are wrong, they are likely to gravely inhibit the autonomy of pregnant women for no objective benefit,[7] while if the abortion defenders are wrong, they are likely to commit or endorse something not too far from murder (this becomes clearer in the infanticide cases). In fact, it is likely that one of these extreme views, both of which are frequently characterized as evil, wicked, corrupt, and so on, are likely correct: that abortion is immoral and should be illegal except when the mother's life is in danger *and* the fetus is likely to die anyway; or else that abortion and infanticide are widely permissible.[8]

So if there are honest, non-culpable, and rational (I call such agents "sincere agents" for shorthand) proponents of both views, it seems that some such people are liable to have a heinous opinion (namely, either that women should be deprived of fairly basic freedoms of bodily autonomy, or that we should condone the killing of members of the human moral community) and probably commit heinous acts on that basis. And it is difficult to deny the premise. Jeff McMahan—who endorses the permissibility of abortion and infanticide—is undeniably honest and informed. As he himself notes, there is little vested interest in publicly and explicitly condoning infanticide. And, while I think he is wrong and that my own position is more reasonable (as most of us presumably feel about our own opinions), it is simply not credible to insist that he is straightforwardly and culpably irrational. His position is extremely well thought out and relies on some credible intuitions about certain thought experiments. Again, I think he is very and dangerously wrong. But to dismiss him as straightforwardly irrational is not plausible (even if we think, as I do, that the arguments opposing his view are stronger).

Yet it is equally hard to deny that there are sincere opponents of abortion. For some of us—especially in the medical profession—vocal opposition to abortion is liable to make us exceptionally unpopular and probably inhibit our career prospects. I can vouch at least for myself when I say that I do not enjoy the unpopularity that comes from voicing my position, and that I would prefer to be more popular. My vested social, professional, and pecuniary interests all lie in adopting the prevailing moral sensibility (although without going as far as condoning infanticide). There are plenty of us—myself included—who have studied the debates in detail and who were only convinced after reading the academic literature on the topic. And, again, it is difficult to simply dismiss us as fundamentally irrational. Just as there are some strong intuitions in favor of the importance of psychological capacities for rights, so there are strong intuitions in favor of the importance of human equality and against the permissibility of infanticide. I think the former intuition can be accommodated readily within my framework, and McMahan thinks the latter intuitions can be accommodated readily within his own (though ultimately rejecting at least the latter as false). But we can at least *understand* why each other's (plausible) intuitions lead to the beliefs they do. Both sides have at least some plausibility behind them. And yet one of us must be heinously wrong—despite our honesty, education, and rationality.

One might be tempted, again, to insist that this is not really a dispute about fundamental ethical facts: Both sides might agree that murdering persons is wrong—they just disagree regarding who counts as a person.[9] Sincere agents would not disagree about the *fundamental* ethical facts—and it is disputes about those which we should forbid. But this is not a feasible move: One could just as well say that Nazis and non-Nazis both agree on the fact that murdering persons is wrong—the former just disagree that Jews (and others) are persons. Obviously if any views are to be banned, it ought to be ones like these—and so one cannot appeal to this reasoning to justify our tolerance of this debate.

There is a sort of middle ground case in this vicinity: Peter Singer was recently protested for his views on disability, since he thinks (roughly) that certain cognitive features are determinants of value—features which some disabled people do not have. His opponents think that he has abhorrent views about disabled people by counting them as less than human, while someone of his view might well plausibly suppose that his opponents have abhorrent views regarding the extent to which we force each other to look after disabled people (e.g., by forcing taxes to help care for them, or by discriminating in favor of them against cognitively comparable animals). Clearly, some people think his views are literally intolerable: They should not be given a place at the academy. Others[10] who find his views contemptible think that they nevertheless should be allowed a place in universities. And even many who find his views on disability repulsive find themselves indebted to his work on global poverty and animal suffering.[11] So we have a useful spectrum of cases—infanticide, disability discrimination, and Nazism—where the personhood of ostensible persons is denied, and where there are differing levels of resistance to the permissibility of these views in academia. If we cannot find significant *formal* differences among these cases (there may be differences in plausibility, but I will later argue that this is likely to be person-relative and is not a good justification for banning some), then perhaps the discrepancy should lead us to re-examine our thoughts about limiting academic speech.

Perhaps you are not convinced by the infanticide example. It might seem obvious to you that infants are persons. It might seem obvious to you that they are not. But for *any* of us, there are going to be at least *some* marginal cases of personhood. Of course, it would be impossible to settle on an uncontroversial example, since we all have different ideas of personhood. But, for example, suppose you think that certain cognitive traits are necessary for personhood. There is such a wide spectrum of cognitive life—a spectrum that is close enough to continuous—that it is virtually inevitable that, somewhere between the two ends (persons vs. non-persons), there will be a grey area admitting of at least some agnosticism. Denying the equality and personhood of some agents in this grey area, on the one hand, risks a heinous crime against them. But granting personhood "just in case" only pushes the problem back a step: What about the agents just below them on the cognitive scale? And in any case, granting personhood "just in case" might well require considerable deprivations of liberty elsewhere—by forcing everyone else to look after them through taxes, and so on. There is simply no easy answer, and risks abound each side.[12]

Maybe there is no entirely uncontroversial example of disagreement among sincere agents regarding heinous acts. In that case, let us think more abstractly. Let us call the formal situation I have described a *contemptible dilemma*—where both sides of a dilemma are, if wrong, committed to a contemptible or heinous position. And, where there are actual proponents on each side of a contemptible dilemma, we have a *contemptible dispute*. I have argued that some such disputes are sincere—that is, they involve sincere agents. Just as McMahan honestly believes that restrictions on abortion are undue violations of women's bodily autonomy, so I honestly believe that abortion is the unjust taking of a human life. Neither of us have much incentive to lie in these ways and every incentive to take more moderate positions. The evidence of sincerity is compelling. The evidence of education and broad rationality is likewise strong, and so we seem to have such cases.

I suggest that there is no theoretical reason why contemptible disputes should be readily soluble, or why all sincere agents should end up on one side of the dispute. What would need to be the case for this to be false? We would need a principle along the lines of: "Any heinous view must be obviously false to all sincere agents." But why think that such a principle is true? Do all heinous views have an epistemic probability of 0? There is certainly no reason in probability theory why this should be obvious. Nor is it clear how any laws of psychology or moral epistemology should lend themselves to this conclusion.

Those views which require some reflection or inference trivially require at least some deliberation regarding their truth—and so clearly must permit at least some debate (even if privately in one's own head), allowing for the initial possibility that the heinous view is, in fact, true. I suspect most of us would concede that there are at least *some* heinous views which we have ruled out by such inference. It appears to follow that such deliberation over whether a heinous belief really is heinous is not necessarily concerning: It is a natural part of our moral knowledge.

And there is no clear reason to prohibit communities from aiding this deliberation.

Perhaps there are some moral beliefs we rightly hold without reflection. But is it the case that *every single* heinous belief possible is excluded by these? And is it the case that *every single* one of these beliefs are known intuitively by every sincere agent, and known with such conviction that they require no deliberation at all? Again, while this is not conceptually impossible, there is no reason to think it is the case. And it seems *prima facie* relatively implausible. Either way, *some* of our core moral beliefs will be held on the basis of some reflection. And both reflective and non-reflective moral beliefs are subject to disagreement among sincere agents. And so it follows that, very probably, there are some contemptible disputes in which a sincere agent has a considerable degree of agnosticism.

Practical Implications

We have contended that there are contemptible disputes, that some such disputes are sincere, and that there is no epistemological reason for thinking that they should be readily soluble. Now let us draw out some implications.

The first implication of these theses is that it is extremely unlikely that all morally wicked views are obviously wrong or implausible—and especially unlikely that all morally wicked views are obviously implausible to *all* sincere agents. This has a further implication uncomfortable for many: that some morally abhorrent views are nevertheless plausible, or even probable (given limited evidence sets). This should not surprise us too much: Most of us have probably held views we later thought to be abhorrent. It is possible that we were simply being irrational at those times—but it is also possible that some of us simply lacked some of the relevant evidence or had different intuitions which were not demonstrably false. In any case, why assume the current zeitgeist is entirely immune to the same limitations that have pervaded human moral thought for so many centuries? And if we are not, then it is likely that even the ethical elite largely hold to some abhorrent views—and perhaps on matters in which they think precisely the *alternative* is abhorrent.

That the relations between moral facts, moral knowledge, and sincere agents generate this uncomfortable structure plausibly has further implications. In the first place, it should prompt us to reexamine any moral discourse that divides people into the essentially decent and the wicked. Sincere agents likely, in some cases, hold abhorrent views, and they should not thereby be discounted as thoroughly wicked or bigoted people on those grounds alone. Likewise, holders of wicked views are not necessarily culpable for their doing so. So, in the first place, there should be greater sympathy and openness to those with ostensibly wicked views on account of their plausible sincerity.

This must obviously be tempered, however. This sympathy and openness is not intended to diminish the seriousness of abhorrent moral views and actions. If we are confident that someone is suggesting something abhorrent, we should be clear about this and, in our actions and policies, oppose them just as robustly as otherwise.[13] For example, I am confident that infanticide is very seriously wrong—so I will continue to labor as an activist against it, I will continue to decry it as evil—including in academic settings, and I would support strong legal punishments for those who commit it. I am not intending a kind of moral skepticism or moral paralysis. How our convictions should prescribe our actions is notoriously difficult to determine (see, e.g., Buchak 2014). But what seems at least clear is that we should still act on at least some of our convictions. And those cases in which we are most confident that we have a strong obligation seem like optimal candidates.

The sympathy is therefore strictly limited: We should try our best to listen to and understand their heinous views and the reasons for them. And, at least in some cases, we should be more hesitant to denounce the person who holds this view as a thoroughly wicked person. For it is simply a fact of life that (relative to average humans, at least), some decent people will have some abhorrent views. Our sympathy should be for hearing and understanding the ideas, and (at least in some cases) for the *person*—not being too quick to judge them as a whole.

This does not make one a "sympathizer" in the sense that one enjoys, is partial to, or encourages their views. It is an objective hearing in a (hopefully) objective academic context. If the view is truly incorrect and therefore detestable, one would hope that an academic setting would provide the best opportunity of soundly refuting it, rather than letting it fester and gain popularity in less critical environments. And if not—on the off chance that it is correct—academia might well be best placed to recognize this and allow it to pick up speed, as well as refining it as appropriate. So we have, too, at least the rudiments of a rationale for being particularly interested in *academic* freedom of speech.

These are surely some interesting results. That sincere agents are liable to have contemptible views from time to time—although inevitable on reflection—is nevertheless surprising. And given the plausible implications—that having a contemptible view, or maybe many contemptible views, does not mean one should necessarily be entirely discredited as a moral thinker or agent[14]—we have substantial work to do in contemporary discourse.

This has generated some reason, therefore, to preserve a relatively liberal conception of academic freedom. There are many practical and theoretical reasons for preserving academic freedom (in a broad sense), some of which I identified at the beginning of this article. But the recognition that the geometry of moral knowledge itself draws a fine—and sometimes evidentially or rationally indeterminate—line between the morally abhorrent and the morally obligatory should give us very strong reason to. For there are a number of reasons to engage with sincere disputants who seem to us to hold contemptible views.

The first is that such engagement is good for them. As described, it is possible that such disputants are still otherwise reasonably good people. And in that case, we ought to help them come around to the more probably correct view—for their own sake and for others (indeed, this is probably true even if they are not otherwise good people—but their being otherwise good is extra motivation). Simply banning their view from discussion is more likely to breed resentment, and is a great injustice to them if they are, in fact, correct.

The second, more pressing reason is that such engagement is good for the pursuit of truth. This was captured most favorably by JS Mill (1859, 33):

> Were an opinion a personal possession of no value except to the owner; if to be obstructed in the enjoyment of it were simply a private injury, it would make some difference whether the injury was inflicted only on a few persons or on many. But the peculiar evil of silencing the expression of an opinion is, that it is robbing the human race; posterity as well as the existing generation; those who dissent from the opinion, still more than those who hold it. If the opinion is right, they are deprived of the opportunity of exchanging error for truth: if wrong, they lose, what is almost as great a benefit, the clearer perception and livelier impression of truth, produced by its collision with error.

For Mill (and I think he is probably right), the chance that the minority opinion-holder is right is an obvious reason in favor of free speech: Convincing the academic community thus would be a great service to it, and probably to the whole world if it should be accepted more widely. But even if it is wrong, Mill suggests, our knowledge is edified, since the nature of its wrongness helps to illuminate the truth. Returning to our earlier examples, suppose we think that McMahan is wrong about infanticide. Nevertheless, his work on the topic is extremely sophisticated, and his discussion may help us to navigate moral territory better. Suppose we think he is right, for example, that certain psychological connections in an agent (which he thinks is an embodied mind) give that agent some interests to be respected, but find that his arguments elsewhere are lacking. This gives us considerable reason to rethink our attitude towards animals and the harmful ways in which we treat them. Locating our disagreement most precisely gives us moral and practical clarity in other domains, and so serves truth. Even cases where our disputant is most obviously wrong—say, in denying the Holocaust—thinking about what *exactly* is so contemptible about such a position (it could be the result of culpable ignorance or intellectual laziness, or it could be subconscious racism, or it could be simply correlated with antipathy towards Jews, and so on), prompted by such discussions, may help us in other areas of ethics. So truth, too, is served.

Finally, returning to the possibility that our disputant is correct, it helps all of us. For it might just correct our views and might, indeed, prevent us from committing heinous acts on the basis of them. Of course, this will be very unlikely in some cases. And it might be that our views are relatively harmless even if false, and so we are playing a low-risk game. But there is always at least the risk of the injustice of moral carelessness and wrongful condemnation. Since this is in some cases extremely unlikely, this benefit may reasonably be weighed against the risks of academic freedom. Fortunately, for the reasons I gave earlier, *inter alia*, the risks of academic freedom seem low in almost all cases, and indeed there are other benefits to academic freedom.

Nevertheless, I concede there is some reason against academic freedom, and that the reason I have given for academic freedom here is of varying strength depending on these various other factors. And indeed, my argument does not suggest that academic freedom should be *maximized* at the expense of other resources: Universities ought not spend large amounts of resources on inviting disputants in many cases, for example. But I continue to note that what has seemed incredible to past generations has turned out to be both true and morally crucial. There have been plenty of societies where it has been inconceivable that members of other races or tribes or groups have been just as morally valuable as one's own, for example. And, nevertheless, showing the wrongness of this view is a crucial foundation of modern liberal moral thought. If the worst that can happen is not so bad, if there are other benefits to academic freedom, and if or when there is a relatively low cost to allowing such views to be heard, the chance seems well worth it.

Objections

Let me conclude with a few thoughts on our intuitive resistance to academic freedom and, by doing so, clarify my position. I am no less repulsed by some opinions than everyone else, and I have not forgone the instinct to simply declare some opinions anathema and not give them the time of day. So let us briefly consider some possible bases for such dismissal.

One possible thought behind no-platformers, protestors, and those who hold to narrower conceptions of academic freedom is that whether a view should be discussed is a function of how appalling the view is, in which case any view—no matter how plausible—which is probably appalling should not be discussed. The anxiety may be that by discussing a view, we are tacitly conceding that it is not really appalling.

Of course, my previous discussion attacks at precisely this juncture: There simply is no reason to think that every heinous opinion will be very improbable. So when can we say that an opinion is too heinous to be discussed? If the probability of its heinousness if 0.51, is that sufficient? But then there is a perfectly reasonable chance that we are completely wrong. In that case, it seems clear that to prohibit its discussion would be imprudent. So appallingness simply cannot be a sufficient criterion for banning a view from the academy.

But this suggests that the principle itself is simply wrong. It is simply not the case that to think a view should be discussed is to tacitly concede that it is not really appalling. Perhaps whether a view is worth discussing is not just a function of how appalling it is but of how plausible it is. Might heinousness combined with a certain degree of implausibility ground academic restrictions?

There are a number of reasons why this might not be so simple. First, there is the problem of arbitration. Who decides how implausible a view is? Sincere experts might disagree, and in any case it is not commonplace for experts in relevant fields to be in charge of policy on academic freedom. What we would need is for the view to be implausible to all sincere agents, and this simply casts the net too wide to generate much more than minimal restrictions on academic claims. Secondly, showing that a view is implausible in the first place will require some engagement with it, and so some academic engagement with implausible heinous views is necessary to begin with. There is, moreover, the problem of new evidence and arguments: It is always possible that new arguments may overturn even a very implausible view, and unless we are prepared to countenance those arguments, we cannot reasonably maintain that no strong counter-arguments to our position exist.

The problem is that once we have accounted for these (e.g., by finding cases where all sincere agents do agree), there will not be much left to censor—and it is particularly unlikely that reasonable censorship will line up with what many contemporary activists are attempting to censor (for example, debates on abortion or transgenderism).[15]

What seems more reasonable than trying to consistently censor views on more nuanced grounds than this, therefore, is simply to be clear from the outset that discussing an appalling view is not to concede that it is worth discussing, plausible, or less than appalling. If this proviso is understood from the outset, we can circumvent the problem of heinous and implausible academic views being seen to have academic credibility or moral legitimacy.

Mulhall (2002, 16) describes a second possible objection as anticipated by Anscombe: "She thereby expressed a (highly controversial but hardly unintelligible) fear not only of evil actions, but of thinking evil thoughts—a fear of the dulling and degrading of moral sensibility that such acts of contemplation can encourage and express." It is not difficult to agree that there is something unnerving about ruminating on evil actions. The Christian tradition—shared by Anscombe, Mulhall, and myself, as well as many of the foremost respondents and critics of the unpopular views of Singer and his company—is clear about fleeing from sin and about the importance of purity in one's thoughts just as well as one's deeds.

But this intuition may be preserved—in the Christian tradition and outside of it—without suggesting that we literally need not think about evil propositions at all, or in detail. For there is a huge difference between *deliberating* over evil actions (perhaps pleasurably) and *thinking* about them in a descriptive, analytical way. The former warrants avoidance; it is far from clear that the latter does too.

Nevertheless, it is still open to wonder whether discussing such views dulls our moral sensibilities, as if encouraging us to consider them as academically respectable or mere differences of opinion. This is a reasonable concern that I share. It might even be that discussing the views is not for everyone—those who are worried about this effect might want to voluntarily abstain from the debate. But that is no reason to prevent *anyone* from taking part in the debate, especially not those who are able to hold their condemnation of evil views and actions quite firmly in the context of academic debate, as many of us are.

Finally, we might offer some further ways of resolving this tension. One of which has been indicated already: Part of the solution is surely to insist on being clear on the heinousness of the view one is addressing. Another solution might be to resist the strong division of academia and polemics. This will need to be done carefully, since there are clearly strong advantages to the civility and (relative) objectivity of academia. But for those who think there are equally strong advantages of polemics against and stigmatization of truly evil views, I note simply that my thesis is consistent with them.

Practical considerations aside, I doubt very much whether it is even possible to avoid thinking at least some evil thoughts. In fact, there is likely to be at least some rudimentary cogitation about virtually all our moral beliefs (even our belief that heinous beliefs are false requires at least some thought about them). And, plausibly, there are inevitably some cases where detailed thought about evil ideas is required: where important *prima facie* inconsistencies arise in our moral thinking, for example (see, e.g., McMahan 2013). Thinking about evil opinions is inevitable, and we cannot piously avoid it. And it is plausibly safer to do so in a community where they can be corrected and shown for what they are.

All these considerations—that we can be clear about a heinous view while discussing it, that moral rumination is inevitable, and so on—count finally against a final intuitive thought: that, if my thesis is correct, then whether or not we should do some evil act is "up for debate." This is, indeed, an uncomfortable thought. But, in addition to the arguments I have given for my view, we might also give an alternative explication of this thought which helps to smoothen any inconsistency.

One such interpretation might be to say that, once we have arrived at a conclusion[16] regarding, e.g., the dignity and rights of a certain category of humans, the issue is no longer "up for debate" in the sense that we allow such humans to be mistreated or violated by others just in case those others disagree with us on their status. We could say that there is no "debate" when it comes to how to treat them, given their humanity. We do not allow court defenses based on their lack of humanity, nor do we suddenly revoke their rights if we have transient or shallow doubts about their status. So there are credible interpretations of the intuition which are consistent with genuine epistemic uncertainty about an ostensible person's rights and their grounding.

In any case, it is difficult to see what alternative there is. All of us feel deeply, deeply disturbed by the contention of a certain demographic group's humanity, and at the need to defend it. But given that some people will inevitably disagree—sometimes sincere agents, no less—disturbance is inevitable. The issue is how we respond to it. One possibility is to simply refuse to endorse their concerns with debate. This is terribly dangerous, especially if the movement gains ground and becomes more popular. And we cannot get away with saying that such views never would become popular: They have done so all too recently and devastatingly. The alternative is to engage in the uncomfortable debate. As I suggest, this might require the inclusion of polemics or stigma in our academic discourse. This is perhaps not ideal either: But if it is what is required to defend the humanity of those in doubt, it might well be warranted.

Conclusion

These considerations may not be sufficient to justify unrestricted academic freedom, but they do constitute a good reason to significantly expand the range of views we are willing to entertain.[17] And supposing we find no reasonable threshold of plausibility with which to adjudicate, or supposing that almost any view may be plausible to at least one sincere agent, perhaps the most promising solution is to extend academic freedom unrestrictedly. The most sensible and sensitive way to do this is to undermine the implication that discussing a view tacitly assumes its decency. I suggest that my initial considerations serve this purpose as well.

In short, a view's being appalling is not good reason to think it is also extremely improbable. Yet contemporary discourse—probably from all political vertices—by its attitude towards those with ostensibly contemptible views, and especially its failure to interact with those views, does not often faithfully represent the fact that some abhorrent views are plausible.

My argument therefore recommends informal sympathy and a hearing for sincere agents expressing contemptible views, and moreover it recommends that such hearings extend to the academy. By giving plausible alternative interpretations of common intuitions and slogans against academic free speech, one can hold the spirit of these consistently with my proposals, even if this requires some modification of academic discourse.

These debates are uncomfortable, no doubt. And I do not hereby intend to credit the depraved—morally and intellectually—views which surely exist in the academy. But I do hope to have shown that despite our discomfort and despite their depravity, debate simply cannot be avoided on consequential or principled grounds. So let us have the debates and subject our core moral beliefs, along with depraved ones, to such academic tests. If we are indeed right, we can be confident that we will pass them.[18]

Notes

1. McMahan himself has always extended grace to those with whom he strongly disagrees: The first time we met, I presented a paper arguing for a fetal "right to life"— the conclusion of which he rejected emphatically but met with most helpful and kind comments.
2. My overall thesis does, in fact, link very clearly with this point. So although it can be seen as an independent reason in favor of academic freedom, I note that it is heavily augmented (and so deserves further reflection) by the arguments developed in this paper.
3. Clearly all these ideas deserve considerably more working out, and I regret that I am unable to offer more than a tip of the hat in their direction in this paper.
4. A few examples of increasingly invasive university/academic actions from the last few years are worth mentioning: the journal *Hypatia* was berated and encouraged to retract an article in which Rebecca Tuvel argued for a symmetry between transgenderism and transracialism (Weinberg 2017); a number of events put on by Oxford Students for Life, a pro-life group at the University of Oxford, were cancelled or required police intervention to proceed (Oscroft 2017); the University of Strathclyde's Students' Association banned a pro-life group (Gray 2016); feminist writer Julie Bindel was banned from a University of Manchester event she had been invited to because of (impolitely expressed) skepticism about transgenderism she had expressed in the past (Palmer 2015); a Sheffield University student was removed from his course for stating on Facebook that homosexuality and same-sex marriage were sinful (Grierson 2017); a Wilfrid Laurier graduate student was interrogated by university officials after playing a clip of Jordan Peterson in a class she was teaching (Joseph 2017); Bret Weinstein was told by police at Evergreen State College that they could not guarantee his safety after he objected to a day event encouraging white people to stay off campus (Weiss 2017); a faculty member was injured after a protest against Charles Murray prevented his speaking at Middlebury College (Weiss 2017); a Bath Spa University student was prevented from research on transgenderism on the basis that the results might be "politically incorrect" (BBC 2017); and so on. It is not difficult to find many similar cases in the news, although each must be taken with pinch of salt.
5. It may be unclear to you that Tobias's family are justified in making these claims. If so, very well, for this is essentially my point. The reason it is important is that those who defend the innocence of accused parties in parallel

contexts are often met with scorn akin to that of Tobias's family, even when the evidence is either inconclusive or poor. See, e.g., the backlash at football clubs for considering signing footballer Ched Evans even after the overturning of his rape conviction after new evidence came to light (BBC 2016). Along similar lines, see efforts to overturn the presumption of innocence in related cases (Rayner and Gardner 2015; Real Clear Politics 2015): a well-intentioned move, we should be absolutely clear, but again seeming to confuse the heinousness of the alleged crime with the plausibility of its veracity.

6. Let us suppose, for the sake of argument, that they reject Thomson-style violinist arguments which suggest that even adult humans would not have a substantive right to life if dependent on another human. Reasonably comprehensive responses to such arguments can be found in Greasley (2017) and elsewhere.
7. Plausibly, too, they are liable to the charge of "speciesism"—perhaps on a par with racism—for prioritizing human life above animal life.
8. Of course, not everyone agrees that one or the other extreme view is correct. Unfortunately, I do not have space to defend this view. But in any case, it is not strictly necessary, since all I am arguing is that both these extremes have opinions which might be heinous if wrong. In fact, perhaps most debates regarding who counts as a person count as similar instances.
9. Of course, it is equally possible that they disagree on more fundamental ethical facts too—I am just highlighting a possible informative case.
10. See for example George and West (2017), a public statement which, though not explicitly mentioning the Singer case, appeared to be in response to it and was signed by Singer himself.
11. I am grateful to Donald Downs for making this point to me.
12. In case you are tempted to think that this could be escaped with a different criterion of personhood—being a human being, for example—run through the exercise again, with hypothetical cases if necessary. There will always be difficult cases. In that case, what about ET? He is not biologically human but nevertheless plausibly counts as a person. But then our criterion includes human-*like* organisms. And again, the relevant likeness will admit of both so many degrees and so much agnosticism that the problem is bound to recur.
13. This obviously admits of substantial variety. From my own Christian tradition, grace and forgiveness are always to be extended for even the most heinous of crimes, and vengeance is strictly forbidden. But for others, heinous crimes are to be met with very severe punitive measures. Nothing in my argument turns on this.
14. I leave open the question of whether it can *ever* be sufficient to discredit one as a moral thinker or agent. Certainly, one contemptible view can cause great suffering and lead to absolutely heinous acts—that is not in dispute. And certainly, we should treat the doer accordingly. But my point here is to emphasize that ethics can be heavily *compartmentalized*—evil though the one view may be, it simply does not entail in every case that the person is thoroughly evil. And my view here does take seriously the idea that we should appreciate the good in someone who might have committed terrible acts.
15. One wonders if—even aside from questions of how to ground the restrictions—there is a more transparent inconsistency in the way metaethical views are treated: We suggest it is heinous and perhaps censorable to deny that rape is objectively wrong if one is a moral realist, but it is less common to suggest that moral nihilism is morally heinous or censorable, even though it entails precisely the same denial.

16. Recall that in at least some cases there will *inevitably* be some reflection or inference, so one cannot respond to this by suggesting that we do not need to "conclude" that certain of our core and important moral beliefs are true. It is simply a fact—whether comfortable or not—that some of our most important beliefs about human dignity are genuinely concluded rather than, e.g., directly perceived or intuited.
17. I leave open for now the question of the extent to which other factors might be important: for example, the otherwise creditable nature of a disputant's work or career. My thanks to Donald Downs for drawing my attention to the importance of this point.
18. I am grateful to George Tarr, Donald Downs, and Joshua Blanchard for their detailed and helpful comments on this paper.

Works Cited

Anscombe, G. E. M. "Modern Moral Philosophy." *Philosophy*, Vol. 33 (1958): 1–19.

"Bath Spa University 'Blocks Transgender Research.'" *BBC News*. September 25, 2017. www.bbc.co.uk/news/uk-41384473

Buchak, Lara. "Belief, Credence, and Norms." *Philosophical Studies*, Vol. 169 (2014): 285–311.

"Ched Evans: Footballer Found Not Guilty of Hotel Rape." *BBC News*. October 14, 2016. www.bbc.co.uk/news/uk-wales-37659009

Dworkin, Ronald. *Life's Dominion: An Argument About Abortion and Euthanasia*. London: Harper Collins, 1993.

George, Robert P. and West, Cornel. "Truth Seeking, Democracy, and Freedom of Thought and Expression—a Statement by Robert P. George and Cornel West." *Princeton University Website*. March 14, 2017. https://jmp.princeton.edu/statement

Giubilini, Alberto and Minerva, Francesca. "After-Birth Abortion: Why Should the Baby Live?" *Journal of Medical Ethics*, Vol. 39 (2013): 261–263.

Gray, Jasmin. "University of Strathclyde Student Union Bans Pro-Life Group for Violating 'Safe Space.'" *Huffington Post*. December 5, 2016. www.huffingtonpost.co.uk/entry/university-of-strathclyde-student-union-bans-pro-life-group-for-violating-students-safe-space_uk_5845420ce4b061fb97e5eddd

Greasley, Kate. *Arguments About Abortion: Personhood, Morality and Law*. Oxford: Oxford University Press, 2017.

Grierson, Jamie. "Christian Thrown Out of University Over Anti-Gay Remarks Loses Appeal." October 27, 2017. www.theguardian.com/uk-news/2017/oct/27/christian-felix-ngole-thrown-out-sheffield-university-anti-gay-remarks-loses-appeal

Joseph, Rebecca. "Wilfrid Laurier Admits It Mishandled Lindsay Shepherd Academic Freedom Case." *Global News*, December 18, 2017. https://globalnews.ca/news/3923478/wilfrid-laurier-no-complaint-lindsay-shepherd/

McMahan, Jeff. *The Ethics of Killing: Problems at the Margins of Life*. Oxford: Oxford University Press, 2002.

———. "Infanticide." *Utilitas*, Vol. 19 (2007): 131–159.

———. "Infanticide and Moral Consistency." *Journal of Medical Ethics*, Vol. 39 (2013): 273–280.

———. "Philosophical Critiques of Effective Altruism." *Effective Altruism Forum*. May 3, 2016. http://effective-altruism.com/ea/x4/philosophical_critiques_of_effective_altruism_by/

Mill, John Stuart. *On Liberty*. London: John W. Parker and Son, West Strand, 1859.

Mulhall, Stephen. "Fearful Thoughts." *London Review of Books*, Vol. 24 (2002): 16–18.

Oscroft, Alex. "WomCam Protesters Try to Shut Down Anti-Abortion Talk." *Oxford Student*. November 2, 2017. http://oxfordstudent.com/2017/11/02/womcam-protesters-try-shut-anti-abortion-talk/

Palmer, Ewan. " 'Transphobic' Feminist Julie Bindel Banned From Manchester Student Union Talk on Free Speech." *International Business Times*. October 8, 2015. www.ibtimes.co.uk/feminist-julie-bindel-banned-manchester-student-union-talk-free-speech-1522670

Rayner, Gordon and Gardner, Bill. "Men Must Prove a Woman Said 'Yes' Under Tough New Rape Rules." *The Telegraph*. January 28, 2015. www.telegraph.co.uk/news/uknews/law-and-order/11375667/Men-must-prove-a-woman-said-Yes-under-tough-new-rape-rules.html

Real Clear Politics. "Hillary to Sexual Assault Victims: 'You Have The Right to Be Heard, You Have the Right to Be Believed.' " *Real Clear Politics*. September 14, 2015. www.realclearpolitics.com/video/2015/09/14/hillary_clinton_women_should_be_believed_when_they_claim_rape_have_to_increase_prevention.html

Singer, Peter. *Practical Ethics*. Cambridge: Cambridge University Press, 1993.

Tooley, Michael. "Abortion and Infanticide." *Philosophy & Public Affairs*, Vol. 2 (1972): 37–65.

Weinberg, Justin. "Philosopher's Article on Transracialism Sparks Controversy (Updated with response from author)." *Daily Nous*, May 1, 2017. http://dailynous.com/2017/05/01/philosophers-article-transracialism-sparks-controversy/

Weiss, Bari. "When the Left Turns on Its Own." *The New York Times*. June 1, 2017. www.nytimes.com/2017/06/01/opinion/when-the-left-turns-on-its-own.html

20 Safeguarding Academic Freedom on Campus Through Faculty Governance

Rima Najjar Kapitan

Introduction

As an attorney who represents faculty in tenure appeals, disciplinary cases, and litigation, I often find myself wishing that the university in question had stronger structural protections for faculty. Indeed, in many cases I have dealt with, stronger protections would have likely precluded the necessity of internal appeal or litigation altogether. In particular, stronger protections for academic freedom would have helped greatly.

It is hard to be optimistic about improvements in this department being forthcoming, however. In fact, academic freedom is emerging as one of the casualties of the ever-expanding power and corporatization of university administrations. Academic freedom is losing ground due to the decreasing number of tenure line positions, the scarcity of jobs relative to the number of applicants, and the willingness of some administrators to terminate the positions of even tenured faculty members when their power is challenged.

In the face of the weakening of structural protections for academic freedom such as tenure and faculty mobility, faculty must adapt and develop alternate means of preserving a realm in which intellectual inquiry and critical thought can flourish, as well as develop means of ensuring adequate working conditions. One way to do this is through reform of university policy documents (typically referred to herein as "faculty handbooks") and effective mobilization of faculty legislative bodies (referred to herein as "faculty senates") to achieve such reform.

In the hopes of providing useful advice and taking solace from the fact that other contributors to this volume offer many valuable theoretical insights, this chapter errs on the side of practicality. It takes for granted the value and importance of increasing faculty freedom and self-governance in the academic setting, and is written from a perspective of faculty advocacy. The protections proposed in this chapter would not only reinforce the autonomy of faculty members but also enhance the overall health of academic life. They could provide much-needed stability by disincentivizing administrative overreach and minimizing litigation.

I do two things in this chapter. First, I outline the current judiciary status quo, which is at best indifferent and at worst outright hostile to academic freedom. The courts, unfortunately, provide meager guarantees of due process. This, when accompanied by inadequate due process and academic freedom protections in faculty handbooks, creates a situation where the academic freedom of individual faculty members gets overridden. Second, I make concrete suggestions about what types of protections can and should be instituted through internal reform spearheaded by faculty governments. Although these suggestions are the result of years of experience representing professors and a survey of faculty handbooks at public and private universities in the US, no individual institutions are identified.

The Courts and Institutional Autonomy: A Get-Out-of-Jail-Free Card for University Administrations

I begin with a brief description of the general hesitancy of US courts to interfere with university affairs, whether when enforcing contracts or civil rights statutes. In doing so, I hope to stress the importance of creating strong internal policy documents for the regulation of university life.

Although such judicial interference is sometimes the only way academic freedom and other faculty rights can be protected, courts are often less concerned with the individual rights of faculty and students and more concerned with the "institutional right of self-governance in academic affairs." *Urofsky v. Gilmore*, 216 F.3d 401, 412 (4th Cir. 2000). Moreover, absent contractual provisions to the contrary, the courts do not recognize a right of faculty governance. *Minnesota State Bd. for Cmty. Colleges v. Knight*, 465 U.S. 271, 288 (1984) ("Faculty involvement in academic governance has much to recommend it as a matter of academic policy, but it finds no basis in the Constitution."). As the Fourth Circuit Court of Appeals infamously put it in 2000, "[T]o the extent the Constitution recognizes any right of 'academic freedom' above and beyond the First Amendment rights to which every citizen is entitled, the right inheres in the University, not in individual professors." *Urofsky*, 216 F.3d at 410.

To many courts, professors are merely ordinary employees and like in the corporate model, those who run the university may curtail their speech as they see fit. "After all," wrote Judge Laurence Silberman of the DC Circuit in 2008, "the state can be said to 'speak' through its employees." *Emergency Coal. to Defend Educ. Travel v. U.S. Dep't of the Treasury*, 545 F.3d 4, 19 (D.C. Cir. 2008) (Silberman, J., concurring). The infamous *Garcetti* case, although it did not arise in the academic context, ominously held that speech made by public employees in the scope of employment does not come within the ambit of the First Amendment. *Garcetti v. Ceballos*, 547 U.S. 410, 421 (2006). The Supreme Court has not yet ruled on whether academic speech is subject to the "*Garcetti* exception" to the First Amendment.

The Fourth and Ninth Circuit courts of appeal subsequently held that *Garcetti* does not apply to teaching and academic writing, however, meaning that speech made during the course of teaching or in scholarship would continue to be analyzed using the traditional First Amendment test. *Demers v. Austin*, 746 F.3d 402, 412 (9th Cir. 2014); *Adams v. Trustees of the Univ. of N.C.-Wilmington*, 640 F.3d 550, 563 (4th Cir. 2011). The Seventh Circuit applied *Garcetti*'s reasoning to faculty speech made in a teaching environment, although it did seem to recognize that it is required to balance the teacher's right to speak against the employer's interest in regulating the speech, signaling it would not preclude a First Amendment analysis in academic employment cases. *Piggee v. Carl Sandburg Coll.*, 464 F.3d 667, 672 (7th Cir. 2006).[1] Even if the Supreme Court chooses to adopt similar reasoning as the Fourth and Ninth Circuits in holding that faculty members have academic freedom in teaching and research despite their status as employees, it is not clear whether speech made in the context of faculty service to the university would be considered protected speech. The Fourth Circuit noted that faculty speech may not come within the scope of the First Amendment when it is made while "declaring or administering university policy, as opposed to scholarship or teaching." *Adams*, 640 F.3d at 563. And indeed, the Third Circuit applied *Garcetti* to preclude First Amendment protection to the speech of a professor who supported a student charged with a policy violation and disinvited the university president from a fraternity prayer breakfast. *Gorum v. Sessoms*, 561 F.3d 179 (3d Cir. 2009). The court reasoned that the speech was not related to scholarship or teaching and therefore did not imperil academic freedom. *Id.* at 186; see also *Sadid v. Idaho State Univ.*, 154 Idaho 88, 97, (2013) ("Academic freedom is irrelevant in this case, because [t]he speech complained of involves potentially slanderous statements regarding the qualifications, experience, and performance of his colleagues as administrators—not even as scholars").

But for some courts, institutional autonomy means that faculty members are held to an even higher standard than ordinary employees in establishing employment claims, especially when it comes to challenging tenure decisions. The Seventh Circuit, although it acknowledges there is no tenure review exception in statutes such as Title VII of the Civil Rights Act, believes that the complex and high-stakes academic context makes it nearly impossible (and undesirable) to ascertain whether discrimination is at play in tenure decisions. Judge Richard Posner explained that "practical considerations make a challenge to the denial of tenure at the college or university level an uphill fight—notably the absence of fixed, objective criteria for tenure at that level." *Blasdel v. Nw. Univ.*, 687 F.3d 813, 815 (7th Cir. 2012); see also *Hosty v. Carter*, 412 F.3d 731, 736 (7th Cir. 2005) ("Let us not forget that academic freedom includes the authority of the university to manage an academic community and evaluate teaching and scholarship free from interference by other units of government, including the courts."). With all due respect to Judge Posner, it is hardly the case that professors are unique in being subjected to sometimes subjective or complex standards, nor is it the case that it is always—or even usually—impossible to compare the relative performance of tenure candidates based on fixed, objective criteria. Nonetheless, the practical effect of these decisions is that faculty should not rely solely on the First Amendment and civil rights statutes to safeguard their employment and academic rights; universities have not only institutional power but a high level of deference afforded by the courts.

The due process clause of the Fourteenth Amendment protects professors at public universities from termination for cause mid-contract (or termination for cause despite having tenure) unless they are first afforded notice and an opportunity to respond to the allegations. *Cleveland Bd. of Educ. v. Loudermill*, 470 U.S. 532, 542 (1985). The Constitution's due process clauses are not likely to be of much use for many other kinds of employment actions, however. That is because there is no general right to due process floating around by which faculty members can claim a right to be treated fairly. As the Supreme Court put it,

> Property interests, of course, are not created by the Constitution. Rather they are created and their dimensions are defined by existing rules or understandings that stem from an independent source such as state law—rules or understandings that secure certain benefits and that support claims of entitlement to those benefits.[2]

In other words, the due process clause will often not apply unless faculty handbooks explicitly incorporate specific procedures guaranteeing fair process.[3]

So, faculty members should not assume that the courts will protect them if they are treated unfairly or arbitrarily, or if they are silenced because of their viewpoints. Even when they do face situations with clear legal recourse, litigation is lengthy, cumbersome and costly. It is far preferable to develop effective internal mechanisms for securing faculty rights.

The Faculty Handbook as a Contract

When there is tension between the "academic freedom" of institutions and that of faculty members, faculty members should ensure they have recourse to effective contractual remedies that even Judge Posner would find unambiguous as well as strong internal mechanisms for conflict resolution designed to minimize litigation. Faculty members should also ensure that changes to the faculty handbook do not conflict with the university bylaws or charter.

In an attempt to foreclose contract claims, some universities include a disclaimer in the faculty handbooks stating explicitly that the document is not a contract. Such provisions may not be enforceable—in some states the courts refuse to honor them when the university requires faculty adherence to the requirements of the handbook but seeks to avoid being bound itself. *Arneson v. Bd. of Trustees, McKendree Coll.*, 210 Ill. App. 3d 844, 851 (5th Dist. 1991). As it was eloquently stated in a Washington state court decision,

> An employer may expect, if not demand, that employees abide by policies expressed in employee handbooks or manuals, and create an atmosphere where employees justifiably rely on those expressed policies and justifiably expect that the employer will abide by those same policies. . . . We reject the premise that this disclaimer can, as a matter of law, effectively serve as an eternal escape hatch for an employer who may then make whatever unenforceable promises of working conditions it is to its benefit to make.[4]

In some states, however, courts give effect to these disclaimers, or give effect to them under certain circumstances such as when the disclaimer is given prominence in the handbook. See, e.g., *Bouwens v. Centrilift*, 974 P. 2d 941, 947 (Wyo 1999). Regardless of whether such provisions are enforceable in a particular state, however, it is better to oppose their inclusion so as to foreclose arguments about them in court or otherwise. There is no reason, especially in light of the already unequal power dynamic, that a university should be permitted to create a document that establishes binding rules for employees while rendering its own obligations optional.

The requirements for the formation of a contract are similar across states. Although faculty members should consult the case law in their own state if they want to be sure the faculty handbook would be construed as a contract, here is a general summary of what is normally required:

- First, there must be a clear promise in the form of written rules.
- Second, the policy statements must be disseminated to the employee in such a manner that s/he is aware of its contents and would reasonably believe it to be an offer. For example, the handbook may be routinely referenced in employees' annual contracts or accessible to faculty on the university website.
- Third, the employee must accept the offer by commencing or continuing to work after learning of the policy statement.[5]

The handbook should be reviewed periodically and systematically by the faculty senate to make sure that it includes sufficient basic guarantees of faculty rights, adapts to reflect institutional experience, and takes into account developments in academic life and technology. As part of this process, faculty senate committees should be encouraged to report on their experiences in their respective areas and suggest improvements.

The task of negotiating changes to a handbook is not always an easy matter. At minimum, faculty should ensure they are granted a meaningful role in the drafting and approval of changes to policy documents that affect faculty. Some universities grant the administration or Board of Trustees veto power over changes to the handbook. The role of the faculty senate should not be less than that of the administration in terms of determining the contents of the faculty handbook. And if anyone should have veto power, it should be the faculty. At minimum, the faculty should have the power to override an administrative veto by a vote.

Now we turn to what is actually *in* the handbook, a matter that overworked faculty members often do not give much attention until a problem arises.

Academic Freedom

Given that statutes, the Constitution, and case law offer meager protection for the academic freedom of faculty, faculty members should have specific internal recourse for academic freedom violations.

Handbook provisions often explicitly incorporate the American Association of University Professors (AAUP) academic freedom standard, especially the AAUP's 1940 "Statement of Principles on Academic Freedom and Tenure." This is indeed an excellent place to start, but elaboration is warranted, especially since the Statement does not say explicitly whether professors are protected when they speak in their service capacity, such as when they oppose the decisions of administrators or participate in university governance. So, whether or not the university extends academic freedom protections to faculty service should be spelled out in the faculty handbook.

Another AAUP document, which addresses more fully the right to academic freedom in university governance, is its 1994 Statement, "On the Relationship of Faculty Governance to Academic Freedom." That Statement recognizes that freedom of speech in institutional governance "is a prerequisite for the practice of governance unhampered by fear of retribution." It concludes:

> [T]he academic freedom of faculty members includes the freedom to express their views (1) on academic matters in the classroom and in the conduct of research, (2) on matters having to do with their institution and its policies, and (3) on issues of public interest generally, and to do so even if their views are in conflict with one or another received wisdom.

If the faculty handbook does not explicitly reference this Statement, it should incorporate the Statement's inclusion of faculty speech made in the course of academic governance and other service into its academic freedom protections. Otherwise, faculty will be left with very little institutional power and empty promises of faculty participation in governance.

Exceptions to Academic Freedom

The 1940 statement also says that in public statements, professors should exercise appropriate restraint. Handbooks should elaborate about what this "restraint" requires. The AAUP itself provides significant guidance in the context of its publications on collegiality.

Faculty handbooks also often restrict speech unreasonably when they require excessive politeness. In particular, any attempt to police civility should not make use of subjective standards. Handbooks which prohibit "harassment," "bullying," create "safe spaces," or which require faculty members not to cause offense to others can be and often are abused. Subjective standards are also impossible to follow consistently. For example, sexual harassment provisions which prohibit "unwanted attention" or "propositions" are too subjective and do not provide adequate notice of the type of conduct that is prohibited. The focus for such policies should be on conduct that is objectively offensive—in other words, conduct that the faculty member knows or should know would, in itself, cause offense to a reasonable audience, regardless of the mental state of the audience. Subjectively offensive conduct can certainly be addressed, but it should not be deemed an automatic violation of policy. In fact, subjective civility or behavioral provisions, which were ostensibly created to protect vulnerable individuals and oppressed groups, are usually used against those very individuals and groups, or against those who offend the egos or sensibilities of the powerful, their professional or financial interests, or simply resist the orthodoxy.

In sexual harassment policies, even provisions prohibiting objectively offensive conduct can sometimes go too far. Universities should think carefully about whether they want someone who uses "sexual humor" or "innuendo" to be subjected to the university disciplinary process. The focus of such policies should be on conduct that is both subjectively and objectively offensive, and for the more annoying but innocuous behavior, it should only be prohibited if repeated after a warning.

Many handbooks include the AAUP's requirement of "respect for the opinions of others." Any such requirement should be limited and carefully defined. It is debatable whether civility should be a universal goal in academia, even if it were possible to do it in an even-handed manner. Not all opinions are worthy of respect. Nor is it clear why there should be a general duty to respect all opinions. Should the opinions of those who advocate for and rationalize unjust wars and genocide be respected? Should the opinions of those who believe that the Cambodians, the Armenians, the Jews and the Poles, the Tutsi, the Bosnians, or the Iraqis "had it coming" be respected? As Professor Norman Finkelstein said in a speech at the University of Chicago after he was denied tenure for being uncivil in his academic speech about Israel-Palestine, there are certain types of strong emphatic outrage and protest that should be expressed, especially when there are lives at stake. He said, "There are moments that require breaking out of the constraints of polite discourse to sound the alarm that innocent people are being butchered while we speak due to the actions of our government."[6] Faculty members should oppose any such restrictions, and "respect for the opinions of others" should be understood in its most minimal sense: the recognition that their right to hold and defend such opinions is protected by the same framework as everyone else's.

Along similar lines, policies which require impartiality, journalistic objectivity, or viewpoint "balance" should be opposed. First, at state institutions such restrictions may be unconstitutional; just as the Constitution generally does not allow universities to prohibit particular types of speech, it is also a violation to *require* certain types of speech. *Roberts v. United States Jaycees*, 468 U.S. 609 (1984) (the freedom of speech presupposes the right not to speak). As Professor Akeel Bilgrami put it, when viewpoint balance becomes a requirement, we embrace "a conception of education as a sort of chronic dithering" (Bilgrami 2016, 15.) It may even be worth including affirmative statements to that effect within academic freedom provisions in handbooks, since not all administrators take for granted that professors should not be required to offer "balanced" lectures.

Finally, some institutions circumscribe academic freedom by requiring that faculty members adhere to the norms of their respective professions. Because such a standard can be interpreted to mean that views or methodologies outside the accepted traditions or prevailing norms of the discipline should be excluded, the provision may unintentionally hamper academic freedom. In particular, such restrictions can result in the suppression of new and innovative but useful methods, or arbitrary imposition of research methodologies that have nothing to do with the quality of the work. For example, I have represented professors in both the sciences and humanities who were denied tenure partly on the basis that the focus or scope of their peer-reviewed and acclaimed scholarship was "too broad" or "too narrow" based on what were deemed to be the norms of the profession but bore little relationship to available objective measures of the merit of the work. In his book *On Fact and Fraud: Cautionary tales from the front lines of science*, David Goodstein describes the problem as follows:

> [G]overnment agencies used to define scientific misconduct as "practices that seriously deviate from those that are commonly accepted within the scientific community." . . . But rapid progress will be more likely if different investigators have different attitudes toward appropriate methods. . . . Thus, attempts to define misconduct in

> terms of deviations from commonly accepted practices are doubly misguided: Not only will such commonly accepted practices fail to exist in many cases, but also it will be undesirable to enforce the conformity that such a principle would require. More generally, we can see why attempts to discover "the" scientific method fail. There are deep, systematic reasons why all scientists should not follow some single, uniform method.
>
> (Goodstein 2010, 13)

So, academic freedom should also protect against excessive academic rigidity, even when well-intentioned. Tenure standards in particular should be sensitive to this concern. Faculty should ensure that there is sufficient flexibility in the standard to accommodate methods of measuring excellence in research while still maintaining rigor. Faculty can thereby preserve academic freedom without letting go of high academic standards.

Tenure

In the tenure cases I have litigated, negotiated, appealed, or reviewed, the most common problem has been the inadequate notice of deficiencies in the applicant's record. Sometimes, of course, those alleged deficiencies are simply excuses and *post hoc* rationalizations, not the actual reasons for the tenure denial. However, even when the justification for denial is sincere, senior faculty or administrators do their junior colleagues no favors if they refrain from criticism when they first identify the deficiencies that underwrite the denial.

Departmental or college-level tenure policies should be reviewed to ensure that tenure-track faculty members are given (1) clear notice of the requirements for tenure from the beginning of their tenure-line appointments, (2) access to mentors, and (3) regular meaningful reviews of performance. These measures will not guarantee that tenure denials will always be anticipated, since most schools allow the president or members of the board of trustees the final tenure decision, and those individuals rarely weigh in on performance during the probationary period. But clear communication about tenure standards and progress would make it more difficult for decision makers at most levels of review to apply criteria arbitrarily, would allow faculty apprised of deficiencies the chance to improve performance or move on to another institution or endeavor without the stigma of a tenure denial, and would avoid significant investment in faculty members whose contracts should have been terminated several years earlier than the ultimate tenure review year.

During the tenure review process itself, there should be a mechanism for ensuring that professors who are denied tenure were given fair notice of deficiencies in their performance. Probationary evaluations should be included in the tenure portfolio to allow determination of whether such notice was given. In the case of professors who have not met the standard for tenure but were never warned about the relevant deficiencies in their performance in time to make improvements, something should be done to remedy the failure of the previous reviews. For example, in close cases a professor could be given the opportunity to reapply for tenure in the following year and demonstrate improvement in the deficient area(s).

And as elusive as Judge Posner seems to think such an endeavor may be, objective tenure criteria should be devised and communicated to the extent possible. Although it is usually difficult to draft a sufficiently specific set of criteria at the university level, colleges and/or departments should be required to establish tenure criteria in writing and update those requirements periodically. It is important to keep in mind, though, that if a faculty member's contract of hire incorporates an exception to those norms, that contract should be controlling. Assurances to incoming faculty that vary from the standard departmental or university procedures should be reduced to writing. Although it is important to allow universities to adjust the tenure requirements to allow for changing standards in the field and shifting institutional priorities, faculty members should be protected from scenarios where they invest a significant portion of their probationary periods working under specified tenure requirements and then suddenly are notified of changed requirements when it is too late to shift gears. The faculty handbook should contemplate this possibility and provide academic units with guidance about how to approach it. For example, a rule could be devised whereby substantial changes to the tenure standard may not be made if the faculty member is in at least his or her third academic year. Or, faculty members should be given additional time to meet the new standard. To the extent that institutions base tenure denial on changing "institutional needs" as opposed to performance, faculty should, whenever possible, be informed of those changing needs in advance of the tenure review process, and be given a reasonable amount of time to make adjustments or move to another institution. Moreover, faculty should be included in the process of determining if and how those institutional needs change.

Once those criteria and procedures are established, they should of course be followed. Someone at each level of the review process should be assigned the dry but important task of ensuring that tenure procedures are adhered to. This same person or committee can also be charged with ensuring that the university follows through on promises it made to the candidate that entail variation from the standard procedures. For example, universities sometimes allow extensions of the length of the probationary period for illness, family leave, and other reasons, but then evaluate the candidate's scholarship as if that leave had not been granted (in other words, by holding the candidate to a higher standard due to the increased duration of the probationary period). This failure is often inadvertent, such as when an outside evaluator or even an internal personnel committee member is simply not informed that an extension was granted.

At each level of review, the reviewing committee or administrator should be required to specify reasons for its/his/her recommendation, and that report should be shared with all other reviewing committees as well as the faculty member. The primary purpose of this explanation of reasons is to afford the faculty member and/or department the opportunity to respond prior to the next level of review, or to appeal. Lack of transparency serves no purpose other than to make it more difficult for the faculty member to challenge the decision and foster an environment in which administrators can retaliate against faculty who use their academic speech in ways that are contrary to the administration's perceived interests.

Finally, tenure evaluators should be required to marshal objective evidence in support of claims. Tenure decisions which raise "questions" about a particular area of a scholar's performance but do not attempt to answer those questions suffer from a lack or reliability and are often the result of manipulation by decision makers who lack sufficient objective bases for their views. Whenever possible, "questions" should attempt to be answered, and the opposing view should be considered when deciding whether any remaining "concerns" are sufficiently serious and justified to warrant tenure denial. For example, if an external reviewer criticizes the scholar's published work, but other reviewers address and rebut that specific criticism, that criticism should be disregarded unless the evidence in response to that criticism is lacking. Or if qualitative comments by students or external reviewers are cherry-picked to give a skewed sense of the scholar's deficiencies or merit, evaluators should consider whether those comments are anomalies or reflective of substantial deficiencies that have not been corrected. Of course, not all evaluators will come to the same conclusions, even based on objective indicators, when attempting to assess whether a concern is indicative of a substantial deficiency in performance. If tenure standards emphasize the requirement that concerns be tied to actual deficiencies in performance, though, departmental reviews will be more useful to upper-level committees and administrators, and the latter will not merely rely on stated concerns or positive statements about the candidate but rather assess whether concerns or compliments are warranted based on the evidence.

Solicited Reviews

Professors should have the opportunity to respond to evidence used in the tenure review. Many universities solicit feedback from external reviewers about professors' scholarship. Others also solicit letters from graduate and undergraduate students. There are several reasons this type of evidence could be unreliable. In external reviews, for instance, ideological biases, or substantive disagreement with the scholar's conclusions as opposed to reasoned critiques of their methodology or reasoning process can cloud the objectivity of the review. Or, slight disciplinary differences can lead to misunderstanding of the goals of the scholar's research portfolio. In the case of students, displeasure with the grade a student received or personal dislike of the professor can lead to retaliatory reviews. Such reviews can of course also provide a fuller sense of the quality of the scholar's work.

One of the ways these benefits can be retained while mollifying the potentially unfairly damaging impact is to allow the scholar to respond to any solicited review. While many institutions prefer to keep these reviews confidential to encourage frankness, the anonymity of the reviewer can often be preserved while disclosing the content. And even if a candidate is likely to infer the identity of the letter from the content, the benefit of affording the faculty member fair process in such an important decision is significant enough to overcome discomfort that reviewers might feel about the lack of anonymity. Allowing the scholar to respond to alleged deficiencies as summarized in the department or college letter is insufficient. First, if the departmental-level review is conducted without the benefit of the scholar's response to negative feedback and is unfairly negative, all the remaining reviews could be tainted by that assessment, even if the scholar is able to respond to the departmental review itself. Second, the departmental summary of the solicited review may substantially misrepresent it. At no time should a faculty member be denied tenure without the opportunity to respond fully to evidence used against him or her. This protection is a basic requirement of due process which is for good reason enshrined, respected, and practiced in virtually every corner of litigation practice, and the fact that some universities routinely deny it with destructive effect to academic speech is indicative of need for serious reform.

Teaching Standard

Some tenure reviews fail to evaluate teaching in an empirically sound manner, particularly because they rely too heavily and too uncritically on student evaluations. Although the limitations of the quantitative component of student evaluation are well-documented (Stark 2014), they are sometimes the main or even the exclusive vehicle through which universities evaluate faculty for tenure. In particular, the numerical component of student evaluations is devoid of empirical meaning unless it is understood in the context of a data model, which requires correlating it to specific measures of pedagogical success or deficiencies as observed by other experts in the field. Otherwise, the numbers either can't be said to reliably measure anything, or can be said to measure only pedagogically irrelevant characteristics such as race, age, national origin, accent, gender, or strictness of grading criteria.

Indeed, some studies suggest that even the previous description might be overly optimistic, and quantitative student evaluations might actually do little more than gauge how the physical appearance of the instructor is received by the students. The study was based on an experiment, which involved showing thirty-second or shorter—*and completely muted*—segments of the video footage of lectures by more than a dozen Harvard University instructors, and asking the students to quantitatively rate these instructors in fifteen categories that are used as standard measures of teaching effectiveness in student evaluations. The students' ratings not only strongly correlated with one another, but *also with the end-of-semester evaluations for the same instructors* (Ambady and Rosenthal 1993).

If these findings are correct, the quantitative component of student evaluations should not be used for hiring, renewal, promotion, and tenure decisions. If numerical averages from student evaluations have to be used to judge faculty performance, they should at most be a small and complementary component of this judgment. Moreover, the departments should be required to ascertain *reasons* for low or high student evaluation numbers, determine whether the causes of the high or low numbers are indicative of positive or negative performance, and provide specific advice about what the professor can do to improve as well as what s/he is doing that works well. Both peer evaluations and the written portion of student evaluations can assist in this regard. Moreover, peer reviews should be spaced throughout the professor's tenure-track period to ensure that improvements are tracked and accounted for in the tenure review.

Due Process

Many university handbooks have inadequate procedural protections for faculty who are facing termination or are charged with misconduct or other policy violations. Rather than reinvent the wheel, which has not served accused faculty well, universities that offer adjudicative or appellate procedures should incorporate basic due process principles from the US judicial system into their procedures. The main due process deficiencies universities often embrace are: (1) excessive and selective confidentiality, (2) failure to preserve evidence, (3) failure to provide impartial decision makers, and (4) failure to provide the opportunity to defend oneself.

Misconduct and grievance procedures should be carefully set forth and reevaluated periodically based on institutional experience. All faculty, whether full-time, contingent, tenure-track, or tenured, should have access to procedures for meaningfully contesting their termination, nonrenewal, discipline, or other job-related action.

Often, well-meaning handbook drafters provide for confidentiality for complainants. The rationale is that it may be desirable to encourage reporting and protect the complainant from retaliation by the accused. The laudability of this type of confidentiality ends when it implicates the rights of a specific individual, or is used to make some employment-related decision. Allegations may be untrue, the result of misunderstandings, or may unfairly restrict another individual's academic freedom. Faculty members should always have the right to defend themselves against allegations, and this right implies access to means of effective defense. Mounting an effective defense, however, is often impossible when the nature of the allegations and the evidence in support of these allegations are withheld from the defendant because revealing it may also reveal the identity of the accusers or witnesses.

Clearly, universities should also maintain strong policies against retaliation so that those who do report violations are assured they will not be punished as a result. This should involve informing complainants of their right to be free from retaliation for making complaints. Another important protect for complainants is to ensure that they are not disciplined unfairly for making complaints. Some universities include provisions which prohibit bad-faith complaints. It is not sufficient for disciplinary action if the sole evidence for "bad faith" is that the university found the complaint not to be warranted, however. Simply because the university found the complaint to be unwarranted does not mean the complainant had a nefarious motive in bringing the complaint. At minimum, policies should require a high standard of proof before taking any action against an employee for making a "false report" of discrimination or harassment.

Academic freedom is also imperiled when accused faculty members are presumed guilty by administrators eager to eradicate discrimination and other violations. For example, the "I believe you" mantra in sexual harassment cases has no place coming from administrators or other adjudicators who have responsibility for determining whether sexual harassment or sexual violence allegations are well-founded. At a minimum, investigators should maintain neutrality, or preferably presume innocence, which is perhaps the most fundamental due process right in Western democracies. Saying "I believe you" before evidence warranting belief is presented, impartially evaluated, and freely questioned, is just a positive-sounding euphemism for the presumption of guilt, which is virtually extinct today outside the kangaroo courts of dictatorships. Therefore, it has no place at the university, no matter how grave the accusations are, and no matter what the institutional power dynamic among the respective parties to the complaint is.

Relatedly, faculty members should be apprised of the *evidence* against them. It is not sufficient to know the nature of the accusation if the evidence is kept confidential. In order to provide a meaningful response that will allow the decision maker to ascertain what happened and whether misconduct occurred or some remedial action should be taken, all evidence, witness statements, and relevant documents should be exchanged between the parties, just as in the civil and criminal judicial contexts (the governmental "secret evidence" exception, in cases where claimed compelling government interests such as national security are at stake, notwithstanding.)

Other rules that prohibit faculty access to evidence should be resisted. For example, handbooks that prohibit faculty members from making a record of a disciplinary meeting or hearing are failing to protect the rights of the faculty member. Some institutions prohibit note-taking or transcripts during hearings, insist on collecting the notes at the end of the session, or maintain policies for shredding documents following a personnel decision. These are all terrible practices because not only do they preempt the due process rights of the defendant, but they also render any attempt at consistency through time, building on precedent, and administrative transparency and accountability impossible. Even during less formal disciplinary meetings such as meetings with one's supervisor, the faculty member should be apprised of the subject matter of the meeting in advance and permitted to be accompanied by a colleague or neutral administrator if requested.

Finally, handbooks should be reviewed to ensure there is an adequate level of meaningful faculty involvement in all personnel decisions, or at minimum the opportunity to review minor personnel actions on appeal. Moreover, there should be faculty representation on the university's board of trustees, as well as on committees involved in selecting important administrator positions such as deans and provosts. Since administrators are generally unaccountable to the faculty, this would allow some faculty oversight in the administration of the university.

Faculty should also be wary of procedures that allow administrators to circumvent the faculty in making personnel decisions. For example, the "for cause" procedure for terminating the employment of faculty members should be reserved for cases where the inadequate performance is of the type for which the standard review process is not equipped or for cases where the matter is urgent. These situations should be carefully set forth. And even then, faculty should be given a role in the process of determining whether cause exists.

In particular, there has been pressure on certain campuses to make it easier for administrators to terminate the employment of tenured faculty members. These changes should be resisted with utmost determination. One particularly nefarious technique that has been gaining popularity is the use of fitness-for-duty psychological examinations to attempt to manufacture a pretext to terminate or otherwise marginalize unpopular faculty members or pressure them to leave. Employment contracts or applications that require professors to acknowledge that they agree to be subjected to psychological testing should be resisted.

The Americans with Disabilities Act regulations set limits on the use of this method to ensure that mandatory psychological assessments are not used for improper purposes.[7] Faculty handbooks should create their own procedural limits on the use of psychological evaluations as well; for example, by requiring that a neutral faculty committee evaluate and approve requests for the imposition of a mandatory psychological examination. If it is found that such an examination is warranted due to incompetency or potential safety issues, during the pendency of the examination the faculty member should not be suspended from employment unless that faculty committee determines there is credible objective evidence that the faculty member is a safety threat. Such cases will be exceedingly rare.

Elimination of Programs and Positions Due To Financial Exigency

Administrators can reshape universities through the elimination of faculty positions, programs, and even departments based on claims of financial exigency. Faculty should have a role in shaping the goals and composition of the institution. Faculty should therefore participate in developing sections in handbooks about the elimination of units or positions.

First, handbooks should make clear that dramatic cuts (e.g., the elimination of tenured faculty lines and the elimination of academic units) should never be purely administrative decisions. Handbooks should contain detailed procedures that the administration must follow when it seeks to make such cuts. They should also identify detailed criteria for the selection of which programs or faculty lines to eliminate when there is a need for cuts. The faculty senate should appoint a faculty committee to assist in weighing proposals or making cuts to academic programs.

When the university is weighing a proposal for dramatic cuts due to financial exigency, faculty should be permitted to hire an outside economist to conduct a financial analysis and assess the validity of the claims of those suggesting the cuts. As part of that process, the economist (and the faculty) should be permitted full access to the relevant financial documents. The economist should be permitted to consider whether the university's budget is excessively bloated due to administrative and other waste. In addition, when cuts to a particular program are being considered, the faculty in the affected program should be permitted to respond to any proposal and the Handbook should specify systematic and fair means of evaluating the proposal. When dramatic cuts are necessary, the affected faculty members should be offered alternative positions within the university if at all feasible. These safeguards will help protect against the use of claims of financial exigency as masks for ideological bias, and usurpation of judgments that should be made by the faculty.

Conclusion

Through concerted action and the development of adequate governance documents, faculty members can prevent administrations from acting as corporate human resources departments and promote a freer intellectual environment. Of course, for any of these reforms to have any value, they must be scrupulously enforced, which itself often requires commitment and concerted action on the part of an organized faculty.

Notes

1. In a case decided before *Garcetti*, however, that same court rejected the idea that the First Amendment protects faculty speech made in the course of their performance of their duties as employees. *Omosegbon v. Wells*, 335 F.3d 668, 677 (7th Cir. 2003) ("Because academic freedom rights must ultimately flow from the First Amendment, claims of their violation are subject to all the usual tests that apply to assertions of First Amendment rights.")
2. *Bd. of Regents of State Colleges v. Roth*, 408 U.S. 564, 577 (1972).
3. *Spuler v. Pickar*, 958 F.2d 103, 107 (5th Cir. 1992) ("Because the faculty handbook bestowed no contractual rights on Spuler and no concomitant obligations on the University, and because Spuler points to no other source of entitlement to tenure, Spuler enjoyed no property interest the deprivation of which merited procedural or substantive due process protection.")
4. *Swanson v. Liquid Air Corp.*, 118 Wash. 2d 512, 532 (1992).
5. See, e.g., *Green v. Trinity Intern. University*, 344 Ill.App.3d 1079, 1089–1090 (Ill. App. 2nd Dist. 2003); *Klinge v. Ithaca Coll.*, 634 N.Y.S.2d 1000, 1003 (Sup. Ct. 1995), *aff'd as modified,* 652 N.Y.S.2d 377 (1997).
6. www.youtube.com/watch?v=1fgFSX89oh4
7. 42 U.S.C.A. § 12112(d)(4); see also *Wright v. Illinois Dep't of Children & Family Servs.*, 798 F.3d 513, 523 (7th Cir. 2015) (internal quotations removed) ("Courts consequently require that an employer provide significant evidence that could cause a reasonable person to inquire as to whether an employee is still capable of performing his job."). The employer must have "a reasonable belief based on objective evidence that a medical condition will impair an employee's ability to perform essential job functions or that the employee will pose a threat due to a medical condition." *Wright*, 798 F.3d at 522–523.

Works Cited

Ambady, N. and Rosenthal, R. "Half a Minute: Predicting Teacher Evaluations From Thin Slices of Nonverbal Behavior and Physical Attractiveness." *Journal of Personality & Social Psychology*, Vol. 64 (1993): 431–441.

American Association of University Professors. 1994. "On the Relationship of Faculty Governance to Academic Freedom."

Bilgrami, A. "Truth, Balance, and Freedom" In *Who's Afraid of Academic Freedom?*, edited by Akeel Bilgrami and Johnathan Cole. New York: Columbia University Press, 2016.

Goodstein, D. *On Fact and Fraud: Cautionary Tales From the Front Lines of Science*. Princeton, NJ: Princeton University Press, 2010.

Stark, P. "An Evaluation of Course Evaluations." *ScienceOpen*. September 26, 2014. www.stat.berkeley.edu/~stark/Preprints/evaluations14.pdf

"Statement of Principles on Academic Freedom and Tenure." *American Association of University Professors*. 1940. www.aaup.org/report/1940-statement-principles-academic-freedom-and-tenure

Cases Cited

42 U.S.C.A. § 12112(d)(4)

Adams v. Trustees of the Univ. of N.C.-Wilmington, 640 F.3d 550, 563 (4th Cir. 2011)

Arneson v. Bd. of Trustees, McKendree Coll., 210 Ill. App. 3d 844, 851 (5th Dist. 1991)

Bd. of Regents of State Colleges v. Roth, 408 U.S. 564, 577 (1972)

Blasdel v. Nw. Univ., 687 F.3d 813, 815 (7th Cir. 2012)

Bouwens v. Centrilift, 974 P. 2d 941, 947 (Wyo. 1999)

Cleveland Bd. of Educ. v. Loudermill, 470 U.S. 532, 542 (1985)

Demers v. Austin, 746 F.3d 402, 412 (9th Cir. 2014)

Emergency Coal. to Defend Educ. Travel v. U.S. Dep't of the Treasury, 545 F.3d 4, 19 (D.C. Cir. 2008)

Garcetti v. Ceballos, 547 U.S. 410, 421 (2006)

Gorum v. Sessoms, 561 F.3d 179 (3d Cir. 2009)

Green v. Trinity Intern. University, 344 Ill.App.3d 1079, 1089–1090 (Ill. App. 2nd Dist. 2003)

Hosty v. Carter, 412 F.3d 731, 736 (7th Cir. 2005)

Klinge v. Ithaca Coll., 634 N.Y.S.2d 1000, 1003 (Sup. Ct. 1995), *aff'd as modified*, 652 N.Y.S.2d 377 (1997)

Minnesota State Bd. for Cmty. Colleges v. Knight, 465 U.S. 271, 288 (1984)

Omosegbon v. Wells, 335 F.3d 668, 677 (7th Cir. 2003)

Piggee v. Carl Sandburg Coll., 464 F.3d 667, 672 (7th Cir. 2006)

Roberts v. United States Jaycees, 468 U.S. 609 (1984)

Sadid v. Idaho State Univ., 154 Idaho 88, 97, 294 P. 3d 1100, 1109 (2013)

Spuler v. Pickar, 958 F.2d 103, 107 (5th Cir. 1992)

Swanson v. Liquid Air Corp., 118 Wash. 2d 512, 532 (1992)

Urofsky v. Gilmore, 216 F.3d 401, 412 (4th Cir. 2000)

Wright v. Illinois Dep't of Children & Family Servs., 798 F.3d 513, 523 (7th Cir. 2015)

Contributors

Jason Brennan is the Robert J. and Elizabeth Flanagan Family Chair of Strategy, Economics, Ethics, and Public Policy at Georgetown University. His is the author of eight books, including most recently *In Defense of Openness*, with Bas van der Vossen, and *Against Democracy*. He is currently writing *Cracks in the Ivory Tower: The Bad Business Ethics of Higher Ed*, with Phil Magness, for Oxford University Press.

Andrew J. Cohen is an associate professor of philosophy and founding coordinator of the Bachelors of Interdisciplinary Studies Program in Philosophy, Political Science, and Economics at Georgia State University. He is the author of *Toleration and Freedom from Harm: Liberalism Reconceived* (Routledge, 2018) and *Toleration* (Polity, 2014) as well as articles in journals like *Ethics*, *The Canadian Journal of Philosophy*, and in new reference works like the *Cambridge Companion to Liberalism*.

Sarah Conly is an associate professor of philosophy at Bowdoin College. She is the author of *Against Autonomy: Justifying Coercive Paternalism* (Cambridge University Press, 2013) and *One Child: Do We Have a Right to More?* (Oxford University Press, 2016).

Shane D. Courtland is the managing director of the Center for Free Enterprise at West Virginia University. He is also the editor of the philosophy journal *Civil American*. His publications have appeared in *Pacific Philosophical Quarterly*, *Journal of Environmental Philosophy*, *Journal of Applied Philosophy*, *Journal of Mind and Behavior*, *Southwest Philosophy Review*, *Hobbes Studies*, *Reason Papers*, *Utilitas*, *Stanford Encyclopedia of Philosophy*, and Routledge's *Ethics in Politics*. Most recently, Courtland edited a volume, *Hobbesian Applied Ethics and Public Policy*, with Routledge (2017).

Christina Easton is a doctoral researcher in the philosophy department at the London School of Economics and Political Science. Her work is primarily in political philosophy and its application to education policy. Prior to taking up the scholarship at LSE, she spent eight years teaching philosophy and religious studies to 11–18 year olds. Christina recently co-authored *Critical Religious Education in Practice: A Teacher's Guide for the Secondary Classroom* (in press with Routledge).

Bob Fischer is an assistant professor of philosophy at Texas State University. His edited volumes include *The Moral Complexities of Eating Meat* (Oxford University Press, 2015), *College Ethics: A Reader on Moral Issues That Affect You* (Oxford University Press, 2016), *Modal Epistemology After Rationalism* (Springer, 2017), and the *Routledge Handbook of Animal Ethics* (Routledge, forthcoming). He's also the author of *Modal Justification via Theories* (Springer, 2017) and several essays on animal ethics, moral psychology, and the epistemology of modality.

Frank Furedi is emeritus professor of sociology at the University of Kent, United Kingdom. He is well known for his work on sociology of fear, education, therapy culture, paranoid parenting, and sociology of knowledge. His essays are published in *AEON, American Interest, The New Scientist, The Guardian, The Independent, The Financial Times, The Daily Telegraph, The Express, The Daily Mail, The Wall Street Journal, The Independent on Sunday, The Times, The Sunday Times, The Observer, The Sunday Telegraph, Toronto Globe and Mail, The New York Times, The Christian Science Monitor, The Times Higher Education Supplement, Spiked-online, The Times Literary Supplement, Harvard Business Review, Die Welt* and *Die Zeit*, amongst others.

Evan Gerstmann is a professor of political science at Loyola Marymount University. He is the author of two books on constitutional law: *Same-Sex Marriage and the Constitution* (Cambridge University Press, 2003, 2008, 2017) and *The Constitutional Underclass: Gays, Lesbians and the Failure of Class-Based Equal Protection* (University of Chicago Press, 1999), as well as the co-editor of a third book: *Academic Freedom at the Dawn of a New Century: How Terrorism, Governments, and Culture Wars Impact Free Speech* (Stanford University Press, 2006). Among his other publications are "Where Is Equal Protection? Applying Strict Scrutiny to Use of Race by Law Enforcement," *Harvard Journal of Racial and Ethnic Justice* (2013), "Litigating Same-Sex Marriage: Might the Courts Actually Be Bastions of Rationality?," *PS: Political Science and Politics* (April 2005), and "We are the World? What United States Courts Can and Should Learn from the Law and Politics of Other Western Nations," *Journal of International Law and International Relations* (Fall 2005).

John Hasnas is a professor of business at Georgetown's McDonough School of Business, a professor of law (by courtesy) at Georgetown

University Law Center, and the executive director of the Georgetown Institute for the Study of Markets and Ethics. Professor Hasnas has held previous appointments as associate professor of law at George Mason University School of Law, visiting associate professor of law at Duke University School of Law and the Washington College of Law at American University, and Law and Humanities Fellow at Temple University School of Law. Professor Hasnas has also been a visiting scholar at the Kennedy Institute of Ethics in Washington, DC, and the Social Philosophy and Policy Center in Bowling Green, Ohio. He received his B.A. in philosophy from Lafayette College, his J.D. and Ph.D. in legal philosophy from Duke University, and his LL.M. in legal education from Temple Law School.

Edward Johnson is emeritus professor of philosophy at the University of New Orleans. He has published more than a hundred essays in academic books and journals, dealing with a broad range of philosophical issues, especially in applied ethics.

Rima Najjar Kapitan is the principal attorney at an employment and civil rights law office in Chicago. In recent years, she has increasingly focused on academic cases, representing professors and students in internal appeals and litigation of academic freedom and discrimination cases. She has spoken on the topic of academic freedom at California State University–Fresno, the New York University School of Law, the Fordham University School of Law, and the Illinois Conference of the American Association of University Professors, among other venues. She has also published in the AAUP's *Journal of Academic Freedom* and *Arab Studies Quarterly* about free speech in the academic context and the imposition of "balance" on discourse about Palestine/Israel. Her most recent publication is a chapter in the book *Against Apartheid* (Dawson, A. & Mullen, B., Eds.), which advocated for the use of academic boycotts to expand academic freedom both here and abroad, including in Israel.

Michael Joel Kessler is an assistant professor and Raymond Pryke Chair in the Margaret MacMillan Trinity One program at Trinity College in the University of Toronto. He writes about the intersection of morality, political theory, and the law. Recent papers have focused on the law of obscenity and the problem of justifying spending tax dollars on artistic or cultural projects. He is currently working on a book project on legal ethics related to impaired consent in medical, contractual, and intimate interpersonal contexts.

Brian Leiter is the Karl N. Llewellyn Professor of Jurisprudence and director of the Center for Law, Philosophy & Human Values at the University of Chicago. His publications include three books: *Nietzsche on Morality* (Routledge, 2nd ed., 2015), *Why Tolerate Religion?* (Princeton, 2013), and *Naturalizing Jurisprudence* (Oxford, 2007).

J.K. Miles is an associate professor of philosophy at Quincy University in Illinois where he teaches applied ethics including medical ethics, business ethics, and political philosophy. His work centers on the intersection of epistemology and ethics, especially as it pertains to virtue theory. He has published on freedom of speech and pornography and international blasphemy laws in academic journals. He is currently writing a medical ethics textbook.

Calum Miller is a visiting research scholar in bioethics at the Uehiro Centre for Practical Ethics, University of Oxford. He has published a number of papers in bioethics and the philosophy of religion.

Ryan Muldoon is an assistant professor of philosophy at the University at Buffalo–SUNY. Previously he was a senior research fellow in the philosophy, politics and economics program at the University of Pennsylvania. He is the author of *Social Contract Theory for a Diverse World: Beyond Tolerance*. His primary research investigates how we can turn the challenge of increasing diversity into a resource to be tapped for our mutual benefit.

Burkay T. Ozturk is a lecturer in philosophy at Texas State University. He does research in ethics, philosophy of science, and mathematical philosophy. His recent publications are "The Negotiative Theory of Gender Identity and the Limits of First Person Authority" in *The Philosophy of Sex* (ed. R. Halwani), "Of German Tanks and Scientific Theories" in *Southwest Philosophy Review*, and "Facsimiles of Flesh" in the *Journal of Applied Philosophy* (co-authored with Bob Fischer).

Arianne Shahvisi is a Kurdish-British academic, writer, and activist. She holds a doctorate in the philosophy of science from the University of Cambridge and is a lecturer in ethics and medical humanities at the Brighton & Sussex Medical School. Her current research spans a diverse set of topics in applied philosophy, focusing on reproductive ethics, the intersection of race and gender, and social epistemology. Arianne serves on the editorial board for *Kohl: A Journal for Body and Gender Research*, a feminist journal on gender and sexuality in the Middle East, South West Asia, and North Africa regions, and is science editor for the literary magazine *The Offing*.

Peter Singer is the Ira W. DeCamp Professor of Bioethics at Princeton University, and a laureate professor in the School of Historical and Philosophical Studies at the University of Melbourne.

James R. Stoner, Jr. is the Hermann Moyse, Jr., Professor and director of the Eric Voegelin Institute in the Department of Political Science at Louisiana State University. He is the author of *Common-Law Liberty: Rethinking American Constitutionalism* (Kansas, 2003) and *Common Law and Liberal Theory: Coke, Hobbes, and the Origins of American*

Constitutionalism (Kansas, 1992), as well as a number of articles and essays. A senior fellow of the Witherspoon Institute, he has co-edited three books the institute published: *The Thriving Society: On the Social Conditions of Human Flourishing* (with Harold James, 2015), *The Social Costs of Pornography: A Collection of Papers* (with Donna M. Hughes, 2010), and *Rethinking Business Management: Examining the Foundations of Business Education* (with Samuel Gregg, 2007). He chaired his department from 2007 until 2013, and in 2013–2014 he was Garwood Visiting Professor and Visiting Fellow in the James Madison Program at Princeton University. He earned his A.B. from Middlebury College and his M.A. and Ph.D. from Harvard University. His current research is on the nature of legislative power as well as freedom of speech in American constitutionalism.

Keith E. Whittington is the William Nelson Cromwell Professor of Politics at Princeton University. In addition to casebooks and edited volumes on constitutional law and history, he is the author of *Constitutional Construction: Divided Powers and Constitutional Meaning*; *Constitutional Interpretation: Textual Meaning, Original Intent, and Judicial Review*; *Political Foundations of Judicial Supremacy: The Presidency, the Supreme Court, and Constitutional Leadership in U.S. History* (which won the C. Herman Pritchett Award for best book in law and courts and the J. David Greenstone Award for best book in politics and history); *Judicial Review and Constitutional Politics*; and *American Political Thought: Readings and Materials*. He is editor (with Gerald Leonard) of *New Essays on American Constitutional History* and editor (with Maeva Marcus, Melvin Urofsky, and Mark Tushnet) of *Cambridge Studies on the American Constitution*. His latest books include *Speak Freely: Why Universities Must Defend Free Speech* and *Repugnant Laws: Judicial Review of Acts of Congress from the Founding to the Present.*

Index

For Product Safety Concerns and Information please contact our EU representative GPSR@taylorandfrancis.com
Taylor & Francis Verlag GmbH, Kaufingerstraße 24, 80331 München, Germany

www.ingramcontent.com/pod-product-compliance
Ingram Content Group UK Ltd.
Pitfield, Milton Keynes, MK11 3LW, UK
UKHW022004180926
475701UK00003B/187
9780367591021